The economic theory of structure and change

The economic theory of structure and change

edited by
Mauro Baranzini
University of Verona
and
Roberto Scazzieri
University of Padua

CAMBRIDGE UNIVERSITY PRESS
Cambridge
New York Port Chester
Melbourne Sydney

CAMBRIDGE UNIVERSITY PRESS
Cambridge, New York, Melbourne, Madrid, Cape Town,
Singapore, São Paulo, Delhi, Mexico City

Cambridge University Press
The Edinburgh Building, Cambridge CB2 8RU, UK

Published in the United States of America by Cambridge University Press, New York

www.cambridge.org
Information on this title: www.cambridge.org/9781107405035

First published 1990
First paperback edition 2012

A catalogue record for this publication is available from the British Library

Library of Congress Cataloguing in Publication Data
The economic theory of structure and change / edited by Mauro
Baranzini and Roberto Scazzieri.
p. cm.
ISBN 0 521 34516 2
1. Economics. I. Baranzini, Mauro. II. Scazzieri, Roberto.
HB171.E248 1990
330.1–dc20 89–78202

ISBN 978-0-521-34516-3 Hardback
ISBN 978-1-107-40503-5 Paperback

Contents

List of figures *page* viii
List of contributors ix
Preface xi
Acknowledgements xiii

Introduction 1
Mauro Baranzini and *Roberto Scazzieri*
1. Alternative uses of structural concepts. 2. Structure as the 'fabric' of economic society. 3. Structure as the set of relationships among economic magnitudes. 4. The institutional framework of economic structure. 5. Structure, change and economic theory. 6. The organization of the volume and the contributions. 7. Epilogue.

PART I: STRUCTURE AND INSTITUTIONS IN POLITICAL ECONOMY

1 **Economic structure and political institutions: a theoretical framework** 23
Lorenzo Ornaghi
1. Introduction. 2. Political institutions as a 'terminal problem'. 3. Political economy and the 'modern' organization of power. 4. State and economic structure: a fallacy. 5. 'Order' and 'transformations'. 6. The temporal horizon of creative economic action. 7. Concluding remarks.

PART II: SINGLE-PERIOD RELATIONSHIPS AND ECONOMIC THEORY

2 **Economic structure and the theory of economic equilibrium** 47
Takashi Negishi
1. Introduction. 2. Logical structure of Walrasian theory. 3. Time structure of Walrasian theory. 4. Time structure of

Marshallian theory. 5. Equilibrium industry with disequilibrium firms. 6. Edgeworth's equivalence theorem. 7. Communication structure of duopoly. 8. Conclusions.

3 **Structure and change within the circular theory of production** 64
Heinrich Bortis
1. Introduction. 2. Production as a circular and social process. 3. The 'linear' view of production and its comparison with the 'circular' view. 4. Economic activity and the circular view of production. 5. Economic activity and the 'linear' view of production. 6. Institutions, structure and actions. 7. Structure and change. 8. Concluding remarks: determinism and choice.

PART III: STRUCTURAL DYNAMICS AND THE ANALYSIS OF ECONOMIC CHANGE

4 **Specification of structure and economic dynamics** 95
Michael A. Landesmann and *Roberto Scazzieri*
1. Introduction. 2. Structural invariance and economic change. 3. The descriptive–analytical and the deductive–behavioural approaches to structural change analysis. 4. Methods of dynamic analysis. 5. Time structure, sequential causation and motive forces. 6. Productive interrelationships and economic dynamics. 7. Concluding remarks.

5 **Vertical integration, growth and sequential change** 122
Jean Magnan de Bornier
1. Introduction. 2. A general formulation for sector- and time-based models of production. 3. A survey of past controversies about the time structure of capital. 4. The problem and models of traverse.

6 **The structural theory of economic growth** 144
Harald Hagemann
1. Introduction. 2. Six decades of structural analysis of real capital formation: Adolph Lowe and the Kiel School. 3. Structural analysis of dynamic equilibria in Lowe's 'tripartite scheme'. 4. Structural analysis of traverse processes. 5. Force analysis as a necessary complement to structural analysis in Lowe's political economics. 6. Advantages and drawbacks of the inter-industry approach compared to the vertical integration approach in the analysis of economic change. 7. Concluding remarks.

PART IV: A FRAMEWORK FOR STRUCTURAL ANALYSIS

7 **Economic theory and industrial evolution** 175
Michio Morishima
1. Introduction: the congruence between economy and economics. 2. Ricardian and anti-Ricardian premises. 3. Ricardo and Walras. 4. Keynes. 5. Identification of the epochs.

8 **Production process and dynamic economics** 198
Nicholas Georgescu-Roegen
1. An epistemological exordium. 2. The analytical representation of production process. 3. The flow–fund representation. 4. The epistemology of dynamic economics.

9 **Economic structure: analytical perspectives** 227
Mauro Baranzini and *Roberto Scazzieri*
1. Introduction. 2. Economic structure in economic theory. 3. Institutions in economic theory. 4. Persistence and change in the analysis of structure. 5. The features of economic dynamics: representation and method. 6. Vertical integration and the circular flow: perspectives on the evolution of dynamic theory. 7. 'Anatomy' and 'Physiology' of the economic system: a framework for economic dynamics.

Name index 334
Subject index 340

Figures

2.1	The Edgeworth box diagram	*page* 59
3.1	Concepts of horizontal and vertical causality	87
4.1	Commodity flows in the pure circular-flow model	110
4.2	Time interdependencies and horizontal interrelationships	112
4.3	Vertically integrated processes and the Hicksian time structure of production	114
4.4	The Hicksian traverse	115
4.5	Vertically integrated sectors of production	117
8.1	Flow and fund utilization	216

Contributors

Mauro Baranzini *Professor of Economics, University of Verona and Catholic University of Milan; formerly lecturer and tutor in economics, The Queen's College, University of Oxford*

Heinrich Bortis *Professor of Economics, University of Fribourg, Switzerland*

Nicholas Georgescu-Roegen *Professor of Economics, Vanderbilt University, Nashville, Tennessee*

Harald Hagemann *Professor of Economics, University of Hohenheim; formerly Professor of Economics, University of Bremen*

Michael A. Landesmann *Senior Research Officer, Department of Applied Economics, University of Cambridge*

Jean Magnan de Bornier *Professor of Economics, Université de Bourgogne, Dijon*

Michio Morishima *Sir John Hicks Professor of Economics, The London School of Economics and Political Science*

Takashi Negishi *Professor of Economics, University of Tokyo*

Lorenzo Ornaghi *Professor of Political Science, Catholic University of Milan and University of Teramo*

Roberto Scazzieri *Professor of Economics, University of Padua; formerly lecturer in economics, University of Bologna*

Preface

It is the purpose of this volume to inquire into the general field of structural economic analysis by linking it with the conceptual foundations of theory building on the one hand and with the specific requirements of factual analysis on the other. This area is part of a wider research programme that has led to the publication of *Foundations of Economics, Structures of Inquiry and Economic Theory* (ed. M. Baranzini and R. Scazzieri, Basil Blackwell, Oxford and New York, 1986). In this volume attention was drawn to the fact that the structure of economic theories may be traced back to a number of primitive elements that are essential in determining the general shape of the conceptual set-up, as well as the particular propositions to be analytically derived within it. Building on that ground we came to think that the way in which these primitive elements may be combined into general theories is related to the criterion adopted in specifying the basic features of the relevant economic descriptions, that is in identifying the underlying structure of the economic system under consideration.

An important implication of such an approach is that the analysis of actual economic systems critically depends on the type of structural specification adopted. It then follows that the study of economic change may be more comprehensively considered when an explicit assessment is made of the distinct types of economic structure adopted in describing the economy under consideration. This volume aims at assessing the different aspects of the concept of economic structure, in particular by emphasizing the mutual dependence between economic structure as a set of objective magnitudes and economic structure as a frame for existing institutional arrangements and their pattern of transformation. In this connection, the distinction between 'circular' and 'vertical' representations of the objective stock -flow network of economic activities is assigned a prominent role. Indeed it is found that such a distinction proves helpful in analysing the way in which the institutional set-up is itself related to the objective features of economic structure, and thus with the dynamic behavioural principles at the basis of the actual motion of the economic system through historical time.

The contributions gathered in this volume have been specifically written with the aim of assessing the above framework of research.

Mauro Baranzini
Roberto Scazzieri

Acknowledgements

The preparation of this volume has been made possible by a number of institutions and persons who have supported our research in different ways. First of all thanks are due to our present academic institutions, respectively the University of Verona (in particular the Institute of Economic Sciences) and the University of Padua (in particular the Faculty of Statistics). We would also like to thank the University of Bologna, the University of Cambridge, the Catholic University of Milan and the University of Oxford (in particular The Queen's College) for providing, at various stages of the preparation of this volume, research facilities and an intellectual environment that has stimulated our work in an important way. Additionally, our research has taken advantage of the support of the Centre for Research in Economic Analysis (CRANEC) of the Catholic University of Milan and of the Institute for the Dynamics of Economic Systems (IDSE) of the Italian National Research Council (CNR). Finally, research help has been provided, at different stages, through grants from the Italian National Research Council, the Italian Ministry for the University and the Swiss Science Foundation. Indexing and bibliographic contribution has been provided by Maria Cristina Bacchi, senior assistant librarian at Bologna University Library.

Introduction

MAURO BARANZINI AND ROBERTO SCAZZIERI

1. Alternative uses of structural concepts

Our discipline is characterized by a plurality of ways in which it is possible to describe events as elements of a particular structure. An examination of economic literature suggests a fundamental distinction.

On the one hand, 'structure' is conceived as the network of interpersonal relationships on which the economic *fabric* of society is founded. Such relationships describe the social rules and personal and collective beliefs that provide the framework for the actions of economic agents. Institutions provide an important example of the way in which this notion of structure can be used in economic analysis. (This notion of structure provides the backbones of Adam Smith's, Alfred Marshall's and John Maynard Keynes's works on the working of market society.)

On the other hand, 'structure' is conceived as a set of relationships among *economic magnitudes* such as sectoral outputs, population and technology. Such relationships describe in the first instance the outcome, not the motivations, of agents' aggregate behaviour, thereby expounding the mutual compatibility among global components of economic activity. For instance, a particular structure could be described by the association of a given technique, the consumption/saving ratio and the rate of growth of the system. (This notion of structure appears in the writings of Charles Davenant, William Petty, François Quesnay, Wassily Leontif, and Richard Stone.)

2. Structure as the 'fabric' of economic society

The emergence of the notion of economic society presupposes the identification of a network of interpersonal obligations and mutually compatible beliefs within a specialized sphere of social life. In the absence of such a precise network the descriptions of varous aspects of economic life belong to the fields of (i) moral philosophy, as in the case of Aristotle's *Nichomachean Ethics* or St Thomas Aquinas' *Summa Theologiae*; (ii) practical philosophy, as in the case of Xenophon's *Oeconomics* or Niphus's writings; (iii) treatises on commercial and banking practices.

The emergence of 'market laws' provides an important instance of the process by which the notion of economic society was born in European thought. It also provides an instance of the interaction between obligations and beliefs and of the resulting rise of a specialized and institutionalized sphere of social life, which comes to be regulated by a specific set of legal rules (commercial law). This process marks the development of trade in the towns of medieval Europe. There the *ius mercatorum* ('the law of the merchants') takes shape as a specialized set of legal arrangements that regulated the relationships of the merchants among themselves as well as the relationships between merchants and non-merchants. This latter set of relationships substituted the general rules with a specialized set of norms to which non-merchants were obliged to abide: this is the so-called *privilegium mercaturae* ('privilege of trade'). (An early discussion of these bonds is to be found in Bartolus's *Commentaria* (first half of the fourteenth century); see also Scazzieri, 1988, p. 151.)

Slowly this process led to a sophisticated and institutionalized system of rules of behaviour that came to be regarded as a natural framework for economic actions. This lengthy process provided the backbones of the notion of 'civil society', the economic structure of which was considered in Smith's *Wealth of Nations*. For Smith civil society is seen as a stage in the evolution of humankind characterized by the ethical rules considered in the *Theory of Moral Sentiments*. In the *Wealth of Nations* Smith considers the specification of this social structure in the field of economic relationships.

Smith's general set-up was taken up in David Ricardo's view of modern society, in particular for what concerns the existence of entitlements of different social classes to a particular share of the product. Later on Smith's general view of economic structure was replaced by John Stuart Mill's and Karl Marx's conception that more than one set of social arrangements is possible in modern society.This point of view was taken up in Marshall's idea that the working of the market may be supplemented by the introduction of explicit ethical rules; and in Keynes's view that the 'market laws' may in given cases be replaced by direct economic policy. From this point of view *economic* structure no longer provides a self-contained system of laws that completely regulate economic activities.

3. Structure as the set of relationships among economic magnitudes

A different notion of economic structure emerges from the work of seventeenth-century writers in the field of 'political arithmetics', such as Charles Devenant, William Petty, Gregory King, John Graunt. Such writers stress that it is possible to describe the economic system in quantitative terms by measuring magnitudes such as wealth, revenue, population and capital stock. From what appears to be a work in the field of national accounting there slowly emerges a definite theory of the fundamental relationships among these economic magnitudes. An important instance is that of Petty's economic writings, in which the notion of net product is explicitly identified as the difference between the measure of national product and that of the resources employed to produce it.

The same concept of economic structure is used by Leontief in his *Structure of the American Economy 1919–1939* (1941), in which the production process at the national level is described in terms of a flow of inter-industry relationships. Attention is focused on the commodities that each sector of productive activities receives from the other sectors as well as on the commodities that it in turn provides for the other sectors. This type of approach has often led to particular ways of representing the technology of a productive system by means of the unit requirements of each particular input that may be computed directly from inter-sector relations. However, as L.V. Kantorovich points out, although this method of describing technology

> is of special interest, this approach may be considered sufficiently satisfactory for calculating valuations of products. Indeed, instead of actual methods of production, broad averages are used here and the results obtained depend essentially on the methods chosen for aggregation. (Kantorovich, 1965, p. 281)

Leontief's notion of economic structure is basically a 'production-oriented' one. Its scope appears to be widened by subsequent works and in particular by Richard Stone's idea that final consumption can be related to income levels by means of a definite structural relationship (Stone's *linear expenditure system*).

4. The institutional framework of economic structure

The two different notions of economic structure outlined above are not always clearly separated, for in a number of cases economic analysis has dealt with the structural specifications in terms of the relationships among magnitudes such as wealth, revenue and capital stocks by making assumptions about the institutional set-up of economic society. Among modern economists Keynes, Piero Sraffa and Luigi L. Pasinetti dealt with the way in which particular institutional aspects bring about a given outcome. For example, in Keynes the form of the consumption function could be made to depend on the level and distribution of income. This is of course reflected in the value of the expenditure multiplier, which, in the case of a given autonomous expenditure, leads to a particular increase in national income for any given set of structural relationships among economic magnitudes.

Another example is provided by the treatment of the relationship between structural specifications and institutional assumptions in Sraffa's *Production of Commodities by Means of Commodities*. Here the author considers how a particular structure of production (i.e. a given set of productive methods) is not in itself sufficient to fully explain the set of relative prices; in fact the latter is also determined by assuming a particular criterion for the distribution of the net product among the various productive sectors of the system. In the special case of a capitalist economy the set of relative prices is determined by assuming either an exogenously given wage rate or 'by the level of the money rates of interest' (Sraffa, 1960, p. 33).

The relationship between the analysis of structure and institutional assumptions is elucidated in Pasinetti's (1964/5) inaugural lecture. Here the author states that a set of fundamental properties concerning economic structure (such as the relationship between the maximum rate of profits and the maximum growth rate or the 'natural rate of profits' – which allows the long-run equilibrium expansion in the output of the various final commodities according to Ernst Engel's law – cf. Pasinetti, 1981) can be analysed independently of the institutional set-up. This set-up does however become relevant as soon as one moves to the consideration of more specific features of economic systems, such as the interplay between relative prices and the distribution of income.

The idea that structural analysis ought to be separated from consideration of the institutional set-up (that is, the social, political and legal features of an economic system) has not always been perceived by scholars interested in the structural features of the economic system.

Going back to the Physiocrats one may consider Quesnay's *Tableau économique* in which the analysis of the circular flow of the social product is carried out by examining the way in which this social product is reproduced from one period of production to another by means of transactions between social classes. The latter are determined partly by the type of productive activity that is exerted and partly by the ownership of a productive factor (land). The two social classes of the former type are those of the agricultural and manufacturing producers; the third is that of the landlords. In this system there is a basic congruence between the way in which the social fabric is established and the mechanism by means of which the reproduction of social wealth is carried out. This feature is no longer to be found in Marx's work, where the reproduction of the social product requires the fulfilment of equilibrium conditions – such as those shown in his reproduction schemes – that are not necessarily consistent with the long-run coexistence of all social classes.

Keynes underlines the critical role of the entrepreneurs' class in a modern economic system (and this element will later be taken up by post-Keynesian writers and Michal Kalecki). On the one hand the entrepreneurs' class is, as such, the engine of growth of the system; but entrepreneurs as consumers do play a different role: Keynes stresses this in two distinct passages. First he states that 'in contemporary conditions the growth of wealth, so far from being dependent on the abstinence of the rich, as is commonly supposed, is more likely to be impeded by it' (Keynes, 1973, p. 373; 1st edn 1936); secondly he points out that while the scale of investment may be promoted by a low rate of interest, at the same time 'it would mean the euthanasia of the rentier, and, consequently, the euthanasia of the cumulative oppressive power of the capitalist to exploit the scarcity-value of capital' (Keynes, 1973, p. 376; 1st edn 1936).

Another type of inconsistency between social structure and long-run equilibrium conditions of the system as determined by a specific requirement on the accumulative process or structure (more precisely both capitalists and workers must provide enough savings to let their capital stock grow at the steady state growth rate) is provided by James Edward Meade (1966) and by the Samuelson Modigliani (1966) model of distribution. In particular when the saving propensity of the workers is higher than a given limit, the pure capitalists' class asymptotically disappears from the system.

This brief account shows that, although it is useful to distinguish between the two fundamental notions of structure to be found in economic analysis, it is equally important to examine their pattern of interaction. For example, a number of structural analyses show that the social and institutional structure behind an economic system is an important element for the determination of its productive structure; while the way in which production and accumulation are carried out could well influence the social structure as represented by, for instance, class composition.

5. Structure, change and economic theory

It is the purpose of this volume to contribute to the identification of the scope of structural methods in economic inquiry by:

(i) outlining the 'common core' of structural analysis;
(ii) examining the conditions under which particular specifications of economic structure can be useful for different purposes;
(iii) considering alternative ways in which such structural specifications have to be dealt with when examining the framework for dynamic analysis.

It is the editors' opinion that this field of inquiry deserves a thorough investigation both from the point of view of the different methods of structural analysis and from that of their application to specific problems of economic dynamics.

The relationship between the concept of economic structure and the analysis of economic change is of critical importance for the study of economic dynamics, but it has seldom been explicitly evaluated in a comprehensive way by economic theorists. Economic structure is the most fundamental set of relationships among economic units providing the basic framework for economic life. As a matter of fact most economic events are both the result and the cause of the underlying economic structure. Interdependence among economic units brings about results that may vary according to the type of structure being considered; on the other hand, the structure itself can often be seen as the background against which a certain class of economic outcomes is to be expected. Within a certain framework the relationships associated with any type of structure constrain interactions among economic agents and tend to bring about a determinate pattern of aggregate behaviour.

There are a number of ways in which the analytical device of economic structure has been used by economic theory. In particular one may refer to the utilization of economic structure in both the research line dealing primarily with allocation and 'rational' decisions of individuals (theories based on the pure exchange model) and the research line dealing primarily with the objective stock–flow network and wealth and income distribution among classes of individuals (theories based on the pure production model – see Baranzini and Scazzieri, 1986). The former type of theory is based on the identification of the interaction and communication scheme among economic agents and draws attention to the role of the structural framework in providing suitable restrictions on the behaviour of individuals, thus leading to determinate social outcomes. (On this point see Allais, 1986; Hildenbrand, 1983; Kirman, 1989.) On the other hand, the theories of the pure production type focus upon interdependence among the objective conditions moulding the 'system of events' to which human actions belong; here the role of the structural set-up is to provide a framework in which the mutual compatibility of objective conditions may be assessed quite independently of individual or collective objective functions.

6. The organization of the volume and the contributions

The organization of the volume reflects the approach we adopted in dealing with the above-mentioned issues. In particular we have attempted a comprehensive investigation of the relationship among institutional set-up, structural specification and the time structure underlying the identification of fundamental economic relationships. This strategy of inquiry leads to the analysis of the connection between structural dynamics and the analysis of economic change. The contribution in Part I ('Structure and Institutions in Political Economy') provides a critical framework for the assessment of the relative position of economic structure and institutional arrangements in moulding the pattern of economic behaviour. The contributions in Part II ('Single-Period Relationships and Economic Theory') and in Part III ('Structural Dynamics and the Analysis of Economic Change') provide an assessment of the role of uni-periodal and dynamic concepts of structure in alternative theoretical frameworks; first by investigating the 'static' specification of structure characterizing pure-exchange and pure-production models; secondly by outlining a framework in which the specific requirements for the analysis of dynamic structures (that is of structures generating structural change) may be considered. Part IV ('A Framework for Structural Analysis') aims at providing new conceptual perspectives on the foundations of the economic theory of structure and change. This is done by outlining a comprehensive framework for the relevant types of structural specification, by identifying a number of critical features characterizing the historical dynamics of economic systems and by assessing the associated patterns of structural change.

The contribution in Part I is by Lorenzo Ornaghi on 'Economic Structure and Political Institutions: A Theoretical Framework'. This chapter starts from the consideration, from a methodological point of view, of what may be called 'terminal problems' of economics, that is problems located on the borderline between economics and other social disciplines. Ornaghi deals with his topic by showing how the consideration of political institutions has always performed a major role in moulding the relationships between structures of inquiry and economic theory. As a matter of fact, the interdependence between politics and economics has represented a major theme for economic analysis since the age in which the modern state organization took shape and 'political economy' replaced the ancient Aristotelian tradition of 'œconomics' concerning the rules for the good administration of the household. At this point it is argued that a general theoretical framework relative to the relationship between economic structure and political institutions presupposes an essentially dynamic approach to the interaction between economics and politics. Here the author stresses that political institutions, considered as a system of goal-oriented procedures, are fundamental for the interpretation of the internal as well as the global dynamic of economic structure. A critical role is performed by the consideration of time: first, political institutions play a role in determining the time horizon of economic actions; secondly, such institutions are directly related to innovative transformation of the fundamental economic structure. This perspective suggests a theoretical framework with distinct methodological and analytical features. On the one hand, a 'terminal problem' of political economy is dealt with by opening up the conceptual domain of economics to concepts and hypotheses deriving from other social disciplines. On the other hand, it may be possible to highlight the specific role of modern political institutions in providing an essential cohesive framework for a type of economic structure that is revealing itself to be increasingly complex and sophisticated. As a result the relation between political institutions and economic structure appears to provide an important starting point for a reflection on the distinct and autonomous foundations of economics and politics.

Part II introduces a critical analysis of the issue of structural specification in economic theory by considering in particular those theoretical frameworks in which economic structure is identified as a given network of relationships without explicitly dealing with time-related issues of structural change. The first chapter of this part is by Takashi Negishi on 'Economic Structure and the Theory of Economic Equilibrium'. Negishi discusses the structure of Walrasian general equilibrium theory and Marshallian partial equilibrium theory, which form a large part of the traditional 'core' of marginalist or neoclassical economics. Negishi develops his analysis by following two distinct, but interlinked, issues. The first concerns the reconstruction of seemingly uni-periodal concepts of economic structure underlying the core elements of general and partial equilibrium theories. Here Negishi argues that an implicit dynamic framework underlies such theories and that in this connection it may be helpful to consider the contribution of Sir John Hicks 'who integrated Walrasian and Marshallian implicit dynamic concepts, along with more explicit Swedish ones, into a unified theory' (see p. 47 below). However, as the author underlines, the whole set of implications of a number of these explicit dynamic concepts have not been exhaustively pursued by modern economic theorists.

The second major issue taken up by Negishi concerns the comparison of

Walrasian and Marshallian theories with the theory of the market put forward by Francis Edgeworth and William Stanley Jevons. Negishi stresses that the communication structure of the Walras–Marshall model differs from the Jevons–Edgeworth model of cooperative market games. More precisely, while the two models coincide in the case of a large economy with a great number of agents, in the case of competition among a few one obtains fundamentally different results. A major point stressed by the author is that '[i]mplicit dynamic concepts are hidden in the time structure of Walrasian and Marshallian theories, which are generally regarded as uni-periodal economic theories' (see p. 62 below). Some of these concepts, according to Negishi, clearly correspond to the more refined concepts of modern dynamic theories. However, the implications of Marshall's idea that the equilibrium of the industry may be compatible with the disequilibrium of individual firms have not yet been fully developed by modern theorists, and a step in this direction is to be considered. After showing the dynamic implications of Marshall's contribution, Negishi moves on to consider equilibrium theories characterized by a different communication structure among agents, such as those of Jevons and Edgeworth. He concludes that, in the case of an economy with a large number of agents, one obtains the same results concerning the dynamics of the economic system independently of its communication structure, thereby establishing the general applicability (for the large economy case) of dynamic results obtained within the Marshallian framework.

The second chapter of Part II is by Heinrich Bortis on 'Structure and Change Within the Circular Theory of Production'. In this contribution the author discusses the different meaning of terms such as structure and change in classical and Keynesian theory on the one hand, and in neoclassical or marginalist theory on the other. It is argued that, in the former, structural elements, technology and institutions directly govern the outcome of economic events. For example, natural prices depend upon the conditions of production and on institutionally fixed distribution (profit rates). Objective factors that partly determine the actions of individuals thus play a crucial role. This is different in neoclassical economics where institutions and technology belong to the framework surrounding the market place. The latter, if functioning 'satisfactorily', is supposed to coordinate the rational actions of individuals in such a way that a determinate outcome is achieved. In the neoclassical theory, factor markets play a prominent role with respect to functional income distribution and employment. If the long run is being considered, the absence of 'factor markets' in the classical (Ricardian) approach perhaps represents the main conceptual difference between the classical and the neoclassical way of looking at economic phenomena.

The author argues that the different perspective associated with either approach is essentially due to a different treatment of production and exchange. In classical political economy, the conceptual starting point is provided by the consideration of production processes, and exchange plays a relatively minor role. In particular, deviations of market prices from prices of production emerge as a result of structures of production that are inappropriate with respect to the structure of needs. Neoclassical economics, on the other hand, starts from the principle of exchange, which is subsequently extended to other spheres of economic life including, of course, production. Bortis's contribution considers in particular the implications of the concepts of 'structure' and 'change' in the circular view of production that is embedded in economic theory of the classical type. First, the classical approach to production is characterized: production emerges here as a social process based on horizontal interdependencies. Then the consequences of the classical approach in view of explaining important economic phenomena (such as distribution, value and proportions among sectors) are set forth. It appears that the typically Keynesian problem of employment determination can be neatly integrated into the classical theoretical scheme.

At this point the paper attempts to formulate a general analytical framework within which the concept of structural change is grafted onto a new appraisal of the concept of economic structure. Here Bortis suggests that institutions 'do not *entirely* explain the phenomena in question, but only their constant or slowly changing parts' (see pp. 80–1 below). As a matter of fact economic structure consists of the institutionalized parts of economic life and includes the techniques of production and the various institutional arrangements that give a certain degree of regularity to the interplay of human actions within any given economic system. More specifically, it is maintained that institutions are associated with repetitive actions 'in relation to which the time element does not play an essential role' (see p. 83 below), whereas time is essential in a theory of structural (and institutional) change. The paper finally advances a new conceptual framework within which the relationship between structure and human action is linked with the distinction between two different types of causal analysis: 'vertical causality' in which time plays no essential role, and 'horizontal causality', in which time is a critical component of economic explanation.

Part III of the volume presents a critical assessment of structural specification in relation to the analysis of economic transformation in general and structural change in particular. Here the issue of the way in which the consideration of time moulds the theory of economic dynamics takes on a specific character since the role of time is linked with the principle of relative structural invariance, which emerges as a critical feature in the economic theory of structural change. The first contribution is by Michael Landesmann and Roberto Scazzieri on 'Specification of Structure and Economic Dynamics'. The starting point of this chapter is the idea that the identification of a specific 'structural mapping' is an essential prerequisite for describing any given economic system in a way that is compatible with the appraisal of the most abstract and general features of such a system. The role of 'simplifying assumptions' in moulding the field of economic analysis takes on a critical dimension when the prerequisites for dynamic analysis are considered. In particular, the authors argue that if the 'relative persistence' of economic structure is not explicitly considered, dynamic analysis tends to inquire into the conditions for the stability of any given equilibrium state, rather than into the characteristics of adjustment paths associated with parameter changes. An important example of the role that such a relative persistence may perform is provided by the analysis of structural economic dynamics. Here Landesmann and Scazzieri maintain that the identification of 'time-differentiated' processes of transformation is a necessary condition for the analysis of 'dynamic structures'. These are defined as structures in which the change of a given set of relationships takes on a definite shape because other relationships are changing at a different speed, or do not change at all.

This perspective leads the authors to identify two distinct approaches to the analysis of the time structure of a transformation process. One is Marshall's time-period analysis, in which any actual state of the economy (different from the stationary state) is described as a combination of adjusted and non-adjusted structures. The other is the analysis of economic movement as a sequence of transformation stages as carried out in economic theories of the 'sequential causality' type, such as the 'cumulative process' analysis started by Knut Wicksell and the 'theory of continuation' considered by Hicks.

At this point, a number of different approaches to structural specification are examined, and the authors address the issue of which type of specification is more suitable for structural change analysis. In this connection it is maintained that the utilization of a pure 'circular-flow' model may be compatible with the analysis of structural dynamics, provided dynamic behavioural principles allow for the consideration of a whole sequence of 'circular states'. However, a completely dynamic treatment of structural transformation leads to the appraisal of dynamic structures, which may alternatively be based on horizontal or vertical interdependencies, according to the specific form taken by the relative persistence of structures and by the dynamic principles determining the movement of the economic system through historical time.

The issue of structural change, in relation to the type of descriptive–analytical approach adopted in economic analysis, is the central focus of attention in the contributions by Jean Magnan de Bornier and Harald Hagemann, which consider the economic theory of structural change when the structural-invariance criterion is associated with complementarities over time (Magnan de Bornier) and when it is associated with the combination of horizontal and vertical structural rigidities (Hagemann).

The chapter by Magnan de Bornier ('Vertical Integration, Growth and Sequential Change') presents an inquiry into the fundamental analytical characteristics of the vertical and time-based specification of economic structure, and on the implications of such a structural specification on aggregate economic behaviour. The author first describes and compares the 'intratemporal' and 'intertemporal' approaches to the identification of a structural-invariance criterion and argues that the intertemporal model, which is based on the description of complementarities over time, is especially suited for the consideration of dynamic problems involving rigidities over time, such as those associated with non-transferable capital goods. In particular, Magnan de Bornier points out that the strength of the time-based vertical model of economic structure, of which the foremost example in modern economic theory is presented in Hicks's *Capital and Time* (1973), may be associated with the analysis of transitional paths (Hicks's own 'traverses'), in which 'the present situation appears as a *datum*, where the capital stock is given' (see p. 131 below). In this case, the reproducibility conditions considered in the circular flow and the associated network of horizontal interdependencies recede into the background, and the most critical economic issue becomes that of ensuring the transformation of a given economic structure by building up new capital equipment on the basis of an existing fund of productive resources. Complementarities over time are considered as the defining characteristics of structural change, especially if attention is focused upon short- and medium-term dynamics. Such a feature of economic structure is then grafted onto the assessment of capital controversies and of the way in which dynamic features and patterns are dealt with in economic theory.

In the former case, it is argued that most criticisms of the Austrian theory of capital lead to the consideration of the capital stock as 'an *abstract and permanent fund* generating an equally permanent flow of income' (see p. 135 below). In the case of dynamic theory, it is maintained that intertemporal complementarities introduce an important difference between planned and spontaneous traverses, and are, in general, a critical source of economic instability.

The last chapter of Part III is by Harald Hagemann on 'The Structural Theory of Economic Growth'. In this essay the comparative advantage of vertical and circular (inter-industry) approaches are highlighted. Hagemann draws attention to the specific contribution of the Kiel School in establishing a rigorous working relationship between the roles of horizontal and vertical rigidities in the analysis of structural transformation in general and cyclical growth in particular. A leading member of that School, Adolph Löwe, has proposed a theoretical set-up for the structural analysis of production. On the one hand this draws from Marx and the study of interdependencies among sectors, and on the other hand it remains open to the vertical integration of productive activities. The originating elements of the Kiel research programme may be traced back to the 'construction of a theoretical model of cyclical growth with the basic working hypothesis that a satisfactory explanation of industrial fluctuations must fit into the general framework of an economic theory of the circular flow as it was developed by Quesnay and Marx' (see p. 148 below). The appraisal of cyclical growth within an integrated theoretical framework including both circular and vertical features is achieved by adopting a stage-structure description of individual productive processes and, at the same time, an inter-industry representation of the productive network holding together the different sectors of an economic system. Such an approach allows for a treatment of complementarities over time that are rooted in the circular mechanisms of causality characterizing intersectoral flows.

Hagemann then considers the specific feature of a comprehensive approach to the analysis of structural transformation. He maintains that the full strength of such an approach may be appreciated by examining the critical role of the machine-tool sector in determining the conditions for the feasibility of any given transformation process and the specific shape taken by such a process in the course of historical time. In particular, Hagemann stresses the need for integrating the descriptive analysis of structural relations and economic dynamics in actual economic systems with an appraisal of the necessary conditions that any given structural transformation path must fulfil if a certain policy goal has to be attained. This would require an integration of structural analysis with 'force analysis', in which economics 'is raised above the level of a mere engineering science'.

This perspective suggests that the combined utilization of the circular and vertical approaches in the formulation of a theory of structural transformation may be associated with the specific problems of historical transformation processes carried out as definite goals of economic policy. Such a result opens the field of structural analysis to the consideration of economic and political institutions, which appears to be necessary in the assessment of actual processes of structural change and of their goal-adequate characteristics.

Part IV ('A Framework for Structural Analysis') outlines a general framework within which a number of critical issues raised in the volume may be given a new perspective. In particular, the relationship between 'objective' (for instance technological) and institutional features of economic structure emerges as a most important element in determining paths of structural economic change. This aim is pursued by assessing the relevance of specific clusters of historical features in determining the suitable theoretical framework for dynamic analysis (also including the role of the representation of productive structure to be adopted); by proposing a general approach to the analysis of the relationship between institutional constraints and the dynamic of production processes; and finally by setting into perspective the way in which the distinction between horizontal and vertical approaches to the analysis of economic structure may be related to the investigation of the linkage between objective and institutional features of economic structure.

The first chapter of Part IV is by Michio Morishima on 'Economic Theory and Industrial Evolution'. The author proposes a rigorous analytical framework in order to explain what he calls 'fatal structural changes', that is changes constraining a given economic system along a path of transformations leading to a completely different structure. Such changes might in turn explain the succession of different economic theories. In this perspective, Morishima considers the classical, marginalist (or neoclassical) and Keynesian paradigms and he builds for each of them a comprehensive theoretical model within which he considers in detail the properties of all relevant variables. According to Morishima, the transition from classical to neoclassical economic theory was achieved by substituting one set of characterizing assumptions for another, and in particular by replacing the Ricardian wage-fund theory with the theory of inter-sectoral repercussions (marginalists). On the other hand, the transition from marginalist to Keynesian theory is associated with Keynes's denial of Say's law (marginalist) so that full-employment equilibrium is not automatically realized, and also with his rejection of the 'free-good rule' in factor markets (especially for labour) via the introduction of an investment function, partly consisting of autonomous investment and partly of induced investment. (Investment and savings will be equated with each other after necessary adjustments have been made, and the equilibrium activity levels are made to depend on the level of autonomous investment.)

At the end of his paper, Morishima tries to identify the characterizing features of each type of model by summarizing as follows: 'the Ricardian model is a model for an economy where (1) the wage-fund theory is valid and (2) Say's law prevails, while the Walrasian model is based on (2) but gets rid of (1) and the Keynesian is free from both (1) and (2)' (see p. 193 below). Thus Ricardo's economics is suitable for the analysis of a system at an early stage of development, when agriculture is still a significant sector of the economy. In this connection, Morishima quotes two sets of data relative to Great Britain. The first refers to the ratio of workers engaged in agriculture (including forestry and fishing) to workers engaged in the manufacturing industry; the second refers to the share of agricultural output in total gross national income. These data lead Morishima to identify the age of Ricardian economics with the period between 1810 and 1850, because during this historical phase agriculture is still significant, at least 'until the repeal of the Corn Laws in 1846' (see p. 193 below).

However, during the second part of the nineteenth century, the Ricardian model becomes increasingly inappropriate and the Walrasian model based on the consideration of simultaneous inter-industrial relationships increases its influence. In order to assess the degree of applicability of Say's law to the real world Morishima divides actual investment into three parts: first, the investment made by capitalists who are themselves entrepreneurs and who will invest the whole amount of their savings; secondly, the investment undertaken by entrepreneurs on the basis of credit from banks or the issue of new shares or bonds; and thirdly, the autonomous investment made by the state or other public bodies. In connection with such a distinction, Morishima relates Say's law to investment of the first type and considers the latter two types of investment as making up the 'anti-Say's law part' (Morishima). Consideration of economic history suggests the inapplicability of Say's law for modelling the economic system after the 1920s.

The above comparison of the Ricardian, marginalist and Keynesian sets of 'characterizing assumptions' leads Morishima to argue that there is at present no general theoretical framework that may provide an explanation for the transition from one type of economic structure to another. In particular it is maintained that '[i]t is indeed difficult to theorize an object of investigation that is quickly changing in its basic features; we are not provided with enough repetition of similar phenomena, on the basis of observations of which we may construct a theory' (see p. 195 below).

The second chapter of this part is by Nicholas Georgescu-Roegen on 'Production Process and Dynamic Economics'. This contribution presents a critical assessment of the way in which production phenomena are analytically represented in economic theory and highlights the implications of such analytical representation for the theory of economic dynamics and structural change.

Here the issue that emerges concerns the complex descriptive requirements associated with the analysis of economic change. Any given economic system consists of a cluster of institutional features that may lead to analytical model building after a number of particular characteristics have been selected from the set of historically and technically identifiable features. At this point the method of structural analysis takes on a specific character, since the process of structural specification is carried out by explicitly considering the implications of alternative analytical representations in the analysis of dynamic processes and 'qualitative change'.

This task is carried out by providing a comprehensive assessment of the relevance of 'intended and planned production', which is considered 'a human activity far older and, moreover, far more critical than participation in a stock exchange market' (see p. 199 below). In the connection it is pointed out that productive activity lends itself to analytical treatment in terms of the concept of 'material process'. However 'no definition of "process" is to be found anywhere' and there is a thorough investigation of the specific analytical requirements to be satisfied by the concept of process in production theory.

The author points out that a satisfactory analytical representation of production activity must take into consideration that '[e]verywhere there is some action, some change, some vibration, far too many happenings for a manageable description (see p. 207 below). Here a necessary condition for economic inquiry is a suitable carving of the relationships that one wants to examine; in particular a fundamental distinction is introduced among the factors of production: '[t]he factors that enter the process and also come out of it are *funds*; those that enter but do not come out or come out without having entered are *flows*' (see p. 209 below).

Finally, the implications of the flow–fund representation for the epistemology of dynamic economics are investigated. Here Georgescu-Roegen challenges the utilization of Newtonian dynamics and points out that, in the case of economics, qualitative change rather than motion is the distinguishing feature of dynamic processes. In particular a theory of economic dynamics ought to consider that '[w]e cannot produce commodities from commodities; we can produce commodities only by accomplished production processes' (see p. 222 below). This point allows Georgescu-Roegen to highlight an important relationship between the analytical representation of production technology used in Leontief's input–output model and certain issues taken up in the vertically integrated representations of the productive system. More specifically, the production of productive processes come to the fore as a critical feature in the explanation of changes in the rate of change of any given economy. In this connection it may be suitable to substitute a process-based dynamic framework for a commodity-based identification of production technology; as a matter of fact the consideration of dynamic processes leads Georgescu-Roegen to stress the important role of morphogenesis in explaining the most critical features of dynamic economic paths.

The final chapter of this volume ('Economic Structure: Analytical

Perspectives' by Mauro Baranzini and Roberto Scazzieri) attempts a critical assessment of the different intellectual strands of structural analysis, provides a first systematization of such contributions and suggests a number of lines of further research. This task is carried out in a sequence of steps. The treatment of economic structure in economic theory is considered by focusing upon two distinct ways of classifying economic magnitudes: one describing the horizontal network of mutually dependent activities and the other considering the representation of the economic system as a set of vertically integrated sub-systems that cut through the network of horizontal interdependencies. At this point we consider the position of institutions in the theory of economic structure by arguing that institutional arrangements provide an essential element in the identification of the behavioural features of any given objective stock–flow network of economic magnitudes (such as the input–output pattern of production interrelationships). In this connection the special relevance of institutions in describing the morphology of economic systems and in analysing their qualitative patterns of transformation is stressed. The theory of economic structure lends itself to the formulation of analytical frameworks for the analysis of structural transformation in which a critical role is performed by the relationship between persistence and change. Here it is maintained that a complete theory of structural dynamics requires the integration of an endogenous pattern of structural change and external dynamic impulses or forces. The above conceptual framework is followed by an appraisal of the most important dynamic features of economic systems and by the identification of the connection existing between the analysis of such features and the utilization of particular methods of theoretical investigation. In particular, the relationship between conceptual frameworks and objects of analysis is examined by considering the specific types of dynamic issues that may be investigated by concentrating upon the vertical integration of economic activities or upon the circular (horizontal) network of economic interrelationships. This task is attempted by presenting a rational reconstruction of the history of dynamic economic theory based on the distinction between horizontal and vertical approaches to economic structure. Finally, it is argued that the above distinction may provide a unifying framework for assessing the mutual compatibility between the identification of structural features, institutional arrangements and patterns of economic dynamics.

7. Epilogue

The concept of economic structure emerges as the unifying theme of the different contributions of this volume. In particular, the structure of any given economic system appears as the network of features giving identity to that system and providing the necessary elements on which task-specific theoretical tools may be constructed. As a result, these theoretical tools are to be grafted onto historically definite characterizing assumptions. The identification of economic structure is thus a critical step in establishing a connection between economic theory and factual economic analysis. More precisely, a relationship comes to be established between, on the one hand, the choice of simplifying assumptions underlying any given theoretical framework and, on the other hand, the identification of characterizing assumptions relevant for the description of any determinate historical framework. In this way, a new perspective is introduced: the analysis of actual economic systems comes to be associated with what may be called 'theoretical empiricism', a method of inquiry in which factual observation is not independent of the explicit utilization of theoretical frameworks, while the latter are supposed to incorporate the specific characterizing assumptions relevant to each particular case.

The concept of economic structure suggested in this volume allows for a reassessment of the coexistence of distinct theoretical frameworks in economic inquiry from many different perspectives. In particular a new interpretation may be proposed concerning the respective role of the 'pure-exchange' and 'pure-production' models in the construction of economic theory. Such an interpretation draws on the relationship between the analytical simplification implicit in theoretical models and the historical characterization often implied by the adoption of a particular set of primitive assumptions. As a matter of fact, actual economic events may reveal themselves to be approximations of given sets of theoretical preconceived schemes. For example, the 'society of exchange' of a certain stage of early capitalism approximates the cluster of features characterizing the pure-exchange model. In a similar way, the 'capital-accumulation society' of a more advanced industrial economy approximates the characterizing features of the pure-production model. This implies that the process of analytical simplification often suppresses actual institutional characteristics and replaces them with those institutional elements relevant for the theoretical framework under consideration. It then follows that an exhaustive assessment of distinct research lines may not be carried out as long as historical and institutional characteristics are not adequately considered.

The implications for the analysis of change are far-reaching. As a matter of fact, economic dynamics may be considered in different ways depending on the type of structural specification. More precisely, the motion of any given system reflects both the 'anatomy' and the 'physiology' of that system, that is the way in which the objective stock–flow network has been described and the manner in which definite behavioural principles may be grafted onto such an objective structure. At the same time, given behavioural principles act upon the motion of the system in a different way according to whether the objective structure of the system is described as a circular flow or as a one-way flow from primary resources to finished goods. It is at this point that the institutional arrangements supporting any given economic system come into play. As a matter of fact, it may be argued that a fundamental behavioural principle, such as the propensity to save, is associated with different types of economic dynamics and that more sophisticated institutional arrangements are required to ensure the process of physical capital accumulation and hence economic expansion. The one-way description of economic structure is generally associated with the identification of institutional arrangements concerning the availability of primary resources, their free disposal (property rights) and the way they lead to the satisfaction of human needs. On the other hand, the circular representation of economic structure requires a set of institutional arrangements that permit the linkage between saving and physical productive accumulation by means of specific rules for the distribution of produced commodities among individuals and across different time periods.

In this perspective, the theory of economic change turns out to be associated with three fundamental elements of analysis: the specification of 'objective' economic structure (that is the objective stock–flow network), the identification of particular institutional arrangements and the selection of given types of economic transformation. The way in which the above three elements of analysis are combined may lead to greater or lesser emphasis on particular instances of economic behaviour and type of motion, thus allowing for the construction of economic theories that are suitable for the investigation of different features of dynamic economic paths.

References

Allais, M. (1986) 'The Concepts of Surplus and Loss and the Reformulation of the Theories of Stable General Economic Equilibrium and Maximum Efficiency', in *Foundations of Economics. Structures of Inquiry and Economic Theory*, ed. M. Baranzini and R. Scazzieri, Basil Blackwell, Oxford and New York, pp. 135–74.

Baranzini, M., and Scazzieri, R. (1986) 'Knowledge in Economics: A Framework', in *Foundations of Economics. Structures of Inquiry and Economic Theory*, ed. M. Baranzini and R. Scazzieri, Basil Blackwell, Oxford and New York, pp. 1–87.

Hicks, J. (1973) *Capital and Time. A Neo-Austrian Theory*, Clarendon Press, Oxford.

Hildenbrand, W. (1983) 'Introduction', in G. Debreu, *Mathematical Economics. Twenty Papers of G. Debreu*, Cambridge University Press, Cambridge.

Kantorovich, L.V. (1965) *The Best Use of Economic Resources*, Pergamon Press, Oxford (Russian original 1959).
Keynes, J.M. (1973) *The General Theory of Employment, Interest and Money*, Macmillan, London (1st edn 1936).
Kirman, A. (1989) 'The Intrinsic Limits of Modern Economic Theory: The Emperor has no Clothes', *Economic Journal*, 99, pp. 126–39.
Leontief, W.W. (1941) *The Structure of American Economy, 1919–1939. An Empirical Application of Equilibrium Analysis*, Harvard University Press, Cambridge, Mass.
Meade, J.E. (1966) 'The Outcome of the Pasinetti Process: A Note', *Economic Journal*, 76, pp. 161–5.
Pasinetti, L.L. (1964–5) 'Causalità e interdipendenza nell'analisi econometrica e nella teoria economica', *Annuario dell'Università Cattolica del S. Cuore*, Milan, pp. 233–50.
(1981) *Structural Change and Economic Growth. A Theoretical Essay on the Dynamics of the Wealth of Nations*, Cambridge University Press, Cambridge.
Samuelson, P.A., and Modigliani, F. (1966) 'The Pasinetti Paradox in Neoclassical and More General Models', *Review of Economic Studies*, 33, pp. 269–301; and 'Reply to Pasinetti and Robinson', ibid., pp. 321–30.
Scazzieri, R. (1988) 'Economic Theorizing', in *Contributi di analisi economica*, ed. M. Baranzini and A. Cencini, Casagrande, Bellinzona (Switzerland), pp. 149–57.
Sraffa, P. (1960) *Production of Commodities by Means of Commodities*, Cambridge University Press, Cambridge.

Part I
STRUCTURE AND INSTITUTIONS IN POLITICAL ECONOMY

1 Economic structure and political institutions: a theoretical framework

LORENZO ORNAGHI

1. Introduction

With increasing frequency social scientists are openly regretting the disadvantages of an exasperated 'autonomy' in their respective disciplines. In economics, as in other major social sciences (such as political science and sociology; but the same applies to law) autonomy now carries the risk of an isolation that is less and less acceptable – unless it is regarded as a necessary condition for the progress or very existence of each discipline.[1] Since the end of the nineteenth century, the body of the social sciences has become progressively more fragmented under the pressure of specialization, both by fields of inquiry and by analytical tools. In our day, every 'major' social discipline is unified only in appearance: internally each of them is actually a system (or a more or less coherent set) of methods and techniques, theories, doctrines. Isolation – progressively more worrying as it comes to resemble Hegelian 'alienation' (*Entfremdung*) – thrives now within, as well as between, the disciplines constituting the old and noble – and deceased – *corpus* of the nineteenth-century *Gesamtwissenschaften*.[2]

I am grateful to Massimo Beber for his contribution to the translation of the original Italian manuscript and for his observations.

[1] The isolation of economics, glaringly apparent in relation to history (Hicks, 1986), is increasingly emerging with regard to psychology. It might be worth remembering that Vilfredo Pareto, before separating 'non-logical actions' from 'logical actions', had observed that 'the foundation of political economy and generally of every social science is, manifestly, psychology' (Pareto, 1971, p. 35). Similarly Maffeo Pantaleoni, acknowledging the 'asymmetry' between 'economic problems of *locus*' and those of '*tempus*', had remarked in *Definizione dell'economia. Una prolusione*: 'Notwithstanding the contrary opinion of celebrated modern thinkers, such as Pareto, Keynes, Schumpeter and Cassel, I maintain that political economy should not be denied access to the factual data provided to us by psychology. I cannot see what is to be gained from such privation, but I do see what is lost.' He immediately added, with regard to Pareto's 'contradiction': 'For the present, we should observe that the new route has led to *identical* results when it is pursued by those who had previously followed the old one, such as Pareto.' (Pantaleoni, 1925, p. 8)

[2] An important attempt at preserving this *corpus* – or possibly at substituting a less imposing but more vital one began very early this century, with the attempt to analyse the relations

A peculiar danger, and a paradox, in this state of affairs is that what each social discipline conventionally regards as beyond the boundaries of its 'sovereignty' or 'autonomy' is also what is increasingly perceived as crucial to the growth of the conceptual and theoretical endowment of that discipline. Those very problems on whose solution the development of social knowledge rests are considered to lie outside the specific domain of each discipline (as parameters to be accepted, or constraints to be suffered, without being able to change them). In other words, they may be considered 'terminal problems' – as the Italian economist Emanuele Sella would define them with reference to his own discipline – 'whose solution presupposes the definition of concepts that are *interfering* with concepts not belonging to political economy' (Sella, 1904, p. 401).

It is mainly when approaching contemporary economic, political and social 'transformations' that such 'terminal problems' appear in all their relevance. For all social disciplines, and particularly for political economy, the analysis of change is indeed the field in which the need for rigorous and powerful concepts is most urgently felt. Undoubtedly, social disciplines appear to participate in a *koiné* of ideas.[3] But the concepts of wider currency – when they do not rebound, uncontrolled, between disciplines – turn out to have limited use in the exploration of one of the fundamental mechanisms governing the current changes: the increasing number and strength of *factual* 'interferences' between economic, political and social factors. If 'terminal problems' are to be correctly formulated, they need 'interfering concepts' that are suitable for their analysis.

Political institutions are certainly among the major factors in those interferences. Compared with other institutions, political ones have a sort of 'surplus value' (*Mehrwert*), consisting in their actual or virtual power to directly affect the boundaries of the economic structure and also (we shall later see how importantly) the temporal horizon of economic actions as *creative* actions.

Through the permanent interaction between political institutions and

between politics and economics and to identify the elements of a 'philosophy of economics' (Tönnies, 1907–8; Freyer, 1921). However, such a 'period of constructive synthesis in the social sciences' had already well and truly ended by the early 1930s, as repeatedly remarked by Adolph Löwe in his attempt at elaborating a 'realistic theory of the modern economic system', which was to be informed by the 'dynamic chain of reciprocal causation between the economic process and its social environment' (Löwe, 1935, pp. 138–9).

[3] Thus the most current concepts of the social disciplines today appear extraordinarily 'cosmopolitan': e.g., 'institution', 'structure', 'power', 'exchange', 'welfare' and so on. In any case, this continuous wandering of concepts is the product of a lack of dialogue among social disciplines – exception made for the rare instances where the original identity of the concept is still clearly recognized, as maybe in 'value': and it is the more dangerous the more it entrenches the habit or convention of taking for valid the 'results' of neighbouring (but methodologically 'autonomous') disciplines.

structure,[4] individual and collective actions coalesce into a specific 'economic system' that can be historically identified and represented.

Again through this interaction, in every historically identified system the economic structure is founded upon (and perceived as) a *durable* framework of relations providing the basic framework for economic activity. It is precisely the 'surplus value' (*Mehrwert*) of political institutions that permits the existence and durability of correspondences and symmetries between politics and economics. Moreover, if indeed – as in Max Weber's definition of 'the concept of economic action' – 'an "economic system" (*Wirtschaft*) is an autocephalous system of economic action. An "economic organization" (*Wirtschaftsbetrieb*) is a continuously organized system of economic action' (Weber, 1947, p. 31),[5] then the integrating role of political institutions appears to increase with the degree of complexity and organization of economic action. The relation of political institutions with economic structure then becomes essential for two distinct reasons. First, it provides a better analytical–historical perspective on the links between political economy and 'political order' (the latter is not coincident with the type of 'order' that is associated with the existence of the State). Secondly, it contributes to a 'dynamic' interpretation of the contemporary relations between State institutions and economic order. In turn, this is the only route to an analysis emphasizing the link between order and transformation in a theory of the intersections between economic and political cycle.

This also explains why, with much prior hesitation and armed only with the analytical tools of their own discipline, political scientists should now dare trespass into the occasionally awkward territory of economics.

[4] In Marxist terminology, 'structure' has often been used as a substitute for 'basis' (*Base*, *Basis*, in German). But precisely because, in our later discussion of 'economic structure', the emphasis will be on the totality of individual 'actions' and on the 'interrelations' among the activities of production and distribution of goods and services, this meaning must be distinguished from the one implied by Marx (Marx–Engels, 1845–6, p. 311), when defining the 'mode of production' as the 'real basis' (*reelle Basis*) of the State; or in considering the 'social organization' immediately unfolding from the mode of production and exchange as the 'basis' of the State and of any other 'superstructure' (*Superstruktur*).

[5] Max Weber pointed out that '[a]n "organization" (*Betrieb*) is a system of continuous *purposive* activity of a specified kind'; thus in its more general form 'a "compulsory association" (*Anstalt*) is a corporate group the established order of which has, within a given specific sphere of activity, been successfully imposed on every individual who conforms with certain specific criteria'. Accordingly, the *Anstalt* is distinguished from the *Verein* or union, which is described as 'a corporate group originating in a voluntary agreement and in which the established order claims authority over the members only by virtue of a personal act of adherence'. Both 'compulsory association' and 'union', Weber concludes, possess a '*rationally* established order' (Weber, 1947, p. 28). The arduous – and most interesting – question is, however, to what extent 'rational' and 'systematic' are strictly coextensive for every economic structure.

2. Political institutions as a 'terminal problem'

In the current frame of ideas in the social sciences 'institution' is associated with a plurality of meanings, its constant use (and misuse) having almost worn it down to a generic synonym of 'organization'. It may still have a sufficiently precise meaning in law, where it retains traces of its ancestry in late Roman ecclesiastical law,[6] but in sociology and anthropology, as well as in political science and even in the sociology of law, the concept of institution has dissolved into a myriad of definitions and meanings. In an attempt at classification, they seem to fall into two broad categories. In the first class one finds those acceptations that stress the existence of organized groups and sets of roles related by specific and relevant functions; in the second group are those usages that emphasize the existence and formation of norms, customs and beliefs, symbolic systems functional to the discipline of social behaviour.

However, both cases (that of 'pure norms' and that of 'organization', which requires the existence of goods as well as of pure norms) imply the existence of 'regularities', and thus of individual 'expectations' that certain events should recur with constant and known characteristics. In François Perroux's definition: 'Institutions are durable frameworks of actions, durable rules of the social game and collective habits, in contrast to later unconnected actions or events' (Perroux, 1960, p. 118).

These 'regularities' can be 'artificial' (in the sense of being constructed on purpose by people) as well as 'natural'. Political institutions come under the former type of regularity: they are constructed on purpose by people (or retained when they are the outcome of 'general and contingent circumstances' rather than 'the product of a design').[7] As a result, they appear to

[6] The meaning of 'what has been instituted' is a (relative) 'novelty' originating from France. Its paternity is almost certainly to be attributed to the French translation of Samuel von Pufendorf's *De iure naturae et gentium* (1672), first published in 1706 thanks to Jean Barbeyrac. At the outset of Book I.1.4, Pufendorf wrote: 'Moreover, just as the original mode of production of physical entities is creation, so the mode of production of moral entities can hardly be better described than by the word *impositio*'. The Latin '*impositio*' is rendered with '*Institution*' by Barbeyrac, who thus significantly expands in footnote 2: 'I have not been able to find a better term for "*impositio*"... As a substitute, the term "institution" is generally used for what is constructed and put in place, as opposed to what comes from *nature*. I accept there is a difference between the normal acceptation of this distinction, and that intended by our Author when he maintains that moral phenomena are such *by imposition*, not *in themselves, or by their nature*' (see Orestano, 1982–3, pp. 174–5).

[7] A reading of the political institutions of the modern State mainly in terms of the outcome of these 'general contingent circumstances' has been stressed – quite correctly in my opinion – by Michael Oakeshott (1975, pp. 267, 185). Hayek, in his stringent critique of constructivism, moves in the same direction, concluding that 'a large part of social formations, although the result of human action, is not of human design' (Hayek, 1978, p. 5; see also Hayek, 1973). In this connection, it is worth mentioning Gerhard Oestreich's view that the modern State can 'only partially be described in terms of centralization and institutionalization as essential components of rationalization' (Oestreich, 1969, p. 338).

be goal-oriented: they are basically agreed upon procedures of a game with a general aim – reducing the domain of and degree of uncertainty – as well as a game-specific aim, the concrete objective of each such procedure.

If the 'object' of politics is a guarantee against expected future needs (see Miglio, 1988, vol. 2, p. 793), the role of institutions in politics is to give the rules of the game, in that, by reducing the uncertain and unforeseeable character of interpersonal relations, insurance is mutually provided.[8] In one sense, political institutions define and make possible the 'normal situation' of the order of a community out of a wider range of activities. Indeed, they constitute the fundamental guarantee of the functioning and legitimacy through time of such an order. Being convened upon procedures, which are finalized to the construction and preservation of intended situations, political institutions shape a community's 'normality' and largely determine its concrete working.

In their relation to the actions performed within any given economic structure political institutions also appear to bound the set of normality. However, in this case the aim of the game played by political institutions seems considerably more difficult to define than that for other forms of human action.

The minimal aim is to provide the security that, within the domain of economic structure, interpersonal relations will respect the fundamental rule disciplining all 'private' relations: that is, the rule of *pacta sunt servanda*. At higher levels, however, the same aim can be defined – as indeed has historically been the case – as a range of modifying or controlling interventions in some constituent parts of the economic structure: instances of this are the redistribution of income and wealth, state monopoly – or the concession of privileges – on some raw materials, or positional changes in the hierarchy of social groups (with the inherent discrepancy between *status* position and contract position)[9] achieved through the political use of inflation.

[8] In a political science perspective, the reduction in the variance of human behaviour is possibly the most important element in the analysis of institutions (see also, from an economic viewpoint, Heiner, 1983). In the view of 'constitutional political economy', on the other hand, the relevance of a set of institutional rules lies above all in their capacity to foster and preserve 'equilibrium'. Precisely because the political process is seen – like the market – as a 'system of interacting individuals from which outcomes emerge as equilibria', the fundamental argument in the study of those rules 'depends on the recognition of the role rules play in isolating an equilibrium outcome or pattern of outcomes for a community of social agents with given capacities and objectives' (Brennan and Buchanan, 1985, pp. 15–16).

[9] The move from 'status' to 'contract' was central to the analysis of Henry Sumner Maine (1861, p. 141). What we are witnessing today is really a twofold – and in no way contradictory, appearances notwithstanding – phenomenon: on the one hand the 'contract', in its perpetual flexibility, becomes the most effective instrument for regulating the relations between statuses and between these and political institutions; on the other hand 'statuses' tend to coalesce, increasingly often, on political as well as on economic and social grounds.

The difficulty in assessing the relation between political institutions and the economic structure is due not only to the variety of relevant historical experiences; rather, in theoretical terms, it fundamentally depends upon the awkwardness of defining – if indeed it exists – the domain of 'normality' of economic activity.

A first reason for this awkwardness relates directly to the general delimitation criteria between economics and politics. While politics is seen as the sphere of what is 'guaranteed' (including the 'expectation of guarantee', thus a deferment), economics is perceived as the realm of risk and uncertainty.[10] As a direct consequence, while every economic structure is subject to constant change and transformation over time (thus adding to the awkwardness in defining its 'normal' condition, short of equating it with the stationary state), political institutions appear to gravitate towards such a static position. Hence the impression, shared in many a historical setting, of a natural chasm between the width and speed of transformation of the former and the slow rhythm of change in the latter.

There is however a further, and possibly even more important, reason for this difficulty in defining the relation between political institutions and economic structure. Just as the 'structure'–'transformation' duality within the productive system emerges as one of the most powerful elements 'in shaping economic theory and in connecting the dynamics of economic theory with the structural dynamics of the economic system' (Quadrio-Curzio and Scazzieri, 1986, p. 381), so also the '(economic) structure'–'(political) institution' duality may be crucially relevant – not only for an understanding of how some fundamental 'types' of economic system came to be isolated in the development of economic thought (with important theoretical consequences being derived from this), but also for an analysis of the links (and specific influences) between the dynamics of the political system and that of the economic system.

The parallel drawn between this latter dichotomy and the former duality may so far appear haphazard. It may gain plausibility through a cursory sketch of the relations between political economy and the institutions in

[10] These two concepts, explicitly antithetic in Frank Knight's *Risk, Uncertainty and Profit* (1921), have ever since constituted familiar – and still controversial – reference points for economic theorists: the domain and instruments of analysis of their discipline crucially depend on the position adopted along a spectrum ranging from '(post-)Keynesian Fundamentalism' to 'Rational Expectations'. Clearly, an economic methodology built upon the 'stochastic equivalent of perfect knowledge' sits ill at ease with an analysis of the link between political institutions and economic structure on the lines proposed in this work. Thus a successful clarification of the nature of that link appears crucially relevant to a choice between the above-mentioned methodological positions – and, possibly more fruitfully, to the 'sense of direction and significance' of the current explorations into 'Bounded Rationality'.

which the modern organization of political power (the State) has taken shape. This will reveal how political institutions have been an essential factor in determining the extension and temporal horizon of economic activity. It will also help us to understand why at the present time, as the interferences between politics and economics grow, so does the need for an analysis carried out by means of 'interfering' concepts.

3. Political economy and the 'modern' organization of power

The development of modern economics – like that of the political science of the modern age – has been accompanied and punctuated by the question of the organization of power, which is seen as a strong link between politics and economics.

In the tightly knit treatments of this subject by those 'Reasoners' who were mainly responsible for forging the fictitious (and hybrid in origin) 'person' of the State in the late fifteenth and in the sixteenth century,[11] there is a sharp distinction between the 'political' and the 'economic' orders as well as between these two orders and the 'civil' order. However, while reflecting a precise hierarchy of the aims of each sphere in the realm of practical activity, this partition is recomposed through the belief in a 'natural order'. This order founds and legitimizes the correspondences and symmetries between politics and economics. The same order secures the internal consistency and authority of both normative economics and normative politics.[12] Significantly, even as the rise of 'political economy' appears to herald the rapid disintegration of the old *economica* (economics), the very foundations of the economic order are still directly linked to 'policy', 'police' and 'politeness' (Porta, 1988).

After William Petty – who explicitly applied a Baconian methodology in his *Political Arithmetick* – put economic analysis in permanent connection with the activity of the *Body Politick*, the Physiocrats and the classical economists, in order to define the subject matter and aims of political economy, emphasized the theme of the State, its action and its protective

[11] Since the age of the 'Reason of State' (Meinecke, 1924), the State has been seen *as if* it were a 'person': the State – for Machiavelli still the small group of people around the Prince, sharing in his power – is transformed into an abstract entity (Miglio, 1981). Also, during the age of the 'Reason of State', the closest and most lasting links between 'political action' and 'economic action' were forged, transfiguring the Prince's particular, concrete interest in the general interest, and welfare, of the community (Ornaghi, 1984b).

[12] There are several and significant – if not yet fully investigated – connections between normative politics and normative economics in the fifteenth and sixteenth centuries. If the former focuses on the Prince and the latter on the 'head of the family' (see for instance *Georgica curiosa oder Adeliges Land- und Feldleben* by Wolf Helmard von Hohberg, 1682), both locate their theories in the area between 'nature' and (civil) 'order', and between 'rules of nature' and 'institutions'.

aims and its claim to legitimacy in relation both to the natural economic order and to the 'rational' activity of individuals.

Shortly before the publication of *An Inquiry into the Nature and Causes of the Wealth of Nations* by Adam Smith, and several decades after the term *économie politique*, *economia pubblica* and *economia politica* ('political economy') had taken root in European language (King, 1948; Groenewegen, 1987; Perrot, 1988), James Steuart published *An Inquiry into the Principles of Political Oeconomy: being an Essay on the Science of Domestic Policy in Free Nations* (1767). Even more important than the fact that 'political oeconomy' was granted the dignity of being included in the title of an English book is Steuart's analysis of the constituent parts of that 'system of administration' in which the 'Science of Domestic Policy' takes concrete form. This is especially worth mentioning, since Steuart was continuously attracted by what is political ('public spirit', 'the public', 'the public good'). These constituent parts do indeed define – not in the abstract but in continuous relation to the political institutions – the nature and purposes of political economy.[13]

Moreover, if the 'change in the meaning of the word "economics" in spoken language, and the origin of economic science seem to come from the same root, but not to be interdependent' (as Otto Brunner maintained in his study of the concept of *Wirtschaft* and of its gradual extension from 'the totality of the household' to the 'national economy' – Brunner, 1950, p. 118), then one should also remember that, particularly in the German-speaking world, both phenomena presuppose a specific connection between the economic and the political order, with the latter being increasingly identified with the order of the State.

In the whole Cameralistic tradition, and particularly in the Austrian School with Johann Joachim Becher's fundamental *Politische Discurs* (1688), *Policey* becomes the sphere in which action of the Prince and economic thinking are firmly linked. Probably introduced into Germany via the chancellories of Burgundy, and increasingly documented since the late fifteenth century in official papers of towns, principalities, and the Sacred Roman Empire, the concept of *Policey* – also *Polizey*, *Policei* – extends from its original meaning of 'condition of good order of a

[13] This is shown by the rest of Steuart's title: *In which are particularly considered Population, Agriculture, Trade, Industry, Money, Coin, Interest, Circulation, Banks, Exchange, Public Credit, and Taxes.* An interesting comparison can be drawn between this title and those of contemporary Cameralistic works. Even more indicative is to compare Steuart's concept of 'modern oeconomy' as one of the most effective limits upon 'the power of a modern prince' (Steuart, 1966, pp. 278–9) with corresponding ideas in Cameralistic writings, such as Georg Heinrich Zincke's *Cameralisten-Bibliothek* (1751–2). Zincke, who uses the term *Wirtschaft* to indicate both economic activity and economic science, distinguishes *Oeconomic* – that is economic science – from *Oeconomie*, the object of economic intervention: the fundamental aim of *Oeconomic* is the solution of the general economic and financial problems of the State (Small, 1909, pp. 232–66; Schiera, 1968, p. 413).

community', to that of 'rules generating and preserving the condition of good order', to its eventual meaning of 'comprehensive care of the good order and general welfare of the country'. Thus every State activity dealing with economic matters becomes a central and specific theme of *Policey* (Schulze, 1982).

In his *Il principe cristiano pratico* (1680) the Italian Cardinal Giovan Battista de Luca not only distinguishes 'Political' government from the 'Civil' and 'Economic' government; he also makes it clear (chapter 7) that the two latter types of government should mainly deal with 'the abundance of victuals, the preservation of public health, transport, commerce and other similar necessities, or conveniences for the community and for the civil, comfortable and happy life of the People, which has to be the main aim of the Prince' (De Luca, 1680, p. 79).

Thus, in the age of the 'Reason of State' we can identify a problem that was to acquire growing importance for the stability of the modern organization of power: how to make the order of the State not just as rational as possible, but above all as similar as possible to the political order. If rationality and similarity are to be accomplished, it becomes indispensable that the order of the State should be 'symmetric' to the economic order. The quest for this symmetry outlived the *Ancien Régime*; however, in specific connection with the growing consequences of the Industrial Revolution, the economic order appeared less and less as an artificial link between the order of the State and political order and more and more as an autonomous order whose symmetry was directly with the political order.[14]

4. State and economic structure: a fallacy

As the order of the State increasingly interfered with the operation of the economic structure, the economic order seemed compelled to strengthen its autonomous and original character, connecting itself directly with a political order that is not coextensive with the aims and rules of operation of State institutions.[15]

[14] Significantly, in Nicolas de Lamare's famous *Traité de la police*, '*police*', having for objective the realization of 'that good order from which the well-being of States depends', takes form in the following fields of activity: 'Religion; the Discipline of Behaviour; Public Health; Victuals; the Safety and Peace of the Public; Transportation; Sciences and the Liberal Arts; Commerce, Manufactures and the Mechanical Arts; Domestic Servants and Labourers; and the Poor' (Lamare, 1729, vol. I, p. 4).

[15] There thus arose a paradox whose convoluted historical development has been outlined by Karl Polanyi. As the economic order progressively establishes its original distinction from the State order, the identifiability of the latter with the political order becomes more arduous. The consequence of this was that – starting with the latter half of the nineteenth century – while the economy of *laissez-faire* was the product of a deliberate action by the State, later limitations to *laissez-faire* began spontaneously (Polanyi, 1944).

Introducing an 1852 collection of *Trattati italiani del secolo XVIII* by Antonio Genovesi, Pietro Verri, Cesare Beccaria, Gaetano Filangieri and Giammaria Ortes, the Director of the *Biblioteca dell'economista*, Francesco Ferrara, remarked that 'the learned men ... created a new branch of human knowledge, naming it Economics' with the specific aim of thinking through and amending 'all current ideas about the State and its functions'. He added: 'I hope to be speaking to readers for whom the mission of our Science seems incompatible with a system in which the State is anything more than a mere mental abstraction, and anything different from the set of its citizens.' (Ferrara, 1852, p. xxxv.)

As State ends gradually presented themselves as social ends (and consequently the web of interferences between State institutions and economic structure thickened), the direct relation between economics and politics became progressively more crucial (W. Weber, 1952; Wolin, 1987). This question in the discussion of the links between (economic) 'theory' and 'history' (already apparent in the 'debate on methods' (*Methodenstreit*) current in the last quarter of the nineteenth century) fully established its relevance through the debate on the existence of an identical *ratio* in the modern economy and in the modern State. In this regard the positions of Werner Sombart and Otto Hintze are quite significant.

Sombart, who untiringly and scrupulously retraced all interdependencies between the principles of the 'rational' capitalist economy and 'the essence and origin of the modern State', was nevertheless aware that not all economic relations can be fitted historically within the 'modern *Gross-staat* as a unified system' (Sombart, 1921 4th edn, vol. I. 1, p. 338, 1st edn 1902).

Hintze acknowledges that 'Sombart rightfully claims to have first distinguished the ages of economic history according to the different successive economic systems, while up to now the epochs of State life had been utilized also in the periodization of economic history, as done here by Schmoller and Bücher, but also generally in French and English economic history' (Hintze, 1929, p. 1). However, he firmly challenges the 'separation of the fields of economics and politics in the consideration of history (*ibid.*). He then observes that 'the social process through which capitalism arises is sociologically related to that generating the political system of the new world of States, both when it happens through a new foundation – as in the town and territorial States of Italy and Germany – and when it results from a transformation of the grand old State structures'. Hintze finally concludes that there is a very strong 'link between economics and politics, which is therefore also synthesized in the narrower unity of *civilization*, distinguishing this last from *culture* – the culture, that is, of the pure life of the spirit' (Hintze, 1929, pp. 1–2).

The numerous inquiries into the origins and development of capitalism published in the first three decades of this century repeatedly reassessed the existence and the historical forms of the link between economics and politics.

But even then such a link could no longer be solved by a purely historical inquiry. Since the unity of the *corpus* of social sciences had long been broken – and by then even the residual connection through the theme of the State had been severed[16] – that link was correctly perceived as different from the one between economic (capitalistic) structure and modern State (Wieser, 1914). In its essential historical traits the latter contributes to a correct formulation of the analysis of the former: it does not, however, accomplish it. The former problem – and this is the main conclusion of our argument – claims a theoretical character, while finding one of its main instruments of analysis in historical reconstruction.

Theoretically, the problem of the link between economics and politics originates from the relation between '(political) institutions' and '(economic) structure'. As I have attempted to show above, institutions cannot be assimilated with the functions of the State, but must be understood as goal-oriented procedures; and the structure's fundamental character (and its 'materiality') lies precisely in the consolidation of a set of actions and interrelations between economic agents. This has been observed by Karl Polanyi: 'The instituting of the economic process vests that process with unity and stability; it produces a structure with a definite function in society; it shifts the place of the process in society, thus adding significance to its history; it centers interest on values, motives and policy. Unity and stability, structure and function, history and policy spell out operationally the content of our assertion that the human economy is an instituted process. The human economy, then, is embedded and enmeshed in institutions, economic and noneconomic.' (Polanyi, 1957, pp. 249–50)

In this 'consolidation' one should probably seek not only the most important influence from political institutions on the economic structure, but also the starting point for a dynamic interpretation of their relation.

5. 'Order' and 'transformations'

The gravitation of economic actions and interrelations is the product of two distinct dynamic processes: the first unfolds *within* the structure; the second

[16] Beside the distance opened between 'politics' and 'administration', once the unity of the late nineteenth-century theoretical system broke into the two splinters of power (*puissance*) and *service*, there was also 'a radical alteration of the equilibrium between the State and the economic process, fudging the earlier very sharp distinction between administration and economics', as correctly pointed out by Sordi (1987, p. 15).

considers the structure as a unified system and can be defined as the dynamics *of* the structure.

The concept of institutions appears essential for a study of either process. In the first case, however, political institutions mainly represent the set of rules that validate 'in practice' the 'abstract' predictability of economic actions and interrelations; in the second case, political institutions are specifically relevant to the 'proportion' between the apparatus of transformation and the apparatus of structure in a given economic system.[17] Intervening both on the processes of transformation of original resources into consumption goods and on the relation between original resources and potential output (in other words both on the choice of point relative to the production possibility frontier and on the shape of the frontier), political institutions become a (decisive) variable in the analysis of that 'antagonism – coexistence between producibility and scarcity' that is 'at the basis of the actual dynamics of economic systems, just as it is at the bottom of all attempts to understand its functioning and to intervene upon it' (Quadrio-Curzio and Scazzieri, 1983, p. 54).

Analytically, the concept of political institution appears less and less useful in relation to the 'creative producibility'[18] of the structural apparatus. Significantly, it leaves some crucial questions unanswered. It is difficult – theoretically, as well as in empirical analysis – to assess the degree of 'incidence' of political institutions on the main trends of transformation of an economy; but it is nearly impossible to determine whether the role of institutions is currently wider and more relevant in supporting 'conservation' and 'stagnation' than in fostering 'innovation' and 'development'.

[17] The difference between 'structural apparatus' and 'transformational apparatus' and the relevance of their 'proportion' are analysed in depth by Quadrio-Curzio and Scazzieri (1983). From their contribution I have also borrowed the distinction between 'acquisitive behaviour' and 'creative behaviour': a very relevant distinction, it seems to me, for a general theory of action which – furthering a line of inquiry already forcefully addressed by Ludwig von Mises (1940) – can account for both the 'subjective' and the 'objective' dimensions of action. In this context, a decisive contribution towards a theory of the relation between 'action' and 'institution' is that of Michael Oakeshott (1975).

[18] The importance of this distinction had already been recognized by John Rae (1905). After identifying 'instruments' (pp. 15–16) as the means to satisfy future needs, he separated 'accumulation' (the 'non-inventive expansion of instrumental production', always possible but constrained by diminishing returns) from 'augmentation'; the latter, being 'the effect of the principle of invention', is 'the only power on earth that can be said to create. It enters as an essential element into the process of increase of national wealth, because that process is a creation, not an acquisition. It does not necessarily enter into the process of the increase of individual wealth, because that may be simply an acquisition, not a creation.' (p. 151) Very significantly, Rae did not fail to realize, from such a perspective, the importance of the temporal horizon necessary to the unfolding of 'augmentation', as Charles W. Mixter, the editor of the 1905 reprint, stressed: an essential attendant 'circumstance' in Rae's account of the innovative process is 'the existence of a government strong enough to secure at least ordinary law and order, but not so strong as to crush out the spirit of individual initiative' (p. 151, note 1).

In several respects the duality '(political) institutions–(economic) structure' seems to collapse suddenly[19] when applied to the analysis of structural dynamics, leaving in its place a generic and often ambiguous contrast between the adjectives 'political' and 'economic'.[20] This carries a twofold risk. First, the role of political institutions may be reduced (on the basis of a partial analysis of the transformation of the modern State into a gigantic transfer system) to that of a mere instrument of allocation of scarce resources.[21] Secondly, each problem situation of interference between political institutions and economic structure may be formulated in terms (similar, or even identical to those well familiar, to a conspicuous economic tradition) of maximizing a function (efficiency) under a double constraint: the economic (resource scarcity) and the political (the rules of institutions and the efficiency of their outputs). However, in this way we cast aside the fundamental question in the analysis of both processes (gravitation of economic actions and interrelations and dynamics of the structure): what are the interdependencies between 'political' and 'economic order', recognizing that the latter may indeed be an 'order which organizes itself' (Sartori, 1987, p. 145), but which for this precise reason undergoes continuous transformations?

In this respect the theme of the political-economic 'cycle' is clearly very relevant: in virtue of its ambitious theoretical perspective, this theme has lately recaptured the attention of historians and economists (Salvati, 1981; Olson, 1982; Freeman, 1983; Dotsey and King, 1987).

Here 'time' most forcefully emerges as a fundamental element in the analysis not just of all political phenomena, but specifically of the role of political institutions with respect to the economic structure (Morgenstern, 1934, pp. 63–7). Time, being the protagonist of that 'state of choice' that is

[19] This collapse, also in terms of the 'pure' concepts of 'institution' and 'structure', is only apparent. However, it has been observed, in a philosophical perspective, that even when 'institution' and 'structure' are not interpreted 'as two contradictory terms, denoting the same object from two different viewpoints and with different characteristics – the subjective moment, the action whose meaning respects a rule, is stressed in "institution"; while objectivized society, perceived as "nature" in which the action unfolds, is captured by "structure"' – it is only when the two concepts are distinguished that they allow 'at the same time a diachronic and synchronic approach' to the problem of interferences between political and economic phenomena (Matteucci, 1979, pp. 19–20).

[20] The consequences of an 'uncritical acceptance of some summary distinctions of wide diffusion – like the ostensibly self-evident one between the *Economic* and the *Politic*' or the one 'between the *Economic* and the *Social*' have attracted the attention of François Perroux (1973).

[21] This concept of State, current in the literature on the Welfare State and its crisis, is incomplete, mainly because it neglects the historically varying role of the 'political *élite*' in both appropriating and redistributing resources. In some political-economic systems such a role is particularly conspicuous today, underpinning the phenomena – as yet fully investigated by neither political economy nor political science – of the formation of 'privileges' and of 'political rents'.

normally 'a state of uncertainty about how a future self will evaluate the situation in which the choice made now is placing it' (Pizzorno, 1986, p. 366), plays a fundamental role in the system of symmetries and compatibilities between the rules of institutions and the goals of human action (economic action in our case). To the extent that institutions guarantee 'coherence and stability of actions, allow behaviour that is automatic, spontaneous, habitual and secure, on the basis of which, and of the consequent stability, creative action becomes feasible' (Matteucci, 1979, p. 18), the analysis of time appears decisive in assessing whether the strongest interdependence between 'order' and 'transformation' is indeed given by creative action.

It is precisely in the analysis of what makes such action feasible that political institutions fully display the *Mehrwert* mentioned earlier: the power to directly affect the temporal horizon of economic action as creative action.

6. The temporal horizon of creative economic action

The observer is often struck by the fact that, in the operation of today's political institutions, output is perceived in turn as 'close' to and 'remote' from the field of economic actions and interrelations.

This varying perception (whose specifically psychological dimension it would also be interesting to analyse) is a manifestation of an important phenomenon, directly correlated to the political institutions' capacity – or otherwise – to map out a 'reliable' temporal horizon for 'creative' actions.

As political institutions bound the field in which mutual insurance is provided through the reduction of uncertainty, the 'time' of such mutual insurance is a constituent part of the relation between political institutions and economic structure. This is true in two respects: 'time' offers security as to the future preservation of a currently preferred situation, but also with regard to a future 'transformation' of the present situation. The latter aspect, in particular, avoids discrepancies and conflicts between political order and economic transformations, and enables potentially 'creative' actions to fit, both spatially and temporally, within the institutions' procedures.

It would appear, however, that today's institutions are progressively less able to secure a reasonably wide temporal horizon for the unfolding of such transformations, when they do not altogether fail to secure the necessary material preconditions.[22] In politics today, time to come seems to shrink to

[22] Here lies the root of a very remarkable current phenomenon: as the perception of a distinction between the rhythms of economic-social transformation and change in political institutions sharpens, the latter are increasingly seen to converge on a 'natural' stationary state implying a 'physiologic' immutability. Heinrich von Treitschke (1897–8) had already noticed that society necessarily and at all times 'lives faster' than the State.

almost nothing. As a result, political institutions run the risk of being a 'limit' imposed upon the economic structure.

In a general sense, political institutions are a limit because they appear as one of the most powerful determinants of actions (these are defined, praxeologically and subjectively, as relations between uncertain ends and the procurement of means): against this limit there is not even, on occasion, any possibility of 'exit'.[23] More specifically, political institutions are also a limit inasmuch they influence the import and extension of actions, often under the ideological camouflage of a 'primacy' of politics over economics.

Finally, it is important to stress that political institutions can be a limit in a rather similar sense to that used by mathematicians in relation to functions, especially given that, when the independent variable is time, a zero limit denotes stationary equilibrium of the system.

Economists have been increasingly aware of this limit; indeed, such an awareness underlies a fundamental debate around the 'theory of economic policy'. In the vision of its modern founders, from Abba Ptachya Lerner, to James Edward Meade, to Jan Tinbergen, the theory implied a technocratic use of 'instruments' to achieve uniquely defined 'objectives', and the early attacks concentrated on the effectiveness of instruments, without questioning the effectiveness of the political process in formulating objectives.

Yet for quite some time scepticism and, increasingly, outright rejection[24] have characterized the approach of many economists to that political process: the rational economic agent's 'infinite planning horizon' is contrasted with the typically shorter intertemporal maximization exercise of politicians – with the implication that the optimality of economic activity cannot obtain under the political 'limit'. On the contrary, the argument developed in this essay makes it clear that the 'time' of politics, as well as being a limit, is a necessary condition for the unfolding of economic activity with a similar temporal horizon. I will try to illustrate this apparently paradoxical view with one example, taken from what may soon become a major 'interference' between the political and economic structure: the management of the environment. Since Ronald Harry Coase's pioneering study of broadcasting, a complete set of property rights has been proposed as an 'efficient' solution to 'technological externalities'. Yet it is characteristic of the relevant property rights, that they could not be vested or

[23] I use 'exit' in Albert O. Hirschman's (1970) sense, without however taking it – in opposition to 'voice' – as an accurate reflection of the more fundamental distinction between politics and economics. It is indeed this distinction that is to be challenged today, in its traditional theoretical foundations, by the interferences between political institutions and economic structure.

[24] As an instance of the shift in position within the thought of one such influential critic see the two statements by Milton Friedman in his *Methodology of Positive Economics* and, a few years later, in the *Joint Introduction to the Cambridge Economic Handbooks* written with C.W. Guillebaud (Friedman, 1953, p. 5; Friedman, 1957, pp. vi vii).

marketed but for their establishment by the political process. Thus individual intertemporal plans of action may only include externalities for the period over which the political guarantee of the corresponding property rights is expected to hold. There lies a dilemma that is only now – albeit at dramatic speed – becoming apparent. Only if our political institutions stretch 'time to come' well out into the future will they be able to impose effective 'boundaries' to the economic structure's treatment of externalities; conversely, only the establishment of such boundaries would create the conditions for a 'creative' economic endeavour in the use of the environment.

More specifically, if political institutions are perceived as a limit imposed upon the economic structure, they lose the capacity to provide a reliable temporal horizon for 'creative' action. As the temporal horizon shrinks, all creative actions tend to unfold, and to find their rules of gravitation, outside and possibly against the political structure. Moreover, as such a horizon tends towards its zero limit, the effort to fully secure an uncertain present situation dominates efforts to predetermine future outcomes that can be only partially secured; thus acquisitive behaviour inevitably tends to dominate creative behaviour.

It becomes very difficult to interpret economic action – as Löwe already pointed out in 1935 – as 'the model of perfect social interaction' (Löwe, 1935, p. 76).[25] In particular, once we are deprived of the dimension of *time* in our analysis, it becomes increasingly difficult to assess the properly 'creative' dimension of economic actions: that is to indicate the social as well as the economic areas where they 'generate' real changes.

7. Concluding remarks

A synthetic assessment of the argument developed so far is now in order; we shall attempt this by making the main articulations of the argument more explicit and by recalling some of the results.

The relation between political institutions and economic structure, when introduced as a problem in its own right, usually denotes a 'critical' phase in the development of economic theory. This was the case during the passage from *economica* to 'political economy'; and the same happened in the twilight of *Nationalökonomie*, once the prescription imparted by Wilhelm Roscher in his 1854 *Die Grundlagen der Nationalökonomie* (namely, that economics should be considered as a special and important part of

[25] This largely explains not just the *aporia* besetting all present attempts to extend the instrument of economic analysis to political analysis, but also the necessity of a theory of economic action that is fully integrated within a theory of human action.

politics)[26] appeared unattainable. Again, even within economic theory, this has been the case every time one has tried to assert 'the primacy of the problem of the organisation and control of the economic system, that is, its structure of power' (Samuels, 1987, p. 865).[27]

Within the dynamics of economic theory, it is probably excessive (and possibly erroneous) to attribute a meaningful cyclical pattern to the relation between political institutions and economic structure. It is also premature (but not for much longer, given the growing need for a solution) to identify the lines of research[28] into those relations and to explain why they currently appear to be stagnating rather than progressing. It is certain, however, that the reopening of this question indicates methodological dissatisfaction, while a correct setting of the question requires a strong analytical and methodological reorientation. As recently stressed by Luigi L. Pasinetti, there exists a sharp 'discrimination between those economic problems that have to be solved on the ground of logic alone – for which economic theory is entirely autonomous – and those economic problems that arise in connection with particular institutions, or with particular groups' or individuals' behaviour – for which economic theory is no longer autonomous and needs to be integrated with further hypotheses, which may well come from other social sciences' (Pasinetti, 1981, p. xiii). The relation between economic structure and political institutions belongs specifically to this latter type of problem. Along an extended stretch in the development path of 'modern' political economy that relation has been analytically encapsulated within the question of correspondences between 'State order' and 'economic order'; while, in the wider reflections on the 'foundations' of political economy, the same relation fell within the more general problem of circular relations between 'political order', 'economic order' and 'natural order'. Even after the latter problem was surrendered by economics to philosophy, the underlying theme still lurked behind the analysis of links between State institutions and capitalistic system, between State and market.

[26] Roscher observed: '[i]f, by the public economy of a nation, we understand economic legislation and the governmental guidance or direction of the economy of private persons, the science of public economy becomes, so far as its form is concerned, a branch of political science, while as to its matter, its subject is almost coincident with that of Political Economy. Hence it is, that so many writers use the term public economy, or the economy of the state (*Staatswirtschaft*), and National Economy (*Volkswirtschaft*), as synonymous' (Roscher, 1878, p. 91).

[27] Instances of this are the institutional economics of Thorstein Veblen, Clarence Ayres or John R. Commons, as well as other attempts to directly link economic and political variables.

[28] The concept of 'lines of research' and the distinction between 'stagnating' and 'progressing' ones, as well as the above-mentioned notions of 'paradigm' and 'research programme', are used here in the sense given by Baranzini and Scazzieri (1986, pp. 1–4).

If the relation between political institutions and economic structure is today again the starting point for a reflection on the reciprocally distinct and autonomous 'foundations' of economics and politics, it is also the main analytical field for the actual 'interferences' between the economic and political process. In this sense political institutions are, to the economist, a 'terminal problem'; its solution requires interfering concepts and, above all, a 'new' theory of institutions, sensitive to the dynamic aspects and firmly connected to a theory of action.

For this precise reason, the interrelation between 'institution' and 'creative action' has been repeatedly emphasized. Just as the 'production'–'exchange' duality is a 'constituent moment' of political economy, the institution –action duality strongly resurfaces the greater the impulse towards 'transformations' of the relations between the economic and political orders. This, therefore, must be the foundation for an analysis of both the dynamics *within* the structure, and the dynamics *of* the structure, as well as of the actual *loci* of interference between 'order' and 'transformations', 'structural stability' and 'tendencies to change'.

For economists and political scientists alike the effort required is remarkable. The traditional analytical tool kits appear inadequate, and the use of new interfering concepts – if hybrid and facile eclecticism is to be avoided – requires not only rigorous definitions but also a knowledge of the history and variations of those concepts and categories that are still thought to be appropriate and fruitful.[29]

However, such an effort appears to be increasingly indispensable. While political institutions are still considered as a 'limit' upon the economic structure, the way forward to a correct analysis of transformations remains blocked. Above all, this would imply relinquishing the search for those analytical instruments that are required for one of the most important theoretical problems of this day: the problem of the circular relations between 'producibility', 'political institutions' and 'structural change' in their connection with the boundaries and temporal horizon (that is with the current feasibility) of 'creative' economic action.

[29] It would be extremely interesting to reconstruct, historically and analytically, the perceived *interference* of the concept of power (in itself an object of study by Maffeo Pantaleoni (1898), Eugen Böhm-Bawerk (1914), Friedrich Wieser (1914)) with the concepts of monopoly and income distribution (Oppenheimer, 1910), production (Honegger, 1925), economic law (Zwiedineck-Südenhorst, 1925; Morgenstern, 1934). Such a reconstruction effectively represents the main route open for a clarification of one of the strongest methodological intersections between economic and political science (see Ornaghi, 1984a).

References

Baranzini, M., and Scazzieri, R. (1986) 'Knowledge in Economics: A Framework', in *Foundations of Economics. Structures of Inquiry and Economic Theory*, ed. M. Baranzini and R. Scazzieri, Basil Blackwell, Oxford and New York, pp. 1–87.

Becher, J.J. (1668) *Politische Discurs*, J.D. Zunner, Frankfurt.

Böhm-Bawerk, E. von (1914) 'Macht oder ökonomisches Gesetz?', *Zeitschrift für Volkswirtschaft, Socialpolitik und Verwaltung*, 23, pp. 205–71 (reprinted in *Gesammelte Schriften*, ed. F.X. Weiss, Hölder-Pichler-Tempsky, Wien-Leipzig, 1924, pp. 230–300).

Brennan, G., and Buchanan, J.M. (1985) *The Reason of Rules. Constitutional Political Economy*, Cambridge University Press, Cambridge.

Brunner, O. (1950) 'Die alteuropäische "Ökonomik"', *Zeitschrift für Nationalökonomie*, 13, pp. 114–39 (reprinted in *Neue Wege der Verfassungs- und Sozialgeschichte*, Vandenhoeck & Ruprecht, Göttingen, 1968, 2nd edn).

Coase, R.H. (1959) 'The Federal Communications Commission', *Journal of Law and Economics*, 2, pp. 1–40.

De Luca, G.B. (1680) *Il principe cristiano pratico*, Stamperia della Reverenda Camera Apostolica, Rome.

Dotsey, M., and King, R.G. (1987) 'Business Cycles', in *The New Palgrave. A Dictionary of Economics*, ed. J. Eatwell, M. Milgate and P. Newman, Macmillan, London, vol. I, pp. 302–10.

Ferrara, F. (1852) 'Prefazione' in *Trattati italiani del secolo XVIII* (*Biblioteca dell'Economista*, ser. I, vol. 3), Pomba, Turin, pp. v–lxx.

Freeman, C. (ed.) (1983) *Long Waves in the World Economy*, Butterworths, London.

Freyer, H. (1921) *Die Bewertung der Wirtschaft im philosophischen Denken des 19. Jahrhunderts*, W. Engelmann, Leipzig.

Friedman, M. (1953) 'The Methodology of Positive Economics', in *Essays in Positive Economics*, University of Chicago Press, Chicago and London.

(1957) (with C.W. Guillebaud) 'Introduction' to *The Cambridge Economic Handbooks*, Cambridge University Press, Cambridge.

Groenewegen, P. (1987) '"Political Economy" and "Economics"', in *The New Palgrave. A Dictionary of Economics*, ed. J. Eatwell, M. Milgate and P. Newman, Macmillan, London, vol. III, pp. 904–7.

Hayek, F.A. von (1973) *Law, Legislation and Liberty*. Vol. I: *Rules and Order*, University of Chicago Press, Chicago.

(1978) *New Studies in Philosophy, Politics, Economics and the History of Ideas*, Routledge & Kegan Paul, London and Henley.

Heiner, R.H. (1983) 'The Origin of Predictable Behavior', *The American Economic Review*, 73, pp. 560–95.

Hicks, J. (1986) 'Is Economics a Science?', in *Foundations of Economics. Structures of Inquiry and Economic Theory*, ed. M. Baranzini and R. Scazzieri, Basil Blackwell, Oxford and New York, pp. 91–101.

Hintze, O. (1929) 'Wirtschaft und Politik im Zeitalter des modernen Kapitalismus',

Zeitschrift für die gesamte Staatswissenschaft, 87, pp. 1–28 (reprinted in *Soziologie und Geschichte. Gesammelte Abhandlungen*. vol. II: *Zur Soziologie, Politik und Theorie der Geschichte*, ed. G. Oestreich, Vandenhoeck & Ruprecht, Göttingen, 1964, 2nd edn).

Hirschman, A.O. (1970) *Exit, Voice, and Loyalty. Responses to Decline in Firms, Organizations, and States*, Harvard University Press, Cambridge, Mass.

Hohberg, W.H. von (1682) *Georgica curiosa oder Adeliges Land- und Feldleben*, Endter, Nuremberg.

Honegger, H. (1925) 'Der Machtgedanke und das Produktionsproblem (Politik und Wirtschaft)', *Schmollers Jahrbuch für Gesetzgebung, Verwaltung und Volkswirtschaft*, 49, pp. 533–62.

King, J.E. (1948) 'The Origin of the Term "Political Economy"', *The Journal of Modern History*, 20, 230–1.

Knight, F.H. (1921) *Risk, Uncertainty and Profit*, Houghton Mifflin, Boston.

Lamare, N. de (1722) *Traité de la police*, 2 vols., Brunet, Paris (1st edn 1705–38, 4 vols).

Löwe, A. (1935) *Economics and Sociology. A Plea for Co-operation in the Social Sciences*, Allen & Unwin, London.

Marx, K., and Engels, F. (1845–6) 'Die Deutsche Ideologie', in *Marx–Engels Werke*, vol. III, Dietz Verlag, Berlin.

Matteucci, N. (1979) 'La pensabilità dell'economico ovvero delle strutture della prassi', in *La dimensione dell'economico*, Liviana, Padua, pp. 5–27.

Meinecke, F. (1924) *Die Idee der Staatsräson in der neueren Geschichte*, Oldenbourg, Munich and Berlin (English translation *Machiavellism*, Routledge & Kegan Paul, London, 1957).

Miglio, G. (1981) 'Genesi e trasformazioni del termine-concetto "Stato"', in *Stato e senso dello Stato oggi in Italia*, Vita e Pensiero, Milan, pp. 65–86 (reprinted in *Le regolarità della politica*, Giuffrè, Milan, 1988, vol. II, pp. 799–832).

(1988) 'Il tempo come elemento psicologico nel processo politico', in *Le regolarità della politica*, Giuffrè, Milan, vol. II, pp. 791–7.

Mises, L. von (1940) *Nationalökonomie. Theorie des Handelns und Wirtschaftens*, Editions Union, Geneva (English translation *Human Action. A Treatise on Economics*, Yale University Press, New Haven, 1949).

Morgenstern, O. (1934) *Die Grenzen der Wirtschaftspolitik*, Julius Springer, Vienna.

Oakeshott, M. (1975) *On Human Conduct*, Clarendon Press, Oxford.

Oestreich, G. (1969) 'Strukturprobleme des europäischen Absolutismus', *Vierteljahrschrift für Sozial- und Wirtschaftsgeschichte*, 55, pp. 329–47.

Olson, M. (1982) *The Rise and Decline of Nations. Economic Growth, Stagflation, and Social Rigidities*, Yale University Press, New Haven.

Oppenheimer, F. (1910) *Theorie der reinen und politischen Ökonomie. Ein Lehr- und Lesebuch für Studierende und Gebildete*, G. Fischer, Jena.

Orestano, R. (1982–3) '"Institution". Barbeyrac e l'anagrafe di un significato', *Quaderni fiorentini per la storia del pensiero giuridico moderno*, 11/12, pp. 169–78 (reprinted in *Edificazione del giuridico*, Il Mulino, Bologna, 1989, pp. 167–77).

Ornaghi, L. (1984a) *Stato e corporazione. Storia di una dottrina nella crisi del sistema*

politico contemporaneo, Giuffrè, Milan.
(1984b) *Il concetto di "interesse"*, Giuffrè, Milan.
Pantaleoni, M. (1898) 'An Attempt to Analyse the Concepts of "Strong" and "Weak" in Their Economic Connection', *Economic Journal*, 8, pp. 183–205.
(1925) 'Definizione dell'economia. Una prolusione', in *Erotemi di economia*, Laterza, Bari, vol. 1, pp. 1–65 (1st edn 1913).
Pareto, V. (1971) *Manual of Political Economy*, ed. A.S. Schwier and A.N. Page, Macmillan, London and Basingstoke (1st Italian edn, *Manuale di economia politica con una introduzione alla scienza sociale*, Società Editrice Libraria, Milan, 1906).
Pasinetti, L.L. (1981) *Structural Change and Economic Growth. A Theoretical Essay in the Dynamics of the Wealth of Nations*, Cambridge University Press, Cambridge.
Perrot, J.-C. (1988) 'Économie politique', in *Handbuch politisch-sozialer Grundbegriffe in Frankreich 1680–1820*, ed. R. Reichardt and E. Schmitt, Heft 8, Oldenbourg Verlag, Munich, pp. 51–104.
Perroux, F. (1960) *Économie et société. Contrainte – échange – don*, Presses Universitaires de France, Paris.
(1973) *Pouvoir et économie*, Bordas, Paris.
Pizzorno, A. (1986) 'Some Other Kind of Otherness: A Critique of "Rational Choice" Theories', in *Development, Democracy, and the Art of Trespassing. Essays in Honor of Albert O. Hirschman*, ed. A. Foxley, M.S. McPherson and G. O'Donnell, University of Notre Dame Press, Notre Dame, pp. 355–73.
(1987) 'Politics Unbound', in *Changing Boundaries of the Political. Essays on the Evolving Balance Between the State and Society, Public and Private in Europe*, ed. Ch.S. Maier, Cambridge University Press, Cambridge, pp. 27–62.
Polanyi, K. (1944) *The Great Transformation. The Political and Economic Origins of Our Time*, Holt, Rinehart & Winston, New York.
(1957) 'The Economy as an Instituted Process', in *Trade and Market in the Early Empires. Economies in History and Theory*, ed. K. Polanyi, C.M. Arensberg and H.W. Pearson, Free Press, New York, pp. 243–70.
Porta, P.L. (1988) 'I fondamenti dell'ordine economico: "Policy", "police" e "politeness" nel pensiero scozzese', *Filosofia Politica*, 2, pp. 37–67.
Quadrio-Curzio, A., and Scazzieri, R. (1983) 'Sui momenti costitutivi dell'economia politica', in *Protagonisti del pensiero economico (1817–1936)*, ed. A. Quadrio-Curzio and R. Scazzieri, Il Mulino, Bologna.
(1986) 'The Exchange–Production Duality and the Dynamics of Economic Knowledge', in *Foundations of Economics. Structures of Inquiry and Economic Theory*, ed. M. Baranzini and R. Scazzieri, Basil Blackwell, Oxford and New York, pp. 377–407.
Rae, J. (1905) *The Sociological Theory of Capital. Being a Complete Reprint of The New Principles of Political Economy*, ed. Ch.W. Mixter, Macmillan, New York and London (1st edn 1834).
Roscher, W. (1878) *Principles of Political Economy*, ed. J.J. Lalor, 2 vols., Callaghan and Company, Chicago (1st German edn *System der Volkswirtschaft*. Vol. 1: *Die Grundlagen der Nationalökonomie*, Cotta, Stuttgart, 1854).

Salvati, M. (1981) 'Ciclo politico e onde lunghe. Note su Kalecki e Phelps Brown', *Stato e Mercato*, 1, pp.9–45.
Samuels, W.J. (1987) 'Institutional Economics', in *The New Palgrave. A Dictionary of Economics*, ed. J. Eatwell, M. Milgate and P. Newman, Macmillan, London, vol. 2, pp.864–6.
Sartori, G. (1987) 'Mercato e pianificazione', in *Elementi di teoria politica*, Il Mulino, Bologna, pp.139–61.
Schiera, P. (1968) *Dall'Arte di governo alle scienze dello Stato. Il Cameralismo e l'assolutismo tedesco*, Giuffrè, Milan.
Schulze, R. (1982) *Policey und Gesetzgebungslehre im 18. Jahrhundert*, Duncker & Humblot, Berlin.
Sella, E. (1904) 'Della natura logica dei problemi terminali dell'economia politica', *Giornale degli Economisti*, ser. II, 29, pp.401–26.
Small, A.W. (1909) *The Cameralists. The Pioneers of German Social Polity*, The University of Chicago Press, Chicago.
Sombart, W. (1921) *Der moderne Kapitalismus. Historisch-systematische Darstellung des gesamteuropäischen Wirtschaftslebens von seinen Anfängen bis zur Gegenwart*, 4th edn, Duncker & Humblot, Munich and Leipzig, 2 vols (1st edn 1902).
Sordi, B. (1987) *Tra Weimar e Vienna. Amministrazione pubblica e teoria giuridica nel primo dopoguerra*, Giuffrè, Milan.
Steuart, J. (1966) *An Inquiry into the Principles of Political Oeconomy*, Oliver and Boyd for the Scottish Economic Society, Edinburgh and London (1st edn 1767).
Sumner Maine, H. (1861) *Ancient Law. Its Connection with the Early History of Society, and its Relation to Modern Ideas*, John Murray, London.
Tönnies, F. (1907–8) 'Sinn und Wert einer Wirtschaftsphilosophie', *Archiv für Rechts- und Wirtschaftsphilosophie*, 1, pp.36–43.
Treitschke, H. (1897–8) *Politik*, Hirzel, Leipzig (English translation *Politics*, 2 vols., Macmillan, London, 1916).
Weber, M. (1947) *The Theory of Social and Economic Organization*, trans. A.M. Henderson and T. Parsons, The Free Press of Glencoe, New York (1st German edn *Wirtschaft und Gesellschaft*, J.C.B. Mohr (Paul Siebeck), Tübingen, 1922).
Weber, W. (1952) 'Über die wirtschaftsbegrifflichen Grundlagen der älteren "Welfare Economics": Eine dogmenkritische Studie', *Zeitschrift für Nationalökonomie*, 13, pp.582–613.
Wieser, F. (1914) *Theorie der gesellschaftlichen Wirtschaft*, J.C.B. Mohr (Paul Siebeck), Tübingen (English translation *Social Economics*, with a preface by W. Mitchell, Augustus M. Kelley Publishers, New York, 1967; 1st English edn Adelphi Co., New York, 1927).
Wolin, S. (1987) 'Democracy and Welfare State: The Political and Theoretical Connections between Staatsräson and Wohlfahrtstaatsräson', *Political Theory*, 15, pp.467–500.
Zincke, G.H. (1751–2) *Cameralisten-Bibliothek*, 4 vols., C.L. Jacobi, Leipzig.
Zwiedineck-Südenhorst, O. (1925) 'Macht oder ökonomisches Gesetz. Ein Vortrag', *Schmollers Jahrbuch für Gesetzgebung, Verwaltung und Volkswirtschaft*, 49, pp.273–92.

Part II
SINGLE-PERIOD RELATIONSHIPS AND ECONOMIC THEORY

2 Economic structure and the theory of economic equilibrium

TAKASHI NEGISHI

1. Introduction

This chapter discusses the structure of Walrasian general equilibrium theory and Marshallian partial equilibrium theory, both of which form a large part of the traditional or current mainstream economics called neoclassical economics. Beyond the general exposition of these equilibrium theories, we shall particularly pursue two issues.

First, we shall try to clarify implicit dynamic concepts hidden in these theories, which are generally regarded as uni-periodal economic theories. Actually, the start of the development of modern dynamic economics was, at least partially, made possible by John Hicks (1946), who integrated Walrasian and Marshallian implicit dynamic concepts, along with more explicit Swedish ones, into a unified theory. The implications of some of these implicit dynamic concepts have, furthermore, not yet been fully and explicitly developed by modern theories of the dynamic economics.

Secondly, we shall critically compare Walrasian and Marshallian theories with Francis Edgeworth's theory of market, which succeeded William Stanley Jevons's view of market. The communication structure is different between the Walras–Marshall model of non-cooperative market games and the Jevons–Edgeworth model of cooperative market games. While the first two approaches have an identical result in the case of a large economy with infinitely many agents, the latter suggests the possibility of a quite different result in the case of competition among a few, if we can safely ignore the costs of communication, negotiation and organization. In other words, the former theories do not fully consider the implications of non-price competitions.

After this introductory section, the following two sections will be devoted to discussing the Walrasian general equilibrium theory. We shall describe how the core elements of an economic system are successively combined to form the general equilibrium models of exchange, production, credit and capital formation and, finally, money and circulation (section 2). Then, using a simplified model of credit and capital formation, we shall consider the implicit time structure of Walrasian seemingly uni-periodal theory (section 3). One possible interpretation is the stationary equilibrium, while another possibility is to consider the temporary equilibrium.

In the next two sections, the time structure of the Marshallian partial equilibrium theory will be discussed to show, first, that, unlike in the case of Léon Walras, all the core elements of an economic system are already introduced in the simplest model, the market-day model, but most of them are regarded as 'being constant' until sufficient time has past to make them adjust in the short-run or in the long-run model (section 4). Another implicit time structure to be shown in Alfred Marshall's theory is his concept of the stationary equilibrium of an industry in which individual firms are in disequilibrium, clearly a biological analogy with the case of a constant forest and its changing trees (section 5).

Though Walrasian and Marshallian theories have different time structures, they share an identical view of markets: that economic agents are isolated and communicate with each other only in terms of prices and price-related concepts like demand and supply functions. In the last two sections, we shall explain Edgeworth's view of markets, in which individual agents are free to form and block coalitions and make contracts and recontracts not necessarily in terms of the price concept. Results are compared with those of the Walras–Marshall view in the case of a large economy (section 6) as well as in the case of a duopoly (section 7).

The chapter will finish with a brief conclusion.

2. Logical structure of Walrasian theory

Walras (1954) insisted that complicated phenomena can be studied only if the rule of proceeding from the simple to the complex is always observed. Walras first decomposes a complicated economy of the real world into several core elements like consumer-traders, entrepreneurs, consumer goods, factors of production, newly produced capital goods and money. He then composes a simple model of a pure exchange economy by picking up a very limited number of such elements, that is individual consumer-traders and consumer goods, and disregarding the existence of all other elements. Consumer goods to be exchanged among individual consumer-traders are assumed simply to be endowed to them and not considered as produced at cost. There are no production activities in this hypothetical world.

Travel from this simple model to the complex world proceeds by adding one by one those core elements so far excluded, that is first entrepreneurs and factors of production in the model of production, then newly produced capital goods in the model of credit and capital formation, and finally money in the model of money and circulation. In the model of production, capital goods are introduced as a kind of factor of production, but the investment, that is the production of new capital goods, simply does not exist. In all the Walrasian models of exchange, production and credit and capital formation, there exists no money at all; it is finally introduced in the model of money and circulation.

In this journey from the simple to the complex, each intermediate model, enlarged from a simpler one and to be enlarged into a more complex one, is still a closed and self-compact logical system. Even the simplest model, that of the exchange, is already a model of general equilibrium, in which results of interactions among the core elements introduced are to be studied fully and exhaustively. However, each of the Walrasian models is as unrealistic as the starting model of pure exchange, with the exception of the last, into which all the core elements of a real world economy have been introduced.[1]

Those unrealistic models into which have been introduced only a limited number of core elements of the economy cannot, of course, be of practical use in considering what Hicks (1934) called particular problems of history or experience. They are designed to show the fundamental significance of such core elements of the real world economy as entrepreneurs and production, investment and the rate of interest, inventories and money, by successively introducing them into simple models that are then developed into more complex ones. Walras's theoretical interest was not in the solution of particular problems but in what Hicks called the pursuit of the general principles that underlie the working of a market economy.

One can study the problem of the exchange in the most essential form when the model of exchange is abstracted from all the other complex problems. There we can see most clearly Walras's view of a well-organized, highly institutionalized market in which the specialized auctioneer determines the uniform market price and changes it according to the excess demand or supply generated as functions of the price by price-taking traders. The model of production can show the role of entrepreneurs and the mechanism of distribution among factors of production, including capital goods, without being bothered by such time-related problems as investment, saving and the rate of interest. The latter problems can, then, be studied intensively in the model of credit and capital formation, in which the complex problems of money and circulation have not yet been introduced.

If the key of our approach in this volume is the relationship between

[1] For a difficulty in the last model, that of money and circulation, see Negishi (1988) chapter 7, section 5.2.

production and time, then the time structure implicit in Walrasian seemingly uni-periodal theory should be found not in the model of production but in the model of credit and capital formation.

3. Time structure of Walrasian theory

Since the original Walrasian system of equations of credit and capital formation is too complicated to describe, let us consider a drastically simplified version of a two-good (consumer and capital goods), two-factor (labour and capital) economy.[2] Two goods are produced from the input of labour service and the service of capital goods under constant returns to scale. Labour is the sole primary factor of production and there is no inventory investment, nor is there money.

Let X_1 and X_2 be the level of output of the consumer and new capital goods, respectively. The aggregate income of labourers and capitalists is

$$Y = w(a_1X_1 + a_2X_2) + q(b_1X_1 + b_2X_2) \tag{1}$$

where w denotes the rate of wage, q denotes the price of the service of capital goods, a_1 and a_2 are, respectively, the labour input coefficients in the production of the consumer and capital goods and b_1 and b_2 are, respectively, the capital input coefficients in the production of consumer and capital goods. Input coefficients are functions of factor prices, w and q.

At the general equilibrium of credit and capital formation, there is no profit left for entrepreneurs, so that

$$p_1 = wa_1 + qb_1 \tag{2}$$

$$p_2 = wa_2 + qb_2 \tag{3}$$

where p_1 and p_2 are respectively the price of the consumer and new capital goods. Since markets for two goods have to be cleared,

$$D(p_1, p_2, w, q, Y) = X_1 \tag{4}$$

$$H = X_2 \tag{5}$$

where D denotes the demand for consumer goods and H stands for the demand for new capital goods. Factor markets have also to be cleared so that

$$a_1X_1 + a_2X_2 = L \tag{6}$$

$$b_1X_1 + b_2X_2 = K \tag{7}$$

[2] This is a simplified version of the model given by Morishima (1977, pp. 108–12). We cannot, however, agree with Morishima's interpretation of the model (1977, pp. 112–22). See footnote 3, below.

where L and K are, respectively, the given existing labour force and the given existing stock of capital goods. Since there is no money, suppose capitalists own capital goods and lend them to entrepreneurs or sell the service of capital goods to them. If gross saving is defined as the excess of income over consumption, then capitalists save in kind or purchase new capital goods with saving, so that

$$p_2 H = S(p_1, p_2, w, q, Y) \tag{8}$$

where S denotes the aggregate gross saving.

Equations (1)–(8) may be interpreted as the description of a temporary equilibrium in the sense of Hicks (1946), as was done by Morishima (1960; 1977, pp. 70–81). It is assumed that expectations on the future prices are static, that is the elasticity of expectation is 1, in the determination of consumption and saving so that D and S are functions of current prices. There are eight equations to determine seven unknowns, Y, w, q, X_1, X_2, p_2, and H, since we can choose the consumer goods as *numéraire* so that $p_1 = 1$. The eight equations are not independent, however, and one of the equations can be derived from other equations and from Walras's law,

$$Y = p_1 D + S. \tag{9}$$

In the determination of consumption and saving, capitalists assume that goods and services of factors have the same prices in the future as they have at the present moment, and the difference between resultant gross saving and the value of the depreciation of capital goods, that is the net saving, can be either positive or negative. If it is positive, we have the case of a progressive economy, which Walras (1954, p. 269) himself wished to consider. The capital stock K is larger in the next period than in the current period so that temporary equilibrium prices in the former are in general different from those in the latter, even though capitalists in the current period expected unchanged prices through periods.

The assumption of the saving in kind is not necessary if we follow Walras and introduce a commodity E consisting of perpetual net income of a unit of *numéraire*, the price of which is the inverse of the rate of perpetual net income or the rate of interest i (Walras, 1954, p. 274). If this commodity is sold by entrepreneurs or firms wishing to buy new capital goods and is purchased by capitalists wishing to save, the clearance of the market of this commodity through changes in i implies that aggregate gross saving = 'aggregate excess of income over consumption = aggregate demand for (E) × price of (E) = aggregate demand for new capital goods × price of capital goods' (Walras, 1954, p. 21). Therefore,

$$p_2 H = S(p_1, w, i, Y) \tag{8'}$$

instead of (8) since, in the determination of consumption and saving, capitalists are now concerned, not with p_2 and q, but with i. Similarly, (4) may be replaced by

$$D(p_1, w, i, Y) = X_1. \tag{4'}$$

At equilibrium, the rate of net income for capital goods has to be equalized for the rate of net income for the commodity E,

$$(q/p_2) - d = i \tag{10}$$

where d denotes the technically given rate of depreciation of capital goods. This is nothing but Walrasian implicit or degenerate investment function, derived from assumptions that investors are price takers and that expectations are static.[3] Since the introduction of a new unknown i is matched by the introduction of additional equation (10), we still have equality between the number of unknowns and the number of equations.

If the general equilibrium of credit and capital formation is interpreted as a temporary equilibrium, entrepreneurs and capitalists fail to expect future prices in a progressive economy correctly, since changes in prices are induced by changes in K in a series of successive temporary equilibria. If we wish the perfect foresight to prevail and the expectation of unchanged prices to be correct in the general equilibrium of credit and capital formation, then this should be interpreted (see Yasui, 1970, pp. 173–278) as a stationary equilibrium, where K remains unchanged through periods. The reason is that only in a stationary state do the prices of the service of capital goods remain unchanged indefinitely into the future, as Walras assumed in equation (10). Of course, the service of the factors of production can have the same prices in the future as they have at the present, not only in a stationary state but also in a progressive economy of balanced growth. As Wicksell (1967, pp. 226–7) pointed out, however, the latter case is inconceivable, 'as the sum of natural forces cannot be increased'.

The condition for the stationary state is that the aggregate gross saving is equal to the value of depreciation of capital goods, or

$$H = dK \tag{11}$$

in view of (8) or (8′). Since the number of equations are increased by the addition of (11), one more unknown should be introduced. The existing stock of capital goods K is, therefore, no longer an arbitrary given quantity and has to be solved jointly with other unknowns from equations of general equilibrium of credit and capital formation. Then, we have nine unknowns,

[3] It is, therefore, superfluous to introduce the Keynesian investment function. See, however, Morishima (1977, pp. 112–22).

$K, i, Y, w, q, X_1, X_2, p_2$ and H to be solved from any nine equations of ten equations, (1)–(3), (4′), (5)–(7), (8′), (10) and (11), since $p_1 = 1$ and one of the equations is not independent in view of (9). Yasui (1970) first pointed out the necessity of this modification of the original Walrasian theory of credit and capital formation.[4]

Two alternative interpretations of Walras's theory of credit and capital formation – temporary equilibrium and stationary state – correspond respectively to two methods of economic dynamics in modern economic theory: the temporary equilibrium method and the growth equilibrium method, distinguished and evaluated by Hicks (1965, p. 28). Also, it is well known that Walras's theory of capital gives the micro-economic foundation to the so-called neoclassical macro-growth theory developed by Robert M. Solow, Trevor W. Swan, James Edward Meade and Hirofumi Uzawa.

4. Time structure of Marshallian theory

Like Walras (1954) Marshall (1921) also started with a very simple model to study complicated economic phenomena and then proceeded to more complex models. There is an important difference, however, between Walrasian general equilibrium analysis and Marshallian partial equilibrium analysis.

Unlike Walras who started with a general equilibrium model of an imaginary economy, which contains only a limited number of core elements of a real world economy, Marshall begins with the partial equilibrium analysis of a whole complex of a real world economy as such. In other words, every Marshallian model contains all the core elements of the economic system. Of course, Marshall also simplifies his study at first by confining his interest to a certain limited number of core elements of the economy. But he does it not by disregarding the existence of other elements but by assuming that other things remain unchanged. In this sense most of Marshall's models of an economy, though realistic, are open and not self-sufficient, since some endogenous variables (i.e. the 'other things') remain unexplained and have to be given exogenously.

Marshall's simplest model, which corresponds to Walras's model of exchange, is that of the market day, in which goods to be sold are, unlike in the case of Walras, produced goods, although the amount available for sale is, for the time being, assumed to be constant. Since the length of a single

[4] Yasui pointed this out as early as 1936. See Yasui (1970, p. 248) and also Garegnani (1960) Part 2, chapter 2. In spite of Garegnani, however, the fact that the stock of the existing capital goods cannot be an arbitrary given is not the defect of Walrasian theory of credit and capital formation. This is also the case with the classical theory of the stationary economy.

market day is so short, the level of output cannot be changed, even though production does exist in this temporary model. Unlike in Walras's model of production investment is actually undertaken in Marshall's short-run model. The latter is also a model of production, though the amount of currently available capital is given and unchanged, since the length of the period is still not long enough to allow for adjustment in capital equipment. The effects of such adjustments can be fully considered only in the study of Marshall's long-run model.

While money is introduced only in the final model of Walrasian theory, money does exist in all Marshallian models, though its purchasing power or its marginal utility is sometimes assumed to be constant. Walras has to consider the problem of exchange without using money under the unrealistic assumption of *tâtonnement*, that no exchange transaction should be undertaken at disequilibrium prices. Since, however, money is already introduced even in the model of the market day, Marshall can consider the problem of exchange in monetary economy, that is the exchange of a commodity against money, without making any *tâtonnement* assumption. The study of such non-*tâtonnement* exchange is made easy by the assumption of constant marginal utility of money, which makes the final equilibrium price independent of exchange transactions carried out at disequilibrium prices (Hicks, 1946, pp. 127–9).

Thus each Marshallian model corresponds to a different state of the same real world economy. The market-day and short-run models are, therefore, as realistic as the long-run model. They are of practical use in considering what Hicks (1934) called particular problems of history or experience. 'Marshall forged an analytical instrument capable of easier application.' A good example is the concept of consumer surplus. Hicks concluded that Walras and Marshall differ in interest, the former being more interested in principles, the latter in practical applications.

However, even if one is interested in principles alone, Marshall's contributions are important complements to Walras's. For example, of particular and continuing interest is a dynamic element implicit in the equilibrium concept of Marshall, who regards economic biology as the Mecca of the economist (Marshall, 1961, p. xiv). Considering the relation between an industry and its firms as the relation between a forest and its trees, Marshall studied the long-run normal supply price of an equilibrium industry in the case where 'some business will be rising and others falling' (Marshall, 1961, p. 378). Marshall used this concept of equilibrium industry with disequilibrium firms to argue for the compatibility of the increasing returns to scale and competition, considering that individual firms have their life-cycles and do not have enough time to exploit the increasing returns fully.

5. Equilibrium industry with disequilibrium firms

Marshall considered the stationary state of an industry as the first 'step towards studying the influence exerted by the element of time on the relation between cost of production and value' (Marshall, 1961, pp. 315–16). He did not require, however, that every firm in the industry remain of the same size. It is supposed that firms rise and fall, but that the representative firm remains the same size. The representative firm is defined as the miniature of an industry, like the representative tree of a virgin forest. It may not be possible to pick out an actual firm as being representative of the industry. It is, however, a very convenient device in considering the normal supply price of an industry composed of firms behaving differently under different conditions.

The normal supply price of the industry is assumed to be the normal expenses of production (including normal profit) of the representative firm. It is the price the expectation of which is sufficient to maintain the existing aggregate amount of industrial production. A higher price increases aggregate production by increasing the growth of the rising firms and slackening the decay of the falling firms. A lower price diminishes industrial production, since it hastens the decay of the falling firms and slackens the growth of the rising firms.

Why do some firms rise by increasing their output while others fall by diminishing theirs? On the basis of his life-cycle theory of firms, Marshall argues that young firms, like young trees, grow, while old firms, like old trees, decay. It may be considered that a young (an old) firm increases (decreases) its output by expanding (reducing) its capacity, since its normal expenses of production (including normal profit) fall short of (exceed) that of the representative firm, that is, the normal supply price of the industry.[5] In Marshall's stationary state, of course, the condition of the long-run equilibrium is satisfied, so that the demand price equals the normal supply price of the industry, while the supply price of each firm is considered to be its normal expenses of production including normal profit.

When the amount produced is such that the demand price[6] is higher than the supply price, then sellers receive more than sufficient to make it worth their while to bring that amount of the goods to the market. There is an incentive at work to increase the amount brought forward for sale. On the other hand, when the amount produced is such that the demand price is

[5] In other words, short-run average cost including normal profit is higher (lower) than the normal supply price of the industry for the contracting (expanding) firms, while short-run marginal cost is equal to the normal supply price of the industry for all firms.

[6] The demand price for a certain amount of a good is the price that clears the market, i.e. makes the demand equal to the given amount.

lower than the supply price, sellers receive less than sufficient to make it worth their while to bring that amount of the goods to the market. There is, then, an incentive at work to diminish the amount brought forward for sale (Marshall, 1961, p. 345).

Let us denote by x the supply price of a firm and by p the supply price of the industry. A firm increases its output if p is higher than x, and decreases it if p is lower than x. It is assumed that the rate of change in output is proportional to the difference between p and x. Different firms may have an identical value of x or a different value of x. Let $y(x)$ be the total output of firms with the same value of x. Furthermore, let $D(x)$ denote changes (increases if positive, decreases if negative) in y. Then, from this assumption,

$$D(x)/y(x)=(p-x). \tag{12}$$

Since the aggregate output of the industry remains unchanged in the stationary state, that is,

$$\int y(x)dx=\text{constant}, \tag{13}$$

we have from (12),

$$\int D(x)dx=\int (p-x)y(x)dx=0. \tag{14}$$

If we define the proportion of the total output $y(x)$ of firms with the supply price x to the aggregate industrial output as

$$f(x)=y(x)/\int y(x)dx, \tag{15}$$

we have, in view of (15),

$$p=\int xf(x)dx, \tag{16}$$

since from the right hand side of (14)

$$p\int y(x)dx=\int xy(x)dx. \tag{17}$$

From the definition (15),

$$\int f(x)dx=1. \tag{18}$$

Therefore, (16) implies that the normal supply price of the industry or its representative firm is the average supply price of individual firms in the industry.[7]

Marshall considered increasing returns in the sense of internal economy with respect to the long-run average cost of individual firms, since he

[7] It is interesting to see that Marx's market value (1959, p. 178) corresponds in this respect to Marshall's normal supply price of the industry. See Negishi (1988) chapter 6, section 6.

argued that short-run supply price increases with output, but an increase in demand gradually increases the size and efficiency of the representative firm (Marshall, 1961, p. 460). If there exist internal economies and if the supply price of an individual firm is a decreasing function of its output capacity, there is no limit to the expansion of a firm with the largest capacity until the whole industrial output is concentrated in its hands. To prevent concentration of the whole industrial output in the hands of a single firm, Marshall emphasized that the life span of private firms is limited and that expanding young firms with low supply prices are eventually changed into shrinking old firms with high supply prices long before such concentration is actually realized.

Marshall's life-cycle theory of firms insists that firms of the industry, like trees in the forest, have a cycle of birth, growth, decay and death. It is based on the fact that the expansion of an individual firm is eventually arrested by the decay, if not of the owner's faculties, then of his liking for energetic work, of his unabated energy and of his power of initiative (Marshall, 1961, pp. 285–6; Marshall, 1921, pp. 315–16). This life-cycle theory of firms may, therefore, give a realistic picture of nineteenth-century industry, but the question is whether it remains relevant with the development of joint-stock companies, which, as Marshall himself admitted, do not really die.

However, we may revive Marshall's biological concept of equilibrium of an industry by considering the life-cycle of technology in equilibrium growth instead of the life-cycle of firms in stationary state.[8]

6. Edgeworth's equivalence theorem

As was pointed out in section 2, Walras's view of market is that of a well-organized market, in which individual traders do not communicate with each other but communications are exclusively made between each trader and the (perhaps fictitious) auctioneer, who acts as the incarnation of the law of supply and demand. Although Marshall paid more attention to the case of an imperfect market where connections among traders are important (Marshall, 1921, p. 182), his general view of market is still not much different from that of Walras in the sense that the leading role is played by the uniform market price and the law of supply and demand.

An alternative view of market with a completely different communication structure is that of Edgeworth. This succeeded Jevons's view of market, in which an important role is played by the arbitrage behaviour of traders in order to establish the law of indifference. Mutual communication among traders is essential, since in Edgeworth's theory of exchange they are

[8] For an example of such an attempt, see Negishi (1985) chapter 5.

expected to form and block coalitions and to make contracts and recontracts. Contracts are not made necessarily in terms of the uniform price, and supply and demand are not expected to make changes in such price.

However, in the case of a large exchange economy with infinitely many traders on both sides of the market, Edgeworth (1881, pp. 34–42) demonstrated the equivalence of the outcome of two different views of the market (the Walras–Marshall view and the Jevons–Edgeworth view) by using the so-called Edgeworth box diagram. In this section we shall sketch Edgeworth's demonstration, which forms a corner-stone of modern mathematical economics, while a more interesting case of duopoly will be discussed in the next section.

Consider an exchange economy in which two goods are exchanged between two trading bodies. Each trading body consists of infinitely many traders who are identical with respect to tastes and initial holdings of goods. The outcome of exchange can be seen by considering the exchange between the representative trader of each homogeneous trading body through the use of the Edgeworth box diagram.

In Figure 2.1, the quantity of the first good is measured horizontally, that of the second good, vertically; and the quantity of goods given to trader A are measured with the origin at A, those given to trader B, with the origin at B. Point C denotes the initial allocation of goods before trade. This implies also that the total amount of the first good to be exchanged between traders A and B is AC and that of the second good, BC.[9] Curves I, II, etc., are indifferent curves of trader A, curves 1, 2, etc., are those of trader B, and curve DEF is the contract curve, a locus of points where the indifference curves of two traders are tangent.

Point E is the equilibrium of the perfect competition, with the common tangent to indifference curves at E passing through point C. This is the outcome of the exchange if traders are price takers and demand and supply are equalized at the uniform price ratio denoted by the slope of the line EC. Edgeworth's equivalence theorem insists that point E is the outcome of the exchange even if traders are not price takers but form and block coalitions and freely make contracts and recontracts.

It is clear that all the points off the contract curve cannot be stable outcomes of the exchange, since both traders can be better off by making recontracts in order to settle down at some point on the contract curve. On the contract curve only the points between D and F can be candidates for the stable outcome of exchange, since otherwise a trader can be better off by blocking the contract and returning to point C. If A and B are only traders,

[9] Of course, this is a simplifying assumption and in general C can be anywhere in the box.

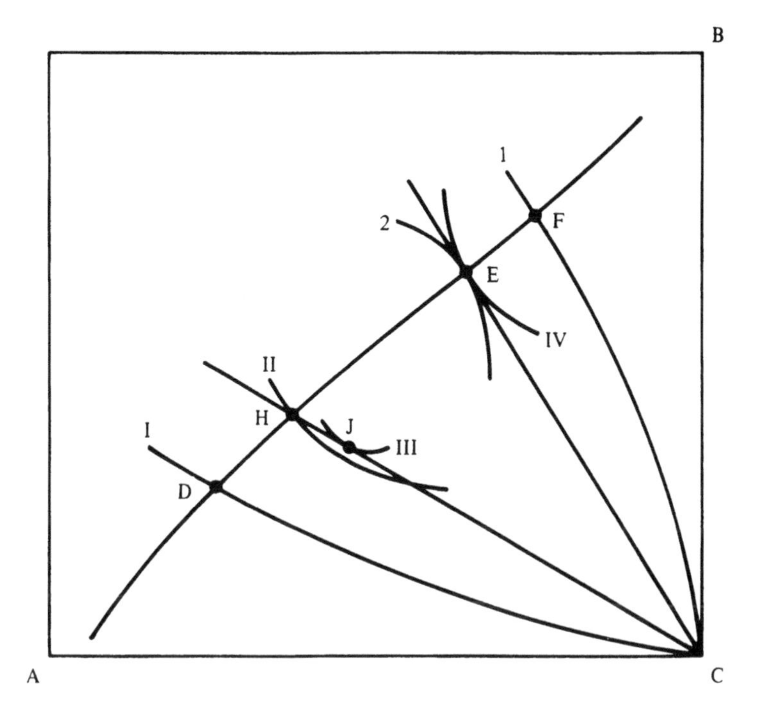

Figure 2.1 *The Edgeworth box diagram*

as in the case of isolated exchange, then all the points on the contract curve located between D and F are stable outcomes of exchange. It should be noted that such points other than point E cannot be reached through exchange with the uniform price ratio.

In the case of a large economy, however, it can be shown that all the points on the contract curve other than point E can be blocked by some coalition of traders that aims to make the participants better off. If so, only point E can be the stable outcome of the exchange, and the outcome of two different views of market are shown to be equivalent.

For example, the contract of point H in Figure 2.1 can be blocked by a coalition formed by all the A-type traders and more than half but less than all of the B-type traders. In the coalition, some A-type traders still continue trade with B-type traders and are located at H, while the rest of the A-type traders have no trade partners in the coalition and are located at C. By sufficiently increasing the number of B-type traders joining the coalition, and therefore increasing the number of A-type traders located at H, we can make the average allocation of two goods for A-type traders (some at H, some at C) so close to H on the line CH that it is located like J, above the indifference curve passing through H. By reallocating among themselves, therefore, all the A-type traders are better off than they are at point H. With some payments to B-type traders in the coalition, all the traders in the coalition are better off than they are at point H, so that an exchange contract H is blocked by a coalition of traders.

Similarly, any point between D and F on the contract curve, where the common tangent to two indifference curves does not pass through the point C, can, if necessary, be blocked by a coalition of traders by changing the roles of A-type traders and B-type traders from those in the case of point H. Obviously only the point E belongs to the core, that is the set of exchange contracts that are not blocked by coalitions of traders.

As far as the case of a large economy with infinitely many traders on both sides of the market is concerned, therefore, different views on the information structure in the market does not matter at all. By Edgeworth's equivalence theorem one may defend the unrealisticness of the neoclassical assumption of no mutual communication among traders and the existence of an auctioneer, since what matters is not the realism of the assumption but that of the outcome.

7. Communication structure of duopoly

Following the suggestion of Farrell (1970) let us now consider the case of duopoly with Edgeworth's communication structure, where there are only two traders of one type and infinitely many traders of another type, though the total quantities of two goods are finite in the exchange economy. Since equal quantities of goods should be allocated to identical traders of the same type, we can still use the Edgeworth box diagram (Figure 2.1), which now describes half of the economy, that of the duopolists and its infinitely many customers.

Suppose first that there are two B-type traders, B_1 and B_2, and infinitely many traders of type A. In Figure 2.1, BC is the quantity of the second good initially held by a B-type trader and AC is the sum of quantities of the first good initially held by half of the A-type traders. Curves I, II, etc., in Figure 2.1 are now aggregate indifference curves of A-type traders, as well as individual ones, which can be constructed if the identical individual curves are homothetic, so that the marginal rate of substitution between two goods depends only on the ratio of the quantities of goods and the Engel curve is a line through the origin.

An exchange contract H in Figure 2.1 can now be blocked by a coalition of one B-type trader (one of duopolists) and more than half but less than all of infinitely many A-type traders. All the A-type traders currently trading with the B_1 trader, who we assume joins the coalition, also join the coalition and keep the contract H with B_1. Some A-type traders currently trading with B_2, who does not join the coalition, join the coalition and cancel the contract with B_2 to return to the initial point C. By sufficiently decreasing the number of the latter group of A-type traders joining the coalition and therefore increasing the number of A-type traders located at H, relative to those A-type traders located at C, we can make the average allocation of two goods for individual A-type traders in the coalition so close to point H on the line CH that it is like an allocation J located above the indifference curve passing through H.[10] By reallocating among themselves, therefore, all the A-type traders in the coalition are better off than they are at the contract H. With some payment to B_1 located at H, all the traders joining the coalition can be better off than they are at H, so that the contract H is blocked.

Suppose next that there are two A-type traders, A_1 and A_2, and infinitely many traders of type B. In Figure 2.1, AC is now the quantity of the first good initially held by an A-type trader and BC is the sum of quantities of the second good initially held by the half of the B-type traders. Curves 1, 2, etc., in Figure 2.1 are aggregate indifference curves of B-type traders. In this case, an exchange contract H in Figure 2.1 can be blocked by a coalition of one A-type trader (one of duopolists) and less than half of infinitely many B-type traders. Then suppose A_1 joins the coalition. Those B-type traders also joining the coalition keep trade with A_1 unchanged so that they can keep the same level of utility as enjoyed at the exchange contract H. Duopolist A_1 cancels trade with those B-type traders who are not permitted to join the coalition, so that A_1 moves on the line HC from H towards C. Unless too many contracts with B-type traders are cancelled, A_1 can be located like J above the indifference curve passing through H. By reallocating among themselves, then, all the traders joining the coalition can be better off than they are at H, so that the contract H is blocked.

Similarly, any contract between D and F on the contract curve, where the common tangent to two indifference curves does not pass through the point C, can be blocked by a coalition of traders, if necessary, by changing the roles of A-type traders and B-type traders from those in the case of the contract H. Again, it is only the point E that belongs to the core. In other words, even a duopoly market ends up with an equilibrium identical to that of the perfect competition if duopolists and infinitely many customers are free to communicate to organize coalitions.

If, on the other hand, there is no such direct communication between duopolists and customers and the latter behave simply as price takers in the

[10] Though H and J are allocations to half of the A-type traders in the economy, they can be considered as allocations to an A-type trader, since indifference curves are homothetic. Alternatively, we can argue more generally by the use of Scitovsky indifference curves.

face of the uniform price offered by the former, it is well known that the equilibrium is in general different from that of the perfect competition, as was shown by Cournot (1897). The structure of communication is, therefore, very important in the case of the theory of duopoly and, more generally, in the case of oligopoly. In view of the prevalence of non-price competition among oligopolists, which implies the existence of direct communication between oligopolists and customers, we have to admit the unrealisticness of the assumption of the traditional theory of oligopoly, which denies the possibility of such communication.

Our consideration suggests, then, that the efficiency of an industry may depend not so much on the degree of concentration (the number of firms) as on the possibility of such direct communication and the cost of information, communication and organization.

8. Conclusions

Implicit dynamic concepts are hidden in the time structure of Walrasian and Marshallian theories, which are generally regarded as uni-periodal economic theories. Some of them correspond clearly to the more developed concepts of modern dynamic theories. The implications of Marshall's equilibrium of industry with disequilibrium firms has, however, not yet been fully and explicitly developed by modern theories of dynamic economics. While Edgeworth's theory of exchange has generally been evaluated as an important contribution to the theory of perfect competition, the implications of its communication structure of the market are considered in the case of duopoly, and it is suggested that the efficiency of an industry depends not so much on the degree of concentration as on the communication structure.

References

Cournot, A. (1897) *Researches into the Mathematical Principles of the Theory of Wealth*, Macmillan, London (French original, 1838).

Edgeworth, F.Y. (1881) *Mathematical Psychics. An Essay on the Application of Mathematics to the Moral Sciences*, C. Kegan Paul, London.

Farrell, M.J. (1970) 'Edgeworth Bounds for Oligopoly Prices', *Economica*, 37, pp. 342–61.

Garegnani, P. (1960) *Il capitale nelle teorie della distribuzione*, Giuffré, Milan.

Hicks, J. (1934) 'Léon Walras', *Econometrica*, 2, pp. 338–48.

(1946) *Value and Capital*, Clarendon Press, Oxford.

(1965) *Capital and Growth*, Clarendon Press, Oxford.

Marshall, A. (1921) *Industry and Trade*, Macmillan, London.

(1961) *Principles of Economics*, ed. C.W. Guillebaud, Macmillan, London (1st edn 1890).
Marx, K. (1959) *Capital*, vol. III, Progress Publishers (German original 1867).
Morishima, M. (1960) 'Existence of Solution to the Walrasian System of Capital Formation and Credit', *Zeitschrift für Nationalökonomie*, 20, pp. 238–43.
(1977) *Walras' Economics*, Cambridge University Press, Cambridge.
Negishi, T. (1985) *Economic Theories in a Non-Walrasian Tradition*, Cambridge University Press, Cambridge.
(1988) *History of Economic Theory*, North-Holland Publishing Company, Amsterdam and New York.
Walras, L. (1954) *Elements of Pure Economics*, ed. W. Jaffé, Allen & Unwin, London (French original 1874).
Wicksell, K. (1967) *Lectures on Political Economy*, Kelley, New York (Swedish original 1901–6).
Yasui, T. (1970) *Walras o megutte* (*Essays on Walras*), Sobunsha, Tokyo.

3 Structure and change within the circular theory of production

HEINRICH BORTIS

1. Introduction

Different uses are made of the terms *structure* and *change* in the social sciences in general and in economic theory in particular. Karl Marx, in the preface to the first volume of *Das Kapital*, insists on the fact that the dynamics of capitalism is governed by rigid laws equivalent to the laws of nature. This implies the presence of a technological and social structure – forces and relations of production – the evolution of which *determines* the actions of individuals leading to changes of given situations, that is to the evolutionary movement in question. This holds true of the most important spheres of economics, that is production, price formation, employment and accumulation. The only domain where some freedom of choice seems to exist is consumption. Neoclassical economics stands in deep constrast to the Marxian vision. Here there is freedom of choice for individuals in the whole realm of economics. Structural elements appear only as flexible constraints. These are, in the main, technological, legal, political and social. The important point is that the constraints and thus the structural elements are *outside* the field of economics, that is outside the market place, thus constituting, in usual parlance, the *framework* within which economic actions take place.

How far, then, does structure determine actions and what are the possibilities of choice – as eventually linked with change – within a given structural framework?

This is, of course, an extremely complex and far-reaching question that can only be sketched here. Perhaps the appropriate starting point is to attempt to clarify the relationship between structure – which implies rigidity – and change as is associated with flexibility. The main point will consist in bringing out some implications with respect to structure and change within the 'circular' theory of production. This will be complemented by some hints at the 'linear' production model; and some of its implications are in order to shed additional light on the meaning of the principal argument. The terms 'circular' and 'linear' theory of production are Piero Sraffa's: the former means 'production of commodities by means of commodities and labour', which corresponds to the *classical* model of production of which the Sraffa–Leontief production model is a modern version. The latter stands for the *neoclassical* view of production, according to which there is 'a one-way avenue from factors of production to final goods' (see Sraffa, 1960, p. 93) as is implied in the neoclassical production function.

In sections 2 and 3 the circular and the linear view of production are presented and some differences between them are brought out. Subsequently, it is sketched how important economic phenomena (distribution, value, proportions among sectors and employment levels) are explained if the circular and the linear view of production are adopted (sections 4 and 5). Behind long-run economic phenomena are specific institutions, and the relationship of these with structure and change are hinted at in section 6. Finally, section 7 is methodological. It deals with the problem of structure and time, that is structural change.

2. Production as a circular and social process

Production plays a fundamental role in economic theory and reality. There are, to simplify, two basically different views on the meaning and on the importance of production in economics. First, there is the classical *circular* view of production, which sees the process of production as an essentially *social* process. Second, there is the neoclassical vision, which leads to interpreting the same process as a *linear* process whereby *individual* (entrepreneurial) economic actions (substitution of labour by capital for example) are coordinated on the so-called factor markets. The meaning of these propositions is to be brought out to some extent in this and in the next section.

The most famous circular production models are those of François Quesnay, Adam Smith, Karl Marx, Wassily Leontief and Sraffa, the properties of which are set out comprehensively in Luigi L. Pasinetti (1977). Looking at any one of these production models it becomes apparent that the social and circular aspects embodied in them are closely interrelated. In fact, these terms describe but two different aspects of the classical vision of production.

The *social* element in the process of production shows up, most strikingly, in extensive *division of labour* in the exploitation of raw materials and in the making of tools, machines and consumption goods. Division of labour, in turn, requires *cooperation* between the various producers. In general, then, an action may be called 'social' if several individuals cooperate in order to reach a common (social) aim. Taking account of this definition it is easy to see why in Sraffa–Leontief models and in their classical precursors, especially Adam Smith in the opening pages of the *Wealth of Nations*, production is seen as a social process: the flows of goods and services between a great number of industries for productive purposes point to considerable, even very extensive, division of labour. This means that producers carry out specific functions within the process of production. The common – social – aim to be achieved here consists in producing, by means of non-produced and produced means of production, a *given* output of final goods such as to minimize the costs of production. In modern terms the latter is equivalent to choosing an optimal technique of production (see on this Pasinetti, 1977, pp. 151ff. and Pasinetti, 1981, pp. 188–98). In Quesnay's *tableau économique*, the social aim is stated in terms of an optimal surplus (see on this the excellent presentation of Quesnay's *tableau* in Oncken, 1902, pp. 314ff.) that would obtain if a natural – optimal – stationary state prevailed, and here Quesnay refers specifically to the French economy in the mid-seventeenth century. In fact, the terms of trade between agriculture and manufacturing, the proportions between sectors and thus the distribution of the labour force between sectors have to be such that the rent on land amounts to 2 billion pounds. The rent on land is equivalent to the surplus that is the difference between the gross production (7 billion pounds) and goods used up in the process of production (5 billion pounds), the latter comprising consumption goods. The spending of rent by landlords sets the process of production into motion. If the above conditions prevail and if there is no saving, gross output will be maximized and full employment will prevail. If rent exceeded its optimal level (2 billion pounds), then agricultural wages would be depressed below their natural level; in addition, agricultural fixed capital could not be maintained as the income of tenants would not be sufficiently high. Both factors would lower agricultural production and, consequently, production in general. If, on the other hand, rent was too low, autonomous expenditures would not be large enough to bring about a full use of available resources, including labour. Quesnay's basic production model has, subsequently, been taken up by the classical economists, some features being simplified, others elaborated. For example, Adam Smith has not dealt with the employment problem at all, but he has described the accumulation of capital (absent in Quesnay) and the interaction between industry and agriculture (Book Three of the *Wealth of Nations*) with much care.

Classical production models not only imply sophisticated social processes, for example division of labour and the resultant necessity of cooperation among producers. These models are also *circular*. Circularity shows up on two levels, that is on the level of intermediate products and on that of final products.

In the first place, in a Leontief–Sraffa model each industry delivers goods and services to other industries. Conversely, in order to be able to carry out production, each industry needs goods and services that are produced in other industries. The so-called input–output models thus record the circulation of goods and services going on in the course of the production process. This is circularity on the level of *intermediate* products. One may note at once that the quantities of goods and services circulating between industries are governed by technological factors. The actions of producers are thus strictly determined with respect to the quantities of intermediate products needed in order to produce a given quantity of some other good. There is no room for free choice here once the technique of production has been selected. In a way, present actions relating to the circulation of intermediate goods and services are determined by *past* technological choices.

In the second place, there is circularity on the level of *final* products as occurs in the *process of circulation*. This comes out clearly from Quesnay's *tableau*, Adam Smith's model of economic development as set forth in Book Three of the *Wealth of Nations* and, above all, from Marx's famous schemes of reproduction (chapters 20 and 21 of volume II of *Das Kapital*). As is well known, these schemes describe the exchanges of final products (circulation) that go on between the capital- (investment-) good sector and the consumption-good sector. On the one hand, the consumption-good sector needs durable means of production in order to replace worn-out machinery and, eventually, if a growing economy is being considered, for accumulation of real capital. On the other hand, the maintenance of the workers engaged in producing capital goods requires a certain amount of consumption goods. Thus, in order to guarantee an equilibrium between the two sectors, consumption expenditures occurring in the capital-good sector must equal gross investment outlays in the consumption-good sector. In this scheme, circulation, that is the exchanges between the consumption- and investment-good sectors, strictly stands in the service of production. In fact, an exchange of goods between the two sectors is required in order to maintain and, eventually, to expand the productive forces of a society as are represented, in Marxian terms, by total capital as made up of *constant* and *variable* capital. The productive forces thus consist of fixed and circulating capital and the labour force. If, now equilibrium in exchange between the consumption- and the investment-good sectors is to be maintained, then both sectors must stand in definite relation to each other. This kind of proportionality is part of the economic structure that governs the behaviour of individuals. Again, there is no question of choice implied in the exchange relation between the two sectors: a *given* amount of investment goods *must be* exchanged against consumption goods if the productive forces of an economy are to be maintained and, eventually, to be expanded. Possibilities of choice arise only in connection with the *composition* of the total amount of consumption goods to be produced.

Two main features characterize, then, the classical view of production, the first being related to space, the second to time. Being social and circular, the classical production process pictures, in fact, the spatial organization of production: the firms pertaining to a certain industry are located somewhere, and therefore the flows of goods and services between sectors and industries imply geographical movement of goods and services (transportation). This spatial feature of production is, of course, closely linked with the social aspect of the production process, showing up in division of labour, in that it requires cooperation between producers. This view of production also implies a certain organization of society. For instance, cooperation might be dictated by a *Planning Bureau* or be enforced by the economic power of a *social class*, for example capitalists. However, cooperation might also be based on mutual agreement between all producers. The specific form taken on by the social organization of production thus broadly corresponds to Marx's *Produktionsverhältnisse*, that is the social relations of production. (Of course, social relations play an even greater role in the distribution and use of the social surplus than in the process of production itself. In fact, both are closely interrelated.) The aspect of circularity, however, describes part of Marx's *Produktivkräfte* (forces of production) in that the technically determined flow of goods and services between industries and sectors is recorded.

A second feature of classical production models is that the production of final goods and the reproduction of social capital (constant and variable) takes place at any moment of time. Indeed, an input–output model might be set up to describe daily, monthly, or yearly production; if the necessity arose, a production model capturing events in the productive sphere over five or ten years might be constructed. In a way, in the social and circular process of production the length of the time period chosen plays no essential role. To be sure, production and reproduction go on in historical time, but the process is repetitive in that the same events, albeit in different forms, are repeated over and over again. Consequently, the passing of time becomes unimportant if the *material content* of production is being considered. This is not so, however, if the *form* of the production process is being considered. The way in which production goes on constantly changes in the course of time; time is thus essential here. These two features of production, content and form, as related to space and time will be taken up again in sections 6 and 7. At this stage it may be mentioned that the social and circular process of production going on at any moment of time implies the *simultaneous* production of consumption and capital goods. There is, then, in any period of time a continuous flow of output of means of production, which, in the next period, become part of the productive forces of an economy (see Burchardt, 1931, p. 547). It is precisely with respect to this last point that the circular view of production is fundamentally different from the linear view of production to which we now turn.

3. The 'linear' view of production and its comparison with the 'circular' view

The picture changes radically if we look at the neoclassical vision of the process of production. Here, the terms 'social' and 'circular' are to be replaced by 'individual' and 'linear'. The neoclassical view can perhaps be brought out best by the schemes of production developed by the Austrian branch of neoclassical economics. (An excellent comparison between Marx's and Eugen Böhm-Bawerk's approach to production and circulation is provided by Burchardt, 1931–2.)

To simplify grossly, the Austrian view may be put like this: the starting point is the *exchange* of consumption goods related to utility-maximizing behaviour of consumers, including, of course, producers. The prices of (first-order) consumption goods are thus determined by exchange, that is supply and demand. As such, prices are proportional to the marginal utilities that consumers attach to the last units of the respective consumption goods. Thus, the principle of 'individualism' as related to 'free choice' enters on the very ground floor of neoclassical analysis, as consumption is an individual action and as pricing of consumption goods is based on individual – utility-maximizing – behaviour, which is coordinated on markets. Now, consumer goods are produced by capital goods (parts of fixed capital goods used up in production and certain quantities of circulating capital goods that include half-made consumer goods), land and labour. *The values of these first-order means of production are determined by the prices of the respective consumer goods.* These (first-order) means of production (or second-order goods relative to consumption goods) are produced, in turn, by second-order means of production. Correspondingly, the values of the latter are determined by the prices of the former, and so on. The main difficulty linked with this theoretical construction is well known: there is, in principle, no beginning of the production process. Means of production of order n are produced by means of production of order $n+1$, and by labour and land. To overcome this difficulty, Böhm-Bawerk has assumed that the means of production of the highest order are produced *by labour alone*.

Given this, Böhm-Bawerk's scheme brings out very clearly the linearity of the neoclassical process of production: in successive stages, means of production are transformed into consumption goods, which means that the production of consumer and producer goods is *not* simultaneous as is the case in the social and circular production model. This specific feature of the linear process of production is closely related with another characteristic: production is, like consumption, an individual process. The price of consumption goods being determined by utility-maximizing exchange, the price of the intermediate means of production is governed by their contributions towards producing the final goods. Given this, individual producers combine the means of production on each stage of production in a cost-minimizing way. This implies free choice in the realm of production whereby the actions of the individual producers are coordinated on factor markets or, in the Austrian model, on markets of means of production of different orders.

Time plays an important role in Böhm-Bawerk's scheme. His 'period of production' indicates, in fact, the time span that elapses from the production of produced means of production of the highest order by labour alone until the production of some (final) consumption good. This is not the place to inquire into the possible analytical uses to which the concept of the period of production might be put in relation to the determination of the rate of interest for example. What is important here is that Böhm-Bawerk describes the *production* of final (consumption) goods and the reproduction of the means of production used up in the production process in terms of a *historical process*. This important point is clearly argued by Burchardt: '*Böhm tries to construct a theory of production and reproduction in terms of the historically grown productive structure of an economy*' (Burchardt, 1931, p. 557; Burchardt's emphasis). The linear view of production in which time plays an important role thus stands in clear contrast to the circular view of production *in which time plays no essential role*: 'the circular view of production may, in principle, disregard time' (Burchardt, 1931, p. 557). This crucial point, already hinted at in the foregoing section, may be interpreted as follows: the *material content* of the circular process of production and of the theory picturing it always remains the same, *regardless* of the length of the time period during which the process of production is observed. This is, of course, *not* to say, as will be seen in section 7 below, that the *form* of the process of production remains the same as time goes by, as there is technical progress linked with structural changes going on in time. From the above it now appears that Böhm-Bawerk's view of the production process is, in fact, *not a theory* but a *historical description* of production. As is well known, most modern neoclassical economists have, for various reasons, abandoned Böhm-Bawerk's view of the production process so that there is no neoclassical theory of production at all. We are in fact back to the mysterious transformation of factors of production into final goods alluded to by modern classical (Sraffian) economists. Of course, a modern neoclassical economist would argue that the process of production is described by the optimizing behaviour of producers and its coordination on factor markets where the production function, marginal products and the law of diminishing returns play an essential role. At this point Sraffian (neo-Ricardian) economists would, however, again ask such awkward questions as have been debated in the course of the 'capital theory debate': How do neoclassical economists take account of the fact that capital is, simultaneously, a final product and a factor of production? Can 'real capital' be measured independently of the determination of the rate of interest, that is of income distribution? How does one take account of intermediate products? Regarding the last question it may be mentioned that, if due account is taken of Sraffa (1960), the pre-Sraffian attempt by Robert Dorfman, Paul A. Samuelson and Robert M. Solow (1958) to integrate input–output models into the neoclassical model of production has failed. The modern neoclassical economist would attempt to counter these questions by pointing out that in equilibrium there are no problems with capital. This may be true of temporary equilibrium models, but these may be incompatible with what is considered to be normal in the long run. For example, equilibrium wages may be below the subsistence level, or profit rates may be unacceptably low in some sectors of production. The question as to the tendency towards a fundamental long-run equilibrium thus arises, and here the capital theory debate has produced definitive results in favour of the classical-Sraffian view of production, distribution and price formation (which allows the subsequent integration of the Keynesian theory of output and employment determination).

The main differences between the classical and the (Austrian) neoclassical view on the process of production can now be summarized like this: in the classical view, production is a social and circular process; time plays no essential role in so far as the material content of the classical theory is considered. Production and reproduction go on at any moment of time; actions related to production are determined as techniques are given, the latter being the result of past choices. Austrian neoclassicals, however, see production as a linear process in which time, that is the length of the 'production period', is essential; free choice (subject to temporary constraints) prevails and individual (entrepreneurial) actions are coordinated on intermediate-good markets.

As has been alluded to above, other versions of the neoclassical view of production have developed alongside the Austrian model, mainly the Marshallian and Walrasian lines. A glance at the latter will permit a comparison with the Austrian and the classical view of production.

The main difference between the Austrian and the Walrasian system lies in the complete lack of the time element in the latter. Here, production is no longer seen as a sequence, but occurs *simultaneously* with consumption. In fact, the actions of producers and consumers are both supposed to be coordinated by factor and goods' markets. Given this, a 'timeless' market equilibrium may now be defined. The Walrasian general equilibrium model characterized by simultaneity thus stands in quite sharp contrast to the sequential Austrian model of production, which is perfectly adapted to describe real world disequilibrium situations as occurring in historical time (see on this Walsh and Gram, 1980, p. 135).

There are two further differences between the Austrian and the Walrasian model: first, the Walrasian model lacks a description of the process of production properly speaking, that is as production of commodities by means of commodities and labour, which, in the Austrian model, appears as a sequential process. This implies that the notion of *linearity* acquires a new meaning in this latter framework: final (consumption and investment) goods are now produced by three factors of production: labour, land and real capital. Here, we have, as already mentioned, Sraffa's 'one-way avenue that leads from [f]actors of production to [c]onsumption [and investment] goods' (Sraffa, 1960, p. 93). Real capital, the produced factor of production, is thus put on a par with the original, non-produced factors of production. This is obviously not so in the Austrian framework where, in the final analysis, only labour (and land) are, properly speaking, factors of production, a fact that has far-reaching implications for distribution as is convincingly shown by Burchardt (1931, pp. 548ff.). Indeed, Böhm-Bawerk has explicitly denied that capital is a factor of production on its own (Burchardt, 1931, pp. 547–8). Quite obviously, this raises questions as to the nature of interest and profit.

Second, there is, albeit implicitly, circularity on the level of final products in general equilibrium models but not in the Austrian framework. This comes out clearly if one aggregates a Walrasian model to two sectors, a consumption-good and an investment-good sector. There are flows taking place between the two sectors which are, formally, equivalent to those described by classical (and post-Keynesian) production theory: investment goods flow to the consumption-good sector and *vice versa*. An important difference with classical theory has to be noted, however. In a neoclassical framework, sector sizes are governed by market forces. For instance, there is a market for new capital goods that determines the size of the investment sector. As is well known, in this market, the demand curve embodies the marginal efficiency of capital. The supply curve, on the other hand, states that the supply of resources that can be invested (savings, that is foregoing of consumption) increases with the rate of interest. This is not so in classical and post-Keynesian models, where sector proportions are regulated by consumption and savings pattern without the interference of factor markets, that is the markets for new capital goods in the case considered here.

To end this section two additional differences between classical models and neoclassical models of the Walrasian type are to be noted. First, although there is simultaneity in a general equilibrium model, exchange resulting in an optimum allocation of scarce goods still dominates production (on production- and exchange-oriented paradigms in economics see Baranzini and Scazzieri, 1986). This appears clearly from the structure of Walras (1952). The theory of exchange developed in sections 2 and 3 is subsequently extended to production (section 4) and accumulation (section 5). Thus, the theory of the optimal allocation of consumer goods is extended to include factors of production as well. As Pasinetti (1981, pp. 8–11) points out, this holds also for aggregate neoclassical analysis. In classical analyses, however, the forces and the relations of production depend on technology and institutions, a point to be developed further in section 5 below. This implies that in this case production is not regulated by market forces.

Secondly, Walrasian economists consider the process of production as the result of individual decisions of producers coordinated on factor markets. Individual producers aim at maximizing profits. To reach this aim they combine, given factor prices, the factors of production in appropriate proportions. Changes of factor prices lead to changes in proportions: relatively expensive factors are substituted by relatively cheap ones. This mechanism tends to bring about an optimal allocation of productive resources, and this implies that there is full employment of available resources. Thus, given tastes, technology and initial endowments, there is, according to the Walrasian model and in virtue of the principle of substitution, a wide scope for individual action.

This stands, as has already been mentioned, in striking contrast to the classical view of production, which implies a considerable amount of determinism. The implications of this statement are to be brought out to some extent in the following sections.

4. Economic activity and the circular view of production

In the previous sections, especially in section 1, it has been argued that classical economists and their modern followers adopt a *circular* view of the process of production, which implies that this process is also seen as a *social* process. In this section we shall briefly sketch the implications of adopting a circular view on production with respect to the most important economic problems. It is convenient to start with distribution and then to go on to value, expenditure of income as linked with the right proportions between sectors and, finally, the determination of the volume of employment.

To bring out the implications for *distribution* implied by the circular view of the production process consider a complete input–output table (for a numerical example see Pasinetti, 1977, p. 38). As is well known, rows indicate gross outputs produced in the different sectors of production, made up of intermediate and final outputs respectively. Columns represent costs of production, that is the value of intermediate goods used up in the various industries plus the incomes accruing to land, labour and fixed capital. The latter represents value added. Now, the input–output table records only factor income *ex post* and leaves open the question as to the principles governing the distribution of value added. Indeed, different possibilities are open and have in fact been proposed. David Ricardo considered as a natural law that workers, in the long run, get a natural wage near the subsistence rate. The fact that the least fertile land gets no rent determines total rents. Consequently, *given* the natural wage rate, profits appear as a residual. Alternatively, some Cambridge post-Keynesians (such as Nicholas Kaldor, Luigi L. Pasinetti, and Joan Violet Robinson) conceive profits or the rate of profits as being determined by investment or the rate of growth (the Cambridge equation) so that wages appear as a residual, rent being neglected in this theory. Marx has argued that, due to the existence of a permanent 'reserve army' of workers, the propertied classes, landlords and capitalists, could hire workers at subsistence wages, thus maximizing surplus value, which takes on the form of profits, including interests, and rents. Finally, when looking at some economically advanced countries today, distribution is, in the long run, presumably regulated by legal prescriptions and by mutual agreements between workers and entrepreneurs. The theories of income distribution alluded to are all of the classical type and have one point in common: they are all based on some political or social mechanisms that show an interplay of institutions. Distribution, as implied by the classical vision of production, is thus governed by the social and political structure, which is made up of various institutions having developed historically. The fact that distribution is the result of an institutional process is perhaps the main reason why economic theories of the classical type may properly be called *political economy*, not just *economics* as in the case of neoclassical economics, where functional income distribution is regulated by factor markets.

Once distribution is determined, a further economic problem may be tackled by classical economics, namely *value*, that is absolute and relative prices. The nature of prices in classical theory may be brought out in the most appropriate way by starting with Pasinetti (1977, pp. 72–4). Suppose, to simplify, that $n-1$ goods are produced by $n-1$ goods and labour. There are, then, $n-1$ price relations. Each of these represents the total costs incurred in producing a unit of output. Costs, in turn, consist of the value of the intermediate goods used up in the (circular) process of production and of value added, that is wages and profits. Thus, there are $n+1$ unknowns: $n-1$ absolute (money) prices, the money wage rate and the rate of profits on (circulating) capital. One of the unknowns may be eliminated by choosing an arbitrary *numéraire* good i in terms of which all the other goods are measured. This implies dividing all prices by p_i. There are now n unknowns: $n-2$ relative prices, the real wage rate (in terms of the *numéraire* good) and the rate of profits. However, there are still only $n-1$ price relations, which means that one of the unknowns must be determined outside the production system. As there is no economic sense in fixing one of the relative prices, either the real wage rate or the rate of profits has to be determined. This can be done with the help of one of the institutionally based distribution theories mentioned above.

Once the real wage rate or the rate of the profit is fixed, that is distribution is regulated, relative prices are determined by the price equations. In fact, relative prices depend upon the conditions of production (the production coefficients) *and* the rate of profit (see, for example, Pasinetti, 1977, pp. 73 and 80). The conclusion that relative prices are governed by the conditions of production *and* by distribution continues to hold if more complex situations are considered, for example if fixed capital is introduced (see on this Pasinetti, 1981, p. 44).

Given this, it now becomes evident why distribution, in a typically Ricardian spirit, has to be dealt with prior to the problem of value. In fact, the fixing of the real wage rate or of the rate of profit is a prerequisite to the determination of relative prices, which means that, in classical theory, distribution is *logically prior* to value.

From the above a rather peculiar feature of classical prices emerges. The prices of production (the classical natural prices) are, in fact, determined in the spheres of production and distribution and are, therefore, known before goods come to the market. The latter only regulates the quantities to be produced. In classical theory, then, supply and demand register only deviations from natural prices, while quantity adjustments tend to bring into line market prices and natural prices.

This brings us to a third economic problem, namely to the theory of *expenditure and demand* implied in certain modern versions of classical theory. In fact, the way in which incomes are spent determine sector sizes and thus the proportions between sectors. This is shown in great detail in Pasinetti (1981).

The fractions of total income saved and consumed bring about a first broad division of final output. As is well known, in macro-economic equilibrium saving must equal investment. This equilibrium condition regulates simultaneously the volume of employment *and* the size of the investment and of the consumption-good sector. Now, the equality between saving and investment implies fulfilling another equilibrium requirement: the demand for consumption goods coming from the investment-good sector must equal the demand for investment goods by the consumption-good sector. This is the Marxian condition guaranteeing equilibrium in the circulation of final goods as well as reproduction and, in a growing economy, expansion of total capital. The significance of this Marxian condition has been briefly discussed in section 1. The above points to the close connection between Marx and Keynes. The work done by both economists is, in fact, essentially macro-economic in character, Keynes's main aim being to explain the volume of employment, whilst Marx attempted to explain, among other things, the sizes of the consumption and investment sectors and thereby the distribution of a *given* labour force among both sectors.

Finally, the way in which consumption expenditures are spent on specific goods and services, as is indicated by Engel curves, determines the detailed structural set-up of the consumption-good sector. The latter governs, in turn, the structure of the investment-good sector as, due to the Marxian conditions just mentioned, both sectors must stand in definite proportion to each other.

Historically speaking the question of proportions between sectors has been dealt with in Quesnay's *Tableau économique*, in Adam Smith's industry-agriculture model in Book Three of the *Wealth of Nations* and, as just mentioned, in Marx's schemes of reproductive circulation; more recently, Leontief and Sraffa have tackled the problem of proportions between sectors in a classical spirit. The issue has perhaps been definitively settled by Pasinetti (1977, 1981).

It should be mentioned that the above is related to so-called 'fully adjusted situations' as governed by constant or slowly changing institutional and technological factors. In a fully adjusted situation there is a structural equilibrium – sectors are in the right proportions – and prices equal natural prices. Of course, fully adjusted situations represent only part of reality. During business cycles and short-term fluctuations, market prices, as determined by supply and demand, will, as a rule, deviate from their natural levels. Simultaneously, sector sizes will not be in line with the fully adjusted situation. However, both natural prices and fully adjusted situations act as gravity centres that attract both market prices and sector sizes. These gravity centres broadly correspond to the *natural features* of an economic system as set forth in Pasinetti (1981).

The classical theories of distribution, value and sector proportions dealt with above can now be neatly linked with the Keynesian theory of *employment and output determination.*

The starting point is a 'fully adjusted situation' in which the right proportions prevail between sectors. This means that the proportions between final goods produced (q_i/q_j) and workers employed (N_i/N_j) are fixed. However, *the scale or the volume of employment* (N) *is yet undetermined.* It is at this stage that classical economic theory must be complemented by the Keynesian theory of output and employment determination. In the short run, the level of output and employment is governed by the Keynesian multiplier mechanism. In the long run, that is in relation with the fully adjusted situations pictured above, the 'supermultiplier' relation will come into play. This relation constitutes, in fact, a theory of the trend. Trend output and employment are, in any period of time, governed by autonomous demand components (government expenditures and exports) multiplied by a 'supermultiplier', the trend growth being equal to the rate of growth of autonomous expenditures (see Bortis, 1984, p. 600). Given this theory of trend output, a post-Keynesian theory of the business cycle along Kaleckian lines and based upon the interplay of investment and profits can, subsequently, be brought in.

Starting then from a circular vision of the process of production, very definite conclusions follow with respect to economic theory. In fact, there emerges a combination of theories of value, distribution and sector proportions based upon the classical approach *and* the Keynesian theory of output and employment determination. Similarly, if the starting point is exchange and a linear view of production then definite conclusions follow with respect to economic theory. To this problem we now briefly turn.

5. Economic activity and the 'linear' view of production

Here, matters are much simpler. In neoclassical analysis the starting point is the individual and its consumption. Exchange is regulated by the utility-maximizing behaviour of individuals. The principle of exchange is subsequently extended to production and distribution. This automatically implies a linear view of production, regardless whether the sequential (Austrian) or the simultaneous (Walrasian) approach is chosen. These crucial points have been brought out in a concise way by J.A. Schumpeter in his *History of Economic Analysis.* The relevant passages are so illuminating that a full quotation is justified:

The first problem that Jevons, Menger, and Walras – Gossen too – tackled by means of the marginal utility apparatus was the problem of barter ... they all ...

aimed at the same goal, which was to prove that the principle of marginal utility suffices to deduce the exchange ratios between commodities that will establish themselves in competitive markets ... They established what A. Smith, Ricardo, and Marx had believed to be impossible, namely, that exchange value can be explained in terms of use value ... The essential point is that, in the 'new' theory of exchange, *marginal utility analysis created an analytic tool of general applicability to economic problems* ... The concepts of marginal and total utility ... carry direct meaning only with reference to goods and services the use of which yields satisfaction of consumers' wants. But Menger went on to say that means of production – or, as he called them, 'goods of higher order' – come within the concept of economic goods by virtue of the fact that they also yield consumers' satisfaction, though only indirectly, through helping to produce things that do satisfy consumers' wants directly ... This analytic device ... enables us to treat such things as iron or cement or fertilizers ... as incomplete consumable goods, and thereby extends the range of the principle of marginal utility over the whole area of production and 'distribution'. The requisites or factors or agents of production are assigned use values: they acquire their *indices of economic significance* and hence their exchange values from the same marginal utility principle that provides the indices of economic significance and hence explains the exchange values of consumable goods. But those exchange values or relative prices of the factors constitute the costs of production for the producing firms. This means, on the one hand, that the marginal utility principle now covers the cost phenomenon and in consequence also the logic of the allocation of resources (structure or production), hence the 'supply side' of the economic problem *so far as all this is determined by economic considerations*. And it means, on the other hand, that, in as much as costs to firms are incomes to households, the same marginal principle, with the same proviso, automatically covers the phenomena of income formation or of 'distribution', *which really ceases to be a distinct topic* ... The whole organon of pure economics thus finds itself unified in the light of a single principle – in a sense in which it never had before. [However, m]ost of the problems that arise from this set-up can be discussed only on a level on which Walras rules supreme. (Schumpeter, 1954, pp. 911–13)

These passages are completed by an exposition of the Walrasian system (Schumpeter, 1954, pp. 998ff.).

The above clearly brings the essence of the neoclassical approach into the open. The principle of individualism associated with exchange necessarily leads to a linear view of production. This is sharply opposed to the classical view as set forth in sections 1 and 2 above. Here, the starting point is society and the social and circular process of production (section 2) from which a specifically classical type of economic theory emerges (section 3).

6. Institutions, structure and actions

In section 3, the classical and Keynesian interpretation of important economic phenomena has been sketched, that is distribution, value, proportions between sectors and the volume or the scale of employment. The starting point has been the circular process of production which, as has been stressed, is seen as a social process by classical economists.

Behind economic phenomena stand individual actions. For instance, (long-term) prices of production depending upon technology and income distribution are set by entrepreneurs. The same holds for market prices that are in line with specific short-term market conditions. This example already points to a first classification of actions relating to their form. Actions may, in fact, be persistent or temporary and rapidly changing. Only the former will be considered here. Persistent actions of some, many or all individuals of a society may be called *institutions*. For instance, Thorstein Veblen has defined institutions 'as principles of action about the stability and finality of which men entertain practically no doubt' (quoted in Roll, 1973, p. 445). Now, persistent actions may again be divided into two subsets. There are, in the first place, persistent actions directed towards *individual* aims. A prominent example is provided by the differing types of consumption pattern of the various individuals commanding comparable incomes, which indicates that the aim of utility maximization may be achieved in different ways. In the second place, there are persistent actions of individuals aimed at *social ends*. These are ends that isolated individuals could not achieve, which implies, as a rule, that individuals carry out specific functions to render possible the achieving of some common aim. Social ends are, of course, also pursued in the economic sphere, the outstanding example of an (economic) social aim being the production of a given gross national product with labour and real capital, the latter being the result of past accumulation. Now, social ends also require social means. If the production of gross national product is being considered, the latter is represented by the social and circular process of production as based on the social division of labour which, in the view of the classical economists, is certainly the most important institution in the economic sphere. However, from a classical point of view there are other institutions that govern the outcome of long-run components of economic events, such as distribution, value, expenditure of income and employment.

It is quite evident that, in the long run, distribution is a social process governed by a very complicated interplay of institutions in which the government, trade unions, employers' organizations and a set of informal groupings participate. Pricing is also basically governed by institutions. In fact, as has been argued in the previous section, prices of production depend upon the conditions of production, that is the forces and relations of production and distribution. Thus, long-run prices depend upon technological and social factors. This does not mean that there is no room for free individual action in the field of pricing. In the short term, entrepreneurs adapt prices to specific market situations; in the medium term, the business cycle may require an appropriate pricing policy. Both factors will cause market prices to deviate from normal long-run prices. In addition, entrepreneurs shape the market by marketing campaigns, by variations of product quality and by introducing new products. In this context, one might mention that the market may also be considered as an institution; in fact, the basic mechanism of supply and demand could be viewed as a *natural*, that is not man-made, institution, whilst specific market forms are institutions shaped by human action.

The way in which income is spent heavily depends upon the institutions governing its distribution, that is by the various social classes and groups and by the state. Starting from this, a theory of spending would have to explain, in a first step, the proportions of income spent on necessary and luxury consumption, government expenditure and investment. This 'macro-theory' of spending could then be followed by studies on the sectoral and micro-level where an enormous amount of work has been and is being done.

Finally, the scale of output and employment also depends, if the long run is being considered, upon a set of institutions linked with autonomous and induced components of effective demand. Aggregate demand, in turn, crucially depends on the way in which income is distributed and this, as has been argued above, is also governed by the interplay of various institutions. The mechanism of long-run output and employment determination can be grasped intuitively by considering the determination of the various magnitudes entering the 'supermultiplier' relations (see Bortis, 1984, p. 600). Here, output and employment appear to be determined by autonomous expenditure (such as government expenditure and exports) multiplied by a supermultiplier depending upon long-run propensities to consume, the terms of trade and the import coefficient and the investment output-ratio, the size of which depends upon the technical dynamism of a society. Perhaps one could say that the institutions governing the foreign trade position of some country are of decisive importance. Indeed, exports, the terms of trade and the import coefficient are crucial determinants of the levels of output and employment.

Institutions, and particularly those directed towards social aims such as production, thus play a very important role in shaping the long-run outcome of economic events. It is indeed a hallmark of classical and partly of Keynesian economic theory, to assert that the most important economic events (such as production, distribution, value, proportions between sectors, the scale of output and employment) are, in the long run, governed by institutions. It should be noted, however, that institutions do not *entirely* explain the phenomena in question, but only their constant or slowly changing parts. For example, the prices that can be directly observed are market prices. These are made up of two main components. Natural, normal or long-run prices are governed by the conditions of production and by distribution, that is by the long-run profit rate towards which there is a tendency in all sectors of production or by a hierarchy of long-run profit rates. The business cycle or short-period market forces may bring about deviations from the normal prices, and these deviations constitute a second element making up prices as observed in the real world. Thus, the institutionally determined parts of prices and employment levels cannot be directly observed. They are hidden, so to speak, below the surface and can be brought to the open only by appropriate theorizing, which guides the economist's observation of reality.

Of course, there are various types of institutions in every society. As was argued in the previous section, the technical and social organization of *production* represents the basic economic (macro-) institution upon which other economic institutions related to distribution and spending are built. The economic institutions form, in turn, the material basis of society, which 'supports' political, legal and cultural institutions in the widest sense. This broadly corresponds to the way the old classical economists and Marx looked at society. According to them the process of production is the basic institution. Part of the gross product (intermediate goods and necessary wages) is used up in the process of production. The remaining surplus is distributed and spent in various ways: non-necessary and luxury consumption, gross investment, public goods and social and cultural purposes. In this view, the surplus emerging from production supports, materially, the social, political and cultural life of society. Of course, the distribution and the use of the surplus is, again, largely governed by institutions.

As is implied in the above, a critical feature of classical and, partly, of Keynesian economics is that institutions *directly* govern persistent or slowly changing parts of economic reality. For instance, it has been said that distribution is, in the long run, the outcome of a complex interplay of institutions. Consequently the most important economic phenomena (such as value, distribution and employment) are not subject to market determination. The latter may govern only the structure of production, *given* normal prices. Therefore, in the long run, markets determine quantities to be produced. In the short and medium term, markets also record fluctuations around constant or slowly changing long-run magnitudes, such as normal prices that are institutionally determined.

Now, all this is essentially different in neoclassical economics, mainly because here institutions play a completely different role. In fact, the starting point is the individual who is acting in different spheres of life – economic, political, cultural. As a rule the actions of individuals are coordinated by some mechanism that represents a natural, that is not man-made, institution. In the economic sphere, this is obviously the market; in the political sphere individual actions are partly guided by voting procedures. As far as the economic sphere is concerned, this implies that the starting point is the principle of *exchange* which, as has been suggested in section 4 above, not only reigns on the markets for consumer goods but also on factor markets. There, relying on Schumpeter, it has been argued that the marginal principle in its different forms (marginal utility, marginal costs, marginal productivity) organizes exchange on all markets. Therefore, supply and demand tend to solve all the important economic problems (value, distribution and employment) *if* markets are working satisfactorily.

In this neoclassical view institutions influence economic events only in an *indirect* way, that is through the market mechanism. In fact, institutions provide the framework for the market mechanism. Indeed, neoclassical economists frequently speak of various types of frameworks that surround, so to say, the market place. There is, first, the technological framework containing the 'technological blueprints' open to choice to enterprises. Consumers' tastes are part of the psychological framework. Trade unions would belong to the social framework. In addition, there is the legal, the political and the cultural framework. Institutions constitute the permanent or slowly changing elements in these frameworks. Some of these institutions are supposed to further the proper functioning of markets; for instance, the legal framework may ensure fair competition. Other institutions like workers' and employers' associations may, however, in the neoclassical view, become disturbing elements in that they may prevent the market mechanism from functioning properly.

The point now is that the institutions contained in the framework exercise only an *indirect* influence upon economic events, namely through the market mechanism. In fact, institutions govern the position of supply and demand curves in the various markets and thus partly determine the rules of the game for economic actions that take place on the market place. Consequently, changes occurring in the institutional framework result in *shifts* of demand and supply curves. For example, in the neoclassical view, growing trade union activity might result in a leftward shift of the labour supply curve. This raises the real wage rate above its competitive equilibrium level and, consequently, brings about unemployment, as, in the view of neoclassical economists, there is now an excess of labour supply over demand.

The differing views on the nature of the process of production, and its relation to exchange, in classical (and partly in Keynesian) theory, on the one hand, and in neoclassical economic theory, on the other, thus lead to a completely different interpretation not only of economic events but also of institutions that influence these events. This will become somewhat clearer if we have, in the next section, a brief look at the relationship between institutional structure and institutional change going on in historical time.

7. Structure and change

Economic structure comprises, broadly speaking, the institutionalized part of economic life. Thus, the technique of production and the various institutions in the different spheres of individual and social life that, in the classical view, directly influence the outcome of economic events make up the economically relevant structure (see sections 4 and 6 above). The fact that 'extra-economic' institutions, political institutions say, may directly influence economic events (that is without interference of the market) implies that society is a structured entity that cannot be split up into pieces at will.

Now, in the previous section, it has been mentioned that institutions represent persistent individual and social behaviour. Institutions thus represent repetitive actions in relation to which the time element does not play an essential role. Also, if institutions are working properly there is almost no uncertainty about the future with respect to institutionalized actions. On the other hand, time is very important in economics and in other social sciences as there are structural changes going on that may be accompanied by uncertainty and expectations. This apparent contradiction may be overcome by making use of the concept of *causal relation*, whereby it will be appropriate to distinguish between two kinds of causality: *vertical causality* in which time plays no essential role and *horizontal causality* where time is essential.

Formally speaking classical and Keynesian economic theory represent a set of causal relations. The hallmark of such relations is that they are unidirectional (see on this Pasinetti, 1964–5): predetermined variables govern determined variables while no significant feedback of the *same* causal type is occurring (an eventual feedback would have to be captured by a different causal relation). The most prominent causal relation is perhaps Keynes's multiplier relation. Here, autonomous variables and the multiplier (the predetermined magnitudes) govern output and employment (the determined variables). This causal relation thus states that effective demand determines output and employment at any moment of time. (Here, one might mention that the accelerator captures the feedback triggered off by the multiplier effect; in the former investment depends upon changes in output.) The circular process of production, dealt with extensively in section 2, also represents a causal relation. Final commodities, the dependent or determined variables, are produced by basic commodities (on this Sraffian conception see Pasinetti, 1977, pp. 104–11) and labour, that is the independent or predetermined variables. Again, different feedbacks, to be represented by corresponding causal relations, are possible. For example, if a significant part of the surplus is put into research and development, the process of production may be modified, since a larger surplus may eventually be produced with constant land and labour inputs.

Now, as suggested above, one may distinguish between two basic types of causality: vertical and horizontal causality lead to two different kinds of causal relations. Causal relations embodying vertical causality describe links existing between different spheres of reality. As such, causal relations of the vertical type are linked to *space*. These relations shed light upon the spatial organization of parts of the real world. For example, the Keynesian multiplier links the investment-good sector to the consumption-good sector: incomes are created in the process of producing capital goods in the former sector, and the partial spending of these incomes leads to a cumulative process of production and income formation in the latter sector. Also, the circular and social process of production pictures aspects of the transformation of labour and land and intermediate products, including the using up of parts of the fixed capital stock, into final output. This amounts to picturing the whole spatial network of inter-industry relations.

Now, why the term 'vertical' causality? This can perhaps best be explained by looking at some economic phenomenon, say a price. A price is, in a way, a result embodying the effects of various causal forces to be found in the real world, that is in space. In fact, every price consists of different components that are governed by differing causal forces. In the first place, there is the normal price, the price of production, and, as has been hinted above, this is governed by the conditions of production and distribution. The latter represent constant or slowly changing technological and institutional factors that are of a long-run nature. A second price component is given by deviations from the normal price, as may occur in the course of the business cycle. For instance, in a cyclical upswing an entrepreneur may stick to the normal price and increase the utilization of existing capacity; or, if capacity utilization is above normal, prices may be put up. These are medium-term causes influencing prices. Finally, market prices may reflect a host of short-run market forces. As a rule these short-run price components depend heavily upon expectations.

The various causal forces governing prices may now be ordered according to their stability in the course of time. This gives rise to forming different *layers of reality*. The top layer would consist in rapidly changing market forces, that is the vagaries of the market. A second layer would contain forces at work as linked to the business cycle. Thirdly, there are persistent institutional and technological forces. All these underlying causal forces determine the price of some good. This also holds for other economic phenomena, such as the level of employment, which consists, in the main, of a trend component and of a cyclical component. These are complemented by short-run components due to the vagaries of markets.

The direction of causality thus goes from the underlying causal factors, the layers of reality, to the visible surface as represented by economic phenomena, prices and employment levels for instance. This is the reason why one might speak of vertical causality. As has been mentioned already in the context of the circular process of production, vertical causality goes on in every moment of time so that the time element does not play an essential role here. Thus, one may consider 'the production of commodities by means of commodities' and labour, the processes of price formation or the multiplier process for one day, a year or five years. Essentially these processes remain the same as time goes by. Thus, one might say that vertical causality embodies the essence, the material content or the substance of some causal relation that is independent of time.

The vertical aspect of classical and Keynesian causal relations thus makes up the *content* of these theories; these set out to explain economic phenomena by the causes underlying them. The classical theory of production, then, states that final output is produced by intermediate goods, including part of fixed capital used up in the process of production, land and labour; in the short and medium terms varying degrees of capacity utilization come in to determine output. Distribution is, in the long run, governed by the interaction of a set of socio-economic and political institutions. Prices depend, as has been mentioned above, upon a host of long-run, medium and short-term forces. Finally, effective demand governs the level of output and employment through the multiplier relation.

While the *content* of classical and Keynesian economic theory represented by the 'vertical' aspect of causality embodied in the corresponding causal relations remains the same as time goes by, the *form* in which causality is effected may change in the course of time. For example, in the multiplier relation, the size of the multiplier may vary as the multiplier process goes on in time. An increased production of capital goods (additional investment) may, in a first step, lead to an increase of prices and profits in the consumption-good sector if capacities are fully utilized there. This reduces the multiplier below its normal level as higher profits imply a larger savings coefficient. As time goes by, however, the capacity effect gradually works out. Productive capacities in the consumption-good sector are thus expanded. This may be accompanied by falling prices and profit rates leading to a decline of the savings coefficient, which, in turn, increases the size of the multiplier. Gradually, a permanent change in the level of investment will thus lead to a permanent change in output and employment where the size of the latter is governed by the normal (average) size of the multiplier coefficient. Similarly, if we have a look at the circular process of production, the production coefficients linking the determined variable (final output) and the predetermined variables (land and labour) constantly change in the course of time, due to technical progress. In addition sector sizes are varying because of changes in the way incomes are spent (Engel's law).

The changes of parameters linking the determined and predetermined variables of causal relations reflect changes going on in the real world. What happens is that the underlying causes governing economic phenomena as situated in the various layers of reality defined above are changing. The changes in question thus go along the time axis. This is the reason why one may speak of horizontal causality. Thus, the content of a causal relation is equivalent to vertical causality whilst the changing form of a causal relation gives rise to horizontal causality. Figure 3.1 should to some extent clarify the meaning of these terms.

Of course, in any causal relation *vertical* and *horizontal* causality occur *simultaneously*. Two examples illustrate this. The first is related to the Keynesian multiplier, the second to the circular process of production.

In his *General Theory* Keynes distinguishes between the 'logical theory of the multiplier, which holds good continuously, without time-lag, at all moments of time, and the consequences of an expansion in the capital-goods industries which take gradual effect, subject to time-lag and only after an interval' (Keynes, 1973, p. 122). It seems evident that the 'logical theory of the multiplier' refers to vertical causality whilst the way in which the multiplier effect works out in the real world is pictured by horizontal causality. This may be illustrated by Keynes's own words: 'The relationship between these two things can be cleared up by pointing out, firstly, that an unforeseen ... expansion in the capital-goods industries does not have an instantaneous effect of equal amount on the aggregate of investment but causes a gradual increase of the latter; and, secondly, that it may cause a temporary departure of the marginal propensity to consume away from its normal value, followed, however, by a gradual return to it.' (Keynes, 1973, p. 123) Keynes provides an example to bring out the meaning of these propositions:

The explanation of these two sets of facts can be seen most clearly by taking the extreme case where the expansion of employment in the capital-goods industries is so entirely unforeseen that in the first instance there is no increase whatever in the output of consumption-goods. In this event the efforts of those newly employed in the capital-goods industries to consume a proportion of their increased incomes will raise the prices of consumption-goods until a temporary equilibrium between demand and supply has been brought about partly by the high prices causing a

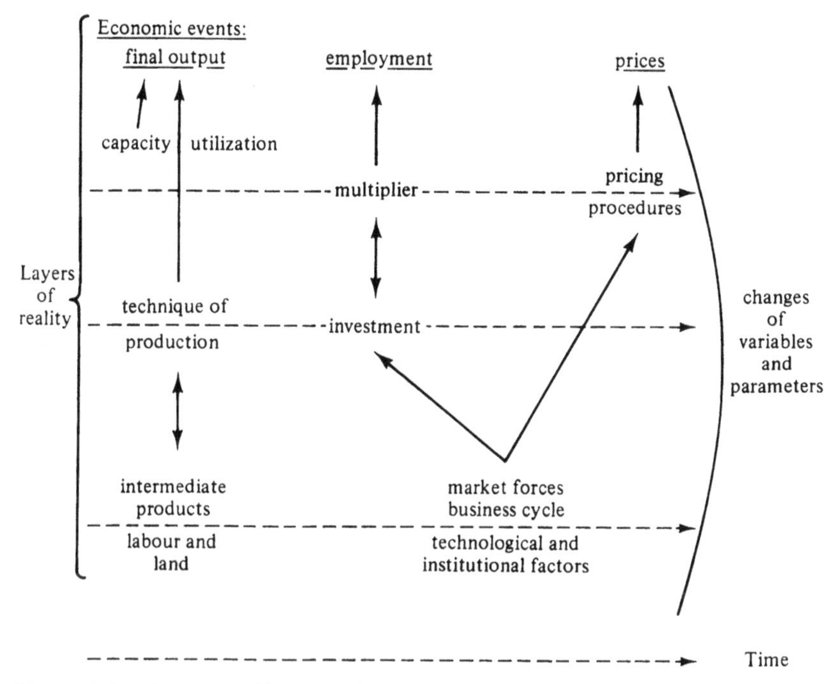

Figure 3.1 *Concepts of horizontal and vertical causality*

postponement of consumption, partly by a redistribution of income in favour of the saving classes as an effect of the increased profits resulting from the higher prices, and partly by the higher prices causing a depletion of stocks. So far as the balance is restored by a postponement of consumption there is a temporary reduction of the marginal propensity to consume, i.e. the multiplier itself, and in so far as there is a depletion of stocks, aggregate investment increases for the time being by less than the increment of investment in the capital-goods industries – i.e. the thing to be multiplied does not increase by the full increment of investment in the capital-goods industries. As time goes on, however, the consumption-goods industries adjust themselves to the new demand, so that when the deferred consumption is enjoyed, the marginal propensity to consume rises temporarily above its normal level, to compensate for the extent to which it previously fell below it, and eventually returns to its normal level; whilst the restauration of stocks to their previous figure causes the increment of aggregate investment to be temporarily greater than the increment of investment in the capital-goods industries ... The fact that an unforeseen change only exercises its full effect on employment over a period of time is important in certain contexts ... But it does not in any way affect the significance of the [logical] theory of the multiplier as set forth [here]' (Keynes, 1973, pp. 123–4).

This important passage from the *General Theory* shows that the concepts of vertical and horizontal causality (for which perhaps more appropriate terms will have to be found) are by no means new. Furthermore, the fact emerges that while the logical theory of the multiplier as associated with vertical causality is extremely simple, its concrete application to a real world event set in historical time (horizontal causality) may be very complex. This is, in fact, a hallmark of classical (mainly Ricardian) and Keynesian theoretical tools: the individual pieces of theory (the substance of a theoretical argument) are of a striking simplicity, prominent examples being the basic Ricardian model of value and distribution as set forth in Pasinetti (1974, pp. 1–28) or the Keynes–Kahn multiplier. These pieces of theory may, however, be put to very complex uses to analyse real world situations evolving in historical time. This last point, finally, indicates that the concepts of vertical and horizontal causality are a starting point for the bringing together of theory and history; vertical causality being associated with theory and horizontal causality with history. Historians of economic thought know that the classical economists, Adam Smith, in the main, and Karl Marx, have excelled in this as is illustrated by the *complete dynamics* embedded in classical and Marxian political economy.

This leads to the second example to be given here to illustrate the concepts of vertical and horizontal causality. The example refers to the circular theory of production, the importance of which in classical economic theory has been alluded to in the preceding lines. The circular theory of production has, in fact, been dealt with in Pasinetti (1977, 1981) in a way that neatly integrates the concepts of vertical and horizontal causality. Pasinetti's main theme is precisely the theme of the present volume: *structure* and *change*. In fact, Pasinetti (1977) deals with vertical causality as is contained in circular (Sraffa–Leontief) production models. These models explain how production, including of course the production of surplus, and reproduction go on in every moment of time; in fact, these production models picture the material content or the essence of the circular process of production. On the basis of this, Pasinetti shows how income distribution comes in and how normal prices, that is the prices of production, are formed. Pasinetti (1981) presents a simplified picture of the process of production in that the concept of vertical integration is brought into the picture. Here, original factors of production (i.e. labour, land being eliminated in the Ricardian way) are directly linked with final goods at any instant of time. This production model, too, is a causal model embodying vertical causality in that it informs us about the substance or the material content of the process of production as it goes on at any instance. Again, starting from his vertically integrated production model, Pasinetti derives a theory of prices of production and shows how distribution comes into the picture. Starting from this theoretical basis a variety of socio-economic problems, technical progress and international trade, are dealt with, albeit very generally, in a classical spirit. There is absolutely no difficulty in bringing in the Keynesian employment problem as Pasinetti's model is about proportions between sectors, leaving open the question as to the scale of employment alone.

In addition, Pasinetti (1981) deals with horizontal causality, and this is even the essential feature of this work. In fact, as time goes by, the coefficients of production and demand slowly but continuously change and new products and new production coefficients come into being. This implies changes in the form of the processes of production and reproduction, distribution and price formation.

The way in which both types of causality are integrated is set forth in Pasinetti (1981, chapter 6, pp. 109–17). This ingenious device of bringing together vertical and horizontal causality in the field of classical theory – if properly combined with the Keynesian theory of employment and output determination as hinted at above – could become the starting point for integrating theory and history. This would be tantamount to the revival of a method of investigation that has featured prominently in classical and Keynesian political economy. More specifically, reconciling theory and history implies that we must look at structure (as linked with theory) and change (as linked with history) simultaneously. Theory makes sense only if it helps to comprehend historical processes; but, on the other hand, history cannot be understood without theory.

8. Concluding remarks: determinism and choice

In the introductory remarks the problem of structure and action (linked with free choice) was hinted at. Now, from the overall argument as set forth in these notes it emerges that historically grown structures as represented by technology and institutions play an important role in determining individual actions and thus limit the scope for free choice. This is particularly true if a circular view of production is adopted and if the implicit consequences for economic theory are drawn. It then becomes apparent that, in classical and Keynesian economic theory, technology and institutions govern *directly* (that is without interference of the market, which is a natural, not man-made, institution) the outcome of (long-term) economic events, that is prices of production, functional income distribution and trend levels of output and employment. Here, a fundamental difference with neoclassical analysis appears. In the latter, institutions and technology form the so-called framework of the market mechanism through which economic phenomena are determined. The market, it has just been said, is a natural, not man-made, institution. Institutional change also produces its effects through the market resulting in a shift of supply and demand curves. Therefore, in neoclassical analysis, institutions and technology have only an *indirect* influence on economic events. This implies that there is much more scope for choice according to neoclassical theory than according to classical and Keynesian political economy. According to the former, there is, in fact, free choice with respect to economic events subject to (flexible) budget constraints. The market, if working satisfactorily, is then supposed to coordinate individual economic actions appropriately.

Compared to neoclassical economics, the possibilities of choice are much more restricted in classical and Keynesian economics. Here, institutions govern global economic magnitudes. For example, the scale of output and employment is determined by effective demand; the overall quantities of goods and services to be delivered from one sector to another are fixed by technology as the result of past choices. Similarly, certain quantities of final output require that technologically fixed amounts of intermediate goods are used up in production. Normal prices are determined by the conditions of production and by functional income distribution, which is itself governed by institutions.

However, there remains considerable scope for choice within a given structural framework. First, while *global* economic magnitudes are institutionally governed and thus determined by objective factors, the *composition* of these magnitudes is largely undetermined, and this makes the door wide open for the intervention of subjective factors as linked with possibilities of choice. For example, *given* the scale of employment, the occupation of the various work places is largely a matter depending upon subjective factors, although objective factors, as pertaining to some social class, may come in more or less strongly. Similarly, the firms surviving in a strongly competitive market will be able to do so on the basis of the quality of work performed by workers and managers. In the second place, institutions do not work rigidly, which means that there is a choice to be made between the different ways an institution can function. For example, to say that distribution is governed by associations of workers and employees, on the one hand, and employers' associations, on the other, does not yet fix the *form* in which determination is exercised. There may, in fact, be conflict or mutual consent, both of which are, to some extent, open to choice.

Thirdly, there may be institutional change brought about by deliberate action. Once again subjective factors, for example the aims pursued by individuals initiating changes, are likely to play an important role. In this the comparison of a given situation with some desired state of affairs is presumably of decisive importance. Finally, temporary deviations from institutionally determined economic variables are to some extent open to choice. For instance according to classical theory prices are, in a long-run view, governed by the conditions of production and by functional income distribution (the rate of profits). In addition, capacities are supposed to be utilized normally. In the short run, however, entrepreneurs may fix prices and/or degrees of capacity utilization that deviate from their respective long-run normal levels in order to adapt them to specific market conditions.

Then, in a classical and Keynesian view, there is no rigid determination of social and economic events as is present in parts of Marx's work. Nor is there free choice subject only to extra-economic constraints, as in neoclassical economic theory. Determinism and choice are simultaneously present: some economic actions, production being a prominent example, are largely determined by existing structures while other actions, consumption for instance, are associated with wide possibilities of choice. There are also economic actions where determinism and choice are inextricably mixed up, as is the case with structural change in production: given the heritage of past capital accumulation, entrepreneurs continuously change the shape of the forces of production by introducing new techniques. In fact past decisions on institutional arrangements provide present structures within which individuals act. This means that history influences the present in an important way without entirely determining what is going on now.

References

Baranzini, M., and Scazzieri, R. (1986) *Foundations of Economics. Structures of Inquiry and Economic Theory*, Basil Blackwell, Oxford and New York.

Bortis, Heinrich (1984) 'Employment in a Capitalist Economy', *Journal of Post Keynesian Economics*, 6, pp. 590–604.

Burchardt, Fritz (1931–2) 'Die Schemata des stationären Kreislaufs bei Böhm-Bawerk und Marx', *Weltwirtschaftliches Archiv*, 34, pp. 525–64; 35, pp. 116–76.

Dorfman, R., Samuelson, P., and Solow, R. (1958) *Linear Programming and Economic Analysis*, McGraw-Hill, New York.

Keynes, J.M. (1973) *The General Theory of Employment, Interest and Money*, Macmillan, London and Basingstoke (1st edn 1936).

Oncken, A. (1902) *Geschichte der Nationalökonomie – Die Zeit vor Adam Smith*, Hirschfeld, Leipzig.

Pasinetti, L.L. (1964–5) 'Causalità e interdipendenza nell'analisi econometrica e nella teoria economica', *Annuario dell'Università Cattolica del Sacro Cuore*, Milan, pp. 233–50.

(1974) *Growth and Income Distribution. Essays in Economic Theory*, Cambridge University Press, Cambridge.

(1977) *Lectures on the Theory of Production*, Macmillan, London.
(1981) *Structural Change and Economic Growth. A Theoretical Essay on the Dynamics of the Wealth of Nations*, Cambridge University Press, Cambridge.
Roll, E. (1973) *A History of Economic Thought*, Faber & Faber, London and Boston.
Schumpeter, J.A. (1954) *History of Economic Analysis*, ed. from manuscript by E. Boody Schumpeter, Allen and Unwin, London.
Sraffa, P. (1960) *Production of Commodities by Means of Commodities*, Cambridge University Press, Cambridge.
Walras, L. (1952) *Eléments d'economie politique pure ou théorie de la richesse sociale.* Librairie Générale, Paris (4ème édition définitive, revue et augmentée par l'auteur, 1900).
Walsh, V., and Gram, H. (1980) *Classical and Neoclassical Theories of General Equilibrium*, Oxford University Press, Oxford and New York.

Part III
STRUCTURAL DYNAMICS AND THE ANALYSIS OF ECONOMIC CHANGE

4 Specification of structure and economic dynamics

MICHAEL A. LANDESMANN AND
ROBERTO SCAZZIERI

1. Introduction

In this paper we shall emphasize the importance of structural specification for dynamic analysis. Such a specification is strongly linked to the notion of relative invariances of patterns of interaction among components of an economic system as well as of their characteristics. Such patterns and characteristics, as the notion 'relative' implies, are not immutable but are changing within clearly specified boundaries. These boundaries impose a definite pattern of adjustment to change within an economic system. Consequently, structural specification is an essential element of the analysis of economic dynamics. We shall explore this issue in section 2.

It will also be emphasized that there is a correspondence between the concepts of structural invariance used in theoretical models and the factual analysis of time patterns of relative adjustment of different characteristics of actual economies. This correspondence is considered in section 3. In section 4 we distinguish a number of methods of dynamic analysis that have been widely used in theoretical economics and are based on distinct analytical treatments of interdependencies through time within an economic system. These distinct approaches to dynamic analysis could, in principle, find applications in most spheres of economic and social activity. In section 6, however, we shall explore how different specifications of the production structure of an economic system have led to distinct theoretical formulations of structural dynamics.

2. Structural invariance and economic change

In economic analysis, description is associated with a certain degree of simplification of the economic system that is being considered. Many characteristic features of that system may be disregarded for the sake of theoretical investigation. Indeed, descriptive simplification is generally carried out in terms of a standard set of categories (such as 'productive process', 'commodity', 'price'), so that abstract reasoning may be applied and general propositions formulated. The analytical description of *economic structure* may be considered as a mapping of the set of features characterizing any given economic system into a set of general and relatively simple characteristics common to a number of distinct economic systems under different circumstances. The utilization of such a structural mapping is a necessary condition for deductive and hypothetical analysis. For the latter requires the consideration of an analytical framework 'in which certain elements of the state (or process) that we desire to examine (or to contemplate) are selected such that the interrelations and interactions of those elements may be deduced by reasoning' (Hicks, 1965, p. 28).

The analysis of dynamic processes is influenced in an essential way by the type of structural mapping adopted, that is by the type of structural specification that is implicit in the economist's description of any given economic system. In particular, economic structure is generally described in such a way that certain elements of it are considered to be fixed while other elements are allowed to change. As a matter of fact, the analysis of structural dynamics is associated with a general postulate of *relative invariance*, according to which any given economic system subject to an impulse or force is allowed to change its original state by following an adjustment path that belongs to a limited set of feasible transformations. In fact, the set of feasible transformations is the consequence of both the characteristics of certain elements of an economic system that are taken as constant and certain patterns of interrelationships among the different components that are assumed as invariant in the structural specification of the system. In this way, the impulse from which the original state of the economy is modified may be purely exogenous but the actual process of transformation can be explained in terms of the 'dynamic' characteristics of the existing structure (that is in terms of the specific paths of feasible transformations that are compatible with its description).

For the purpose of identifying a set of feasible transformations it is necessary that the structural specification of an economic system includes an account of the temporal characteristics of economic interrelationships. A 'time-differentiated' description of the interrelationships among the different elements of the economic system is a necessary condition for the identification of 'dynamic structures'. In other words, the different economic magnitudes must be related with one another in terms of a specific ranking of their respective motions. Such a ranking identifies a virtual sequence of transformations that must be followed whenever the system under consideration is subject to a source of change.

This virtual time structure imposes a constraint not only on the specific direction of change followed by any given economic system, but also on whether such a system is or is not allowed to change its characteristics at all. The reason for this is that, given a virtual time arrangement of feasible transformations, it may be that structural change is blocked whenever there is a source of change that would affect the economic system in a way incompatible with the existing structure and its potential for change.

In the following analysis, we shall define as *dynamic structures* a type of structural description in which the (virtual) time structure of feasible transformations is explicitly considered. As a result, we may say that a dynamic structure is by definition a type of structure in which the possibility of change is explicitly accounted for, in the sense that an essential element of the corresponding structural specification is the description of specific time sequences of feasible transformations. The dynamic identity of an economic system depends on the set of feasible transformations that are compatible with the given specification of dynamic structure. Any two systems are *structurally equivalent* in a dynamic sense if they are associated with the same set of feasible-transformation paths.

Just as an essential element of any concept of a static economic structure is its definition in terms of a pattern of relationships among the different elements of the given structure within a well-defined time interval, the dynamic counterpart of such a concept is the system of sequential (time-dependent) relationships among the rates of change of the different elements that identify the static structure.

The above conceptual framework implies that two distinct but complementary logical steps may be distinguished in the analysis of structural change:

(i) the assumption of invariance of the economic system under a given structural description (such an assumption, which is essential in order to generate determinate transformation paths, is associated with the identification of a specific dynamic structure, as defined above);

(ii) on the other hand, to allow for structural change the same economic system has to be 'open' with respect to other types of structural descriptions. That is, if certain 'blockages' that are inherent to the particular features of structural invariance associated with an economic system are overcome, a switch to a new type of structural characterization must be feasible.[1]

[1] The features of 'relative structural invariance' are not just inherent in a theoretical structure but reflect rigidities in actual economies. The notion of structural invariance thus allows, potentially, a close interaction between the theoretical formulation of features of an economic system and its empirical counterpart. This issue will be elaborated in the next section.

In other words, in order to undertake structural change analysis, the economic system may or may not be mutable under a number of structural descriptions, but it needs to be invariant with respect to at least one type of structural characterization. The property of invariance inherent in such a characterization identifies the dynamic structure in terms of which the analysis of structural change may be carried out.

3. The descriptive–analytical and the deductive–behavioural approaches to structural change analysis

For the purpose of clarifying how the analysis of structural change may be carried out, it is worth distinguishing between two alternative concepts of structure. One is that of an equilibrium or 'settled' constellation of individual actions, based on a clearly stated set of behavioural principles that are essential in determining the way in which such a position is achieved and possibly maintained. The other is an analytical specification of patterns of interrelationship that is obtained by adopting as a starting point what may be called a 'descriptive–analytical' approach. In this case, factual and statistical material is used to describe the basic characteristics of an economic system.

Concerning the first concept of structure, it has often been maintained that the formulation of a concise set of behavioural principles (such as utility maximization and profit maximization) and a working out of their implications for the attainment of a final position of interrelated individual actions is the only way a set of economic interrelationships can really be understood. Of course the pattern of adjustment and the final equilibrium position is not simply a result of the set of behavioural principles at work but also of the initial conditions, of the institutions governing the way in which economic interaction takes place and of certain parameter constellations that provide the environment in which individual actions are planned and executed. However, behavioural principles act as the driving forces behind the adjustment patterns, and the compatibility of a final equilibrium outcome with the persistent pursuit of the implications of such behavioural principles lies at the root of what an 'understanding' of a particular pattern of interrelationships means within this approach. Critics, however, have often pointed out that the set of behavioural principles associated with this approach is too narrow and not supported by empirical tests of individual behaviour; that the set of behavioural principles guiding human behaviour is broader and more unstable as well as subject to environmental influences. The latter fact would mean that the single-minded pursuit of the implications of a given behavioural principle as a stable guide through the various stages of an adjustment process would be misplaced.

The other concept of structure starts with a descriptive assessment of primary factual and statistical material in extracting a picture of the internal characteristics of individual parts of an economic system (such as production units and households) and of their pattern of interaction. If this approach is adopted, it cannot be claimed that the structure is really 'understood'; there are not even grounds at this stage to claim that the features selected in such a descriptive–analytical exercise are in any sense more fundamental than others that could have been selected. The relevance of a particular structural description of an economic system can be judged only at the next stage of analysis. That stage consists in using the structural description in the form of a model that can be 'put to work'. Different parts of the structural description of an economic system are taken as given and particular degrees of structural invariance are attached to them depending on the type of issues that one wants to investigate. In particular, we may mention the analysis of the comparative–static type, in which particular components that featured in the original description of the 'structure' of an economy are changed (such as the composition of output or a particular tax rate or the structure of relative prices) and the responses to such discrete changes by the individual units and their patterns of interrelationships are examined. We may also mention the analysis of the *structural–dynamic* type, in which the evolution of the structural features of an economic system is analysed when it is subject to the operation of 'continuously operating forces' (see section 5 below). In both types of analysis, assumptions will be made about the relative structural invariance of particular components of the system and of their patterns of interrelationship. Different components and relationships of an economic system will not be invariant to the same degree and, furthermore, the degree of their relative invariance will be dependent upon the particular dynamics introduced into the model.

The postulate of relative structural invariance is, in principle, a testable hypothesis. The relative structural invariance of different components of the model in a particular exercise such as the analysis of the effects of a tax rate change may, in the first instance, be the outcome of a particular theoretical–deductive exercise. For example, when the implications of a tax rate change are analysed, the theoretical investigation may limit itself to studying the effects on incomes and relative prices, but it may be assumed that production technology is unaffected. However, also, in this case the theoretical–deductive exercise is conducted by using units of analysis that are descriptive in character, that is by using the categories and classifications of national income accounting, input–output tables, insights obtained from cross-section studies, and so on. Hence the results of a comparative–static or comparative–dynamic theoretical analysis are immediately translatable back into categories that are conducive to statistical analysis and tests. For example, we may take a particular historical experience of a change in the tax rate and examine whether the responses of the system conform to the predictions made by the theoretical–deductive exercise worked out above. The testing of theoretical arguments – which themselves assumed the structural invariance of different components of an economic system – thus comes natural to this type of approach.

It is often the case that theoretical analysis would reveal that further statistical information about an economic system might be useful in addition to, or substituting for, the one originally obtained at the descriptive–analytical stage. The reason could be, for example, that certain complexities of dynamic interrelationships of the adjustment to a change in the tax rate could not otherwise be followed up, or that a certain refinement of the distributional implications of such a change could not be analysed. In this case, the framework for structural description of the economic system at the descriptive–analytical stage will be changed, further refined in some respects and, if some classification details turned out to be redundant, simplified in other respects. Theoretical–deductive and descriptive–analytical work thus becomes an interactive process.

For the *deductive–behavioural* approach testability represents a different problem. It seems to be from the outset a 'fictive' exercise. It proceeds by asking: let us look at a world in which certain behavioural principles have fully worked themselves out; we can then understand the final equilibrium constellation in which certain types of interaction take place among different individuals. In reality, however, it is generally recognized that these behavioural principles are not operating in their pure form and, furthermore, different behavioural principles operate with changing weights as environmental conditions change and as the pattern of interaction unfolds. The stability and determinacy that is provided by assuming the single-minded pursuit of the implications of particular behavioural postulates when setting up a model of interdependent actions is thus not justified when confronted with the pattern of interaction in the real world. However, one might argue that the pursuit of such behavioural principles in the real world may indeed be relatively stable and that a deviation from such an ideal picture is in principle testable. This could be done by testing whether the pattern of interaction predicted by the model deviates strongly from the one actually observed.

At this stage, there would, however, be another problem. It is generally acknowledged that, in most instances, the patterns that can really be 'understood' are only the finally adjusted positions, since the mechanisms of coordination in the process of adjustment are not adequately understood (see Hahn, 1982, and Fisher, 1983). If this is the case, then the question of testability becomes severe indeed. One is supposed to test simultaneously that the deviation from a single-minded and stable pursuit of a narrow set of behavioural principles is not too severe, and whether an assumption that we are very close to an adjusted position (the only one about which precise theoretical predictions can be made) would not be rejected by the data.

4. Methods of dynamic analysis

In economic theory three fundamental approaches to dynamic analysis may be distinguished depending on the way in which 'dynamic structure' is identified. First, a time-differentiated description of the various elements of any given economic system may be obtained by considering a sequence of distinct time intervals. The dynamics of the economic system may then be fully investigated by considering how the state of the economy within each period reflects the data received from the past and the agents' projections about the future. As a result, the analysis of a dynamic path may be carried out period by period, and the mechanism of dynamic interrelationship operates only when considering the junctures between successive periods.

Secondly, the time differentiation of the economic structure may be introduced by considering a hierarchical description of the different dynamic processes operating within the economic system. This approach requires that the actual economic system be partitioned into a certain number of sub-systems, each identified by a particular time horizon (such as Marshall's short-short, short and long period). In this case, the dynamics of the whole system is analysed by considering distinct patterns of motion (for example, different adjustment paths) that are hierarchically related to one another.

The identification of sub-systems can be closely related to the application of the descriptive–analytical approach, since the different elements of economic structure are in reality associated with a different timing of the corresponding motions. For example, trading processes with given stocks of commodities can be analysed within the shortest time horizon, the change in production levels (that is the change of these stocks) is the next stage, and finally the change of productive capacities may be considered as the longest lasting type of economic adjustment. Factual observation leads to the analytical decomposition of the economic system into separate sub-systems whose motions are hierarchically related. One recognizes the partiality of the dynamic processes analysed within each sub-system, since emphasis is laid upon the dynamics taking place within a single sub-system, while the other sub-systems are considered to be unchanged for the purposes of theoretical investigation. The analysis may then shift to the consideration of the motion within the sub-system that comes next in the hierarchy of motions, by assuming full adjustment within the sub-system with the shorter time horizon and acknowledging that the sub-systems with the slower pattern of motion are still unadjusted. Only in long-period analysis may all different types of motion be considered, and the partiality of dynamic analysis gives way to a complete picture of structural economic dynamics.

A third approach to the identification of dynamic structures considers patterns of interrelationship of continuously operating factors of change ('forces'), such as investment activity, technical progress and population growth. Any given dynamic structure is identified by the way in which each force, by interacting with the other forces, determines the path of the economic system as a whole. Here, time differentiation of the economic structure is an inherent feature of the pattern of interrelationship of a given set of forces. Each force is associated with a particular rate of change, and any particular dynamic structure is also described by the set of feasible dynamic paths, given the set of functional relations among the different dynamic variables. In general, the interrelationship of dynamic forces is unlikely to lead to steady-state dynamics; rather the most interesting features of economic dynamics emerge from changes in the rates by which the various 'motive forces' grow or decline. Any change in such rates has clear implications upon the dynamics of the other forces with which they are interrelated. The identification of a certain dynamic structure results from the fact that any such structure is compatible with a given set of different feasible paths of overall dynamics. However, this approach also lends itself to the analysis of structural change, for, under certain conditions (such as parameter changes), a particular dynamic structure may break down and a new pattern of interrelationship among dynamic forces may emerge.

The sensitivity of such dynamic structures to both parameter changes and stochastic shocks is the subject of recent developments in the area of dynamical systems analysis. (For applications to economics, see for example Anderson et al., 1988, and Lorenz, 1989.)

5. Time structure, sequential causation and motive forces

The purpose of this section is to discuss a number of different approaches in dynamic economic analysis that employ the different notions of 'dynamic structure' discussed in the previous section.

5.1 Temporary equilibrium and the analysis of time interdependencies

An explicit linkage between dynamic economic theory and the splitting of time and economic processes into distinct but also related intervals can be found in Knut Wicksell's study of the 'cumulative process',[2] which may be considered as the starting point of the type of *sequential analysis* that was subsequently taken up by other economists of the Swedish school, such as Erik Lindahl and Gunnar Myrdal, as well as in those parts of Sir John Hicks's work in which the concept of sequential causality is adopted.[3] More recently sequential analysis has been further elaborated in recent work on temporary equilibrium theory (see Radner, 1972; Grandmont, 1977).

The sequential causality approach (of which other instances may be found, for example in Dennis Holme Robertson's theory of industrial fluctuations and in Richard Ferdinand Kahn's theory of the sequential multiplier) introduces into economic theory a dimension that is still absent from Marshall's time-period analysis. It is the explicit consideration of the 'order of sequence' (Myrdal) that the effects of any given impulse must follow if we want the repercussions of such an impulse to be conducive to a type of analysis that explicitly considers the structure of an existing set of economic relationships. From our specific point of view, it is important to recall that the theory of the cumulative process implies 'not only certain causal relations [between the different price levels] but also a *given order of sequence in their movements*' (Myrdal, 1939, p. 27).

The method of sequential causality presupposes the identification of a specific dynamic structure (as defined in section 2 above), and it is this structure that makes the succession of the different states of the economic system determinate from the causal point of view. The analysis of economic dynamics in terms of sequential causality requires the splitting of time into intervals and the assumption that economic interdependencies take place

[2] In Myrdal's words, Wicksell's cumulative process describes 'a race of different "price levels": of prices for real capital, factors of production, and consumption goods', which is supposed to follow any given discrepancy between the 'natural rate of interest' and the money rate of interest (see Myrdal, 1939, p. 27).

[3] This is especially the case with Hicks's theory of capital accumulation, as was originally expounded in chapter 12 of *Value and Capital*. There Hicks overcomes the 'self-containedness' of each single time period by considering that there are certain 'repercussions of economic change' that 'take some time to work themselves out', not because of 'slowness of communication or imperfect knowledge' but because they are delayed by the technical duration of productive processes (see Hicks, 1946, p. 283). Delays due to imperfect knowledge or deficient communication do not necessarily involve the existence of sequential causation mechanisms, for a delay in the agent's response to any given signal may systematically be related to a *process* that brings that particular agent to react to any given signal in a specific way. On the other hand, delays due to the technical duration of the productive process derive from the stage structure of productive activity and are thus a result of the causal mechanism that brings a specific decision to produce a particular outcome. In terms of Hicks's distinction between 'prior lag' (the lag between the signal and the decision) and 'posterior lag' (the lag between the decision and the action consistent with that decision), sequential causation processes are only implied by the latter. (The distinction between 'prior lag' and 'posterior lag' is expounded in Hicks, 1979.)

over a sequence of such intervals, so that a clear pattern of precedence or sequentiality is established. In Hicks's theory of temporary equilibrium, the emphasis is initially laid upon the formation of plans at the beginning of each single period (Hicks's 'week') and upon the pattern of plan revision that is brought about as plans are or are not realized. In this connection, the existence of a specific dynamic structure may be taken for granted when the process of a plan formation is considered. However, the fact that, following a certain impulse, a given plan is revised cannot be purely explained in terms of sequential causation for, in that case, one is simply considering 'the relation between those actions devoted to present ends, and those actions which are directed to the future' (Hicks, 1946, p. 127). On the other hand, one is not explicitly examining how the unfolding of actions through time itself constrains the sequence of repercussions that follow a specific impulse and brings that sequence to a particular final outcome.

Sequential causality is explicitly at work when the unfolding of actions (for example during a capital accumulation process) is directly considered. The Lindahl–Hicks theory of temporary equilibrium thus lends itself to two rather different interpretations depending on whether we stress the *formation* of plans or their *execution*. In the former case, the future must be 'telescoped' into the present, and the interdependencies among observed variables presuppose contemporaneous causality, that is a type of causality in which both cause and effect belong to the same time period (see Hicks, 1979, p. 19). In the latter case, the future must be maintained separate from the present, since each time period refers to a specific stage of causation, giving rise to a sequence of hierarchically linked stages in which the outcome of actions of one stage imposes a set of constraints on the next. Sequential causality thus performs a critical role in the analysis of the execution of plans; whereas in the case of plan formation a dynamic structure may be presupposed, but causal relationships work themselves out within each single period. In temporary equilibrium analysis of the contemporaneous–causality type, economic interdependencies are analysed as if they would all occur simultaneously, whereas in temporary equilibrium of the sequential type clear dependency relationships are established through precedence in time.

5.2 The dynamic method of Marshall

Another approach, which may be complementary to the Hicks–Lindahl type of sequential analysis, is Marshall's decomposition of the overall system dynamics into the interdependent dynamics of hierarchically related sub-systems. Here, the starting point is provided by the description of a given state of the economy that reflects a combination of adjusted and non-adjusted structures. The state of the economy at any given time reflects the intensity of operation of 'economic forces' (Marshall), their rates of change and the way in which they influence the different elements of an economic system:

[I]n the world in which we live ... every economic force is constantly changing its action, under the influence of other forces which are acting around it. Here changes in the volume of production, in its methods, and in its cost are ever mutually modifying one another; they are always affecting and being affected by the character and the extent of demand. Further *all these mutual influences take time to work themselves out*, and, as a rule, *no two influences move at equal pace*. (Marshall, 1961, p. 368; our italics)

In Marshall's framework, actual economic systems are undergoing a continuous process of change. Marshall's way of dealing with this from an analytical point of view is to consider an economic system as one in which, at any point of time, adjusted and unadjusted sub-systems coexist side by side. In this perspective, equilibrium analysis may be applied to each individual sub-system but cannot be used for the economic system as a whole. The reason for this is that, when a complete system of interconnected markets is described, it must be recognized that different factors of change operate at various intensities upon different markets or connected subsets of markets. Such differences are ultimately due to the fact that any factor of change modifies the existing economic structure by initiating a sequence of transformations. As a result, at any point of time, the economic system is characterized by the simultaneous existence of markets and production structures (such as inventory levels, capacities, etc.) that are at different stages of adjustment. This feature of actual economic systems is at the root of Marshall's use of partial equilibrium analysis in association with his 'time-period' analysis of economic equilibrium. In particular, prices are 'transaction specific', in the sense that the current price of any commodity reflects the stage of adjustment of the corresponding market at any point of time.[4]

5.3 *Harrodian dynamics and the interrelationship of motive forces*

The first attempt to explicitly identify the dynamic structure of an economic system with the pattern of interrelationship of dynamic forces is due to Roy Forbes Harrod (1939; see also 1948 and 1973). However, important

[4] An important feature of Marshall's approach has recently re-emerged with Allais's 'surplus approach' to economic equilibrium, where 'the unrealistic model of the market economy, in which the fundamental assumption is that a unique price obtains at all times' is substituted by 'the model of the economy of markets in which all transactions are carried out at prices which are specific to them' (Allais, 1986, p. 141).

contributions to this tradition of dynamic analysis were also made by earlier economists such as Thomas Robert Malthus (1820) and John Bates Clark (1899).

Harrod's approach is clearly distinct from those of Lindahl–Hicks and Marshall, for it overlooks the complex structure of adjusted and unadjusted elements that characterizes Marshall's 'decomposition' of overall economic dynamics, and it also overlooks Hicks's analysis of the sequence of stages of adjustment that follow a once-over impulse. As a matter of fact, Harrodian dynamics is specifically concerned with the consideration of 'the effects of continuing changes' (Harrod, 1948, p. 9), and such changes are associated with the operation of 'motive forces', such as capital accumulation or technical progress, which are assumed to affect the economic system without interruption.

Harrod's approach lends itself to the formulation of a specific concept of dynamic structure, which is largely his own even if it had been anticipated by a number of previous economists. This concept of dynamic structure is based upon consideration of the interdependencies of motive forces through time. In particular, and this is an important distinguishing feature with respect to Marshall and Hicks, Harrod is interested in the types of change in interdependencies that occur because variables alter their *rate of change*.[5]

Harrod's method leads to the analysis of interdependence among different economic *forces*, which are defined as particular variables characterized by their rates of growth or decline through time. Harrod emphasizes how changes in the rates of change of such variables (such as an increase in the rate of accumulation or in the rate of population growth) may affect the nature of interdependence of dynamic forces and bring about a new type of dynamics for the whole economic system.

The approaches to dynamic analysis discussed above are in principle applicable to the study of dynamic interrelationships in most spheres of economic activity. In the following, however, we shall point out that the analysis of production relationships played a critical role in the evolution of these approaches.

Marshall's distinction between the short-short, the short and the long period is based upon the relative speeds of adjustment of inventories, production levels with given capacities and capacities themselves. The reference here is directly to physical material properties that can be observed in production units when examining the time it takes to change

[5] In this connection, Harrod criticized Hicks's approach to dynamic theory by pointing out that 'Mr Hicks appears to be analysing the effects of a once-over change in fundamental conditions. There is no recognition that a different technique may be required for analysing the effects of continuing changes.' (Harrod, 1948, p. 9)

inventory levels, adjust production levels to order and install new capacities. While Marshall was clearly interested in the implications these various elements of relative persistence or variability have for market interactions (that is price–quantity relationships on markets in the short-, medium- and long-run), the use of factual material about the nature of various time dimensions of economic activities (and of production activities in particular) is clearly evident.

The Hicksian and Swedish attention for economic actions observed over sequences of time periods found its first application in the temporary equilibrium method. There, the additional innovative elements brought into the analysis are not production-side phenomena but plan formulation by individual decision-making units, expectations formation and plan revision as a result of new information obtained over time and of environmental changes. Nonetheless, the heritage of the early Austrian (Böhm-Bawerkian) time structure of production is visible in the genesis of this approach, and it is clear that while the realization of actual trades as a process occurring in historical time is at the centre of such an approach, the analysis is enriched by the introduction of production-side phenomena, such as the irreversibility of certain investment processes and the binding character of certain productive conditions. More recently, stage analysis has been revived directly in the area of production theory (see Georgescu-Roegen, 1971, Hicks, 1973). The analysis of the time structure of production can also play an important role in the analysis of technological change.[6]

Harrod's interest in dynamic structures as patterns of interdependence of dynamic forces (such as the propensity to accumulate, productivity growth, population growth, demand growth) found its first application in macro-economic analysis. However, Harrod's approach can be extended not only by looking at the dynamic interrelationships of macro-economic variables but also by keeping track of the effects that the evolution of such variables has upon production structures. The study of dynamic forces, complemented by a consideration of the evolution of productive structures, has been anticipated in many contributions of the classical economists. An example is Adam Smith's analysis of the expansion of demand and its relation with an evolving structure of production characterized by different degrees in the extent of the division of labour. Another example is David Ricardo's analysis of the movement towards a stationary state where population

[6] For example, in Nathan Rosenberg's studies of patterns of technological change, the dynamics of inventive and innovative activity in an industrial system is often regulated by the structure of interdependencies among different production activities and the constraints and bottle-necks that emerge as such activities interact over time (see, in particular, Rosenberg, 1969).

growth requires an expansion of agricultural output, and this – given a particular 'structure' in the availability of different types of land – has important implications for the overall growth rate of an economic system and its technological characteristics.

In principle, however, the above approaches may be applied to a variety of spheres of economic activity. Production activities are generally carried out by groups of individuals interacting within particular forms of organization, which may show a relative persistence over time and a limited responsiveness to market signals at any given time. Persistence and limited responsiveness to market signals is also a characteristic feature of other types of social interaction, such as the consumption patterns prevailing in certain social settings, the mode of operation of bureaucratic organizations, codes of professional behaviour in business. The relative persistence of such behavioural and organizational patterns has been considered by researchers in other social sciences (see, for instance, Etzioni, 1973 and 1980). As regards the study of structural dynamics in these social or organizational set-ups, as compared to production relationships more narrowly identified, one may find it more difficult to detect clear hierarchies of relative invariance. In particular, the ranking of different speeds of adjustment may be less stable than in the case of production structures. This might explain why the analytical foundations for the analysis of structural dynamics in other spheres of social and economic behaviour may be more difficult to construct.

6. Productive interrelationships and economic dynamics

In this section we shall apply the methods discussed in the two previous sections to the analysis of the dynamics of the production structure of an economic system. As a matter of fact, a number of theoretical tools developed for production analysis may be directly associated with the above methods of dynamic analysis. These methods were applied, in particular, to the study of the dynamic interrelationships across different time intervals as well as to ways of decomposing an economic system into constituent parts that show differentiated, although interrelated, dynamics.

We shall distinguish the following analytical frameworks that are centrally built upon a representation of production relationships:

(i) a circular-flow model without any specification of the time structure;
(ii) a model that considers horizontal interdependencies while taking account of the time structure of these interdependencies;
(iii) a model in which each productive process is vertically integrated along the time dimension but production stages are distinguished;

(iv) a model based upon vertically integrated sub-systems, in which each sub-system 'cuts through' the network of horizontal interdependencies.

6.1 *The pure circular-flow model*

The circular-flow model without specification of time structure has a long history as a tool in economic analysis. Classical examples are François Quesnay's *Tableau économique* (Quesnay, 1758) and Marx's schemes of reproduction (Marx, 1885). These two schemes are based on the consideration, within a particular period (say, one year), of the flows of commodities among different sectors and income groups (see Figure 4.1).

In the pure circular-flow model, interdependencies among productive sectors (S_i) refer to the sum of commodity flows within each accounting period. No 'descriptive–analytical' tool is used to obtain information concerning the time structure of interrelationships among the different sectors. Without additional elements, such accounting schemes cannot be identified with proper dynamic structures in the sense of section 2 of this chapter. Neither do these schemes explicitly consider the evolution of individual productive processes over time, nor do they present a picture of the economic system as a whole evolving over time. Nevertheless, the circular-flow model has given rise to a large number of contributions to the analysis of the dynamics of economic systems. In particular, circular schemes have been used for a wide range of comparative–static and comparative–dynamic exercises by Quesnay himself (on this point see Eltis, 1984) as well as by subsequent writers such as Marx (1885, Vol. 2), Tugan-Baranovsky (1913) and Luxemburg (1951). Further analytical refinements have given rise to a large number of modern contributions to the study of multi-sectoral economic growth based on the use of the pure horizontal-flow model (see, in particular, the developments arising from Jan von Neumann, 1945–6, such as Michio Morishima, 1964, 1969, Los and Los, 1974 and, for a recent assessment, Mohammed Dore, Sukhamoy Chakravarty and Richard M. Goodwin, 1989).

In the light of these developments one is bound to ask how a tool that by itself could not be classified as a 'dynamic structure' could find such a wide and successful application in dynamic analysis. The reason, as we understand it, is that, for purposes of dynamic analysis, the circular-flow model was always complemented by certain dynamic behavioural principles that allowed the authors to extend the view of a productive system from a single accounting period to a whole sequence of circular-flow descriptions of an economic system. In Marx's schemes of extended

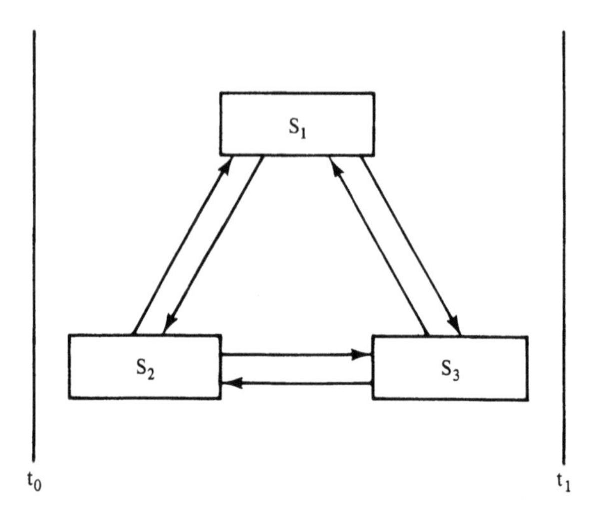

Figure 4.1 *Commodity flows in the pure circular-flow model*

reproduction (and also in models of the von Neumann type) it is the analysis of the determinants of the proportion of the surplus accruing in a particular accounting period and used to expand capacities and production levels in the next period, that is the element that provides such a behavioural principle. The combination of such behavioural analysis with the structural description of features of the productive system provided by the horizontal-flow model allowed the authors in this tradition to study certain aspects of structural dynamics. For example, the consideration of a particular parameter change that acts as an impulse or shock (such as a once-for-all change in the tax rate or in the terms of trade) allows for the analysis of a sequence of adjustment processes. The analysis of these adjustment processes makes use in turn of the information contained in the circular-flow model of structural interdependencies. The use of the latter for dynamic analysis implied, furthermore, the adoption, to some degree, of the principle of relative structural invariance.[7] It is the combined use of relative

[7] Notice that, while the original von Neumann model or Marx's model of expanded reproduction adopted a principle of 'strict' structural invariance (with no change in technology or in the real wage rate in von Neumann's model, or no change in the organic composition of capital and rates of surplus value over time in Marx), later models allowed for technology or the real wage rate to change, while still adopting the assumption of structural invariance for the analysis of interdependencies within each accounting period. Indeed, the assumption of strict structural invariance, while allowing us to show certain dynamic features of an economic system (such as in von Neumann's model of semi-stationary growth), does not allow for the study of truly structural dynamics, that is dynamics with structural change.

structural invariance and of some behavioural analysis of certain dynamic variables that allows the utilization of the circular-flow model in dynamic analysis.

In the above examples we have discussed the use of the horizontal-flow model in combination with the operation of a particular dynamic force or impulse. Another application of the horizontal-flow model for dynamic analysis is when it is combined not only with a particular dynamic force (or a number of such forces), but also with a relatively rigid 'structure' that acts as an additional constraint for the dynamic behaviour of the economic system. A classical example of this type of analysis is Ricardo's theory of the traverse towards a stationary state.

Ricardo's analytical framework consists of three essential elements: a horizontal-flow model, which shows the interdependencies among productive sectors and income flows within any given accounting period; the existence of a particular structure of non-produced inputs (lands of different types), which constrain the technological options of the economic system as a whole when it operates at different levels of activity; and the consideration of a combination of dynamic forces such as population growth and the accumulation of part of the net product generated within each accounting period.

Without going into the details of his analysis (see, in particular, the analytical formulation of the Ricardian problem in Quadrio-Curzio, 1986) we can see that Ricardo's analysis of structural dynamics contains a parametrically given structure of constraints (the quantities of different types of available land) in addition to the sectoral interdependencies that are described in the horizontal-flow model. These additional constraints impinge upon the technological and growth options of the economic system as a whole as it expands over time.

6.2 Horizontal interdependencies with a time structure

A model that considers horizontal interdependencies combined with the time structure of inter-sectoral flows does qualify as a properly 'dynamic–structural' representation of the economic system.

An example may be provided by the consideration of two industrial sectors or productive processes P_1 and P_2, which are supplying, within any given accounting period, commodities to each other, if we make the additional assumption that there are specific time intervals in which P_1 supplies P_2 and the same or other intervals in which P_2 supplies P_1.

This type of model, particularly in the general setting of many sectors or processes supplying one another, has been put to important uses in structural–dynamic analysis. It differs from the pure circular-flow model in

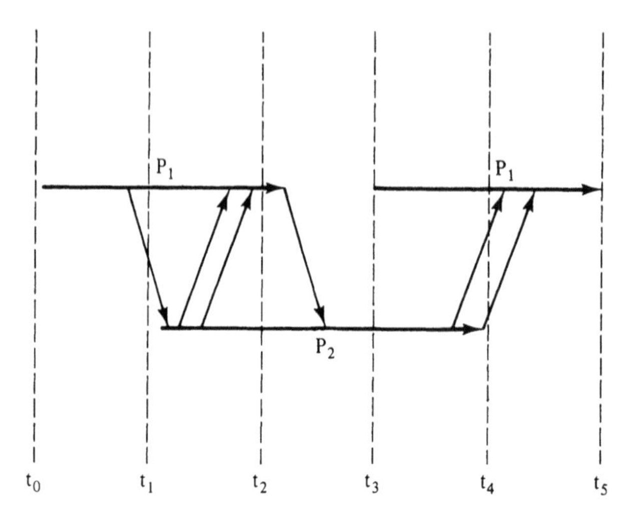

Figure 4.2 *Time interdependencies and horizontal interrelationships*

the reactive response of an economic system to the operation of particular dynamic forces that cause a richer adjustment pattern resulting from the explicit consideration of the time structure of horizontal interdependencies. This particular aspect of the dynamic specification of an economic structure gives rise to what Ragnar Frisch called propagation mechanisms (see Frisch, 1933).

This approach has been adopted in the analyses of Burchardt (1931–2) and Lowe (1976), who extended the use of reproduction schemes by allowing for interdependencies between the capital-good sector and the consumption-good sector through historical time. These schemes are subjected in Lowe (1976) to the operation of a number of dynamic forces, such as population growth or technical progress, which generate uneven growth patterns, given the 'lead and lag' pattern implicit in the specification of the production structure of the economic system. Leads and lags also feature prominently in the various formulations of the dynamic Leontief system (see, for instance, Leontief (1953, 1970), Johansen (1978), Duchin and Szyld (1985)) in which the horizontal-flow description of the static Leontief system is supplemented by the specification of construction and delivery lags. The system is then subjected, in analytical exercises, to a number of shocks such as changes in the level of investment or in the level and composition of final consumption, and the implications for the growth path of the economic system are analysed in terms of the resulting complex propagation mechanism. (Important themes of this line of research may be traced back to Lloyd Appleton Metzler's and Goodwin's early work on the dynamic multiplier; see Metzler, 1945, and Goodwin, 1949.)

The above approaches can be considered as an application of the Hicks–Lindahl method of sequence analysis to a production model that does consider horizontal interdependencies but also takes account of the sequential or precedence patterns of such interdependencies.

However, while the above approaches work through the implications of the operation of an exogenously given dynamic force or impulse upon the productive structure of an economic system, it is also conceivable that the mechanism by which such an initial impulse works itself out will react back upon the behaviour of the dynamic force. For example, the complex dynamics of the propagation mechanism, following an initial increase in the propensity to invest, may itself affect the behaviour of investment in the course of time. This will particularly be the case if the analysis of the propagation mechanism allows for temporary bottle-necks (such as those considered in Hicks, 1965) or capacity constraints in the different industries or sectors (see Duchin and Szyld, 1985). A further analytical possibility may be that of integrating the emphasis on expectations formation that characterizes the early Hicks–Lindahl approach with the more 'mechanical' consideration of leads and lags in the productive system. Both expectations formation and learning processes as well as production linkages are important components of a sequential analysis of the horizontal and intertemporal interdependencies in an economic system.

6.3 Stage-structure theory and traverse analysis

This approach overlooks horizontal interdependencies among productive processes or sectors and emphasizes instead the detailed time structure of the transformation processes involved and of the inputs engaged in such processes. An example is Hicks's use of vertically integrated process analysis in his development of the neo-Austrian method (see Hicks, 1973). In this context, Hicks develops the concept of a productive process with an explicit time profile of the flow-input flow-output type, and characterizes the productive structure of the whole economic system by the successive (and partially overlapping) starting and completion of such processes in the course of time (see Figure 4.3).

Hicks distinguishes between the 'construction' and the 'utilization' phases of each temporally integrated process P, whereby the latter starts (and the former ends) when the first outputs of type *i* are being produced. In this case, the productive structure of the economic system is described in terms of sequentially related stages of input construction and utilization. It may thus be considered as a properly 'dynamic structure' in the sense of

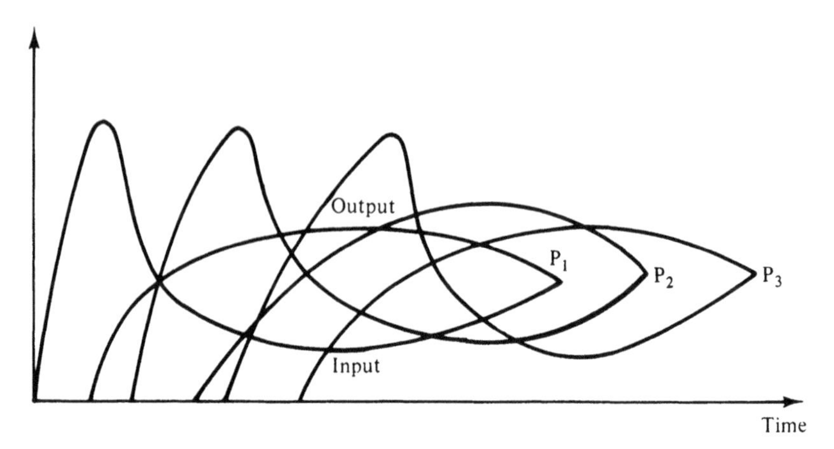

Figure 4.3 *Vertically integrated processes and the Hicksian time structure of production*

section 2 above. However, as it stands, it is simply an analytical description of an economic system and does not by itself produce structural dynamics. The latter is introduced, as Hicks himself has pointed out (see Hicks, 1977), when certain dynamic behavioural mechanisms are associated with the temporally integrated productive structure. The specific mechanism considered by Hicks is that of a once-over impulse, but one could similarly consider dynamic forces that operate in a continuous manner.

An impulse *à la* Hicks, such as the invention and introduction of a new technique of production, leads to a changeover process (or *traverse*) from one technology to another. For example, analysing the changeover process from a single old process P^O to a new process P^N, which starts at t^*, we have the situation shown in Figure 4.4.

We can see from Figure 4.4 that from t^* onwards only new processes will be introduced, but until $\bar{t}^*$ (the end of the traverse) old and new processes will coexist.

Hicks analyses interesting dynamic sequences induced by such changeover processes. For example, he considers how different distributive relationships (such as a constant wage fund or a constant real wage rate) may affect the rate of introduction of new techniques of production and how this in turn affects the rate of expansion of the economic system and its levels of employment (see Hicks, 1973, chapters 8 and 9).

Magnan de Bornier (1980) considers additional elements, such as temporary blockages of traverse paths. Various contributions have also been made that generalize Hicks's use of the neo-Austrian method by maintaining a full picture of horizontal interdependencies, which comple-

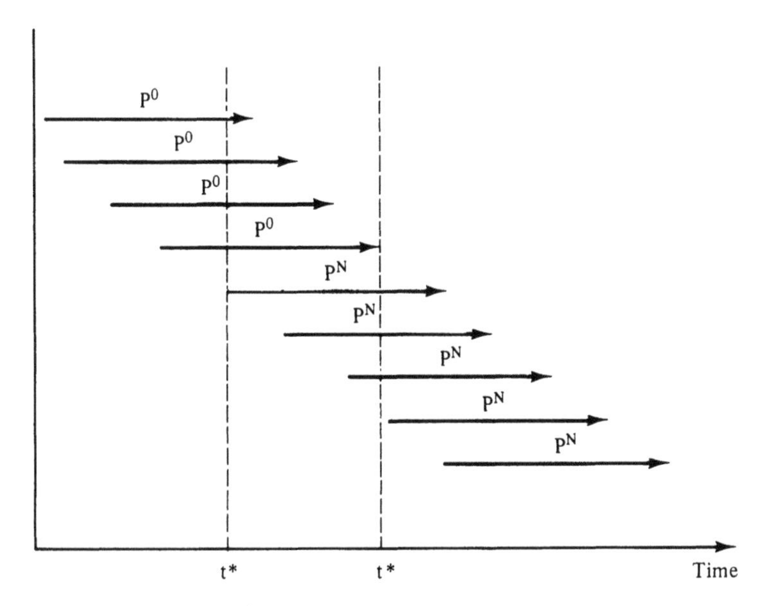

Figure 4.4 *The Hicksian traverse*

ments the stage structure of productive activity (see Belloc, 1980, Baldone, 1990).

Furthermore, it can easily be shown that the Hicksian traverse analysis does not lend itself solely to the study of single (exogenous) impulses (see Hicks, 1973, chapter 12), but also to the analysis of continuously operating forces, such as those that regulate the rate of supply of a labour force or the rate and characteristics of technological innovation.

6.4 Vertically integrated sub-systems and structural change analysis

We may now turn to the identification of productive structure by means of vertically integrated sub-systems that 'cut through' the network of horizontal interdependencies, thus allowing the economist to keep track of any given impulse as it works itself out through the system of input–output relationships.

A precise formulation of the requirements for a vertically integrated representation of the production system is due to Pasinetti (1973) who elaborated the earlier insights provided by Sraffa (1960, Appendix A). Pasinetti's notion of vertical integration leads to the consideration of a productive system consisting of independent production activities producing n final commodities. These commodities feature in the final consumption vector $c(t)$, but they can also be used as intermediate inputs.

Suppose that the demand for the different components of final consumption, that is the elements of $c(t)$, grow at different but constant exponential rates r_i:

$$c_i(t) = c_i(0).e^{r_i t} \quad \text{where } i = 1, 2, \ldots, n$$

One can then try to examine how the production rates of the different but interdependent activities are affected by such an uneven (or disproportional) growth process. Pasinetti proposes a particular decomposition of the overall production system, which makes the uneven growth process and its implications (for the employment structure, relative prices, etc.) particularly visible. He proposes to partition the economic system into *vertically integrated sectors*. Each vertically integrated sector reveals in an integrated manner all the production capacities (stocks of intermediate inputs) and labour that are directly or indirectly engaged in producing a particular final commodity i. In fact, such integrated production capacities and labour requirements are portions of the capacities and labour operating in the production activities or industries originally distinguished, but they can be identified as being directly or indirectly involved in producing the different final commodities. Summing up over all the vertically integrated sectors, such intermediate input and labour requirements must account for the inputs used in the system as a whole.[8] (See Figure 4.5.)

Pasinetti finds that such a decomposition of a production system into vertically integrated sectors is particularly conducive to analysing the impact of two sets of continuously operating *forces* upon an economic system (see Pasinetti, 1981):

(i) technical progress that leads to a relatively continuous reduction of labour input coefficients in the different production activities, which translate themselves into changing labour input requirements of the different (vertically integrated) production sectors, and

[8] Algebraically such a decomposition of an industrial system into vertically integrated sectors can be represented in the following way:

$$x^{(i)}(t) = [B - (l + r_i)A]^{-1} c^{(i)}(t)$$

$$l_i(t) = a_n[B - (l + r_i)A]^{-1} c^{(i)}(t) \qquad i = 1, 2, \ldots, n$$

$$s^{(i)}(t) = A[B - (l + r_i)A]^{-1} c^{(i)}(t)$$

$$\Sigma c^{(i)}(t) = c(t), \quad \Sigma x^{(i)}(t) = x(t), \quad \Sigma s^{(i)}(t) = s(t), \quad \Sigma l_i(t) = l(t)$$

where A and B are respectively input and output coefficients matrices, a_n is the row vector of direct labour input coefficients, x is the vector of physical quantities produced, l is the total labour used (a scalar), and s is the vector of stocks of intermediate inputs.

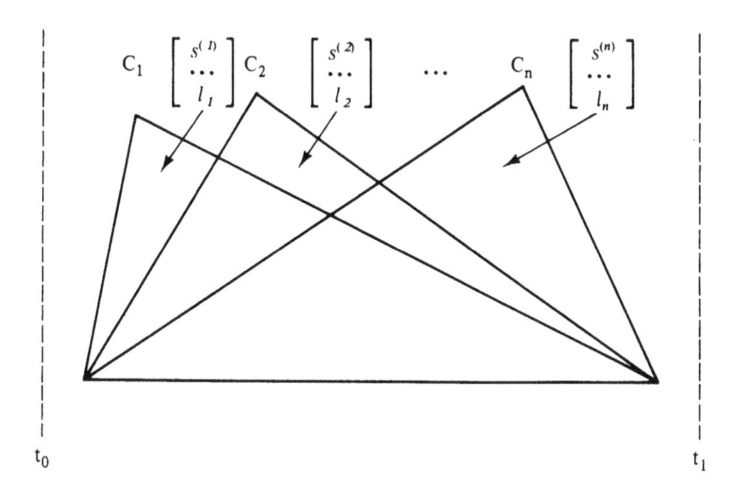

Figure 4.5 *Vertically integrated sectors of production*

(ii) changes in the composition of demand in the form of continuous shifts in the basket of commodities demanded by final consumers and which gives rise to differential growth rates r_i.

Pasinetti's framework represents a case of structure–force analysis and is used to study an important aspect of structural dynamics, that is non-uniform or *disproportional growth*. His analytical representation of the structure of a productive system in the form of vertically integrated sub-systems serves to clearly describe the features and implications of that pattern of growth.

This analytical approach has a remarkable tradition in economic theory. For example, certain features of Smith's theory of value may be traced back to Smith's attempt to formulate a theoretical framework in which value analysis could be applied to derive significant propositions about the wealth of nations and its dynamics through time. In particular, the measurement of national wealth in terms of 'labour commanded' may be considered as an ad hoc analytical tool permitting the identification of the growth potential of the economic system in a simple and powerful way. A first analytical representation of vertically integrated sub-groups of production activities can be found in Arthur Cecil Pigou's work on industrial fluctuations (see Pigou, 1927).

Vertically integrated sub-systems may also feature in other types of structural–change analysis. For example, Quadrio-Curzio (1986) has introduced primary-resource based sub-systems (or what one may call 'forwardly integrated sub-systems') in an attempt to relate structural economic dynamics with a changing pattern of resource utilization. In his model, changeover processes in the technological characteristics of the productive system lead to patterns of non-steady growth.

7. Concluding remarks

This chapter has attempted to develop a framework for the identification of dynamic structures and their utilization in the analysis of structural change. The essential elements of the analytical method we have been expounding may be described as follows.

It has been maintained that an important starting point in the analysis of a dynamic structure is a 'descriptive–analytical' account of the economic system under investigation. The next step is to set up particular 'experiments' in the field of dynamic behavioural analysis, which amount to specifying the dynamic behaviour of particular variables or parameters and studying the interaction between the structural specification of any given economic system and the dynamic behaviour of these variables.

In this connection, the concept of relative structural invariance performs a critical role. In particular, to introduce an 'empirical postulate' of structural invariance with respect to specific elements or layers of the given structural specification is itself a result of inductive inference from factual knowledge about relative rigidities of specific features of the economic system with respect to particular types of motion.

In the application of the above principles of analysis, the productive structure has emerged as a prominent feature determining given patterns of relative structural invariance, and thus allowing for determinate paths of structural transformation. Indeed, it seems that certain assumptions about relative structural invariance may naturally be assessed with respect to specific features of productive activities. Nevertheless, the descriptive–analytical approach may also be applied in the analysis of dynamic structures relative to other spheres of economic life. For example, scholars interested in economic institutions and organization theory have long pointed out that exchange relationships or communicative and power relationships are subject to the principle of relative structural invariance, and also that factual material about structural invariance may be introduced into an analysis of social and economic change (see, for instance, Etzioni, 1973 and 1980).

The above perspective suggests that the identification of resilient elements in the analysis of the productive structure may point to more general features in the economic theory of structural change.

References

Allais, M. (1986) 'The Concepts of Surplus and Loss and the Reformulation of the Theories of Stable General Economic Equilibrium and Maximum Efficiency', in *Foundations of Economics. Structures of Inquiry and Economic Theory*, ed. M. Baranzini and R. Scazzieri, Basil Blackwell, Oxford and New York, pp. 135–74.

Anderson, P.W., Arrow, K.J., and Pines, D. (eds) (1988) *The Economy as an Evolving Complex System*, Santa Fe Studies in the Sciences of Complexity, vol. V, Addison-Wesley, Redwood City, Cal.

Baldone, S. (1990) 'Vertical Integration, The Temporal Structure of Production Processes and Transition Between Techniques', in *Dynamics in Production Systems*, ed. M. Landesmann and R. Scazzieri (forthcoming).

Belloc, B. (1980) *Croissance économique et adaptation du capital productif*, Economica, Paris.

Burchardt, F.A. (1931–2) 'Die Schemata des stationären Kreislaufs bei Böhm-Bawerk und Marx', *Weltwirtschaftliches Archiv*, 34, pp. 525–64 and 35, pp. 116–76.

Clark, J.B. (1899) *The Distribution of Wealth. A Theory of Wages, Interest, and Profits*, Macmillan, New York.

Debreu, G. (1959) *Theory of Value. An Axiomatic Analysis of Economic Equilibrium*, Wiley, New York.

Dore, M., Chakravarty, S., and Goodwin, R. (eds) (1989) *John von Neumann and Modern Economic Theory*, Oxford University Press, Oxford.

Duchin, F., and Szyld, D.B. (1985) 'A Dynamic Input–Output Model with Assured Positive Output', *Metroeconomica*, 37, pp. 269–82.

Eltis, W. (1984) *The Classical Theory of Economic Growth*, Macmillan, London.

Etzioni, A. (1973) *Social Change. Sources, Patterns and Consequences*, Basic Books, New York (2nd edn).

(1980) *A Sociological Reader of Complex Organisations*, Holt, Rinehart and Winston, New York.

Fisher, F. (1983) *Disequilibrium Foundations of Equilibrium Economics*, Cambridge University Press, Cambridge.

Frisch, R. (1933) 'Propagation Problems and Impulse Problems in Dynamic Economics', in *Economic Essays in Honor of Gustav Cassel*, Allen, London.

Georgescu-Roegen, N. (1971) *The Entropy Law and the Economic Process*, Harvard University Press, Cambridge, Mass.

Goodwin, R. (1949) 'The Multiplier as a Matrix', *Economic Journal*, 59, pp. 537ff.

Grandmont, J.M. (1977) 'Temporary General Equilibrium Theory', *Econometrica*, 45, pp. 535–72.

Hahn, F.H. (1982) 'Stability', in *Handbook of Mathematical Economics*, ed. K. Arrow and M. Intriligator, North-Holland Publishing Company, Amsterdam, Vol. II, pp. 745–93.

Harrod, R.F. (1939) 'An Essay in Dynamic Theory', *Economic Journal*, 49, pp. 14–33.

(1948) *Towards a Dynamic Economics. Some Recent Developments of Economic Theory and Their Application to Policy*, Macmillan, London.
(1973) *Economic Dynamics*, Macmillan, London.
Hicks, J. (1946) *Value and Capital. An Inquiry into Some Fundamental Principles of Economic Theory*, Clarendon Press, Oxford (1st edn 1939).
(1965) *Capital and Growth*, Clarendon Press, Oxford.
(1973) *Capital and Time*, Clarendon Press, Oxford.
(1977) *Economic Perspectives*, Clarendon Press, Oxford.
(1979) *Causality in Economics*, Basil Blackwell, Oxford.
Johansen, L. (1978) 'On The Theory of Dynamic Input–Output Models with Different Time Profiles of Capital Construction and Finite Life-Time of Capital Equipment', *Journal of Economic Theory*, 10, pp. 513–41.
Leontief, W. (1953) 'Dynamic Analysis', in W. Leontief et al., *Studies in the Structure of the American Economy*, Oxford University Press, New York, pp. 53–90.
(1970) 'The Dynamic Inverse', in *Contributions to Input–Output Analysis*, ed. A.P. Carter and A. Brody, North-Holland Publishing Company, Amsterdam, vol. I, pp. 17–46.
Lindahl, E. (1939) *Studies in the Theory of Money and Capital*, Allen and Unwin, London.
Lorenz, H.-W. (1989) *Nonlinear Dynamical Economics and Chaotic Motion*, Springer, Berlin.
Los, J., and Los, M.W. (eds) (1974) *Mathematical Models in Economics*, North-Holland Publishing Company, Amsterdam.
Lowe, A. (1976) *The Path of Economic Growth*, Cambridge University Press, Cambridge.
Luxemburg, R. (1951) *The Accumulation of Capital*, Routledge and Kegan Paul, London.
Magnan de Bornier, J. (1980) *Capital et déséquilibre de la croissance*, Economica, Paris.
Malthus, T.R. (1820) *Principles of Political Economy*, John Murray, London.
Marshall, A. (1961) *Principles of Economics*, ninth variorum edition ed. C.W. Guillebaud, Macmillan, London (1st edn 1890).
Marx, K. (1885) *Das Kapital. Kritik der politischen Oekonomie*, vol. II, Meissner, Hamburg.
Metzler, L.A. (1945) 'Stability of Multiple Markets: The Hicks Conditions', *Econometrica*, 13 (October), pp. 277–92.
Morishima, M. (1964) *Equilibrium, Stability and Growth. A Multi-Sectoral Analysis*, Clarendon Press, Oxford.
(1969) *Theory of Economic Growth*, Clarendon Press, Oxford.
Myrdal, G. (1939) *Monetary Equilibrium*, William Hodge and Company, London, Edinburgh and Glasgow.
Neumann, J. von (1945–6) 'A Model of General Economic Equilibrium', *Review of Economic Studies*, 13, pp. 1–9 (German original 1936–7).
Pasinetti, L.L. (1973) 'The Notion of Vertical Integration in Economic Analysis', *Metroeconomica*, 25, pp. 1–29.

(1981) *Structural Change and Economic Dynamics. A Theoretical Essay on the Dynamics of the Wealth of Nations*, Cambridge University Press, Cambridge.
(1988) 'Growing Subsystems, Vertically Hyper-Integrated Sectors and the Labour Theory of Value', *Cambridge Journal of Economics*, 12, pp. 125–34.
Pigou, A.C. (1927) *Industrial Fluctuations*, Macmillan, London.
Quadrio-Curzio, A. (1986) 'Technological Scarcity: An Essay on Production and Structural Change', in *Foundations of Economics. Structures of Inquiry and Economic Theory*, ed. M. Baranzini and R. Scazzieri, Basil Blackwell, Oxford and New York, pp. 311–38.
Quesnay, F. (1758) *Tableau économique*, Versailles. Republished and translated in *Quesnay's Tableau Economique* (1972), eds Marguerite Kuczynski and Ronald L. Meek, Macmillan, London.
Radner, R. (1972) 'Existence of Equilibrium of Plans, Prices, and Price Expectations in a Sequence of Markets', *Econometrica*, 40, pp. 289–303.
Rosenberg, N. (1969) 'The Direction of Technological Change: Inducement Mechanisms and Focusing Devices', *Economic Development and Cultural Change*, 18, pp. 1–24.
Sraffa, P. (1960) *Production of Commodities by Means of Commodities*, Cambridge University Press, Cambridge.
Tugan-Baranovsky, M.I. (1913) *Les crises industrielles en Angleterre*, M. Giard and E. Brière, Paris. (Russian original 1894.)

5 Vertical integration, growth and sequential change

JEAN MAGNAN DE BORNIER

1. Introduction

This paper deals with the vertical structure of production and its consequences on aggregate economic behaviour. Most models of production are stated in terms of horizontal relationships between industries and firms, and do not consider the time dimension of production. However, there is a long theoretical tradition in this direction, which can be traced back to David Ricardo and William Stanley Jevons, and is mainly associated with Eugen Böhm-Bawerk and other Austrian economists. This approach has recently been presented by Sir John Hicks (1973a) as an alternative to the sector-based models and as a specific method of studying the dynamic problems associated with changing economic conditions.

The influence of the time dimension of production will be presented in the three following sections. In section 2 the two approaches of production structure – horizontal and vertical – are described and compared; the vertical model is shown to be suited for dynamic problems involving intertemporal rigidities – that is, non-transferable capital goods. Section 3 is a review of past controversies concerning the nature of capital and the (vertical or non-vertical) structure of production since Böhm-Bawerk. And section 4 is a rapid summary of some models of traverse using the vertical view of production.

2. A general formulation for sector- and time-based models of production

In this section we present two production models, one horizontal in structure, the other vertical. We will also show how both models are related

I wish to thank Mauro Baranzini and Roberto Scazzieri who made useful comments on an earlier version of this chapter but are in no way responsible for remaining imperfections, and also Cindy Klimek who kindly looked over the English language of the text.

and up to what point it can be asserted that they represent different views of fundamentally the same thing. We start with the more usual sector-based horizontal model and then contrast it with the time-based vertical one.

(a) *The horizontal model* can involve many production and/or consumption goods. Production takes place within *activities* or *sectors* with each sector producing mainly one type of good, though joint production is not excluded. Although this is not necessary, for the sake of simplicity we will assume that there are as many sectors as goods. Each sector is characterized by technical relations linking the quantities of inputs (labour and production goods) to the quantities of outputs, that is by a production function. If we admit constant returns to scale, this production function is described by the following set of coefficients:
for sector j ($j=1$ to n), a_j is the quantity of labour necessary, a_{ij} the different quantities of goods ($i=1$ to n) necessary to produce the output quantities b_{ij} ($i=1$ to n). The units are so set that a unit of activity produces one unit of the good with which it is mainly associated: that is, $b_{ij}=1$.

If we write a^j and b^j, respectively, for the (column) vectors of inputs (a_{ij}) and of outputs (b_{ij}), the production function can simply be represented this way:

$$a_j, a^j \rightarrow b^j$$

The whole economy's productive structure can be perceived by putting together all activities:

$A_0=(a_1, \dots a_j, \dots a_n)$ is a (line) vector describing the labour requirements of all sectors;
$A=[a_{ij}]$ is the matrix of all factor requirements;
$B=[b_{ij}]$ is the matrix of outputs.

Each column of matrices A and B indicates (respectively) factor and product coefficients relating to one particular sector j, whereas each line describes (respectively) uses and production of a good i.

This model allows for *simple* as well as for *joint production*: the sector's output can consist of more than one type of good, as is the case when wool and lamb meat are the result of sheep breeding. In the case of joint production, the vector b^j will have more than one strictly positive element; to put it another way, in the case of simple production matrix B is a unit matrix (with ones in the main diagonal and zeros everywhere else) while in the case of joint production it has ones in the main diagonal and non-negative numbers elsewhere.

In this model we can also find two sorts of inputs. Some are totally consumed or destroyed during one production operation (circulating capital), while the others are (suddenly or not) worn out only after several productive operations (fixed capital). In the former case, there is nothing in the economy but *flows* of labour and goods. In the latter case, there will exist at every moment a *stock* of capital as well as flows. However, it is possible to treat the capital stock as a flow. To do this, simply consider that a new machine is a particular good (i), the same machine when it is one-year-old is another good ($i+1$), which is itself different from the two-year-old machine (good $i+2$), etc.

When an activity makes use of the new machine, we will say it destroys it totally and has as an output (among other goods) the one-year-old machine; then another activity makes use of the one-year-old machine and has in its output the two-year-old machine, and so on. This procedure, invented by Robert Torrens and revived more recently by Jan von Neumann and Piero Sraffa, permits the treatment of fixed capital without introducing stocks in the model. It may seem a bit heavy as it makes several sectors out of one real sector, but it has the advantage of not assuming that the physical productivity of capital goods is constant over time (because the coefficients of these artificially different sectors may differ).

It is generally assumed, though seldom in an explicit way, that production within activities takes time, and that all activities have *a uniform production period*. This period extends from the application of the factors, a_j and a^j, to the product achievement. It can be of any length but, for many reasons, the year is the most usual reference as the unitary period of production.

When it is said that all activities in the model have a uniform production period, this could be taken as an assumption about the real world, an obviously false and untenable one, or it can (and we think must) be taken as an analytical device permitting a homogeneous definition of the sectors. A 'real' activity may last more or less than this uniform period, but it is possible to reconstruct activities that have exactly this period of production. For example, the activity of raising twenty-five-year-old trees implies a production period of twenty-five years, but it can be divided into twenty-five one-year activities, each producing trees of a different age. Following this line of thought, we see that the number and nature of the sectors appearing in this model are functions of the chosen production period (this was already obvious from the treatment of fixed capital); the shorter the period, the more numerous the sectors will be. In fact, the goods and activities in the model are fictive. They are an abstract construction and do not relate to what empirical input–output models describe. This has the important consequence that the activities as fictive entities cannot be taken as firms in the real world, that is we are not allowed to think of them as decision centres, with, for example, a profit-maximizing behaviour. Rather, the decisions are diffuse throughout the whole economic structure, and we are bound to study the behaviour of the structure as a whole.

The sector-based models stress the interdependence between activities: production appears as a somewhat circular process whereby activity 1 may make use of good 2 as an input while activity 2 makes use of good 1 as an input, etc. Some goods, directly or indirectly, are essential to the production of the other goods: in Sraffa's terminology they are basic. Of two such goods, it cannot be said that one is of a higher order than the other; the two are necessary for each other's production, a possibility that has important consequences. If such goods exist in a production structure, no good can be produced with labour alone. In 'closed' models the labour inputs do not appear directly; labourers are supposed to be rewarded by means of a consumption-good basket. These goods can enter in a modified form of matrix A, called the 'socio-technical' input matrix. The closed model is an extreme case whereby goods are produced by goods alone, without any apparent labour.

Finally, note that in sector-based models the output consists of all consumption goods, plus all newly produced goods, *plus all partially used machines*.

(b) *The vertical (time-based) model* can now be contrasted with the horizontal model. In the vertical model the underlying vision is that capital goods are nothing but previously invested labour, so that ultimately all consumption goods are made up by labour. While there is an apparent cooperation between labour and produced means of production, this can be more appropriately described as cooperation between today's and the preceding periods' labour. If production can be considered this way, produced inputs need not appear explicitly, but of course time must be taken into account. However, this is not to say that time, or 'waiting', is considered a factor of production, that is has a productivity by itself.

According to this view we can write the production function as a relation between dated labour inputs and dated final outputs, beginning at time 1. The labour input at date t will be written λ_t, and the final output at the same period will be χ_t; if we remain in the constant-returns-to-scale world, the production function is simply:

$$(\lambda_1, \lambda_2, \dots \lambda_T) \rightarrow (\chi_1, \chi_2, \dots \chi_T), \text{ or more concisely}$$

$$\lambda^t \rightarrow \chi^t$$

Note that time is an element of the definition of these vectors but is not itself an input.

Of course these vectors must be semi-positive, but it seems difficult to be more specific as to what their structure should be. One can say nothing about necessary conditions for the productive system to be physically viable, as are the Hawkins–Simon conditions for the sector-based model (if we leave aside the truism that *there must be at least one positive* χ_t), because inputs and outputs are not commensurable. It would only be possible to rule out certain production structures if a real wage rate is introduced, but this would be economic not physical feasibility. This quite important contrast between the horizontal and the vertical model can also be expressed by the fact that in the latter *there does not exist a maximum rate of profit* (the wage-profit frontier is only asymptotic to the profit axis) (Magnan de Bornier, 1980, pp. 131–2).

Leaving feasibility questions aside, however, several general structures have been defined and studied for the temporal model. They depend on a simple characteristic of the vectors of labour and goods: these vectors can have one or more than one non-zero element:

— when labour is necessary in only one period (the first period, obviously, or the product would be freely available), the λ^t vector has the following form: $\lambda^t = (\lambda_1, 0, 0, \dots, 0)$, with $\lambda_1 > 0$. In this instance the production process is said to be 'point-input'; in the other cases, the process is said to be 'flow-input'.

— a similar distinction exists for the product: if it appears in only one period τ, then $\chi^t = (0, 0, \dots \chi_\tau, 0, \dots)$, with $\chi_\tau > 0$. The process is 'point-output'; otherwise it is 'flow-output'.

A production process can, then, be:

— flow-input flow-output (FIFO), the most general case;

— flow-input point-output (FIPO): this is an interesting structure, where the labour of many periods produces goods in only one period; this structure can in most cases be identified with production with circulating capital only, because it seems to be unuseful to build 'machines', that is capital lasting many periods if only one output is to be produced. Early proponents of the time-based model, such as Jevons and Böhm-Bawerk, found it convenient to discuss it mostly in terms of this FIPO structure, but, generally speaking, their discussion is not invalidated by this assumption (just as many correct insights about capital can be and have been drawn from circulating capital models).

— point-input flow-output (PIFO);

— point-input point-output (PIPO);

A recurrent example of the PIPO structure is the growing of a tree: at time one the tree is planted, and at time twenty-five it is ready for its final use *without any additional labour*, even to cut it down. This is obviously a bad description of the production function for trees: it is difficult to conceive that in a lengthy process labour would be necessary only at the beginning. Selling and delivering the product must be labour-consuming parts of the process. This lack of an empirical content is why these point-input structures are seldom studied.

Within the general FIFO structure, Hicks has defined a special type of process that he called 'simple profile'. This is a process with two successive periods: the first is a 'construction period', during which no output appears; the second is a 'utilization period', during which there are outputs and labour is still necessary. These periods, of course, last several unitary periods. The input and output coefficients are constant within the two periods: the labour coefficients are λ_c and λ_u and the product coefficients are 0 and 1, in the construction and utilization periods, respectively. The 'simple profile' structure permits elegant results but is indeed too simple and necessitates some strong hypotheses, like that of machines having a constant efficacity over all their life, during the utilization period, etc.

In the time-based models, processes have a beginning and an end, which means that only 'original' factors are involved. We have until now considered only labour, but land (or nature) is also a non-produced factor; so our input, often named labour, may in fact be any non-produced economic good or service.

This has two obvious consequences: first, there can be no closed version of the time-based model; second, inputs can be heterogeneous. We will admit here that different inputs (outputs will be dealt with below) always appear in the same proportion, so they can be treated as scalar quantities – but a more sophisticated treatment could be provided.

The vertical model, by its very construction, presents some degree of aggregation. It does not describe the activities of an isolated firm, but instead combines the production processes of many firms. The flows of inter-firm trade are thus disregarded, and production is seen as a 'vertically integrated' process: firms (or parts of firms) cooperating in the same final product are in the same integrated process, more or less 'downstream' or 'upstream'.

But this vertical model need not have any degree of 'horizontal integration'. It is horizontally integrated if we consider only one final good (or a basket of final goods with a constant structure). In many cases this is a useful simplifying assumption, but it is not essential to the model. We can build a 'meso-economic', rather than a macro-economic, model, separating the final demand into as many markets (or types of needs) as we wish (say n), and consider the n integrated production functions for these markets, or 'filières' (no English equivalent seems to exist for this French word). The process i ($i=1$ to n) can be described by a set of coefficients:

$$(\lambda^i 0, \lambda^i 1, \ldots, \lambda^i T) \to (\chi^i 0, \chi^i 1, \ldots, \chi^i T)$$

These horizontally disaggregated – but vertically aggregated – 'filières', as we can theoretically construct them and as we can practically search for them (Rainelli, 1982; Montfort and Dutailly, 1983), are by definition independent of each other; there are no exchanges between them. When one particular firm produces intermediate goods that have uses in many final activities, this firm's production is imputed to all these processes in due proportion. (This is theoretically possible as long as constant returns to scale are assumed.) It must be stressed that in this model the *summa divisio* is the different final goods or needs, and that the identification of intermediate goods or production sectors is, according to the analytical viewpoint chosen, quite irrelevant.

If the structure of final demand is known, it is possible to write this model as a fully integrated one: let α^i be the (vertical) vector of final demand intensities $\alpha^i = (\alpha^1, \alpha^2, \ldots, \alpha^n)$; the aggregated production function then has as coefficients:

$$\lambda_t = \lambda^i{}_t . \alpha^i \quad ; \quad \chi_t = \chi^i{}_t . \alpha^i$$

It may be noted that in a similar context Hicks treats the production of two different consumer-good baskets in the same way as we do, namely as resulting from different technologies; this is a useful procedure only in the horizontally aggregated case (Hicks, 1973a, chapter 12).

(c) *Comparing both models*: In many respects, the two models are different ways of saying the same thing, and there is an obvious symmetry between 'several sectors and one period' and 'one sector and several periods', suggesting that they are ultimately equivalent. Some studies have shown how the vertical model can be translated in terms of the horizontal model (i), while others treated the problem the other way round (ii). After presenting these analyses, we try to go beyond these formal exercises and reflect upon the substantive qualities of these models (iii).

(i) From the vertical to the horizontal model

As an example, take an Austrian model with the following coefficients:

$$\lambda^t = (\lambda_1, \lambda_2, \lambda_3)$$

$$\chi^t = (0, \chi_2, 1)$$

Let us interpret these coefficients thus: in the first year a machine is built; it will be operated in the second and third periods, together with λ_2 and λ_3 units of labour, to produce χ_2 and 1 units of final goods. There are two intermediate goods: a new machine, which will appear as output in the first year and as input in the second year (it will be 'good 1'), and a one-year-old machine ('good '), output of the second year and input in the last year; the final good is 'good 3'. In each of the periods the coefficients relating the three goods are specific, so we can think of each year as a special activity. (It has already been shown that activities are defined on a temporal basis.) We can then write this model with the notations of the sector-based model:

$$A_0=(\lambda_1, \lambda_2, \lambda_3) \quad (=\lambda')$$

$$A=\begin{bmatrix} 0 & 1 & 0 \\ 0 & 0 & 1 \\ 0 & 0 & 0 \end{bmatrix} \quad B=\begin{bmatrix} 1 & 0 & 0 \\ 0 & 1 & 0 \\ 0 & \chi^2 & 1 \end{bmatrix}$$

the lines of both matrices being ordered as the three goods.

The 'Austrian' (or non-circular) character of the model is revealed by some striking facts, which can always be shown to be true when this translation is performed:

(a) no good is an input and an output in the same activity ($a_{ii}=0$ for all i);

(b) if good i is an input in activity j, good j is not an input in activity i (A is – or can be arranged – such that $a_{ij}=0$ if $i>j$. Points (a) and (b) can be synthetized by writing $a_{ij}=0$ if $i \geqslant j$;

(c) B also has a particular structure; it is such that $b_{ij}=0$ if $i<j$ (a 'downstream' activity cannot produce a good that is needed in an 'upstream' activity).

This example shows that a time-based model can always be translated into a sector-based model, but then the latter will have a special structure. This does not imply that any horizontal model can be interpreted as the translation of a vertical model. The horizontal model is theoretically a more general one; it allows for circularity, while the other does not. If we analyse the symmetric problem of how to translate a sector-based model into a time-based one, this will appear more precisely.

(ii) From the horizontal to the vertical model

Starting from a sector-based model, we can try to put the emphasis on successive labour input leading to some definite final product, and perform a 'reduction to dated quantities of labour'. We exclude here joint production in order to make this reduction easier, but this is not essential (on all this, see Sraffa, 1960; Pasinetti, 1965, 1973).

From the definition of the production function we know that if X is a vector of total production and Y a vector of final product, $X-Y$ is the vector of intermediate goods that are necessary to obtain Y, and it is given by $X-Y=AX$, or:

$$X=(I-A)^{-1}\,Y \tag{1}$$

Similarly the quantity of labour L^0 needed for Y is A_0X, or

$$L_0=A_0(I-A)^{-1}\,Y \tag{2}$$

X and L^0 are the factors of production required at the beginning of the period to get Y at the end; X is a stock of produced factors, for which we can determine what factors have been necessary in the preceding period, using (1) and (2). Designating the labour and capital goods vector by L^1 and X^1 respectively, we can write:

$$X^1 = (I - A)^{-1} X = (I - A)^{-2} Y \quad (3)$$

and

$$L^1 = A_0 X^1 = A_0 (I - A)^{-2} Y \quad (4)$$

Clearly this calculation can be repeated as many times as desired, 'reducing' the physical inputs of preceding periods into labour. If we perform this operation T times, we get a production process that contains (for one unit of output) the following inputs:

$$X^T, L^T, L^{T-1}, \ldots, L^1, L^0$$
$$\text{with } X^T = (I - A)^{-T-1} Y, \text{ and } L^t = A_0 (I - A)^{-t-1} Y$$

We can thus obtain a temporal model, with only labour (or non-produced) inputs in every period, *with the exception of the first period, during which capital goods are necessary*. But for this difference, this looks exactly like the Austrian model, and it can be shown that this capital-good basket can be made arbitrarily small by lengthening the period T. If we are looking for insights about value and distribution in the Ricardian spirit, this small difference is of enormous importance because in the Austrian model there is nothing like a maximum (physical) rate of profit. But if we are mostly interested in the building of a dynamic theory of the economy, this point may be of little importance. Let us now try to compare both models from this point of view.

(iii) Comparing both models for a theory of stability and change

Which of our two models would better fit the needs of a study of the economics of stability and change? According to Hicks, the time-based model should be chosen:

> The Austrian theory develops its main strength when we pass beyond that sort of equilibrium, to what I have elsewhere called the problem of Traverse. This was a problem which could be envisaged when one was thinking Walrasianly (i.e., in a sector-based model), but which turned out to be by no means suitable for handling by that method. (Hicks, 1970, pp. 257–8)

Von Weizsäcker expressed his opinion on this point in these terms:

> I disagree therefore with the view of Hicks that Walrasian general equilibrium theory is suited for static analysis and Austrian capital theory for dynamic analysis. I take the opposite view: Austrian capital theory is a good starting point to analyse

the time pattern of production and its implications under conditions of tranquillity, where transitions between techniques do not take place. Walrasian equilibrium theory will have to be used to study these transition problems, because under such conditions intermediate products have to be considered in their own right. They are no longer just manifestations of a certain amount of past labour inputs or future consumption goods. (von Weizsäcker, 1971, p. 2)

These two statements clearly indicate that the choice of one model over the other is to be determined by the type of hypotheses that we will make about capital goods. If it is believed that these goods can 'jump out' of their process to go into another process, that they are in a sense malleable, then they must appear in the picture and be duly taken into account. If on the other hand, one supposes that processes must be finished as they start, that production goods are *specific*, then it is unnecessary that they appear, as they will not be exchanged in any sense.

Precisely, the Austrians who put forward the vertical model certainly thought in terms of non-transferable capital goods; the main argument of Austrian capital theory is not that production takes time, a point that few would contest, but that it is a *process with strong intertemporal complementarities*, and that capital goods are generally specific to one process. For such a theory, which may be a good or a bad representation of reality, the vertical or time-based model is best suited, while for the opposite theory the horizontal model will be preferred. The formal properties of both models are poor guides for the choice of the best model to study stability and change if compared to underlying theoretical viewpoints.

It remains that the vertical model may seem limited by its neglect of the circular nature of production and the hypothesis that only 'originary' factors are necessary for production. Although we believe that this is a shortcoming when considering distribution problems, when dealing with properly dynamic questions, and particularly short- or medium-term dynamics, this criticism is not relevant. For in this case, we study situations where the present situation appears as a *datum*, where the capital stock is given. In such a context, the capital stock, the goods in process, can be treated as if they were primary, or perhaps as free goods. The important points to consider, then, are how to use these goods, what new sorts of goods (and in which proportions) to produce, and *when* to produce them. For this the time-based model is certainly most suited.

Stated another way, our argument here is that the sectoral model is of use when we consider the productive sphere as a self-regulating whole, an organic entity that does not need decision-making and for which past and future are quite symmetric; on the other hand, the temporal model describes an economy in which human decision and human action are relevant, and where there is no systematic symmetry between past and future because 'bygones are bygones'. It is therefore not surprising that this view of production and capital is closely associated with two of the founders of neoclassical economics – Jevons and Carl Menger (and his followers of the Austrian School) – if we contrast their general approach of economics as a science of human decision with the classical view.[1] It is also natural that Ricardo, after 'discovering' the Austrian theory of capital, made so little use of it (1817, chapter 1, section 4).

3. A survey of past controversies about the time structure of capital

We will limit this historical survey to discussions between Austrian and other economists (thus leaving out important contributions in this field, like that of Jevons) and start with Böhm-Bawerk's work. Böhm-Bawerk wanted to elucidate the nature of interest and refute Marx's views about capital. He thus proceeded to show that more time is necessary for a greater production, and that this 'higher productivity of roundabout methods of production' is at the basis of an explanation of interest. By higher productivity of roundabout methods of production, Böhm-Bawerk did not mean that time is in itself a factor of production. He wanted to explain that the capitalist is earning an income because he can, for some reason, start a production process and face the necessary costs during this production lag. The ability to wait and the higher productivity or roundabout methods of production are two necessary conditions for capitalistic production, and it is thus quite natural to relate time to capital and say that more time-consuming methods are also more capitalistic. Böhm-Bawerk proceeded to provide a way to measure the length of a production process: the well-known average period of production (APP), which has caused so much confusion. In the case of a point-output process, it is defined as the average length of time elapsing between the use of the different factors and the product achievement, the lengths being weighted by the input intensity. If the process is:

$$(\lambda_1, \lambda_2, \ldots, \lambda_T) \rightarrow (0, 0, \ldots, 0, 1)$$

the APP would be:

$$\mathrm{APP} = \Sigma_i \, \lambda_i . (T - i) / \Sigma_i \lambda_i .$$

If the process is flow-output, which Böhm-Bawerk did not consider, the

[1] The neoclassical view in its purity implies methodological individualism, and in this respect the vertical aggregation that we use to describe processes could seem inappropriate. We should examine firm behaviour rather than process behaviour. The aggregation level chosen here certainly tends to minimize certain coordination problems, but, like any model, it highlights other facts.

APP is the difference between the average duration of the output flow and the average duration of the input flow:

$$APP = \Sigma_i \chi_i.(T-i)/\Sigma_i\chi_i - \Sigma_i\lambda_i.(T-i)/\Sigma_i\lambda_i$$

Böhm-Bawerk could state the following propositions:

(i) The period of production is a good indicator of capital intensity; it was later proven that the APP is equal to the capital/output ratio (Marschak, 1934; Allais, 1947; Dorfman, 1959b);

(ii) Increases of the APP yield increases in the quantity of the product;

(iii) At equilibrium, a shift in the rate of interest induces a shift of the APP in the other direction.

The criticisms addressed to these propositions have been of several kinds:

(a) The APP is ill-defined;

(b) It is irrelevant;

(c) There is no direct relationship between the APP and the volume of production;

(d) There is no production lag at all.

Let us review these questions.

(a) The average period of production is ill-defined because in Böhm-Bawerk's formula compound interest is neglected. Knut Wicksell (1901) was the first to point this out, and it later appeared that if interest is correctly introduced, the APP is no longer a physical property of the production process and proposition (iii) is not always true.

(b) The APP is meaningless when fixed capital (or a FIFO process) is considered. We can define the APP of a *single* product but not that of a flow of products. This criticism has been best stated by Hicks in *Value and Capital* (1939, chapter 17). However, we believe that this criticism applies not to Austrian capital theory but only to the APP, a small element of it. In fact, Böhm-Bawerk did not neglect fixed capital; on the contrary, he spent many pages commenting on the durability of goods (either capital or consumption goods) and on John Rae's related theory of interest (Böhm-Bawerk, 1959a, chapter 11; 1959b, chapter 3). Similarly, among early 'Austrians', Gustaf Åckerman tried to define the optimal duration of fixed capital, and Friedrich August von Hayek replaced the concept of the production period by that of the 'investment period', the period during which a particular factor will remain invested. (It must be noted that both concepts were present in Jevons's *The Theory of Political Economy*, 1871.) In the light of these remarks, it can be seen how excessive is Hicks's separation between 'Austrian' (or point-output) and 'neo-Austrian' (with fixed capital) models (Hicks, 1973a, p. 8).

(c) The third point is more serious. It concerns the link that Böhm-

Bawerk established between the productivity of primary factors and the (physical) length of the production process. Misunderstandings have been numerous on this. Some critics, like A. Landry and Otto Effertz, attributed to Böhm-Bawerk the idea that *any* lengthening of the production process would increase productivity. This led him to point that only *wisely chosen*, more roundabout methods would allow such a result (Böhm-Bawerk, 1959c, p. 2).

Others put forward that more capital frequently means a *shortening* of the production process: building a nest will quicken the catching of a fish. Böhm-Bawerk's exposition is undoubtedly confused about this (1959b, p. 82). Nevertheless, it is clear that those who proposed this argument thought in terms of a shortening of the final operation (e.g. fishing), or of the operations taking place in the firm nearest to the final product, and not in terms of the whole production process, as did Böhm-Bawerk. So this argument was due to a misunderstanding of the theory.

Others again, more numerous, opposed Böhm-Bawerk's theory on the ground that an increase of production can follow from many other circumstances than a lengthening of production: for example, if more primary factors are used or if some technical progress occurs. Although these points are perfectly valid, they do not contradict Böhm-Bawerk's theory. As for the use of more factors, it is crucial to understand that the theory says that *productivity* (not production) is increased by more roundabout methods. The reasoning relies on a given quantity of factors. Obviously, with more factors one can get more product. Böhm-Bawerk replied quite early (1909) to this criticism, and it is surprising to find that Frank Knight repeated this argument in the thirties (1934, 1935, 1938) in his famous attacks against Austrian capital theory. To put it in modern language, Böhm-Bawerk spoke of capital deepening, not of capital widening. As for technical progress, let us note that Böhm-Bawerk considered a given technology, and his theory is *explicitly ceteris paribus*. (He also tried to examine what would happen to the APP when an invention occurs and thought it possible to conclude from historical evidence that inventions that lengthen the production process are more numerous than those that shorten it (1959c, chapter 2).) To conclude, Böhm-Bawerk's theory was consistent, although sometimes heavy and confusing in its exposition, and most objections against it were misplaced because they neglected its analytical framework. What would the modern economist say of the argument that the Cobb–Douglas production function is incorrect because certain ways of using more labour *could* lead to inefficiencies, or because it is defined for a given technology?

It remains that the concept of shortening or lengthening is not unambiguous: we can have two different production methods, neither of which can be said to be the longest or the shortest. So we must admit as a major shortcoming of this theory that the term 'more roundabout method' is not always clear (but the same is true of the more conventional language in terms of 'more capital-using method', as we know how difficult it is to measure capital). And the 'productivity' of some physical flow of inputs is not itself a clear-cut concept if the product appears in more than one period; its measure should depend on the discount rate.

(d) Finally one of the strangest objections to Böhm-Bawerk was John Bates Clark's argument that no production lag exists because production and consumption are synchronized (Clark, 1899, pp. 308ff.). If the economy is stationary, it is possible to associate today's production and today's consumption and neglect the time necessary for production. If we consider a forest in such stationary conditions, every year *n* trees are planted and *n* trees are cut down, and there is no need to wait. Of course, this quite peculiar view neglects two essential facts: first, that *at the beginning* some time-lag must have elapsed (perhaps through refraining to cut down certain trees); and secondly, that stationary conditions have only a small empirical relevance. And this view implies a special conception of 'true capital' as an *abstract and permanent fund* generating an equally permanent flow of income, the replacement of which is automatic and is to be distinguished from capital goods. While 'capital goods imply waiting for the fruits of labor', true capital 'is the means of avoiding all waiting. It is the remover of time intervals – the absolute synchronizer of labor and its fruit.' (Clark, 1899, pp. 308ff.)

It was easy for Böhm-Bawerk to dispose of Clark's argument against the Austrian view and to call it 'a mythology of capital' (Böhm-Bawerk, 1907a, p. 282), but it was not enough to convince his opponents. And the American conception of capital as an abstract self-maintaining fund was later reasserted by Frank Knight and led to the famous Knight–Hayek controversy (Knight, 1934, 1935, 1938; Hayek, 1935, 1936; Kaldor, 1937, 1938; Stigler, 1941). To give meaning to the synchronization concept, Knight left aside the stationary economy hypothesis and advanced the following arguments:

First, it is not possible to define the total production period: 'If we take a certain small increment of consumption, say, drinking a glass of milk, it would never be possible to give any sensible answer to the question when that glass of milk was produced, or when its production began.' (Knight, 1934, p. 275) We can read that the production lag exists, but it is impossible to measure it: 'In the only sense of timing in terms of which economic analysis is possible, *production and consumption are simultaneous*.' (*ibid.*) That the asserted impossibility to measure something makes its measure zero is certainly a strange view!

Secondly, production can be only 'the rendering of services, and it is self-evident that a service can only be produced when it is rendered, and only enjoyed or consumed at the same instant.' (ibid., p. 276) Here production is defined in a way that is quite different from what the Austrians meant by that word (a process), but of course changing the meaning of words cannot be taken as a serious argument. This is indeed, as Hayek put it, 'an absurd abuse of words' (Hayek, 1936, p. 370).

In the same years, George Stigler attacked Austrians on the ground that they failed to understand the method of stationary economics: 'A more important weakness is Böhm-Bawerk's failure to understand some of the most essential elements of modern economic theory, the concepts of mutual determination and equilibrium (developed by use of the theory of simultaneous equations). Mutual determination (*gegenseitige Interdependenz*) is spurned for the older concept of cause and effect.' (Stigler, 1941, p. 181) Whatever the age of the concept of cause and effect, it seems to remain a useful tool when dealing with economic change, where mutual determination is a poor instrument.

We believe that it was important to review these past controversies. In the first part of this century they were not quite conclusive; in the second part, they remained in the background in at least two respects (see also Hicks, 1974):

(a) The first concerns the most accurate representation of production, as a process or as a circular mechanism. That the circular mechanism (as exemplified in horizontal models) has meaning only in (quasi-) stationary conditions should be clear from what has been said.

(b) The second is the nature of capital. The discussions of the past twenty-five years about capital measure or aggregation can be read as extensions of the debate over capital goods and true capital. Only true capital could have an absolute measure, and, because it is already aggregated, only it could lead to a macro-economic production function.

4. The problem and models of traverse

Traverse is one of the many methods that economists developed to cope with dynamic problems. It is a short- or medium-term method – to be contrasted with (long-term) balanced growth analysis – but it is linked with equilibrium growth as it takes this as a starting point. Hicks was the first to formally define a traverse:

> Suppose that we have an economy which has in the past been in equilibrium in one set of conditions; and that then, at time 0, a new set of conditions is imposed; is it

possible (or how is it possible) for the economy to get into a new equilibrium, which is appropriate to the new conditions? We do not greatly diminish the generality of our study of disequilibrium if we regard it that way, as a Traverse from one path to another. (Hicks, 1965, p. 184)

What characterizes the traverse is the *structural change* that brings it about. In that it is different from the simple stability analysis, which would take any economic situation (not a steady state) as its starting point.

It must be pointed out that even if Hicks gave a name to this method, he was not (and did not claim to be) the first to use the method. In particular (although not exclusively), the Austrians used it in their models of business cycles (Hayek, 1931, 1934, 1942). As a way to scrutinizing the behaviour of a formal model, however, traverse was first used in *Capital and Growth* (Hicks, 1965).

We can distinguish several sorts of traverse, according to the following three criteria:

(1) *The nature of the exogenous change.* The traverse can be caused by various shocks: a change in technological knowledge (technical progress); or a change in the value of some economic variable, such as the wage rate or the rate of growth of the labour force. In this case the change may or may not induce a change in the particular production technique that is used. This constitutes a first classification of the cases of traverse (Magnan de Bornier, 1980):

(a) *Imposed traverse* occurs when an important economic exogenous variable has its value changed.
(b) *Technological traverse* is the process of adopting a newly discovered and better production technique.
(c) *Substitution traverse* is the process of substituting the production technique when a change in an economic variable makes it profitable.

(2) *The result of traverse.* Do we want the economic system to reach the new steady state *actually* or *asymptotically*? In the second case, which has been retained by most studies, the traverse appears as a special case of the study of stability, and the same mathematical methods can be applied. If, on the other hand, it is required that the new equilibrium path is actually reached for the traverse to be performed, specific methods are to be used. Both views are, of course, legitimate, remembering that stability is of interest for the analysis of long-term growth, while the other view tends to stress historical rather than logical time and to remain in the short and medium period.

(3) *The economic mechanism of traverse.* It is possible to consider that only 'economic forces' (like market mechanisms) are working and then to look at how (and whether) the traverse develops: the *spontaneous traverse*.

But one can also see it as a planned mechanism that humankind consciously directs; in this case it is a *planned traverse*.

When dealing with traverse, a complete model of the economy is expected, including various prices, physical constraints and the behaviour of agents. This model must permit a description of the economic process during the whole traverse. If we retain the Austrian hypothesis that capital is not transferable from one process to another, and thus use a vertical model of production, here is how a model of the economy can be constructed (Hicks, 1973a, chapters 3–5; Magnan de Bornier, 1980, chapter 6):

First, we consider that in each period one (and only one) new production process is started, with a definite scale depending on macro-economic variables. Knowing the nature and scale of all past processes, it is possible to calculate the present volume of final production and employment. Then, if the distribution of the product between workers and capital owners and the consumption/saving behaviour of these two groups are known, the overall evolution of the economic system can be outlined.

Secondly, there is one variable that is exogenous to the model. In his neo-Austrian model, Hicks has quite naturally considered that economic development can be limited by two main and mutually exclusive quantitative constraints: the volume of resources that can be employed to pay the wages (or the wage fund) and population size. The first of these constraints has a meaning when the wage rate is exogenously given, while if the wage rate is endogenous the work force must be fully employed. These two possibilities lead to the study of two traverse paths: the *Fixwage Path* and the *Full Employment Path*.

In the *Fixwage Path*, the wage rate w is a datum. Given the past behaviour of the economy, there is at each period t a certain quantity of resources that capitalists can devote to the payment of wages (a wage fund F_t). And there is a determinate number of workers Γ_t that are necessary to operate already existing production processes. From this we can derive that $F_t - w\Gamma_t$ is the portion of the fund that remains for the starting of a new process, and that $(F_t - w\Gamma_t)/w = L^*_t$ is the number of workers to be employed in the new process. The scale of this new process is $x_t = L^*_1/\lambda_t$ (or $x_t = L^*_t$ if we normalize all processes such that $\lambda_1 = 1$). The wage fund itself is determined by the saving/consumption behaviour of agents.

Finally, under these conditions and when social accounting relations are correctly determined, it is possible to show the behaviour of the x_t, which describes economic evolution. So in the *Fixwage Path* the wage fund appears as the most important constraint.

The *Full Employment Path* has a dynamic behaviour that depends on another constraint: the number of workers. In this case, if Γ_t is as before the number of workers that are necessary to continue already started processes, and L_t is total employment, we have $L^*_t = L_t - \Gamma_t$, and the x_t are determined. The wage rate in this hypothesis will depend on both total employment, L_t, and the wage fund:

$$w_t = F_t / L_t \quad .$$

The problem of traverse can be restated in terms of the time structure of the x_t, the birth rate of production processes. Before the traverse, this variable has a constant growth rate at some absolute level, and to the new conditions that are imposed there corresponds a new path for x_t (the growth rate or the absolute level, or both, must be changed). Will this new path be reached and how? Let us review some results of earlier models.

In different models, it can be shown that for some values of the parameters the traverse mechanism can be blocked because the constraint (the wage fund or work force) does not even permit continuing the existing processes (formally x_t is less than zero). This result is quite intuitive when the wage rate is increased (in a *Fixwage Path*) or the growth rate is diminished (in a *Full Employment Path*), but this can occur in other situations. In such cases, the traverse is rather a crash.

In models of *planned traverse*, it is generally possible to reach this new path with the assumption that the planning authority has all the necessary knowledge. This does not imply that this traverse is desirable from the point of view of efficiency, and actually the planning mechanism often implies that the scarce resource (the wage fund or labour force) is not fully employed.

In the models of *spontaneous traverse*, the answer will generally be negative, that is the new path is seldom reached. Intertemporal complementarities are too strong to permit it. But the new path can be asymptotically approached, and Hicks (1973a) shows that if processes are of the simple profile type (see section 2), the conditions for convergence can be stated simply. As a matter of fact, in this case we are quite near to two-sector models and the results are identical (the sector producing the final good must be more capital intensive than the other for convergence to be possible). For more general processes, we know no general result about convergence (see Hicks, 1973a, chapter 12).

This brief account of the models of traverse should make it clear that the time structure of capital is potentially an important factor of economic instability, when it is assumed that intertemporal complementarities actually exist. This does not imply that in a world without such rigidities no crisis would occur, but it must be recognized that a lot of research and development effort is directed towards a greater flexibility of capital, and this suggests that these rigidities are really felt in the business world.

References and bibliography

Abraham-Frois, G., and Berrebi, E. (1979)*Théorie de la valeur, des prix et de l'accumulation*, Economica, Paris.

Allais, M. (1947) *Economie et interêt*, Imprimerie Nationale, Paris.

Arrow, K.J., and Levhari, D. (1969) 'Uniqueness of the Internal Rate of Return with Variable Life of Investment', *Economic Journal*, pp. 560–6.

Belloc, B. (1980) *Croissance économique et adaptation du capital*, Economica, Paris.

Bhaduri, A. (1970) 'A Physical Analogue of the Reswitching Problem', *Oxford Economic Papers*, pp. 148–55.

(1975) 'On the Analogy between the Quantity- and the Price-traverse', *Oxford Economic Papers*, pp. 455–61.

Blaug, M. (1968) *Economic Theory in Retrospect*, Heinemann, London.

Böhm-Bawerk, E. von (1959a) *History and Critique of Interest Theories*. Vol. I: *Capital and Interest*, trans. G. Huncke and H. Sennholz, Libertarian Press, South Holland, Ill. (original 1884).

(1959b) *Positive Theory of Capital*. Vol. II: *Capital and Interest*, trans. G. Huncke and H. Sennholz, Libertarian Press, South Holland, Ill. (original 1889).

(1959c) *Further Essays on Capital and Interest*. Vol. III; *Capital and Interest*, trans. G. Huncke and H. Sennholz, Libertarian Press, South Holland, Ill. (original 1909–12).

(1906) 'Capital vs Capital Goods', *Quarterly Journal of Economics*, pp. 3–21.

(1907a) 'A Relapse to the Productivity Theory', *Quarterly Journal of Economics*, pp. 246–82.

(1907b) 'The Nature of Capital: A Rejoinder', *Quarterly Journal of Economics*, pp. 28–47.

Bousquet, G.H. (1936) *Institutes de sciences économiques*, Rivière, Paris.

Burmeister, E. (1974) 'Synthetizing the Neo-Austrian and Alternative Approaches to Capital Theory: A Survey', *Journal of Economic Literature*, pp. 413–56.

Clark, J.B. (1899) *The Distribution of Wealth*, Reprints of Economic Classics, Kelley, New York (1965).

(1907) 'Concerning the nature of capital', *Quarterly Journal of Economics*, pp. 351–70.

Dorfman, R. (1959a) 'A Graphical Exposition of Böhm-Bawerk's Theory of Interest', *Review of Economic Studies*, pp. 153–8.

(1959b) 'Waiting and the Period of Production', *Quarterly Journal of Economics*, pp. 351–72.

Garegnani, P. (1970) 'Heterogeneous Capital, the Production Function and the Theory of Distribution', *Review of Economic Studies*, pp. 407–36.

Gifford, C. (1933) 'The Concept of the Length of the Period of Production', *Economic Journal*, pp. 611–8.

Harcourt, G.C., and Laing, N.F. (eds) (1971) *Capital and Growth*, Harmondsworth, Penguin Books Ltd.

Hayek, F.A. von (1931) *Prices and Production*, Routledge, London.

(1934) 'Capital and Industrial Fluctuations', *Econometrica*, pp. 152–67.
(1935) 'The Maintenance of Capital', *Economica*, pp. 241–76.
(1936) 'The Mythology of Capital', *Quarterly Journal of Economics*, pp. 355–83.
(1939) *Profits, Interest and Investment*, Routledge, London.
(1941) *The Pure Theory of Capital*, Macmillan, London.
(1942) 'The Ricardo Effect', *Economica*, pp. 127–52.
Hicks, J.R. (1939) *Value and Capital*, Clarendon Press, Oxford.
(1965) *Capital and Growth*, Clarendon Press, Oxford.
(1967) *Critical Essays in Monetary Theory*, Clarendon Press, Oxford.
(1970) 'A Neo-Austrian Growth Theory', *Economic Journal*, pp. 257–81.
(1973a) *Capital and Time*, Clarendon Press, Oxford.
(1973b) 'The Austrian Theory of Capital and its Rebirth in Modern Economics', in *Carl Menger and the Austrian School of Economics*, ed. J.R. Hicks and B. Weber, Clarendon Press, Oxford, pp. 190–206.
(1974) 'Capital Controversies: Ancient and Modern', *American Economic Review*, pp. 307–16.
(1975) 'Review of Political Economy: The Old and the New', *The Economic Record*, pp. 365–7.
(1985) *Methods of Dynamic Economics*, Clarendon Press, Oxford.
Hirshleifer, J. (1976) 'A Note on the Böhm-Bawerk/Wicksell Theory of Interest', *Review of Economic Studies*, pp. 191–99.
Jevons, S. (1871) *The Theory of Political Economy*, Macmillan, London.
Kaldor, N. (1937) 'The Recent Controversy on the Theory of Capital', *Econometrica*, pp. 201–33.
(1938) 'On the Theory of Capital: A Rejoinder to Professor Knight', *Econometrica*, pp. 163–76.
(1939) 'Capital Intensity and the Trade-Cycle', *Economica*, reprinted in N. Kaldor, *Essays on Economic Stability and Growth*, Duckworth, London, pp. 120–47.
(1942) 'Professor Hayek and the Concertina Effect', *Economica*, reprinted in N. Kaldor, *Essays on Economic Stability and Growth*, Duckworth, London, pp. 147–76.
Klundert, Th. van de, and Schaik, A. van (1974) 'Durable Capital and Economic Growth', *De ekonomist*, pp. 206–24.
Knight, F. (1934) 'Capital, Time, and the Interest Rate', *Economica*, pp. 257–86.
(1935) 'Professor Hayek and the Theory of Investment', *Economic Journal*, pp. 77–94.
(1938) 'On the Theory of Capital: In Reply to Mr. Kaldor', *Econometrica*, pp. 63–82.
(1946) 'Capital and Interest', *Encyclopaedia Britannica*, vol. IV, pp. 799–801.
Lowe, A. (1976) *The Path of Economic Growth*, Cambridge University Press, Cambridge.
Lundberg, E. (1937) *Studies in the Theory of Economic Expansion*, Norstedt & Söner, Stockholm.
Lutz, F. and Lutz, V. (1951) *The Theory of the Investment of the Firm*, Princeton University Press, Princeton.

Lutz, F., and Hague, D. (eds) (1965) *The Theory of Capital*, Macmillan, London.
Mackenroth, G. (1930) 'Period of Production, Durability, and the Rate of Interest in Economic Equilibrium', *Journal of Political Economy*, pp. 629–59.
Magnan de Bornier, J. (1980) *Capital et déséquilibres de la croissance*, Economica, Paris.
(1984) 'Production jointe et modèle temporel', in *La production jointe*, ed. C. Bidard, Economica, Paris.
Marschak, J. (1934) 'A Note on the Period of Production', *Economic Journal*, pp. 146–51.
Menger, C. (1976) *Principles of Economics*, New York University Press, New York (original 1871).
Montfort, J., and Dutailly, J.C. (1983) *Les filières de production*, Archives et documents 67, INSEE Paris.
Nuti, D.M. (1970) 'Capitalism, Socialism, and Steady Growth', *Economic Journal*, pp. 32–57.
(1973) 'On the Truncation of Production Flows', *Kyklos*, pp. 485–96.
Pasinetti, L.L. (1965) 'A New Theoretical Approach to the Problems of Economic Growth', in *The Econometric Approach to Development Planning*, Pontificiae Academiae Scientiarum Scripta Varia, Vatican City, pp. 571–696.
(1973) 'The Notion of Vertical Integration in Economic Analysis', *Metroeconomica*, pp. 1–29.
Rainelli, M. (1982) 'Structuration de l'appareil productif et spécialisation internationale', *Revue Economique*, pp. 724–45.
Ricardo, D. (1817) *Principles of Political Economy*, John Murray, London.
Robinson, J. (1956) *The Accumulation of Capital*, Macmillan, London.
(1962) *Essays in the Theory of Economic Growth*, Macmillan, London.
(1975) 'The Unimportance of Reswitching', *Quarterly Journal of Economics*, pp. 32–9.
Samuelson, P.A. (1937) 'Some Aspects in the Pure Theory of Capital', *Quarterly Journal of Economics*, pp. 469–96.
(1962) 'Parable and Realism in Capital Theory: The Surrogate Production Function', *Review of Economic Studies*, pp. 193–206.
(1966) 'A Summing-up', *Quarterly Journal of Economics*, pp. 568–83.
(1975) 'Steady States and Transient Relations', *Quarterly Journal of Economics*, pp. 40–7.
Schaik, A. van (1976) *Reproduction and Fixed Capital*, Tilburg University Press, Tilburg.
Schumpeter, J.A. (1954) *History of Economic Analysis*, Oxford University Press, New York.
Sen, A. (ed.) (1970) *Growth Economics*, Harmondsworth, Penguin Books Ltd.
Solow, R. (1967) 'The Interest Rate and Transition Between Techniques', in *Socialism, Capitalism, and Economic Growth*; *Essays Presented to Maurice Dobb*, ed. C.H. Feinstein, Cambridge University Press, Cambridge, pp. 30–9.
(1974) 'Capital and Time, a Neo-Austrian Theory', *Economic Journal*, pp. 189–92.

Spaventa, L. (1973) 'Notes on Problems of Transition Between Techniques', in *Models of Economic Growth*, ed. J.A. Mirrlees and N.H. Stern, Macmillan, London, pp. 168–87.
Sraffa, P. (1932) 'Dr Hayek on Money and Capital', *Economic Journal*, pp. 42–53.
(1960) *Production of Commodities by Means of Commodities*, Cambridge University Press, Cambridge.
Stigler, G. (1941) *Production and Distribution Theories*, Macmillan, New York.
Weizsäcker, C.C. von (1971) *Steady-State Capital Theory*, Springer Verlag, Berlin.
Wicksell, K. (1934) *Lectures on Political Economy*, Routledge, London (original 1901).

6 The structural theory of economic growth

HARALD HAGEMANN

1. Introduction

In a volume in which the analysis of structural change in economic dynamics is the focus of attention, the life-work of Adolph Lowe, culminating in his *On Economic Knowledge* (1965) and *The Path of Economic Growth* (1976), cannot be neglected. The latter work shows Lowe as the second pioneer in traverse analysis after John Hicks, that is in studying the conditions that have to be fulfilled in order to bring the economy back to an equilibrium growth path after a change in one of the exogenous determinants of growth, such as the supply of labour or natural resources or technical progress. Whereas the elder Hicks, shortly after the publication of his *Capital and Growth* (1965), became dissatisfied with his own analysis because of an inadequate modelling of time and switched over from an inter-industry approach to the vertical integration approach in *Capital and Time* (1973),[1] Lowe has always adhered to the inter-industry approach. Although Lowe remained open to elements of the vertical integration approach to productive activities, as emerges in his discussion of the role of working capital or intermediate products (that is the inclusion of 'linear' production sequences *within* each sector), he maintains his critical stance against the Austrian concept of the 'structure of production'. This is because it concentrates exclusively on the process of transforming original inputs into final consumption goods and thus fails to recognize the need for a special machine-tool sector. Thus the point at issue is the role of fixed capital goods in the structure of production.

The strategic position that real capital holds in the growth of an industrial economy comes out most clearly in the analysis of transition

I am grateful to Christian Gehrke, Heinz Kurz and particularly Allen Oakley for their detailed comments on an earlier version.

[1] 'I now regard the "Traverse" chapter of *Capital and Growth* (XVI) as no more than a demonstration of the incompetence, in that field, of the Sectoral Disintegration Method.' (Hicks, 1973, p. 10)

processes when the problem of structural change is moved to the centre of the stage. The existence of an inherited stock of fixed capital goods constitutes the important structural barrier to short-term responses when changes in the growth rate occur. Since a change in the equilibrium growth rate will change the equilibrium ratios in the structure of production – not merely between capital goods and consumption goods or between capital and labour in general, but also between the different types of capital goods – the dynamic traverse from one steady growth path to another necessarily involves a change in the whole quantitative structure, especially in the rebuilding of the capital stock. The decisive problem that the economy confronts upon departing from a steady growth path is the inadequacy of the old stock of fixed capital goods facing the new constellation of data. The necessary adjustment path for regaining flow and stock equilibrium requires both time and cost, and it faces difficulties that arise from disproportions between sectors and from misleading market signals causing expectational problems.

When the stock of fixed capital goods inherited from the past – comprising a specific sectoral composition of existing productive capacities – differs from the (new) equilibrium structure, then it is historical time that matters and no longer logical time (in the sense of Joan Robinson). A change of the current situation in response to such an out-of-equilibrium position makes necessary a process of formation, maintenance and/or liquidation of real capital. While themselves short-run phenomena, these processes of real capital formation or investment are the links between successive stages of growth, thereby transforming the sequence of discontinuous states into a continuous long-run process. Because real capital is not an 'original' factor of production but is the result of economic processes in which it participates as one of the determinants, the formation of real capital is the central channel through which all other determinants – be they technical progress, changes in labour supply or the exploitation of natural resources – influence the long-run development of an industrial system. The additional capital goods are produced with the help of the initially given quantity and quality of real capital; that is real capital is, indeed, both an input and an output. Thus the analysis of fixed capital goods could not be adequately dealt with in a '*linear*' model of production or a 'one-way street' that leads from original factors of production to final consumption goods, but only in a sectorally disintegrated model that takes into proper consideration the circular process of reproduction. Acknowledging the production of commodities by means of commodities, Lowe analyses growth equilibria and, more importantly, adjustment processes caused by the introduction of dynamic disequilibria on the basis of a structural model of production. This is an elaboration of the schemes of reproduction contained in the second volume of Marx's *Capital* and were themselves inspired by François Quesnay's *Tableau économique*.[2]

2. Six decades of structural analysis of real capital formation: Adolph Lowe and the Kiel School

Lowe found the basis of his later works on the structural theory of economic growth very early in Marx's scheme of reproduction, which he later viewed as 'the only comprehensive macro-economic model of the industrial process of production established before Keynes' (Lowe, 1952, p. 141). He considered Marx's scheme to be especially suited to the study of real capital formation – provided that three defects are corrected (see Lowe, 1955, p. 586). The first correction consists in adding appropriate stock variables because the equations in Marx's scheme make sense only if understood as describing flows. Secondly, the two sectors of Marx's analysis have to be disaggregated into vertical stages so that the scheme can be applied also to working capital goods as goods in process. Finally, and most important, Lowe considered it necessary to extend the two-sector Marxian model to a *three*-sector scheme, through the splitting up of the key sector I of Marx's reproduction model, in which capital goods are produced, into two subsectors: one producing the equipment for the consumer-good group and the other producing the equipment for the replacement and expansion of both equipment-good sectors. This subdivision of the equipment-good group is relevant for investigating the structural conditions for steady growth and, even more, for addressing questions of traverse analysis when the implications of this rather simple extension towards a more 'realistic' representation of industrial structure become fully visible.

The need for a tripartite scheme was already pointed out by Lowe in an article entitled 'How is Business Cycle Theory Possible at All?', which was published in German in 1926.[3] In this 'brilliant article' (Kuznets, 1930b, p. 128) Lowe emphasized not only the relevance of the departmental scheme to the analysis of the trade cycle but also that the concept of

[2] See Lowe (1952) and Lowe (1955), reprinted as essays 1 and 2 in Lowe (1987), and Lowe (1976). Interestingly Lowe, who has always favoured the inter-industry approach, not only criticizes the 'linear Imperialism' of the Austrians, but on the other side also Sraffa for his extreme position of eliminating linear processes of production altogether and Dorfman, Samuelson, and Solow for failing to pinpoint the 'true circularities'. See, for instance, Lowe (1976, p. 34, fn. 6).

[3] See Lowe (1926, p. 190). Lowe's contribution to the study of business cycles, to which the economics profession in Germany had turned in the 1920s, can hardly be overemphasized. With his works, especially his article on 'The current state of research on business cycles in Germany' (1925) and his 1926 paper, he became the *spiritus rector* of the debate on business-cycle theory in the Weimar Republic. The importance of Lowe's contribution was also recognized outside Germany, as can be seen, for example, from the two papers by Kuznets (1930a and b).

equilibrium that has been central in all systems of economics since the Physiocrats is logically bound up with a closed interdependent, and therefore a static, system. Lowe's critical analysis of the existing literature on business-cycle theories led him to this conclusion:

The business-cycle problem is no approach *to* but a reproach *against* a static system, since it is an antinomic problem in it. It is soluble only in a system in which the polarity of upswing and crisis arises analytically from the conditions of the system, just as the undisturbed adjustment derives from the conditions of the static system. Who wants to solve the business-cycle problem must sacrifice the static system. Who adheres to the static system must abandon the business-cycle problem. J.B. Say who consciously took this step, however, vis-a-vis reality got into the logical neighbourhood of Palmström who concludes with shrewdness, '*daß nicht sein kann, was nicht sein darf*'. (Lowe, 1926, p. 193)

Lowe stated the problem clearly: if economic theory is to explain the business cycle satisfactorily, it cannot do so simply by outlining the consequences of a disturbing factor exogenously imposed upon an otherwise static economy. Rather, it must seek some causal factor that is immanent to the system itself and can distort the set of equilibrium interrelationships. Whereas many German (-speaking) economists like Friedrich August von Hayek, Ludwig von Mises and R. Stucken resorted to money as the factor whose introduction broke the equilibrium system and made endogenous fluctuations both possible and necessary,[4] Lowe saw the decisive system-immanent disturbing factor in the era of progressive industrialization to lie with technological change on the goods' side. In his critical evaluation of the monetary explanations of the business cycle he came to the conclusion that no one had succeeded in demonstrating the systematic nature of the monetary fluctuations themselves. He regarded monetary factors as playing, at best, an intermediate causal role and being likely to intensify any disequilibrium induced by non-monetary causes (see also Lowe, 1928). On the other hand, the 'built-in instability' that stems from technological change, carrying sufficient momentum to destabilize the equilibrium of the market, is a characteristic feature of an industrial system of production.

These discussions crystallized in the research programme of the *Kiel School*, which even the Keynesian programme has not made obsolete.[5] On

[4] The discussions on a monetary theory of the business cycle taking place in Germany and Austria ran parallel to and reacted to what was happening in Great Britain, the USA and Sweden where R.G. Hawtrey, Keynes, Irving Fisher, Knut Wicksell and others were working on that subject.

[5] Lowe criticizes Keynes for treating the quantity and quality of available equipment and the existing technology as constants and thus eliminating technical progress from his model, a factor that plays a strategic role for the development of output and employment even in the short run. See Lowe (1965, pp. 232—42).

the contrary, against the background of the current micro-electronic revolution, it turns out that the attempt to develop a theory of accumulation, technical progress and structural change – as well as the methods used – are pronouncedly up to date in many respects. The major research interest of the group[6] concerned the construction of a theoretical model of cyclical growth with the basic working hypothesis that a satisfactory explanation of industrial fluctuations must fit into the general framework of an economic theory of the circular flow as it was developed by Quesnay and Marx. The first step consisted of the construction of a model that incorporated both the physical and the value dimensions and that could be made amenable to dynamic transformation. For Lowe and the other members of the Kiel School the physical and technical aspects represent a fundamental determinant of an economic system, especially as important constraints on structural change and behaviour during transition processes. This structural dimension could only be neglected if the production factors were perfectly flexible, mobile and adaptable in the face of change. In order to develop a frame of reference for a sectoral study of economic growth the attention of the Kiel group was directed back to classical and Marxian analysis, since neither the Lausanne nor the Cambridge School, with their emphasis on price variables and the far-reaching exclusion of the physico-technical structures, offered a fruitful starting point.

It was Lowe's closest collaborator, Fritz Burchardt,[7] who set out to

[6] The term 'Kiel School' refers to the most important section of the *Institut für Weltwirtschaft und Seeverkehr in Kiel* in the years 1926–33. The new department of statistical international economics and research on international trade cycles was founded and led by Adolph Lowe (1926–31), who had managed to bring together a group of extremely talented young economists. Besides Lowe and Gerhard Colm, who served as chairman (1931–3) after Lowe's departure to the University of Frankfurt, such distinguished scholars as Hans Neisser, Fritz Burchardt, Alfred Kähler and, for a period of time, Wassily Leontief (1927–8) and Jacob Marschak (1928–30) were also members of this scientific community.

The work on cyclical growth being done in Kiel was supported by the Rockefeller Foundation, as was the research on trade cycles in Vienna (under the direction of Hayek and Morgenstern) and, for example, the business cycle studies in Berlin (Wagemann), Bonn (Spiethoff), Oslo (Frisch), Rotterdam (Tinbergen) and Stockholm (Ohlin) (see Craver, 1986). The members of the Kiel group, who fought against wage cuts in the debates at the end of the Weimar Republic and later, like Colm, made important contributions as policy advisers within the government bureaucracy in the United States under President Roosevelt and President Truman, are internationally recognized as being among the most important precursors of the theory of employment (Garvy, 1975) and in the development of modern non-neoclassical capital and growth theory. (See Clark, 1984, who has also compared the Kiel group with Keynes's Political Economy group in Cambridge operating at the same time.)

[7] Burchardt (1928), who wrote an excellent study of the history of the idea, had already been Lowe's co-worker in the theoretical discussions of the monetary explanation of the business cycle. Fritz (later Frank) Burchardt (1902–58) emigrated to England in 1935 where for the rest of his life he was closely associated with the Oxford Institute of Statistics and was appointed its Director in 1948.

compare, contrast and combine the two most important alternative ways of conceiving the production system, the schemes of the stationary circular flow in Eugen Böhm-Bawerk and Marx, and thus undertook the first synthesis of the vertical integration approach and the inter-industry approach. Together with Lowe's suggestions that the key investment sector I of Marx's reproduction scheme should be divided into two subsectors – Burchardt's seminal synthesis of the sector model and the stage model, which Lowe later applied to the analysis of real capital formation and transition processes between equilibrium growth paths – this represented a profound contribution to the progress of the Kiel School's research. Though for the most part concerned with the stationary aspects of a scheme of reproduction, Burchardt (1931–2) in his two essays left no doubt about its relevance as an instrument for dynamic analysis.

Burchardt's main point of critique in his attack on the linear model of production originally devised by Böhm-Bawerk was the unsatisfactory treatment of fixed capital goods in the 'Austrian' representation of the structure of production in which a sequence of original inputs is transformed into a single output of consumable commodities. No distinction is made between fixed and circulating capital, both types of capital are 'intermediate products' or 'working capital'. The production process is thought of as being *uni-directional*, that is causal, rather than *circular*. Each stage or circle of Böhm-Bawerk's '*Ringschema*' represents intermediate products, with the highest stage or innermost circle being where original factors (labour and natural resources) continuously produce the first intermediate products of the synchronized production process without the aid of intermediate products (capital goods), and with the lowest stage or outermost circle passing each year into consumption. This way of tracing back the production process to some original combination of labour and land leaves unexplained the reproduction and expansion requirements of the stock of fixed capital goods. Böhm-Bawerk's scheme of production thus proves deficient mainly in two respects. First, Burchardt[8] criticized Böhm-Bawerk for mixing up two entirely different problems, namely the *historical* conditions of the original building up of a capital stock and the *present* conditions of reproduction of the existing capital stock. Secondly, in an industrial system, the physical *self-reproduction* of some fixed capital goods is an important technological characteristic; that is, a particular group of fixed capital goods, which Lowe later called 'machine tools', can be maintained and increased only with the help of a circular process in which these machine tools also act as inputs.[9] The role that these goods play in

[8] See for instance Burchardt (1931, pp. 548 and 557).

[9] 'The crucial point of critique lay in the statement of the technical fact of self-reproduction of certain capital goods.' (Burchardt, 1931, p. 556)

industrial production is thus analogous to the role of seed-corn in agricultural production. Therefore it is not technically possible to trace all finished goods back to nothing but labour and land and to treat fixed capital goods as the output of some intermediate stages in the vertical model, as Böhm-Bawerk and his 'Austrian' followers have suggested. However, it has to be remembered that the vertical model was not developed for its own sake but as a basis for a theory of capital, and that there is a certain justification for the Böhm-Bawerkian view of capital as intermediate products, because capital goods are incapable of serving human wants directly and thus have no intrinsic utility of their own (see Nurkse, 1935, Section III). Neither Burchardt nor Lowe questioned the ability of Austrian analysis to deal with the problem of working capital. Both have emphasized that the downward flow to the lowest or final stage of finished output properly describes the structure of working capital if on the highest stage a stock of fixed capital goods is added to the original inputs of labour and natural resources; that is, in order to account for the reproduction, expansion and structural change of an industrial economy, the vertical model must be supplemented by a classical model of the circular flow that clearly depicts the self-reproduction of certain fixed capital goods.[10] 'It is the failure of most models based on the Austrian concept of the structure of production that they disregard the circular flows, concentrating rather on the linear ones.' (Lowe, 1952, pp. 154–5)[11]

Piero Sraffa's well-known argument that fixed capital generally cannot be reduced to dated quantities of labour and his demonstration of the impossibility of Böhm-Bawerk's concept of the 'period of production' to function as an adequate measure of the quantity of capital may be considered as a continuation and elaboration of the critique raised by Burchardt and Lowe about the problematical role of fixed capital in Austrian theory. In striking contrast to the circular vision of the productive process, the vertical vision of the Austrian approach turns out to be a further variant of neo-classical analysis, which conceives of the production

[10] Interestingly, in his *Theories of Surplus Value* (1905, Part I, pp. 107–50), Karl Marx had already described at length that segment of the industrial process depicted by the Austrian scheme, namely the stage model. It also has to be mentioned that as early as 1899 John Bates Clark gave a brief description of the departmental organization of social production (*The Distribution of Wealth*, chapter 18), which possesses basic similarities to Marx's scheme, although the full potential of this explanatory device was not realized by Clark because he did not develop it as a tool of analysis. Like Marx, Clark recognized that the essential characteristic of a particular group of fixed capital goods is that they are replaced and multiplied by a process of physical self-reproduction.

[11] The Burchardt–Lowe critique was taken up by a variety of authors in the English language debate. See for instance Nurkse (1935) whose study on 'The Schematic Representation of the Structure of Production' discussed several central aspects of Burchardt's work, an intellectual debt that was openly acknowledged by the writer.

process as 'a one-way avenue that leads from "Factors of production" to "Consumption goods"' (Sraffa, 1960, p. 93).

The first application of Burchardt's synthetical model to genuine dynamic analysis was Alfred Kähler's study (1933) of the displacement of workers by machinery. Kähler's analysis is based on a very advanced embryo of input–output analysis, applying it for the first time not only to stationary equilibria, but also to the inter-sectoral shifts required for capital formation. Even today, it can be regarded as a significant contribution to our understanding of the relationship between technological change and employment. Kähler's important work, which even in Germany had long fallen into oblivion, partly because of its high complexity and its cumbersome arithmetical examples, has recently received well-deserved appreciation. B. Mettelsiefen (1983) has clearly shown the high originality of Kähler's pioneering multi-sectoral analysis of displacement and reabsorption effects. Kähler's closed input–output model comprised eight sectors, and thus a 8×8 matrix of inter-industry coefficients, a vector of final demand and a vector of sectoral labour inputs.[12]

3. Structural analysis of dynamic equilibria in Lowe's 'tripartite scheme'

In his two papers published in the 1950s Lowe's thought returned to the research achievements of the Kiel School, which he revived and developed against the background of the rise of modern growth theory. This finally culminated in the traverse analysis of his *The Path of Economic Growth* (1976). While the first paper on 'A Structural Model of Production' (1952) provides a more detailed exposition of the model itself, the following article on 'Structural Analysis of Real Capital Formation' (1955) extends the analysis beyond the comparison of equilibrium positions to the analysis of the adjustment paths that the economy follows in response to once-over changes in one of the determinants of growth and to the capital problems related to continuous change. One of the central issues was the critical examination and assessment of the range of validity of the Harrod–Domar

[12] As is well known, Marx's scheme taking account of the sectional differentiation of the process of production has, since the early 1930s, been expanded by Leontief into a comprehensive input–output scheme, and Leontief's Berlin dissertation, 'Die Wirtschaft als Kreislauf' (1928), was published during his stay in Kiel, Leontief (1963) has pointed out that dependence and independence, hierarchy and circularity are the four basic concepts of structural analysis. The method of *triangulation* of empirical input–output tables, which makes it possible to express in a quantitative figure the linearity or circularity, the dependence or interdependence of the various magnitudes in the economy, can be seen as a late answer to the questions discussed by Burchardt, whether the process of the economic circular flow is of a linear or a circular shape. For an excellent discussion of the linearity and circularity of the economic circular flow and the method of triangulation of input–output matrices see Helmstädter (1965).

formula for steady growth. Lowe showed in his structural analysis that the Harrod–Domar conditions, though necessary, are not sufficient to assure growth equilibrium; that is, although the requirements for dynamic equilibrium are much stricter than traditional growth theory makes them appear, once a steady growth path has been achieved, its inherent stability is considerably greater.[13]

Lowe's 'tripartite' division of the economy into three vertically integrated sectors displays a level of aggregation that is a kind of a quarter-way house between Marx and Wassily Leontief. Leontief's model proves indispensable for the solution of practical problems of comprehensive planning. But in the analysis of complex dynamic processes its great advantage – the high degree of disaggregation – turns into an obstacle because it is extremely difficult to trace the adjustment path for such a large number of variables. Lowe assumes an economy divided into three aggregate sectors, a consumer-good sector, 3, and two capital-good sectors: 2, which produces the capital goods used as inputs only in sector 3; and 1, which produces the capital goods directly used as inputs in sector 2 and in sector 1 itself, representing, in Sraffa's terminology, the 'basic industry'. Sector 1, being the only one capable of self-reproduction, thus plays the key role for any expanding industrial economy, especially during a traverse with its structural reproportioning. This becomes obvious when we look at the technology matrix T representing the technical methods of production, with the machine input coefficients $a_{ji}=F_{ji}/O_i$ and the labour input coefficients $l_i=L_i/O_i$, where F_{ji} and L_i denote the inputs of fixed capital goods of type j ($j=1,2$) and total labour in the production of O_i goods in sector i ($i=1,2,3$).

$$T=\begin{bmatrix} a_{11} & O & l_1 \\ a_{12} & O & l_2 \\ O & a_{23} & l_3 \end{bmatrix}$$

Hicks (1985, p. 137), who, in retrospect, now considers his embryonic traverse analysis based on a two-sectoral fixed-coefficient model, in chapter 16 of *Capital and Growth*, a 'bogy', emphasizes: 'I do not believe ... that the fixity of technique ... is the vital point. The big change occurs ... at the point where we abandon the single capital good.' In the *three*-sectoral fixed-

[13] For a detailed analysis see Lowe (1952, pp. 166–8), Lowe (1955, pp. 610–34), and Lowe (1976, pp. 77–100 and 240–5). It has to be emphasized that Harrod concentrated on the *flow equilibrium* of the economy along its 'warranted growth path'. If, however, one analyses the problem of a traverse caused by a change in technology (or the rate of growth of labour supply), historical time and no longer logical time matters. In that case one has to appreciate the very problem of the relation between *stock equilibrium* and capital theoretic issues caused by the irreversibility of time.

coefficient Lowe model, it is indeed the differentiation between two types of capital goods that introduces a new dimension into the process of production. In this model there is a definite hierarchy of sectors 1→2→3, or, in popular terminology, 'machines→tractors→corn'. The existing stock of machines is the bottle-neck that any process of rapid expansion must overcome, that is, under the assumption of full utilization of the available capital stock, fixed capital in sector 1 (and subsequently in sector 2) must be increased before any increase can be obtained in the production of consumption goods. Thus the restructuring of productive capacity can no longer be accomplished by simply readjusting the relative weight of the different sectors through mere horizontal transfer between them, as in the usual two-sectoral model. It is a characteristic property of the Lowe model that it combines an element of flexibility – arising from the dual utilization of machines, which therefore can be transferred between the two capital-good sectors 1 and 2 – with an element of rigidity – arising from the single use of tractors in the consumption-good sector and thereby excluding the transfer of capital goods between the investment- and consumption-good sectors. The abandonment of the single capital-good assumption and the intertemporal complementarity of the hierarchically ordered sectors will imply an adjustment path in which the sectors become involved during different phases in a sequential process of production and restructuring of the economy. It is an essential characteristic of the Lowe model that there exists a unique intertemporal complementarity that makes possible the analysis of traverse processes in historical time, even if we concentrate totally on the inter-industry side of his model (that is the three vertically integrated sectors) and disregard the fact that in Lowe's scheme of industrial production each sector includes four successive stages.[14]

Next we compare economies that use the same technique but operate under different growth or distribution patterns. At first we concentrate on comparing economies that are in long-run equilibrium, that is we try to make explicit some important characteristics of the *three*-sectoral Lowe model with the help of the techniques Hicks (1965), Luigi Spaventa (1968, 1970) and Donald Harris (1973, 1978) developed for their analyses of the *two*-sectoral fixed-coefficient model. With the aid of this analysis we can compare different capital structures associated with different steady-state growth rates. Each point on the consumption–growth and wage–profit trade-offs implies a particular structure of fixed capital, but with steady growth the composition of investment is the same as the composition of the capital stock. The detailed comparison of various economies (the famous

[14] For a detailed analysis of the stage aspect of the model, especially the role of working capital, see Lowe (1976, chapters 5 and 17) and Wyler (1953).

'islands' or 'planets') growing along a steady-state path with different sectoral allocations of resources and different shares of capital and consumption goods in total output is a necessary prelude for the analysis of the traverse, that is the adjustment path that connects two dynamic equilibria defined by different rates of growth. The comparative analysis shows us the terminal equilibrium positions from a structural point of view. To move from one growth path to another or, analogously, from one distribution pattern to another, requires the restructuring of the economy, especially the rebuilding of the capital stock. Once capital goods are installed, there is only one set of outputs that can be consistently produced with full utilization and full employment. Thus we get the following *quantity equations*:

$$\begin{aligned} a_{11}(g+d)f_1 + a_{12}(g+d)f_2 &= f_1 \\ a_{23}c &= f_2 \\ l_1(g+d)f_1 + l_2(g+d)f_2 + l_3c &= 1 \end{aligned} \tag{1}$$

Considering that the seven technical parameters, that is the three machine input coefficients a_{ji}, the three labour input coefficients l_i and the uniform rate of depreciation d[15] are given, the quantity system provides us with three equations in the four variables c, g, f_1 and f_2, where c denotes the output of corn per unit of labour, g the rate of growth, and $f_j = F_j/L$ the input of fixed capital of type j per unit of labour. The quantity system possesses one degree of freedom and remains open unless one variable is given; that is, once we know one of the four quantity variables, then the other three are fully determined. Expressing all the other quantity variables as functions of g we get equations (2) to (5) for economies that use the same technique but operate under a different growth rate.

$$c = \frac{1 - a_{11}(g+d)}{l_3 + (a_{23}l_2 - a_{11}l_3)(g+d) + a_{23}(a_{12}l_1 - a_{11}l_2)(g+d)^2} = \frac{N_g}{D_g} \tag{2}$$

with $dc/dg < 0$

$$f_1 = \frac{a_{12}a_{23}(g+d)}{D_g} \tag{3}$$

[15] The assumption that the rates of depreciation of the fixed capital goods (that is this 'depreciation by evaporation') are given implies that the economic lifetime of each capital good is a constant determined independently of distribution. An adequate treatment of the economic lifetime of fixed capital goods that takes into consideration different efficiency profiles requires a von Neumann–Sraffa approach. See Hagemann and Kurz (1976), who also show that the return of the same truncation period and a reswitching of techniques are closely linked phenomena.

$$f_2 = a_{23}\frac{N_g}{D_g} \quad \text{with } df_2/dg < 0 \tag{4}$$

and

$$\frac{f_1}{f_2} = \frac{a_{12}(g+d)}{N_g} \quad \text{with } d(f_1/f_2)/dg < 0. \tag{5}$$

Functions (2)–(5) represent comparisons of economies in steady-state equilibrium. Any path of balanced growth requires a special real structure of the economy, identified by given capital and consumption goods, allocation of resources and composition of production.[16] Equation (2) exhibits the well-known, monotonically inverse consumption–growth relationship. Obviously, the size of the output–machine ratio in the basic machine-tool sector 1 places an important upper limit upon the achievable rate of growth. The maximum rate of growth is given by

$$g_{max} = \frac{1}{a_{11}} - d$$

that is, the (theoretical) ceiling of growth is independent of the other sectoral output–machine ratios and of relative prices.

Lowe (1976, pp. 71 and 77) emphasizes a relative shift of inputs from the consumption-good sector to the capital-good sector (as well as to the basic sector 1 taken by itself) as the universal structural characteristic of the transition from stationary to dynamic equilibrium, the required magnitude of this shift being a function of the rate of growth. This can be clearly seen when we look at the system of quantity equations. For example, from equations (4) and (5) one can see that the economy with the higher growth rate has a smaller endowment of tractors and a greater ratio between stocks of machines and tractors. Closer examination also shows that the faster growing economy uses a higher share of its labour force in the production of machines and a lower share in the production of consumption goods and produces relatively more machines than consumption goods. The higher the growth rate, the higher is the weight of sector 1 and the lower the weight of sector 3: this is the usual result of two-sector models. But the two-sector case fails to shed any light on the structural transformations operating within the investment sector itself. In the Lowe model, however, one can see that the trade-off between accumulation and consumption also manifests itself in the proportion between the two sectors producing means of production. The economy with the higher growth rate uses a higher

[16] For a more detailed analysis of the equilibrium quantity and price relations see Hagemann and Jeck (1984).

percentage of its machines and its labour in sector 1 than in sector 2 and produces relatively more machines than tractors. But some open questions, like the share of sector 2 in total employment, remain, and these questions all have to do with the specific Lowe-sector 2, which uses machine inputs produced in sector 1 and produces tractors used in sector 3, thus operating as the bridge between the basic sector and the consumption-good sector. The reason for this indeterminateness is therefore clear. Sector 2 participates with lower percentages in a 'bigger cake', which the capital-good producing sectors share as a group.

We now go on to introduce the relations governing wages, profits and relative prices in the Lowe model. Competitive equilibrium in a capitalist economy implies that the price of a unit of output covers the sum of gross profits, consisting of net profits and depreciation, on the value of invested capital and of wages, which are assumed to be paid at the end of the period. By choosing the consumption good as the *numéraire* we get the following *price equations*:

$$\begin{aligned} a_{11}(r+d)p_1+l_1w&=p_1 \\ a_{12}(r+d)p_1+l_2w&=p_2 \\ a_{23}(r+d)p_2+l_3w&=1 \end{aligned} \tag{6}$$

The price system, too, provides us with three equations in the four variables w, r, p_1 and p_2, where the prices of machines and tractors, p_1 and p_2, are relative prices and, like the wage rate w and the rate of profit r, are expressed in units of the consumption good. Expressing all the other price variables as functions of r we get equations (7) to (10) for economies that use the same technique but operate under a different net rate of profit (wage rate).

$$w=\frac{1-a_{11}(r+d)}{l_3+(a_{23}l_2-a_{11}l_3)(r+d)+a_{23}(a_{12}l_1-a_{11}l_2)(r+d)^2}=\frac{N_r}{D_r} \tag{7}$$

with $dw/dr<0$

$$p_1=\frac{l_1}{D_r} \tag{8}$$

$$p_2=\frac{l_2+(a_{12}l_1-a_{11}l_2)(r+d)}{D_r} \tag{9}$$

and

$$\frac{p_1}{p_2}=\frac{l_1}{l_2+(a_{12}l_1-a_{11}l_2)(r+d)} \text{ with } d(p_1/p_2)/dr \gtreqless 0 \text{ for } q_1 \gtreqless q_2. \tag{10}$$

Functions (7)–(10) like (2)–(5) represent comparisons of economies in steady-state equilibrium. In the Lowe model, as in other models with only one consumption good or a fixed basket of consumption goods, the wage–profit relationship (7) turns out to be the exact replica of the consumption-growth relationship (2). But in contrast to the common two-sectoral or multi-sectoral (see Pasinetti, 1977, pp. 199–208) models, duality ceases to hold as soon as we compare the relationships between prices and the rate of profit (equations 8–10) with the relationships between quantities and the rate of growth (equations 3–5).

Since Sraffa's contribution, which triggered off the Cambridge controversies in the theory of capital, we know that the key to the movement of relative prices with changes in the rate of profit lies in the inequality of the proportions in which labour and means of production are employed in the various industries. In the Lowe model, the sectoral machine–labour ratios $q_i = a_{ji}/l_i$ play the crucial role of fixing the direction and extent of the price differences associated with different rates of profit. Whereas the technologically given ratios q_1 and q_2 can be compared directly, this is not possible for q_3 because a different type of capital good is used as an input in the production of consumption goods. But the problem can be eliminated when we compare q_1 and q_2 with the *in*direct machine–labour ratio $q_3^* = q_3 l_2/l_1$, which has the same physical dimension.[17]

As is well known, the postulation of a savings function provides a direct link between the quantity system and the price system of the economy, that is between capital accumulation and income distribution. In connection with the Keynesian equilibrium condition of saving–investment equality, it constitutes a relationship between the growth rate and the rate of profit, thereby reducing the degrees of freedom in the system as a whole to one. Whereas in general, this r–g relationship can be rather complex and depends on technology as well as on income distribution, in Lowe's very special case of a 'superclassical' savings function, with saving out of wages and consumption out of profits being zero, the rate of profit and the growth rate coincide.[18]

[17] For a detailed discussion of the price variations with the rate of profit see Section IV in Hagemann and Jeck (1984). This also shows that the special Ricardo–Marx–Samuelson case, where the labour theory of value holds, in the Lowe model takes the form $q_1 = q_2 = q_3^*$. It must be said that the range of traverse analysis in Lowe (1976) is limited by the very fact that he makes the special assumption of identical sectoral machine–labour ratios, thus making the shift of factors between the two capital-good sectors an easy one, because a transfer of machine tools from sector 2 (1) to sector 1 (2) sets free the same amount of labour per machine as can be absorbed by using the machine in the other sector, that is the already very complex traverse analysis is not complicated by an additional employment problem resulting from the transfer of machines when $q_1 \neq q_2$.

[18] 'Equality of aggregate profits with aggregate savings and investments follows from the set-up of our two-strata model, in which only wage earners are supposed to consume, whereas saving and investment are functions exclusively performed by the recipients of profits. Moreover, in accord with our definition of "efficiency of resource utilization" ... dynamic equilibrium is bound up with the "golden rule of accumulation".' (Lowe, 1976, p. 87)

4. Structural analysis of traverse processes

In the Lowe model, the remaining degree of freedom is closed through the exogenously given natural rate of growth. Structural analysis then investigates the traverse process from one natural rate of growth to another in which the capacity augmenting role of investment is at issue. Since Roy Forbes Harrod and Evsey D. Domar, we know that both aspects of investment, the capacity-augmenting and the income-generating one, must fit together (see also Kalecki, 1971, chapter 11). Making the superclassical saving hypothesis, Lowe puts the whole strain of adjustment on the savings ratio. In general, the natural rate of growth consists of two components, the rate of growth of labour supply and the rate of growth of productivity. Accordingly, we shall be concerned, first, with the traverse that leads from an initial dynamic equilibrium to a terminal dynamic equilibrium under the impact of a once-for-all rise in the exogenously given rate of growth of labour supply and, secondly, with the traverse caused by non-neutral process innovations.[19] Thus, superimposing a once-over change on a movement of steady growth, the complex problems that arise during the traverse from one growth path to another resemble the problems one has to face on the path of a once-over growth adjustment after, for example, a single influx of immigrants or a particular technical improvement. When changes in the major growth stimuli – changes in labour supply and productivity – occur, the ability of an economy to react to these changes is limited by the inherited stock of fixed capital goods.[20] In the search for the structural conditions under which economic growth can be balanced, attention therefore is directed to the process of real capital formation.

It is clear that the adjustment process of an economy that experiences an additional influx of labour requires a complementary addition to real capital as the essential precondition for reaching the final equilibrium in which the steady-state quantity relations are again fulfilled; that is, the real structure of the economy – the set of capital and consumption goods, the allocation of resources and the composition of production – is adapted to the higher exogenously given rate of growth of labour supply. During the traverse, for example, the composition of investment differs from the composition of the capital stock, that is the three sectors are growing at different rates on the *adjustment path*, which, as a consequence of the special hierarchy in the Lowe model, can be subdivided into *four phases*.[21]

[19] We are not dealing here with the third type of traverse analysed by Lowe, namely the adjustment paths caused by changes in the supply of natural resources. For an analysis of the dynamics of diminishing returns in the realm of natural resources or recycling of material residuals and the structure of production see Lowe (1976, chapters 19 and 20).

[20] In order to concentrate on the main arguments, we abstract from possibilities of over-utilization or under-utilization of fixed capital goods.

[21] For a detailed formal analysis of this traverse type see the 'core chapter' 14 in Lowe (1976).

Although the appropriate place for an additional supply of labour seems to be the consumption-good sector, in order ultimately to increase employment and the growth rate of output in sector 3, at first a temporary fall in the growth rate of output of consumption goods is necessary. With fixed coefficients of production and full-capacity utilization, the production of more consumption goods unequivocally requires additional tractors that cannot be supplied unless sector 2 has increased its stock of machines. Such an increase must be obtained from the machine-producing sector, that is the key to a higher growth rate lies in increasing the shares of the basic sector 1. The decisive question, therefore, is by what procedure the output of machines can be increased above the net investment and replacement demands in the old growth equilibrium so that the stocks of fixed capital goods can be adapted to the requirements of the new growth equilibrium. Here, a characteristic property of the Lowe model comes into play: the twofold serviceability of machines that can be transferred horizontally between sectors 1 and 2. In the first phase of the traverse therefore, the capacity in sector 2 has to be partly freed from its original task of producing tractors in order to produce more machines and get the expansion process under way.

The phase of partial capacity liberation, in which sector 1 is expanded at the expense of sector 2, is followed by a second phase of self-augmentation of machines in which all savings are invested in sector 1, up to the 'point of maximum expansion from within', where the terminally required addition to the capital stock in the first sector is accomplished. Taking explicitly into consideration the stage aspect of Lowe's industrial scheme of production, it is clear that the self-augmentation must follow a predetermined sequence and start in the earliest stage. Since the twofold serviceability holds not only for the fixed but also for the working capital goods, the working capital goods liberated in the different stages in sector 2 together with parts of the fixed capital stock in the first phase of the traverse can at once be utilized in the augmentation of machines in sector 1. Only after such a shift has taken place can there occur a process of genuine self-augmentation in steady interplay with the expansion of the corresponding working capital goods.

During the third phase of the traverse, capital stock and output in sector 2 are adjusted to the higher rate of growth. The adjustment requirements include an analogous expansion of the stock of working capital. With the higher capital stock in sector 2 the production of tractors increases. The building up of the additional stock of fixed and working capital goods in sector 3 will lead to an increase of consumption output in the fourth phase, until adjustment comes to an end and the traverse is completed. When the terminal equilibrium path has been reached, all sectors will again expand at the same rate: the higher rate of growth of labour supply.

Lowe centres his analysis of the traverse caused by labour and/or capital-displacing innovations on the *compensation for technological unemployment*, that is on the questions of whether the displaced labour will be reabsorbed in the end and what is required for this to occur. Like Hicks, he distinguishes between the short-run and the long-run effects of an innovation and shows that the employment effects depend heavily on investment behaviour during the transitional disequilibria. Both Lowe and Hicks take as their starting point Ricardo's investigation of the 'machinery problem', which according to Sraffa (1951, p. lvii) marks 'the most revolutionary change' in the third edition of Ricardo's *Principles*. In Ricardo's analysis, the economy takes off from a steady-state equilibrium without any indication that it will arrive at another uniquely determined equilibrium, namely the time paths of profits, investment, employment and output that characterize the economy after the introduction of the machine are largely left indeterminate. The abstraction from capital accumulation is an essential characteristic of Ricardo's numerical example. Accordingly, his example can be regarded as an 'early and rude type of traverse analysis' (see Kurz, 1984), which contains a capital shortage theory of temporary technological unemployment.[22]

In his post-classical model, Lowe concentrates on the *effects* of non-neutral innovations on a pre-existing dynamic equilibrium and on the structural and motorial conditions that have to be fulfilled for the reabsorption of displaced labour and the movement along an adjustment path to a new steady-state equilibrium. The method employed equals Ricardo's 'isolation by abstraction approach', that is, in order to study the structural requirements for the absorption of non-neutral innovations in their purest form, Lowe abstracts from the growth of labour supply and uses an input–output model of a stationary economy as the frame of reference. In this model the structural relationships are expressed by the shares of the three sectors in the value of aggregate gross output.[23] Because he recognizes major innovational shocks as occurring mainly discontinuously, Lowe treats them as once-over changes in productivity. Like Hicks, and unlike Harrod, he regards such once-over changes as legitimate problems for dynamic analysis and describes the traverse that the economy pursues under the impact of such non-neutral innovations, concentrating on the structural problems of real capital formation.

[22] Hicks (1973, chapter 8) shows in his Fixwage model, which provides an almost exact replica of Ricardo's assumptions, that the introduction of machinery has an adverse effect on employment in the short run only in the case of 'strongly forward biased' innovations, that is when the construction costs of the new machines are higher than those of the old machines, whereas the utilization costs are smaller. The temporary surge of unemployment caused by the introduction of new machines can be absorbed by increased accumulation.

[23] For a technical analysis see the details in Part IV of Lowe (1976). See also Hagemann (1987).

Lowe recognizes technological change as 'the true stimulus of economic growth' and identifies technological change with *process innovations*, because of the 'practical reason' that 'product-innovation has so far proved refractory to economic analysis' (Lowe, 1976, p. 236). The traverse analysis is thus confined to the study of labour- or capital-displacing innovations and the structural adjustments required for compensation, that is for achieving the macro-goal of full employment growth. Lowe stresses the industry-specific nature of most technical progress and starts with the discussion of a *pure labour-displacing innovation* introduced in the consumer-good sector 3. This is the clearest case through which to study both the initial impact and the structural adjustment processes required for compensation and convergence to a new equilibrium because it is the only case without additional complications arising from the secondary effects of innovations occurring in other sector(s). The traverse analysis starts with the hypothesis that some pioneering firms in sector 3 can produce the same output quantity with the old capital stock but a smaller input of labour. This pure reduction of the coefficient l_3, which is equivalent to an increase in labour productivity, implies a displacement of workers as long as output does not increase with productivity. A process of additional capital formation is the necessary precondition for a successful compensation of the initial temporary unemployment. Lowe assumes that during the first phase of the traverse the price of the consumption good remains constant, that is the gains of the productivity increase are distributed to the innovating firms,[24] which together form the first of two subsectors in the production of consumption goods (the group of non-innovating firms forming the second subsector). Sub-system 1 then comprises these innovating firms and the firms in the two capital-good sectors required for steady reproduction of real capital operating in this sub-system. The main task, according to Lowe (1976, p. 257), 'is to determine the precise proportion in which the displaced labour will, terminally, have to be distributed over all three sectors of both sub-systems if a new stationary equilibrium is to be established'. The reabsorption of displaced workers can proceed only to the extent to which net investment takes place, implying that some workers are transferred to sectors 1 and 2, first for the construction of additional capital goods and later on for their replacement. Structural analysis shows the analogy between the compensation process for technological unemployment in the case of a pure labour-displacing innovation introduced in sector 3 and the traverse to a higher growth rate of labour supply.

[24] Alternative ways of distributing the gains of productivity increases would consist of prices decreasing *uno actu* with the costs of production, as is assumed in traditional compensation theory, or wages increasing with labour productivity in the economy as a whole. The emergence of technological profits in connection with the superclassical saving (investment) assumption is most favourable for compensation.

If a pure labour-displacing innovation is introduced in sector 2, the major modification consists in the secondary effect of the innovation on the consumption-good sector, which is the only one using the output of sector 2 – the tractor – as an input. This implies that in the terminal equilibrium not only the price of tractors but also the price of corn is lower than in the initial steady state. The secondary effect would influence the entire system if a pure labour-displacing innovation occurs in the production of machines. But in both cases of a labour-displacing innovation being introduced in one of the two sectors producing capital goods compensation for the displacement effects is conditional on the additional formation of real capital. Since the elasticities of demand for tractors and, more indirectly, for machines depend in the long run on the elasticity of the final demand for corn, compensation also depends on the latter after the competitive generalization of technical progress, a process in which the technological profits and thus the funds for the financing of net investment gradually disappear, that is the gains of productivity increases are transferred to the buyers of cheapened output.

Contrary to the case of a pure labour-displacing innovation, the introduction of a *pure capital-displacing innovation* in the consumption-good sector has secondary effects for the two other sectors. Since real capital, in contrast with labour, is not only an input but also an output, a decrease of the coefficient a_{23} is bound to reduce output as well as capital input in both capital-good sectors. In a fixed coefficient model of the Lowe type, a capital-displacing innovation in the production of corn thus creates a compensation problem for *indirectly displaced labour* in sectors 1 and 2. In the case of a capital-displacing innovation in the production of tractors, this secondary labour displacement effect would be smaller because it is limited to the machine-producing sector, whereas in the case of a capital-displacing innovation occurring in sector 1, there is no secondary effect at all. This makes it possible to reach the new equilibrium position more rapidly, although there is some displacement of labour, too, because a decrease in a_{11} reduces the machine-input requirements in the basic sector 1, and therefore (initially) the output of machines below the original level, while at the same time increasing the profit margin and the achievable maximum rate of growth.

But there exists a further important difference between capital-displacing and labour-displacing innovations. Whereas in the latter case a process of additional real capital formation is indispensable for compensation of technological unemployment, in the former case displaced machines are available without an additional process of saving and investing – the important question being whether these old machines are sufficient for the absorption of the displaced workers, a question that is answered in the affirmative by Lowe (1976, pp. 267–70).

5. Force analysis as a necessary complement to structural analysis in Lowe's political economics

Lowe makes it clear that his concern is not with the *descriptive* analysis of structural relations and movements as they occur in actual economic systems in historical time, but rather with the structural conditions required to achieve a stipulated goal. His *instrumental* analysis[25] does not involve prescriptive imperatives of the *ought* kind in the usual way of 'normative', but rather sets out what *could* be done in order to achieve the macro-goal of balanced growth, the 'lodestar' (Lowe, 1976, p. 287) of his analysis, in the most efficient way. 'Instrumental analysis is, then, a generalization of Keynes's concern with the requirements for the attainment of full employment.' (Lowe, 1987, p. 171) While the derivation of the adjustment path based on structural requirements is a necessary first step, it has to be supplemented by establishing behavioural and motivational patterns that will set the economy on a goal-adequate traverse. This is the task of *force analysis*, in which neutrality to social relations disappears and economics is raised above the level of a mere engineering science.

Force analysis is especially relevant for the analysis of adjustment processes in free market systems. This becomes clear when we look back at phases one and two of the traverse to a higher growth rate of labour supply. The analysis reveals the *crucial role of expectations* and the significance of a functioning price mechanism that is anything but a mechanical tool.[26] Partial capacity liberation in sector 2 requires a fall in the aggregate demand of consumption goods. This is achieved by the mechanism of 'involuntary' saving, that is it is workers' consumption that is reduced because an increase in labour supply leads to a reduction of the wage rate. In view of the fact that machines serve indirectly as an input in the production of corn, what, then, are the motorial conditions for positive investment decisions in sector 1 at the same time? The investment of all profit incomes in sector 1 presupposes the investors' anticipation of a long-run increase in demand for corn and tractors, despite the current demand

[25] For a detailed discussion of Lowe's instrumental analysis, the core of which consists in deriving suitable means from given ends, see the exposition in Lowe (1965, chapters 5 and 10–12, and the Postscript in the 2nd edn, 1977) and the critical evaluation of his specific method of political economics given by a variety of authors, along with the reply by Lowe, in Heilbroner (1969).

[26] During the traverse, disequilibrium manifests itself also in price changes and a divergence of the sectoral profit rates, and this acts as a strong incentive for the whole adjustment process taking place. Nevertheless the price mechanism alone is not sufficient but must be supplemented by other guides for long-term decisions. Lowe's findings have also been emphasized by Edmond Malinvaud in his recent comments on the flexprice case of Hicksian traverse analysis: 'orderly convergence of economic growth to a steady, sustainable and efficient path could not be taken for granted, and would even appear unlikely, if the price system alone was operating' (Malinvaud, 1986, p. 379).

reduction and price decline, that is *negative* elasticities of both quantity and price expectations.[27] Since it is probable that the expectations that are *required* to assure positive investment decisions according to structural analysis differ from the expectations that are *likely* to be formed in the prevailing situation, it will be the function of public controls as policy instruments to transform actual behaviour into required, goal-adequate, behaviour. Considering that Lowe emphasizes that the precondition for the success of compensating public policy is the understanding and approval of the macro-goals pursued and the policy measures applied, the strengthening of optimistic expectations must be a principal aim.

Whereas structural analysis has demonstrated the analogy between the compensation process in the case of a pure labour-displacing innovation occurring in the consumption-good sector and the adjustment process to a higher rate of growth of labour supply, things look quite different concerning force analysis. The embodiment of the innovation in new productive capacity both decreases the labour requirement per unit of corn output and increases the profit margin. Whereas the first effect may dominate in the short run, it can be superseded by the second – increased employment as the consequence of additional real capital formation – in the long run. The (technologically induced) profits now providing an alternative source of investment funds are, however, the anticipated result of investing in new machines rather than the cause – as in the case of a wage reduction consequent to an additional labour supply originating outside the economic system. Since it is the displaced workers' demand for consumption goods that liberates part of the existing stock of machines for self-augmentation, we can again speak of 'involuntary' saving: the technological profits result from the former money wages of the displaced workers. Considering the at least temporary competitive superiority of the technological pioneers, investors' risks are much lower than in the case of an additional influx of labour, especially since the pioneering firms that have lower costs of production can increase their market share by lowering their price, thereby transferring the compensation problem to the non-pioneering firms.

6. Advantages and drawbacks of the inter-industry approach compared to the vertical integration approach in the analysis of economic change

The most vehement criticism against the Lowe model has been raised by Amendola (1984) who – although conceding that multi-sectoral models

[27] The situation would be even more complicated in an economy with non-identical sectoral machine–labour ratios in which relative prices differ between the new and the old steady-state path, that is the price changes are not limited to the transitional disequilibria.

with a horizontal structure give more information as to the workings of the economy at any point in time – emphasizes that circular relations in production are an 'obstacle' to the analysis of the process of innovation. He correctly points out that in Lowe the innovations considered take the form of a pure reduction of technical coefficients, which leads to a traverse analysis in which adjustment is accomplished through a reallocation of machines and labour between the different sectors in the economy. This means abstracting from innovations that imply the appearance of new, different capital goods. 'What does the trick in multi-sector models, that is what reduces the *different* to the *more*, is the assumption that *old* machines can be used to produce the *new* ones.' (Amendola and Gaffard, 1988, p. 29)

It is precisely the focus on innovations that take the form of new methods for making the same final product that has led Hicks away from the inter-industry approach to the vertical integration approach of his neo-Austrian theory in which inter-sectoral transactions are dispensed with in order to avoid having to deal with the physical transmutation of the capital stock under the influence of the innovations.

Such innovations, nearly always, involve the introduction of new capital goods, new sorts of 'machines', and of other intermediate products. It is here undesirable that these goods should be physically specified, since there is no way of establishing a physical relation between the capital goods that are required in the one technique and those that are required in the other. The only relation that can be established runs in terms of costs, and of capacity to produce final output; and this is precisely what is preserved in an Austrian theory. (Hicks, 1977, p. 193)

The fact that in most cases even process innovations involve the introduction of new capital goods is not disputed by Lowe who, for example, emphasizes the replacement of the original type of machinery in use by a new type as the 'normal case' (Lowe, 1976, p. 266) of a pure capital-displacing innovation. Like Hicks, Lowe regards the lower unit costs of production as the precondition for the introduction of the new machines, but confines his analysis to innovations taking the form of a reduction of technical coefficients because of the complications resulting from product innovations. He perceives the disregarding of the circular flows as the main failure of all those models that are based on the Austrian concept of the structure of production. The treatment of fixed capital goods is the Achilles' heel of the vertical integration approach. By treating fixed capital as if it were working capital Hicks (1973) does not recognize the need for a special machine-tool sector. An important consequence of this is that in (neo-) Austrian models the effects of innovations upon industrial structure are not shown. Whereas this deficiency is admitted by Hicks, it is ignored by Amendola, who advocates the abstraction of the capital goods from the technical specification in the analysis of the innovation process. Amendola thus overlooks the relevance of a basic system, namely the fact that the new machines cannot be produced without the old machines existing at the beginning of the traverse. Lowe has rather early emphasized that 'additional and possibly qualitatively different real capital is created ... with the help of the initially given quantity and quality of real capital' (Lowe, 1955, p. 584). But it was only recently that Baldone (1984) proposed the idea of 'transition' – or 'pilot' – processes in which new goods, initially produced by old means of production, can later on themselves be used as means of production and assume the character of basic products.

While I recognize that each of the two approaches enjoys a sort of comparative advantage in the complex field of traverse analysis, where the effects of an innovation cannot be easily determined without restrictive assumptions, and I therefore share the position of several authors having a complementary perspective[28] to a certain extent, I nevertheless give priority to the inter-industry approach in the analysis of structural change and see its further elaboration as highly desirable. Such an elaboration, for example, requires the consideration of two important dimensions of fixed capital goods: the degree of capacity utilization and the economic lifetime of machines. The latter can best be dealt with on the basis of a von Neumann–Sraffa treatment of fixed capital goods as a joint part of gross output, thus identifying machines of different ages as different commodities. This not only allows the modelling of more complex patterns of the time profile of efficiency but also an additional consideration of the time dimension in the process of restructuring and expanding the capital stock. Over-utilization or under-utilization of fixed capital goods would not only raise the flexibility of the system but also greatly increase the number of possible adjustment paths.

That input–output models emphasizing inter-sectoral interdependencies retain conceptual priority is also not disproved by Pasinetti in his important *Structural Change and Economic Growth* (1981) in which he analyses how an economic system may through time maintain full employment and full capacity utilization when it is subject to dynamic

[28] For an excellent and fair statement of this complementary perspective see Stefano Zamagni (1984), whose main intention is to show the richness and potentialities of the Hicksian traverse as a method for dynamic analysis.

The complementary perspective is also shared by Hicks, who already in 1973 felt that 'it is unwise to commit ourselves, finally, to the one route or to the other' (Hicks, 1973, pp. 11–12). After giving priority to the Austrian model in the seventies, Hicks (1985) again explores both routes in which a productive system can adjust itself when 'horizontal' (chapter 13) or 'vertical' rigidities (chapter 14) are present.

Malinvaud (1986) does not seem to be entirely convinced of the complementary perspective when he recommends the 'occasional use' of the Austrian model in his Hicks lecture because 'it is too neglected nowadays' and 'in theoretical analysis it is indeed often rewarding to look at the same questions through different glasses' (p. 371).

impulses such as technical progress, a growing population and changes in consumers' preferences according to Engel's law. Pasinetti's analysis is conducted on the basis of a vertically integrated model, which he regards as superior for dynamic analysis because of the change of input–output coefficients and the 'breaking down' of the inter-industry system over time (Pasinetti, 1981, chapter 6). But there remains a problem: is it legitimate to express technical progress generally in terms of reduction of the inputs to these vertically integrated sectors? Technical change takes place at the industry level, a characteristic that is completely washed out in vertically integrated models. The industry-specific nature of technical change implies that, contrary to Pasinetti's assumption, rates of productivity growth in the different vertically integrated sectors cannot be thought of as being independent of each other. This is so even if one takes into consideration that diffusion of new technologies is often dependent on the existence of industries interrelated from the technological point of view. The price Pasinetti has to pay for his assumption is (too) high: he has to give up his general model containing basics (see Pasinetti, 1973) in favour of a special model in which, even in its 'more complex' version (involving capital goods for the production of capital goods), no basic product exists and, therefore, the production process is not circular.

7. Concluding remarks

The strategic role of the machine-tool sector pointed out by Lowe is also emphasized in the work of Grigorii Alexandrovich Fel'dman who formalized the notion that investment priority for the capital-good sector was a precondition for attaining a higher rate of growth during the Soviet industrialization debate in the late twenties.[29] Structural incapacity to supply enough capital goods would prevent a rise in the saving ratio from being fully transformed into the desired level of investment in a closed economy, in which the capacity of a very small capital-good sector forms an operative constraint. Thus a major task of planning for raising the rate of growth must be first to direct investment resources towards expanding the capacity of the basic sector(s).

The strategic role of the machine-tool sector has also been stressed by economists discussing the growth and planning problems of underdeveloped countries in the fifties and sixties (see for example Dobb, 1960, pp. 48–103, who made extensive use of the Lowe model,[30] and Mathur, 1965).

[29] See Domar (1957, p. 227) for an early hint at the similarity of the Fel'dman scheme with the schemes which were suggested by Burchardt, Nurkse and Lowe.

[30] The production-theoretic structure of the Fel'dman model in the version of Robinson and Eatwell (1973, pp. 288 92) and of the Dobb model in the version of Chng (1980) are identical with the three-sectoral Lowe model.

Countries like India that lack a self-sufficient machine-tool sector can speed up their transformation process by foreign trade. The Fel'dman constraint would be binding only if the domestic output of machine tools could not be supplemented with imports. M. Merhav (1969) has called attention to the functional role of imports and the problem of 'technological dependence' in cases of the structural inability of an economy to supply the required capital goods, which must then be imported from other countries. Examination of the structural conditions for steady growth and the adjustments required by dynamic disturbances must therefore be extended to the economy's external balance.

That not only the structural analysis but also the force analysis of Lowe's political economics proves pertinent to recent discussions on economic reform is highlighted by Chakravarty (1987) in his analysis of the Indian experience of development planning. Thus I come to the conclusion that Lowe has addressed important and difficult problems. It will prove valuable if it leads more economists to tackle the significant problems with which Lowe has grappled. The inter-industry framework seems to me more suitable for dealing with the complex issues of the relationships between structural stability and economic change. While giving priority to the inter-industry approach and its elaboration, the analysis can without doubt be enriched by a complementary perspective that takes into consideration the comparative advantages of elements of the vertical approach.

References

Amendola, M. (1984) 'Toward a Dynamic Analysis of the "Traverse"', *Eastern Economic Journal*, 10, pp. 203–10.

and Gaffard, J.L. (1988) *The Innovative Choice. An Economic Analysis of the Dynamics of Technology*, Basil Blackwell, Oxford.

Baldone, S. (1984) 'Integrazione verticale, struttura temporale dei processi produttivi e transizione fra le tecniche', *Economia Politica*, 1, pp. 79–105.

Böhm-Bawerk, E. von (1921) *Positive Theorie des Kapitales* (*Kapital und Kapitalzins*, 2 Abt.), Fischer, Jena. (1st edn Wagner, Innsbruck, 1899). Translated as *Capital and Interest*, vols. 2 and 3, Libertarian Press, South Holland, Ill.

Burchardt, F.A. (1928) 'Entwicklungsgeschichte der monetären Konjunkturtheorie', *Weltwirtschaftliches Archiv*, 28, pp. 78–143.

(1931–2) 'Die Schemata des stationären Kreislaufs bei Böhm-Bawerk und Marx', *Weltwirtschaftliches Archiv*, 34, pp. 525–64, and 35, pp. 116–76.

Chakravarty, S. (1987) *Development Planning. The Indian Experience*, Clarendon Press, Oxford.

Chng, M.K. (1980) 'Dobb and the Marx–Fel'dman Model', *Cambridge Journal of Economics*, 4, pp. 393–400.

Clark, D. (1984) 'Confronting the Linear Imperialism of the Austrians: Lowe's

Contribution to Capital and Growth Theory', *Eastern Economic Journal*, 10, pp. 107–27.
Clark, J.B. (1899) *The Distribution of Wealth. A Theory of Wages, Interest and Profits*, Macmillan, New York.
Craver, E. (1986) 'Patronage and the Directions of Research in Economics: The Rockefeller Foundation in Europe, 1924–1938', *Minerva*, 24, pp. 205–22.
Dobb, M. (1960) *An Essay on Economic Growth and Planning*, Routledge and Kegan Paul, London.
(1967) 'The Question of "Investment Priority for Heavy Industry"', in *Papers on Capitalism, Development and Planning*, Routledge and Kegan Paul, London, pp. 107–23.
Domar, E.D. (1957) 'A Soviet Model of Growth' in his *Essays in the Theory of Economic Growth*, Oxford University Press, Oxford, pp. 223–61.
Dorfman, R., Samuelson, P., and Solow, R. (1958) *Linear Programming and Economic Analysis*, McGraw-Hill, New York.
Fel'dman, G.A. (1928–9) 'On the Theory of Growth Rates of National Income', vols I and II, in *Foundations of Soviet Strategy for Economic Growth*, Selected Soviet Essays, 1924–1930, ed. N. Spulber, Indiana University Press, Bloomington, Ind., pp. 174–99 and 304–31.
Garvy, G. (1975) 'Keynes and the Economic Activists of Pre-Hitler Germany', *Journal of Political Economy*, 83, pp. 391–405.
Hagemann, H. (1983) 'Wachstumsgleichgewicht, Traverse und technologische Unterbeschäftigung', in *Technischer Fortschritt und Arbeitslosigkeit*, ed. H. Hagemann and P. Kalmbach, Campus, Frankfurt and New York, pp. 246–95.
(1987) 'Traverse Analysis in a Postclassical Model', Forschungsgruppe 'Technologischer Wandel und Beschäftigung', Working Paper No. 8, University of Bremen.
Hagemann, H., and Jeck, A. (1984) 'Lowe and the Marx–Fel'dman–Dobb Model: Structural Analysis of a Growing Economy', *Eastern Economic Journal*, 10, pp. 169–86.
Hagemann, H., and Kurz, H.-D. (1976) 'The Return of the Same Truncation Period and Reswitching of Techniques in Neo-Austrian and More General Models', *Kyklos*, 29, pp. 678–708.
Harris, D.J. (1973) 'Capital, Distribution, and the Aggregate Production Function', *American Economic Review*, 63, pp. 100–13.
(1978) *Capital Accumulation and Income Distribution*, Stanford University Press, Stanford, Calif.
Heilbroner, R.L. (1969) *Economic Means and Social Ends. Essays in Political Economics*, Prentice-Hall, Englewood Cliffs, N.J.
Helmstädter, E. (1965) 'Linearität und Zirkularität des volkswirtschaftlichen Kreislaufs', *Weltwirtschaftliches Archiv*, 94, pp. 234–59.
Hicks, J. (1965) *Capital and Growth*, Clarendon Press, Oxford.
(1973) *Capital and Time*, Clarendon Press, Oxford.
(1977) *Economic Perspectives. Further Essays on Money and Growth*, Clarendon Press, Oxford.
(1985) *Methods of Dynamic Economics*, Clarendon Press, Oxford.

Kähler, A. (1933) *Die Theorie der Arbeiterfreisetzung durch die Maschine*, Julius Abel, Greifswald.
Kalecki, M. (1971) *Selected Essays on the Dynamics of the Capitalist Economy*, Cambridge University Press, Cambridge.
Kurz, H.D. (1984) 'Ricardo and Lowe on Machinery', *Eastern Economic Journal*, 10, pp. 211–29.
Kuznets, S. (1930a) 'Equilibrium Economics and Business-Cycle Theory', *Quarterly Journal of Economics*, 44, pp. 381–415.
(1930b) 'Monetary Business Cycle Theory in Germany', *Journal of Political Economy*, 38, pp. 125–63.
Leontief, W. (1928) 'Die Wirtschaft als Kreislauf', *Archiv für Sozialwissenschaft und Sozialpolitik*, 60, pp. 577–623.
(1963) 'The Structure of Development, in *Input–Output Economics*, 2nd edn, Oxford University Press, New York and Oxford, 1986, pp. 166–87.
Löwe, A. (1925) 'Der gegenwärtige Stand der Konjunkturforschung in Deutschland', in *Die Wirtschaftswissenschaft nach dem Kriege. Festgabe für Lujo Brentano zum 80. Geburtstag*, Vol. 2, Duncker und Humblot, Munich and Leipzig, pp. 329–77.
(1926) 'Wie ist Konjunkturtheorie überhaupt möglich?' *Weltwirtschaftliches Archiv*, 24, pp. 165–97.
(1928) 'Über den Einfluß monetärer Faktoren auf den Konjunkturzyklus', in *Beiträge zur Wirtschaftstheorie. Zweiter Teil: Konjunkturforschung und Konjunkturtheorie*, ed. K. Diehl, Schriften des Vereins für Sozialpolitik, vol. 173/II, Duncker und Humblot, Munich and Leipzig, pp. 355–70.
Lowe, A. (1952) 'A Structural Model of Production', *Social Research*, 19, pp. 135–76.
(1955) 'Structural Analysis of Real Capital Formation', in *Capital Formation and Economic Growth*, ed. M. Abramovitz, Princeton University Press, Princeton, N.J., pp. 581–634.
(1965) *On Economic Knowledge. Toward a Science of Political Economics*, Harper and Row, New York (2nd enlarged edn, M.E. Sharpe, White Plains, N.Y., 1977).
(1976) *The Path of Economic Growth*, Cambridge University Press, Cambridge.
(1987) *Essays in Political Economics. Public Control in a Democratic Society*, ed. A. Oakley, Wheatsheaf Books, Brighton.
Malinvaud, E. (1986) 'Reflecting on the Theory of Capital and Growth', *Oxford Economic Papers*, 38, pp. 367–85.
Marx, K. (1893) *Capital, Volume II*, Lawrence and Wishart, London, 1956.
(1905) *Theories of Surplus Value, Part 1*, Lawrence and Wishart, London, 1969.
Mathur, G. (1965) *Planning for Steady Growth*, Basil Blackwell, Oxford.
Merhav, M. (1969) *Technological Dependence, Monopoly and Growth*, Pergamon, New York.
Mettelsiefen, B. (1983) 'Der Beitrag der "Kieler Schule" zur Freisetzungs- und Kompensationstheorie', in *Technischer Fortschritt und Arbeitslosigkeit*, ed. H. Hagemann and P. Kalmbach, Campus, Frankfurt and New York, pp. 204–45.

Nurkse, R. (1935) 'The Schematic Representation of the Structure of Production', *Review of Economic Studies*, 2, pp. 232–44.

Oakley, A. (1987) 'Introduction. Adolph Lowe's Contribution to the Development of a Political Economics', in Lowe (1987), pp. 1–24.

Pasinetti, L.L. (1973) 'The Notion of Vertical Integration in Economic Analysis', *Metroeconomica*, 25, pp. 1–29.

(1977) *Lectures on the Theory of Production*, Macmillan Press, London.

(1981) *Structural Change and Economic Growth. A Theoretical Essay on the Dynamics of the Wealth of Nations*, Cambridge University Press, Cambridge.

Quesnay, F. (1972) *Tableau économique*, 3rd edn, Paris, 1759. Ed. M. Kuczynski and R. Meek, Macmillan, London.

Ricardo, D. (1951) *On the Principles of Political Economy and Taxation* (1st edn 1817; 3rd edn 1821), vol. I of *Works and Correspondence of David Ricardo*, ed. P. Sraffa with the collaboration of M. Dobb, Cambridge University Press, Cambridge.

Robinson, J., and Eatwell, J. (1973) *An Introduction to Modern Economics*, McGraw-Hill, New York.

Scazzieri, R. (1983) 'Economic Dynamics and Structural Change. A Comment on Pasinetti', *Rivista Internazionale di Scienze Economiche e Commerciali*, 30, pp. 73–90.

Spaventa, L. (1968) 'Realism Without Parables in Capital Theory', in *Recherches récentes sur la fonction de production*, Facultés universitaires N.D. de la Paix, Namur, pp. 15–45.

Sraffa, P. (1951) 'Introduction' to *The Works and Correspondence of David Ricardo*, ed. P. Sraffa with the collaboration of M.H. Dobb, Cambridge University Press, Cambridge, vol. I, pp. xiii–lxii.

(1960) *Production of Commodities by Means of Commodities. Prelude to a Critique of Economic Theory*, Cambridge University Press, Cambridge.

Wyler, J. (1953) 'Working Capital and Output', *Social Research*, 20, pp. 91–9.

Zamagni, S. (1984) 'Ricardo and Hayek Effects in a Fixwage Model of Traverse', in *Economic Theory and Hicksian Themes*, ed. D.A. Collard et al., Clarendon Press, Oxford, pp. 135–51.

Part IV
A FRAMEWORK FOR STRUCTURAL ANALYSIS

7 Economic theory and industrial evolution

MICHIO MORISHIMA

1. Introduction: the congruence between economy and economics

The features of the economy with which economists are concerned have been changed and will change throughout history. Some of the hypotheses on the basis of which economic theory is constructed may become inappropriate in different circumstances. Say's law of markets, for example, which had been considered as a suitable approximation to reality, was rejected, especially during the Great Depression, when the amount of effective investment was insufficient. Similarly, when new production processes are being constructed the gestation period in the production of commodities is significant, while at a time when the economy is provided with enough facilities of production, the production period is negligible and products will be obtained almost instantaneously.

Thus, where the actual economy is subject to drastic change, economic theory should also change correspondingly; there must be some kind of congruity between the history of the actual economy and the history of the economic theory. Of course, theory can be examined and re-examined independently of the history of human beings to see whether the logic used in the theory is deductively or inductively correct; there is no case where an application of logic to economic theory can at one point be judged to be correct and then later turns out to be wrong, unless the judgement is a mistaken one. However, any theory can become vacuous when the actual economy has been so changed that the phenomena described by the theory never happen in the actual world and, therefore, the applicability of the theory is reduced to nought. While this sort of diversification of theory from reality might be very rare in the physical sciences, it is likely to be more frequently found in human-physical sciences, like medicine, and especially in the social sciences.

Despite this, the response of theory to the evolution of the economy is not instantaneous but delayed. Even more harmful, most economists of the major schools do not specify the epoch to which their theory is applicable. Classical, neoclassical and Keynesian economists have disputed with each other as if their respective theories are either alternative approaches to the same type of economy or alternative theories that have different advantages in investigating different sorts of problems of the same economy. Without specifying the object of investigation precisely and accurately, contemporary economists have the unfortunate habit of constructing a transcendental model of capitalism and deriving absolute economic laws or theorems that they believe hold non-vacuously true everywhere and forever, as long as capitalism persists. There must be a challenge to this belief in the eternity and generality of economic theory.

It has to be pointed out, before I proceed to my own analysis of the subject, that Amiya Kumar Dasgupta (1988) has recently made a brave effort to identify the epochs of major economic theories. His method of establishing congruence between economic history and the history of economic theory is as follows. First, he selects three major economic problems in the order of their appearances in economic history: (1) economic growth, (2) relative prices and resource allocation and (3) unemployment and economic decay. He then identifies classical, neoclassical and Keynesian economics, respectively, as the theories that are aimed at dealing with these different problems. This enables him to divide the history of economic theory into three epochs: the classical era, the era of marginalism and the Keynesian era.

However, this mode of identification leaves unclear, say, how economists should tackle the problem of relative prices and resource allocation in the era of classical economics. Should it be dealt with in the classical way? That is to say, should we accept the Ricardian or Marxist theory of relative prices, instead of the marginal theory? If this question is asked of an orthodox economist such as Frank H. Hahn (1984) the answer will be definitely, 'No'. The same will be true for the Keynesian era.

For those who see the history of economic theory in the way that Hahn sees it, Dasgupta's whole idea of dividing history into epochs is likely to be unacceptable. There can be one and only one scientifically correct theory of economics. Classical economics is a premature crude economics, which is, of course, imperfect, while Keynesian economics is a special, rather than general, theory that is mainly concerned with the depression phase of the economy. The theory supported by the neoclassical economists is more general than the others and nearest to the correct way of dealing with the economy.

I will adopt an entirely different approach in this essay. Each of the major economic theories has been developed as a systems analytic theory, so that it is not only concerned with the determination of the prices of individual commodities and the wage rate, but also with the determination of outputs of the economy. Each is, however, based on a number of specific assumptions, which are of limitational character and have no general applicability. Though economists usually rank theories according to the generality of their assumptions, I propose to examine the congruency between the sets of limitational assumptions and the stages of development of the economy. I shall find, like Dasgupta, three ages: the ages of classical, neoclassical and Keynesian economics. But my age of classical economics, for example, is not identified, as is Dasgupta's, as the phase of industrial expansion, when the problem of capital accumulation and economic progress was of great, practical importance and was, in fact, advocated by classical economists. It is identified as the period in which the basic hypotheses of classical economics were valid in the actual economy. Similarly, after the epochs of classical economics, it is determined whether a given period belongs to the epoch of neoclassical economics or that of Keynesian economics, according to whether the key hypotheses of the respective economics were prevailing in the period or not.

Nevertheless, in deciding on a concrete historical epoch for classical economics, there is not likely to be any big difference between me and Dasgupta. As for the neoclassical age, however, there is considerable disagreement between us. First of all, Dasgupta does not refer to neoclassical economics but to marginalism. Without specifying the period of marginalism clearly, he considers it an 'interlude' that made its appearance in the transition from classical to Keynesian economics. By contrast, I take the marginalist revolution as a revolution in methodology, so that a marginalist model of the classical economy and a marginalist model of the Keynesian economy are both perfectly conceivable and legitimate. By the same account the views of neoclassical economists must be able to be expressed without using concepts of marginalism. I shall identify an epoch of neoclassical economics between the classical and Keynesian eras, the existence of which is independent of the use of the marginalist methodology.

This view of neoclassical economics does not, of course, deny the importance of the problems of relative prices and resource allocation. I consider that these are not problems specific to any particular epoch. They exist universally through all epochs, so that both classical economics and Keynesian economics must have answers to them.

Since the words 'classical', 'neoclassical' and even 'Keynesian' are obscured and contaminated by miscellaneous elements, throughout the following I have tried to purify the economics of these schools by removing the sundry elements that taint them, representing each in the form of a simple and clearly defined model as shown by one or two major works of each school. First, there can be no objection to representing classical economics by David Ricardo's *Principles*, the work that was its culmination. Of course, Léon Walras's *Elements*, especially its third model of general equilibrium of capital formation, can be regarded as representing neoclassical economics, and this would be a very reasonable selection, particularly in view of the fact that Walras's capital-formation model is the prototype of Robert M. Solow's and Hirofumi Uzawa's one- or two-sector growth models, which are popular among contemporary neoclassical economists. Parallel to neoclassical economics, Keynesian economics is represented not by the original static version, but by a more general, dynamic form as formulated by Roy Forbes Harrod.[1] Thus, more specifically or more exactly, what I am concerned with in the following is the periodization of Ricardo's, Walras's and Keynes's economics.

2. Ricardian and anti-Ricardian premises

Let us simplify Ricardian, Walrasian and Keynesian models by reducing the number of industries to two, one producing consumption goods and one producing investment goods. In the case of the Ricardian model, the consumption-good industry is agriculture, while in the Walrasian and Keynesian models it is a manufacturing industry. Where agriculture is present, there are landowners in the economy in addition to workers and capitalists. In its absence it is assumed that there are no landlords because the use of land is negligible and inessential for industrial production. Thus land problems are entirely neglected in our Walrasian and Keynesian models.

This assumption is acceptable for Keynes. One may point out, however, that land, agriculture and landowners exist in Walras's own model. In spite of this fact I abstract all these from the model, because the essential features of agriculture are not highlighted by Walras. The production period for agricultural products is much longer by comparison with that of industrial products. Walras nevertheless treats agriculture, like manufacturing, as producing its products instantaneously. It is merely one of *n* sectors that do not play any crucial role in the working of Walras's model and are, therefore, eliminated in the following argument relating to Walrasian economics.[2]

We adopt the following notation throughout the three models. Price,

[1] See Ricardo (1951; 1st edn 1817); Walras (1874); Keynes (1936); Harrod (1948); Solow (1956) and Uzawa (1961).

[2] Of course, industry too uses land for production. Throughout all sections below, however, I follow Ricardo in assuming that non-agricultural industries do not use land in any of our three models, Ricardian, Walrasian and Keynesian.

quantity and production coefficients referring to the (non-agricultural) consumption-good industry are represented by Greek letters: π is the price of consumption goods, ξ the output, κ the capital coefficient and λ the labour-input coefficient of the consumption-good industry. Those for the capital-good industry are p, x, k, l, respectively. Since no land is used by these industries, constant returns to scale prevail, so that production coefficients κ, λ, k, l are all constant. The unit of capital services is defined in such a way that one unit of capital goods provides capital services of one unit per period, and the price of capital services is denoted by q.

For agriculture in the Ricardian economy, we assume the following production function. First, a constant amount of capital goods is provided for each worker employed, so that capital per worker, say θ, is constant. Secondly, there is a one-year production lag between the input of labour and capital and the output of products (say, corn). Corn per acre is produced with constant returns to scale until the employment of labour reaches a specified level, say μ^0, after which it is subject to diminishing returns. Let η be the agricultural output per acre. The production function per acre may then be written as:

$$\eta = F(\mu, \theta\mu, 1)$$

where 1 signifies the cultivated acreage, being one acre. Let v be the total acreage cultivated; then total output would be $\xi = \eta v$, which is made available at the commencement of the next year.

Let w be the wage rate, δ the rate of depreciation of capital goods and r the normal rate of profit or the interest rate. Then the employment per acre, μ, is determined such that surplus output per acre, that is the difference between the output per acre $\pi\,\eta$ and the corresponding cost, $w\mu + p\delta\theta\mu + r\,(w\mu + p\theta\mu)$, is maximized subject to the production function above, so that we obtain the marginal condition:

$$\pi = [w + p\delta\theta + r(w + p\theta)]\frac{d\mu}{d\eta} \tag{1}$$

where $d\mu/a\eta$ is, of course, the reciprocal of the total derivative of the production function with respect to μ. In (1) both θ and δ are constant, so that where π, w, p and r are given, $d\mu/d\eta$ and hence μ are determined.

Ricardo attributes the surplus output of agriculture to the landowners as rent. The rent equation may then be written in the aggregate form as:

$$\pi\xi = [w\lambda + p\alpha + r(w\lambda + p\kappa)]\xi + R \tag{1*}$$

where R stands for the total amount of rent, ξ for the total output ηv, λ for the employment of workers per output, μ/η, κ for the employment of capital goods per output $\theta\mu/\eta$ and finally α for the depreciation of capital goods per output, which is $\delta\kappa$.

Let T be the total amount of land available in the economy. The total acreage cultivated cannot exceed the total available acreage.

Thus,

$$v \leqslant T.$$ [3]

We have so far implicitly assumed that the agriculturists cannot bring their commodities to market in less than a year. They must, however, pay wages before their products are sold and thus must have a fund to support labour. This is the reason why the marginal cost of agriculture includes interest paid for the wage fund, that is $rwd\mu/d\eta$ in (1).

Similarly, Ricardo, like Jan von Neumann, assumes that it takes one year to produce capital goods. He also, like von Neumann, assumes that constant returns to scale prevail in industry. Then the marginal cost is fixed at $wl+pa+r(wl+pk)$, where l, k, a $(=\delta k)$ are input coefficients that are all constant. Where the price of capital goods p exceeds the marginal cost, output of capital goods x will be increased endlessly and the industry will be in a state of disequilibrium. On the other hand, where p falls short of the marginal cost, there is no production and the industry will be settled at $x=0$. Thus we obtain a von Neumann-like equilibrium condition,

$$p \leqslant wl+pa+r(wl+pk), \tag{2}$$

which is compatible with equilibrium at $x=0$ if it holds with strict inequality, '$<$'. x may be positive only where it holds with equality. This adjustment of x implies that production of capital goods does not take place whenever excess profits are negative. We call this *the rule of profitability*.

In the case of the Walrasian economy, we have a consumption-good industry, instead of agriculture. It is assumed that constant returns to scale prevail there, as well as in the capital-good industry. It is, moreover, assumed that production is instant in each of these two industries, and therefore, they do not need capital to support labour. The term representing interest on the wage fund disappears from the formula of the constant marginal cost. The price-cost equations are written as:

$$\pi \leqslant w\lambda+p\alpha+rp\kappa \text{ for the consumption-good industry,} \tag{1'}$$

$$p \leqslant wl+pa+rpk \text{ for the capital-good industry.} \tag{2'}$$

[3] Where this holds with strict inequality, μ is equal to u^0; otherwise $\mu \geqslant \mu^0$. Since constant returns prevail in agriculture at μ^0, we have $d\mu/d\eta=\mu/r$ at $\mu=\mu^0$. Substituting this into (1) and comparing it with (1*), we obtain $R=0$. Thus there is no surplus output and, hence, no rent, where a part of the available land remains uncultivated.

These two satisfy the rule of profitability; that is to say, if (1′) holds with '<'. ξ is zero, while (2′) with '<' implies $x=0$. The assumption of instantaneous production seems, at first sight, very unrealistic. But, at a stage of development where each firm has been provided with enough intermediate products, machines and equipment necessary for production of the final manufacturing products, the period of production of commodities is very short and can safely be regarded as negligible. The assumption of instant production may be defended under such circumstances.

Let us next concern ourselves with the demand–supply conditions for products. First, in the case of the Ricardian economy, because of the production lag, output of corn is only available in the market one year after the commencement of production. Let the output available be distinguished from current production, ξ, by putting a bar on the top of ξ. Assuming that capitalists do not consume (their total profits are invested) and that landowners spend their whole income (rent, R) on luxuries that have to be imported (since there is no luxury-good industry in the economy), the total wage payment cannot exceed the value of the wage fund, $\pi\bar{\xi}$, so that we have

$$\pi\bar{\xi} \geqslant w(\lambda\xi + lx).^4$$

Under the additional assumption that workers do not save, the right-hand side of this inequality stands for the workers' demand for corn. Where the above inequality strictly holds with ">", the corn market is in a state of excess supply and corn will be a free good: $\pi=0$. Therefore, the left-hand side of the inequality is zero, while the right-hand side is non-negative. Thus we would obtain $0 > w(\lambda\xi + lx) \geqslant 0$, a contradiction. This means that corn can never be a free good and may, therefore, be taken as *numéraire*. We set π at 1 and the above inequality holds as an equation:

$$\pi\bar{\xi} = w(\lambda\xi + lx) \tag{3}$$

This determines the real wage rate w/π at $\bar{\xi}/(\lambda\xi + lx)$, which is the available amount of corn per worker employed.

In the Walrasian economy, where commodities are produced instantly, there is no need for capitalists to have a certain amount of wage funds at the commencement of production. The demand–supply equation for consumption goods is then written in the following form.

$$\pi\xi \geqslant w(\lambda\xi + lx) \tag{3'}$$

It is assumed in (3′) that workers spend the whole amount of wages on the

[4] Note that in the Ricardian model, the employed per output λ is not a constant but equals μ/η, which varies as μ varies.

consumption of corn, while capitalists and landowners make no demand for corn. If (3′) is satisfied with strict inequality, corn is a free good and, hence, w/π is infinitely large, so that (3′) is reduced to $\xi > \infty$, that is a contradiction because $\xi < \infty$. Hence corn is not free; so (3′) should hold in the form of the equation.

Let us assume $\pi > 0$ and (3′) is an equation. It can be seen that there is a substantial difference in implication between the classical equation (3) and the neoclassical equation (3′). In the case of the wage-fund theory (3), as long as the real wage rate w/π remains unchanged, an increase in the production of capital goods x gives rise to a decrease in the production of consumption goods, ξ, because they compete for the limited resources of the wage fund $\bar{\xi}$. On the other hand, in the case of instantaneous production (3′) we have $\pi > w\lambda$.

This is shown in the following way. Suppose $\pi > 0$, so that prices are normalized such that $\pi = 1$. Suppose the contrary, that is either $1 < w\lambda$ or $1 = w\lambda$. In the former case, (1′) holds with strict inequality; hence $\xi = 0$. Therefore, $x = 0$ from (3′). Then there would be an excess supply in the labour market. Thus we obtain $w = 0$, which contradicts the supposition $1 < w\lambda$. In the latter case, on the other hand, we have $\xi = 0$ from (1′) if $p > 0$. Then $x = 0$ from (3′). Hence from (6′) below we obtain $w = 0$ because of an excess supply of labour. Again this is a contradiction. Where $p = 0$, we have $x = 0$ from the rule of profitability applied (2′). This in turn means $\xi = 0$ because the combination, $x = 0$ and $\xi > 0$, contradicts Say's law (4′) stated below. Obviously we have $w = 0$ for the combination, $x = 0$ and $\xi = 0$. This contradicts the supposition $1 = w\lambda$.

Thus we obtain $\pi > w\lambda$, or $1 > w\lambda$ in the normalized form if $\pi > 0$. With $\pi = 0$, we can show that only an absurd, or trivial, unrealistic state of general equilibrium is obtained; we have an equilibrium of no production and no trade, where ξ, x, π, p, w, r are all zero.

Thus $\pi > w\lambda$. Then (3′) must hold with equality; otherwise, $\pi = 0$, a contradiction. From equation (3′) we then obtain

$$\xi = \frac{\frac{w}{\pi} l}{1 - \frac{w}{\pi}\lambda} x,$$

which implies that an increase in x would create an expansion of ξ. Thus the Walrasian School replaces the classical idea of the wage-fund theory of real wage determination by a theory of simultaneous inter-industrial repercussion between the capital-good and consumption-good industries. We thus observe a divergence of view in opposing directions between classical and neoclassical economists. The former expects a decline in the consumption-good industry wherever the capital-good industry is expanded, while the latter concludes that industries will go together in the same direction.

As for the savings–investment equation, we have already assumed in (3) and (3′) that capitalists do save, while workers and landowners, if the latter exist, do not save. Then the total gross savings including depreciation amount to:

$$p(\alpha\xi + ax) + r[w(\lambda\xi + lx) + p(k\xi + kx)] \text{ in the Ricardian model,}$$

or

$$p(\alpha\xi + ax) + rp(\kappa\xi + kx) \text{ in the Walrasian model.}$$

It is noted that coefficients α, λ, κ for agriculture in the Ricardian model are not constant but all depend on the degree of cultivation or the number of workers employed per acre.

Both Ricardo and Walras assume Say's law to the effect that savings are entirely devoted to investment. In the Ricardian economy investment can be made in two ways, one in the form of the wage fund and the other in the capital goods. Landowners who have received rent of the amount R from output ξ spend it in the foreign market on luxuries, and corn of the amount R will be sent to the foreign country as payment. Then the remaining amount of corn, $\xi - R$, will form the wage fund in the next period and the increment, $\Delta\bar{\xi} = (\xi - R) - \bar{\xi}$, represents the investment in the wage fund. px obviously stands for investment in capital goods. Say's law claims that the total value of investment equals the total gross savings. Thus we have in Ricardo's economy:

$$\Delta\bar{\xi} + px = p(\alpha\xi + ax) + r[w(\lambda\xi + lx) + p(\kappa\xi + kx)] \tag{4}$$

In the Walrasian economy, on the other hand, there is no investment in the wage fund. Say's law, which is stipulated as total investment being equal to total gross savings, is put in the form of the following formula:

$$px = p(\alpha\xi + ax) + rp(\kappa\xi + \kappa x). \tag{4'}$$

The final set of conditions consists of the two demand–supply conditions for the stock of capital and the working population, respectively. Let M be the total stock of capital and N the total working population. In the Ricardian economy agriculture and the capital-good industry use capital goods of the amounts, $\kappa\xi$ and kx, respectively, for production. The total sum of these cannot exceed the available amount M, so that we must have

$$\kappa\xi + kx \leqslant M, \tag{5}$$

where κ depends on the intensity of cultivation μ, while k is constant. In case of (5) being a strict inequality we have an excess supply of capital services, so that the price of capital services q (that is rp) vanishes. This rule of pricing is referred to as *the rule of free goods* applied to capital services.

Similarly, we have for labour

$$\lambda\xi + lx \leqslant N \tag{6}$$

with λ depending on μ and l being constant. In this market, too, the rule of free goods prevails. That is to say, where (6) is a strict inequality, w is set at zero.

Finally, we have the same demand–supply conditions in the Walrasian economy too. They may, of course, be written in exactly the same forms:

$$\kappa\xi + kx \leqslant M, \tag{5'}$$

$$\lambda\xi + lx \leqslant N \tag{6'}$$

In this case, however, we assume that input coefficients, κ and λ of the consumption-good industry and k and l of the capital-good industry, are all constant. The rule of free goods prevails both in (5′) and (6′).

3. Ricardo and Walras

Before we proceed to the Keynesian economy let us examine how the Ricardian and Walrasian economies work. We begin with Ricardo, whose model described in the previous section is now restated in terms of seven inequalities or equations:

$\pi = [w + p\delta\theta + r(w + p\theta)]d\mu/d\eta$	the price–cost equation for agriculture,	(1)
$\pi\xi = [w\lambda + p\alpha + r)w\lambda + pk)]\xi + R$	the rent equation,	(1*)
$p \leqslant wl + pa + r(wl + pk)$	the price–cost condition for capital goods,	(2)
$\pi\bar{\xi} = w(\lambda\xi + lx)$	the wage theory,	(3)
$\Delta\bar{\xi} + px = p(\alpha\xi + ax) + r[w(\lambda\xi + lx) + p(\kappa\xi + kx)]$	Say's law,	(4)
$\kappa\xi + kx \leqslant M$	the demand–supply condition for capital,	(5)
$\lambda\xi + lx \leqslant N$	the demand–supply condition for labour.	(6)

Note that $\lambda = \mu/\eta$, $\alpha = \delta\theta\mu/\eta$, $\kappa = \theta\mu/\eta$. Where (2), (3), (5) or (6) is established as a strict inequality, the corresponding variable, x, π, q, w takes on the value 0, respectively, by the rule of profitability or by the rule of free goods. Note that q equals rp.

Let us now be concerned with finding a general equilibrium of full employment of capital and labour. By definition, the capital–labour ratio of agriculture, κ/λ, is equal to θ which is compared with the corresponding ratio of the capital-good industry, k/l, which is denoted by h. We make an assumption that $h<\theta$, which is not essential for the following analysis. H designates the aggregate capital–labour ratio, M/N, which is assumed to be between θ and h.

Suppose both (5) and (6) hold with equality. Dividing (5) by (6) we obtain

$$\theta y + h(1-y) = H$$

where $y = \lambda\xi/(\lambda\xi + lx)$. Solving, we obviously have

$$y = \frac{H-h}{\theta - h}$$

from which we obtain

$$\lambda\xi = l\frac{y}{1-y}x$$

Substituting from this into equation (6), we find that x is determined as

$$lx = N(1-y).$$

Therefore, $\lambda\xi = Ny$.

On the other hand, the total output of agriculture ξ equals the output per acre, η, multiplied by the acreage of cultivated land, v. Substituting this into the above equation and remembering the definition of λ, we finally have

$$\mu v = Ny \tag{7}$$

Now let μ be μ^0, that is the maximum number of workers who can be employed on one acre of land without diminishing output per worker, η/μ. If μ exceeds μ^0, the marginal productivity of labour declines; so $d\eta/d\mu < \eta^0/\mu^0$, while $d\eta/d\mu = \eta^0/\mu^0$ at $\mu = \mu^0$. It is clear that v^0 defined as

$$v^0 = Ny/\mu^0$$

represents the area of land that is needed to produce the full-employment output by employing μ^0 workers per acre. If v^0 does not exceed T, the production by using μ^0 workers per acre and cultivating v^0 acres of land in total is feasible; production will actually be made at $\mu = \mu^0$ and $v = v^0$ and full-employment equilibrium will be established. In this case $d\mu/d\eta = \mu^0/\eta^0$ in the price–cost equation (1). Comparing it with (1*) we obtain $R = 0$.

Substituting from $d\mu/d\eta = \mu^0/\eta^0$ and bearing in mind the definitions of λ, α and κ, the price–cost equation for agriculture (1) may be put in the form:

$$\pi = w\lambda + p\alpha + r(w\lambda + p\kappa). \tag{1}$$

This, together with

$$p = wl + p\alpha + r(wl + p\kappa) \tag{2}$$

determines p and r, because π is fixed at 1 by normalization and the real wage rate w is determined by equation (3) and equation (6) at

$$w = \bar{\xi}/N. \tag{8}$$

Where the w determined in this way is too high, the equations (1) and (2) above are not compatible with a non-negative value of r. Hence either (1) or (2) must be inequality. We can show that in order for r to remain non-negative, condition (2) must hold with strict inequality, while (1) remains an equation.[5] Hence $x = 0$ and M and N are entirely devoted to the production of corn. We then have

$$\kappa\xi < M \text{ and } \lambda\xi = N \tag{9}$$

because $\theta(=\kappa/\lambda) < H(=M/N)$ by assumption. We thus have a general equilibrium where capital stock is underutilized while workers are fully employed.

On the other hand, if $v^0 > T$, cultivation by μ^0 workers per acre is not feasible because of the lack of land. Then μ will be determined by (7) as:

$$\mu^* = Ny/T$$

Thus in (1) $d\mu/d\eta$ is fixed at a value corresponding to $\mu = \mu^*$. Since this value of $d\mu/d\eta$ is smaller than μ^*/η^*, R is positive by virtue of the equation (1*) with $\lambda = \mu^*/\eta^*$, $\alpha = \delta\theta\mu^*/\eta^*$ and $\kappa = \theta\mu^*/\eta^*$. Once $d\mu/d\eta$ is determined at the point of $\mu = \mu^*$, equations (1) and (3) determine p and r, provided w is given by (8) and π is set at 1. Where r thus determined is non-negative, the values of all the variables determined above give a full-employment equilibrium set of solutions. If r is negative, we can show that condition (2) has to be weakened into an inequality in order to keep r non-negative. In the same way as we have seen above for the case $\mu = \mu^0$, we will find that (9) is obtained. While the labour market is in a state of full-employment equilibrium, there remains an excess supply in the capital market.

We can finally show that these equilibrium values of the variables do not conflict with Say's law (4). In fact, where (1*), (2), (3) all hold true, (4) too is satisfied. The economy has enough savings to finance the investment that is required for general equilibrium.

[5] In the case of (1) being turned into inequality, ξ is zero, so that we have $kx = M$ and $xl < N$ because $H < h$. Unemployment of labour thus obtained contradicts (8), which is derived by assuming that there is no unemployment of labour.

So far we have assumed that $\theta \leqslant H \leqslant h$. Where $h < H$, we can show that we have

$$k\xi < M, \lambda\xi = N, \text{ and } x = 0$$

in the state of equilibrium. In this case the capital stock is relatively more abundant than labour, so that full employment of labour is realized, but an excess capacity remains. In the opposite case of $H < \theta$, general equilibrium requires

$$kx = M, lx < N \text{ and } \xi = 0$$

Thus we have unemployment of labour that may be called technical unemployment, because it occurs since workers are equipped only with a stock of capital insufficient for employing all existing workers in either agriculture or the capital-good industry. We may conclude our examination of the Ricardian economy by saying that, except where technical unemployment may occur, we always have full employment of labour.

Let us now turn to Walras. The Walrasian economy is in a state of general equilibrium if the following six inequalities are all fulfilled.

$\pi \leqslant w\lambda + p\alpha + rp\kappa$	the price–cost condition for the consumption-good industry,	(1′)
$p \leqslant wl + pa + rpk$	the price–cost condition for the capital-good industry,	(2′)
$\pi\xi = w(\lambda\xi + lx)$	the demand–supply condition for consumption goods,	(3′)
$px = p(\alpha\xi + ax) + rp(\kappa\xi + kx)$	Say's law,	(4′)
$\kappa\xi + kx \leqslant M$	the demand–supply condition for capital,	(5′)
$\lambda\xi + lx \leqslant N$	the demand–supply condition for labour.	(6′)

The argument that establishes the existence of equilibrium for the Ricardian economy can *mutatis mutandis* be applied to the Walrasian economy too. There is a state of general equilibrium in which all six conditions above are satisfied, and, in particular, workers are always fully employed, except for those unemployed technically. It should be noted that this equilibrium is obtained because the rule of profitability and the rule of free goods are both effective in the economy, as they are in the Ricardian economy. The former implies that no output is produced in an industry in which supernormal profits are negative, while the latter means that if excess supply of a commodity or a factor of production cannot be removed, its price is set as low as zero.

It is true, however, that there is a difference between the Ricardian and

Walrasian models, that is the replacement of the wage-fund theory by the theory of inter-sectoral repercussions as is shown by the fact that (3′), rather than (3), is a member of the model. At first sight it looks to be a small change but in fact it has far-reaching effects. It has caused a drastic change in economists' views concerning the effects that an adjustment of wages may produce. Before the advent of Keynes the change had not revealed its full implications, because both the Ricardian and Walrasian models yield a more or less similar sort of equilibrium due to the rule of profitability and the rule of free goods being common to both models. However, once Say's law has been denied by Keynes and full-employment equilibrium is not automatically realized, the difference in the view of the wage adjustment becomes significant.

At this point let us introduce the concept of the full-employment curve. It is a curve that is traced out on a plane with the horizontal axis being the rate of growth and the vertical axis being the real wage rate. In view of the equation of the wage-fund theory (3), full employment is obtained where

$$\frac{1}{w}\bar{\xi}=N \tag{10}$$

(Note that we take $\pi=1$, so that w stands for the real wage rate.) The real wage rate that establishes this equation is referred to as the full-employment real-wage rate and is denoted by $\bar{w}$. Obviously if $w>\bar{w}$, we have an excess supply of labour and vice versa. As $\bar{w}$ is independent of the rate of growth, the full-employment curvage is a horizontal line through $\bar{w}$.

On the other hand, in the Walrasian model where ξ is flexibly adjusted according to the demand–supply equation

$$\xi=w(\lambda\xi+lx)$$

(again π is fixed at 1), the full employment of labour is obtained where

$$(\lambda\frac{wl}{1-w\lambda}+l)\,x=N$$

Therefore, we have

$$\frac{l}{1-w\lambda}gM=N \tag{10′}$$

where $g=x/M$ represents the gross rate of growth of capital goods. We can trace out the full-employment curve on the plane in which we have w and g as two axes. We designate the full-employment wage rate corresponding to $\bar{g}$ as $\bar{w}$; $\bar{w}$ is not constant but declines where $\bar{g}$ increases.

We then have a surprising result from the above equation to the effect that if $w > \bar{w}$ an excess demand, rather than an excess supply as we have in the Ricardian model, will prevail in the labour market, while a cut in the real wage, $w < \bar{w}$, will create an excess supply of labour. Classical and neoclassical economists would thus assume completely opposite attitudes towards a change in the real wages.

A parallel analysis will lead us to a similar observation concerning the curve of full utilization of capital. Substituting the equation of the wage-fund theory or the Walrasian demand–supply equation of the consumption goods into the full utilization equation of capital, we may write, in view of the definition of g, the curve of the full utilization of capital in the form:

$$\frac{1}{w}\theta\bar{\xi} + (h-\theta)\, lgM = M \quad \text{for the Ricardian economy} \tag{11}$$

or

$$\left[\frac{w\kappa}{1-w\lambda} + h\right] lgM = M \quad \text{for the Walrasian economy,} \tag{11'}$$

respectively, where $\theta = \kappa/\lambda$ and $h = k/l$. Let w^* be the wage rate that establishes the full utilization of capital, (11) or (11′), with g fixed at an arbitrary level g^*. With g fixed at g^*, we have from (11) that there is an excess supply of capital where $w > w^*$, while (11′) implies the opposite relationship, that is an excess demand prevails in the case of $w > w^*$ and $g = g^*$.

In the case of the Ricardian model, we find from (10) and (11) that both labour and capital are in a state of excess supply where w is very high and exceeds both of $\bar{w}$ and w^*. Conversely, if w is too low to reach $\bar{w}$ and w^*, there is an excess demand in both labour and capital markets. In the case of w being between $\bar{w}$ and w^*, there will be an excess supply of labour (or capital), and there will be an excess demand for capital (or labour) if $\bar{w} < w^*$ (or $\bar{w} > w^*$). In the case of the Walrasian model, on the contrary, we have an excess supply in the two markets if $w < \bar{w}$ and $w < w^*$, while an excess demand if $w > \bar{w}$ and $w > w^*$. Where $\bar{w} < w < w^*$ (or $\bar{w} > w > w^*$), we have an excess labour demand for labour (or capital) and an excess supply of capital (or labour).

Let the area where both capital and labour are in excess supply (or excess demand) be designated by A (or C) and the area where labour is in excess supply (or excess demand) while capital is in excess demand (or excess supply) be designated by B (or D). Let the point of intersection of the two full-employment curves of capital and labour be W. Then the areas, A, B, C, D are located anti-clockwise or clockwise around W according to whether the regime is Ricardian or Walrasian. In the next section we shall see that this divergence of view between classical and neoclassical economists concerning the location of these areas is likely to become significant in an economy where Say's law does not hold and full employment is hardly realized.

4. Keynes

In the Keynesian model the rule of free goods is ruled out in factor markets, especially for labour. This is done by introducing an investment function, which consists of a part of autonomous investment and a part of induced investment. Induced investment and savings will change when the outputs of the two industries change. Investment and savings will be equated with each other after necessary adjustments have all been made, and the equilibrium activity levels, ξ and x, depend on the level of autonomous investment. In the special case of the part of induced investment being zero, which we assume below for the sake of simplicity, savings are adjusted to investment, which is kept constant. Thus we have

$$i=(\alpha\xi+ax)+r(\kappa\xi+kx) \tag{4''}$$

where i stands for the autonomous investment and the right-hand side for gross savings. Where all the remaining conditions of the Keynesian model below are fulfilled, it can be shown that gross savings equal the output of the capital-good industry, x. Thus we obtain $i=x$ from (4″), that is to say capital goods that are required for the autonomous investment i will be produced.

When i is set at a level that is lower than the Walrasian equilibrium output of capital goods, we then have an excess supply in capital and labour markets. Keynes assumes that the rule of free goods does not prevail in factor markets, that is the price of capital services $q(=rp)$ and the wage rate w do not vanish even though conditions (5″) and (6″) are established with strict inequality, '$<$'. Moreover, once i is set at a positive level, x and ξ are both positive. Then there is no possibility that the price–cost condition of either of the two industries will become a strict inequality. They are sold at the prices fixed by (1″) and (2″).

We may now put the Keynesian equilibrium conditions in the following form:

$\pi=w\lambda+p\alpha+rp\kappa$	the price–cost equations,	(1″)
$p=wl+pa+rpk$		(2″)
$\xi=w(\alpha\xi+lx)$	the demand–supply equations,	(3″)
$i=(\alpha\xi+ax)+r(\kappa\xi+kx)$		(4″)
$\kappa\xi+kx\leqslant M$	undercapacity	(5″)
$\lambda\xi+lx\leqslant N$	underemployment	(6″)

It should be noted that the formula $\xi = wlx/(1 - w\lambda)$ derived from (3″) is the formula of Keynes's theory of the multiplier for the special case of no worker saving and no capitalist consuming. It should also be noted that the Keynesian and Walrasian models are very similar, except for the fact that the former allows for an independent investment function and denies the automatic investment of savings as well as the rule of free goods for factors, whilst the latter has no investment function and assumes the rule of free goods. Consequently Keynesian economists take the view that a sufficiently low wage rate creates both unemployment of labour and idle capital, provided that the rate of capital accumulation g^* is given at a certain positive level. It is of course true that in the opposite case of a sufficiently high wage rate they will expect an excess demand in factor markets, so that it will result in an inflation of prices.

The Keynesian economy works in the following way. First x is fixed by i. Then by the multiplier theory (4″) ξ is determined provided w takes on a certain value such that $1 > w\lambda$. If w (or $g = x/M$) is set lower than a value determined by g (or w), both (5″) and (6″) would hold with strict inequality. In spite of the excess supply thus created, the wage rate w is not adjusted in the Keynesian economy, so that full-employment temporary equilibrium is generally impossible. Moreover, this unfavourable result cannot be removed even if we take into account a reasonable adjustment of i, for example that according to the adaptable acceleration principle. This principle was introduced by Harrod (1948) to dynamize the Keynesian model. It implies that if the demand for capital equals the existing stock M as a result of investment at the rate $i = x$, then entrepreneurs will be left in a state of mind in which they are prepared to invest at the same rate of investment per capital, i/M, as they have been doing, while if the demand for M exceeds or falls short of M, they have to adjust upwards or downwards. Therefore, i/M is increased or decreased accordingly. This Harrodian premise may be formulated as

$$\text{sign of} \frac{d}{dt}\frac{i}{M} = \text{sign of } (M_D - M), \tag{12}$$

where M_D represents the demand for M, which is $\kappa\xi + kx$.

In view of the multiplier theory (3″) the ratio of the demand for capital to its supply may be written as

$$\frac{M_D}{M} = \frac{\kappa\xi + kx}{M} = \left[\frac{\kappa wl}{1 - w\lambda} + k\right]\frac{i}{M}.$$

Therefore, as long as w remains unchanged, M_D/M becomes smaller and smaller by virtue of (12), once M_D is set to be less than M at the beginning.

Similarly, we have for labour

$$\frac{N_D}{M}=\frac{\lambda\xi+lx}{N}=\frac{l}{1-w\lambda}\frac{i}{M}\frac{M}{N},$$

so that the situation in the labour market is worsened through this process of i/M being decreased, unless M/N increases sufficiently. In any case, i/M will eventually be lower than the rate of depreciation, δ. Then M starts to decrease; therefore, unemployment, $N-N_D$, will increase unless N decreases more than M.

This instability in the full-employment equilibrium is often referred to as the property of the Harrodian knife-edge. It is a new view of equilibrium that totally diverges from the view of classical and neoclassical economists as to how the economy works over time according to their premises. I have examined the Ricardian and Walrasian dynamic processes in detail elsewhere;[6] we now only briefly summarize below the Walrasian process, which is simpler than the Ricardian one.

Prior to showing the stability of the process, it should be noted that we are only concerned with the case of $h<H<\theta$. As before H stands for M/N. At the point of temporary equilibrium (5′) and (6′) hold with equality. Then, in the same way as we have obtained an equivalent equation in the Ricardian case before, we have

$$y=\frac{\lambda\xi}{\lambda\xi+lx}=\frac{H-h}{\theta-h}.$$

Therefore,

$$\frac{x}{M}=\frac{1}{l}\frac{N}{M}(1-y)=\frac{1}{l}\frac{\theta(N/M)-1}{\theta-h}.$$

At the beginning of each period where M/N is given, then the equilibrium value of x/M is determined by the above equation. We assume that the labour force N expands at a constant rate ρ^*. If x/M thus determined is greater than (or falls short of) $\delta+\rho^*$, δ being the rate of depreciation, then M/N will increase (or decrease). Hence by the above formula x/M decreases if $x/M>\delta+\rho^*$, while it increases where we have a converse inequality. x/M eventually approaches $\delta+\rho^*$ and a balanced growth of capital and labour will be established (see Solow, 1956).

In the case of the Ricardian economy, the structure is more complicated. First, diminishing returns to scale prevail in agriculture. Secondly, the model contains an element of time-lag due to the wage-fund theory. Thirdly, Ricardo assumes flexible population growth. Population grows

[6] See Morishima (1989).

where the real wage rate is above its subsistence level w_s. It will decrease if $w < w_s$, while it is stationary at $w = w_s$.

Ricardo has conjectured that the wage rate regulated by M/N will eventually approach the subsistence level w_s, at which point no more change in M and N is created, and the economy is settled in a stationary state. It is true that Ricardo himself has tried and proved this convergence theorem. However, it seems to me that his proof is incomplete. In order to prove the theorem, some additional assumptions may be required. In chapter 10 of my *Ricardo's Economics* (Morishima, 1989) I have specified the function of the shape of the rate of growth of the labour force, $\rho(w)$, in order to establish the convergence to the stationary state. In any case it may be concluded that under Say's law, which prevails in both Ricardian and Walrasian models, the sequence of temporary equilibria is stable and the economy comes, in the long run, nearer and nearer to a stationary equilibrium point or a steady balanced growth path. Without Say's law, however, the economy may be unstable and unemployment of labour and capital becomes greater as time goes on.

5. Identification of the epochs

It has been seen that the Ricardian model is a model for an economy where (1) the wage-fund theory is valid and (2) Say's law prevails, while the Walrasian model is based on (2) but gets rid of (1) and the Keynesian is free from both (1) and (2). Ricardo's economics, emphasizing the role of agriculture, fits the economy at an early stage of development, when agriculture is still a significant sector of the economy. In the case of Great Britain, the ratio of population engaged in agriculture (including forestry and fishing) to that engaged in the manufacturing industry (including mining) was 1.21 in 1801, 1.09 in 1811, 0.74 in 1821, 0.60 in 1831, 0.55 in 1841 and 0.51 in 1851. Afterwards it rapidly decreased to the level of 0.19 in 1901; it further declined to 0.10 in 1951.[7] In terms of output, the share of agricultural output in the total gross national income, which was 36 per cent in 1811, was reduced to 20 per cent by 1851; it thereafter rapidly diminished to 10 per cent in 1881 and 6 per cent in 1901.[8] From these observations we may conclude that in those days when Ricardo was preparing his *Principles* agriculture was still significant in Britain, and it continued to be a sector that could not be ignored until the repeal of the Corn Laws in 1846.

In the second half of the nineteenth century during which period the

[7] See Deane and Cole (1967, p. 142). From this we also obtain the figures: 0.18 for 1911, 0.15 for 1921 and 0.13 for 1931.

[8] See Mitchell and Deane (1962, p. 366).

Ricardian model became more and more inappropriate, the Walrasian model based on simultaneous inter-industrial relationship increased in influence. This transition from the Ricardian to the Walrasian paradigm took place, at least partly, because Ricardo himself advocated that it was beneficial to the British to open their economy to foreign agriculturists. It is under his principle of comparative advantage that Britain's agriculture was replaced by European and other countries' agriculture or by the agriculture of Britain's colonies. By the last decades of the last century, it had been degraded to a minor sector; thus a new model that neglects agriculture becomes more useful in examining the working of the economy. The transition was therefore inevitable once Ricardo's policy had been accepted. It is indeed the very success of Ricardian theory that caused, or at least stimulated, the decline of the Ricardian-type economy.

As for Say's law it is very difficult to determine the degree of its applicability to the real world. Actual investment consists of the following three elements: the first, denoted by i_1, is that part of investment that is made by those capitalists who are themselves entrepreneurs. They will invest exactly the amount that they have saved. The second part, i_2, is the part made by entrepreneurs by borrowing money from banks or capitalists or issuing new shares or bonds. It is decided by the entrepreneurs' investment function $i_2(\ldots)$. The third part, i_3, is the autonomous investment made by the public sector.

We refer to i_1 as the Say's law part and $i_2(\ldots)+i_3$ as the Anti-Say's law part. The ratio of the anti-Say's law part to total investment gives the degree of applicability of Say's law. We term S defined as

$$S = 1 - \frac{i_2(\ldots)+i_3}{i}$$

Say's law index. Where Say's law is perfectly valid, so that $i_2(\ldots)+i_3=0$, S takes on the value of 1, while where anti-Say's law is perfectly correct with $i_1=0$, S is equal to 0.

Obviously, S^* defined as $1-i_3/i$ gives an upper limit to S. On the basis of British historical statistics, S^* is considered as taking on an average value of 82 per cent for the years 1900–20, 70 per cent in the period 1921–38, and 55 per cent in the post-war period.[9] As for the years 1861–99, S^* is roughly estimated as high as 85 per cent. It is clearly observable that there is a declining tendency in S^*. True Say's law index S will *a fortiori* trace out a stronger declining trend, because $i_2(\ldots)/i$ is expected to have been larger and larger during the nineteenth and twentieth centuries. We may thus

[9] See *The British Economy Key Statistics 1900–1970*, Times Newspapers Ltd., p. 13, and Mitchell and Deane (1962, pp. 367 and 396).

conclude that the actual economy is moving from a Say's law world to an anti-Say's law world (see Morishima, 1989, chapter 11).

The statistics show a considerable drop in S^* after the First World War. This suggests that Say's law seems to have become inappropriate for modelling the economy after 1920. If my conjecture is right, we may say that the economy is on the side of Say's law rather than anti-Say's law throughout the nineteenth century. More specifically, the period 1810–50 is the age of Ricardian economics while the period 1851–1913 is the age of the Walrasian economy. I make this identification because throughout these two periods Say's law was not particularly unrealistic and in the first period agriculture still played a significant role, while in the second it was reduced, especially in the relative sense, to a negligible part of the economy. The epoch beginning in 1920 is definitely that of Keynesian economics. One may conclude that the order of succession of Ricardian, Walrasian and Keynesian models in the history of economic thought corresponds to the historical transformation of the British economy. We can confirm that economists, or at least great economists, have, consciously or unconsciously, responded healthily to historical changes in the object of investigation. This is true in spite of the fact that some or many economists regard these models as alternatives to each other and make a discrimination in favour of one against the others from the viewpoint of the problems to be investigated or from that of the logical generality of the models.

We thus have a sequence of economic theories each of which is constructed, as a kind of snapshot, to explain the economy at a particular stage. On the level of theory, a change from one regime to another is a sudden, discontinuous change, so that it is frequently called a revolution, such as the neoclassical or Keynesian revolutions, while at the level of actual economic history the transition from one age to another is smooth and continuous. Unfortunately, at the present stage of development of economics, there is no dynamic theory of structural evolution that can pursue a smooth transition from one structure to the next continuously. It is indeed difficult to theorize an object of investigation that is quickly changing in its basic features; we are not provided with enough repetition of similar phenomena, on the basis of observations of which we may construct a theory.

Of course, there are a few hints by means of which one might be able to explain a transition of the economy from one regime to another. As has been briefly pointed out in relation to the Ricardian regime, there is the case in which the adoption of a particular economic policy may give rise to a fatal structural change, such as a decline of agriculture, and the economy may be transformed into one with a completely different structure. It is also conceivable that the transition from regime A to B may be caused by a trigger effect due to the invention of an important new commodity. A new industry producing the new commodity enters economy A and replaces some of the old industries. The rule of profitability works; those industries whose rates of profit are lower than that of the new industry are closed down. The remaining industries, together with the new one, will form a new system B.

There is a third idea too, which has been familiar to economists for a long period. It can be particularly useful in explaining the transition from a Walrasian to a Keynesian regime. Economic competition among firms will inevitably create winners and losers. The former will become bigger, while the latter will go bankrupt. In order to expand a firm, its owners must raise money by selling new shares to moneyed people or to the general public, and its owners, original or new, will eventually lose the power of controlling the firm, which goes into the hands of general managers or entrepreneurs. These may themselves be managers or hired men. In any case, there develops a separation between capitalists as owners of the firms, and entrepreneurs as managers and decision makers concerning investment. This gives rise to an increase in the ratio $i_2(\ldots)/i$ of the formula of the Say's law index S. This, together with an autonomous increase in i_3/i, would let Say's law be entirely inappropriate to the era of the economy of big firms. We thus have some explanations of economic transition from one phase to another, but they can hardly be called a theory of structural change.

References

Dasgupta, A.K. (1988) *Epochs of Economic Theory*, Basil Blackwell, Oxford and New York.

Deane, P., and Cole, W.A. (1967) *British Economic Growth 1688–1959*, 2nd edn, Cambridge University Press, Cambridge.

Hahn, F.H. (1984) 'The Neo-Ricardians', in *Equilibrium and Macroeconomics*, Basil Blackwell, Oxford, pp. 602–16.

Harrod, R.F. (1948) *Towards a Dynamic Economics*, Macmillan, London.

Keynes, J.M. (1936) *The General Theory of Employment, Interest and Money*, Macmillan, London.

Mitchell, B.R., and Deane, P. (1962) *Abstract of British Historical Statistics*, Cambridge University Press, Cambridge.

Morishima, M. (1989) *Ricardo's Economics*, Cambridge University Press, Cambridge.

Ricardo, D. (1951) *On the Principles of Political Economy and Taxation* (1st edn 1817; 2nd edn 1819; 3rd edn 1821), vol. I of *Works and Correspondence of David Ricardo*, ed. P. Sraffa, Cambridge University Press, Cambridge.

Solow, R.M. (1956) 'A Contribution to the Theory of Economic Growth', *Quarterly Journal of Economics*, 70, pp. 65–94.

Uzawa, H. (1961) 'On A Two-Sector Model of Economic Growth', *The Review of Economic Studies*, 78, pp. 40–7.

Walras, L. (1874) *Eléments d'économie politique pure*, Corbaz, Lausanne; English translation: *Elements of Pure Economics*, ed. W. Jaffé, Allen and Unwin, London, 1954.

8 Production process and dynamic economics

NICHOLAS GEORGESCU-ROEGEN

1. An epistemological exordium

Traditionally, a living creature is expediently defined as an element of nature that feeds itself, defends itself and reproduces itself. The thought that this characterization naturally applies to humans as well opens the way to a more telling substitution, namely that the essential activities of any life-bearing structure are production, consumption, self-defence and self-reproduction. Clearly, any such a structure must produce the elements on which it feeds or with which it defends itself. Production is an essential activity of all living world.[1] Take an oyster (which Plato considered to be the most remote animal from a human); it is engaged in production as it keeps opening and closing its valves to catch the micro-organism on which it feeds. Even a green plant – not to forget – produces its 'food', primarily carbohydrates and proteins, from other 'factors'.

Production of all living creatures other than the human species is an activity governed by instincts, by innate tropisms. The human condition is essentially different. Like all life-bearing species, humankind has evolved biologically; it still does. By contrast, however, the evolution of humankind has not been limited to soma, to the mutations of our biological organs. A million years ago the earliest of our ancestors began to use for everyday needs things that were not part of their soma. They gradually became accustomed to using, say, a club picked up from the woods in order to add more power to the arm. It was through such a simple change at first in the manner of production that the human species embarked on a new and (as it proved later) crucial evolution, namely the exosomatic evolution.

Ever since, humans have been guided to supplement their somatic organs by countless exosomatic – detachable – ones. I consider them 'organs' because a mind different from ours might not distinguish between, say, a

[1] Georgescu-Roegen (1986).

hand that breaks bread and a knife that cuts it. By now these exosomatic organs enable us to run faster than a cheetah, swim faster than any fish and fly higher and faster than any bird, in spite of the fact that we are not endowed with the heart and the muscles of cheetahs, nor with the gills and fins of fish, nor with the hollow bones and the wings of birds.

There is still another upshot of the exosomatic evolution. The minds of natural scientists have been tormented by the question of the origin of the universe or of the origin of life on earth (some, even of the origin of mathematics). Sociologists have also sought an explanation for the origin of society. Only economists seem to have shown no interest in how the economic process began (although the origin of economics has been a constant object of debate). Yet the answer is in hand: because the exosomatic organs are desirable their production increased and spread, and because they are detachable they soon began to form the object of trade.

And because relativism seems the dominant tenor of our day, I should not fail to consider the assertions that in production many animals differ only in kind, not in essence, from *homo sapiens*. In support, our attention is directed especially to the behaviour of many primates. Hard to explain, however, is that the champions of relativism have failed to mention other instances even more impressive. Think of the bees or the beavers, which are clear tool users. A truly striking case is supplied by a Galapagos woodpecker finch (*Cactospiza pallidus*). On discovering a worm inside a tree trunk, that astonishing craftsman looks around for a cactus spine of the appropriate length to reach the worm, cuts it and uses it to bring out its prey. That finch does not only use an exosomatic tool, the spine, but it also makes it. Notwithstanding, these facts and many others of the same nature do not bring any water to the relativist's mill. For humans not only use tools for getting food or for providing comfort, they also make tools to be used for making other tools. Henri Bergson pointed out long ago that humans are the only animals that 'make tools to make tools'. Even in the evolution of *homo* this step represented a momentous mutation. Ever since, 'machines to make machines to make machines' has been the basis of humankind's production activity, as Joseph A. Schumpeter noted with his characteristic penetrating esprit.[2]

It is thus in total reason that production is a fundamentally important activity of ours, far more important than all others. Certainly, intended and planned production is a human activity far older and, moreover, far more critical than participation in a stock exchange market. In addition, several important phenomena of the economic life have their origin in the

[2] More on this theme in *idem*. See also the authoritative essay by J.B.S. Haldane (1956).

production sector. Nothing therefore should be added to make us realize that the production sector needs the preferred attention of the economist. And in a domain as complex as that of production no amount of carefulness could be enough in the approach.

That production of humans or of any other biological species consists of a material process is a truth not susceptible of any formal proof: it is an elemental truth. But what needs unparsimonious emphasis is that no definition of 'process' is to be found anywhere. Alfred North Whitehead, for an illustrious example, does not define it even in his celebrated opus *Process and Reality* (1929). Nonetheless, we do understand what is generally meant by 'the political process', by 'the inventing process', by 'the atmospheric process' and by other similar expressions. But 'process' is also a term much abused, more so than any other of our intellectual disciplines.

When used with sufficient circumspection 'process' constitutes a member of the most numerous class of concepts that are absolutely necessary for our mental contact with reality. It is the class of dialectical concepts, a class discretely distinct from that of the arithmomorphic ones. A dialectical concept always overlaps with its contrary over a dialectical penumbra within which both A and non-A are true, as is, for instance, the frequent case of a political constitution that has both democratic and dictatorial elements. By contrast, an arithmomorphic concept is separated from its contrary by an absolutely vacuous boundary: *tertium non datur*, if we remember that tenacious dogma of the orthodox logic.[3]

Obviously, no variant of the orthodox logic could possibly handle dialectical concepts.[4] This does not mean that correct reasoning with dialectical concepts is impossible, only it requires a substantial dose of what Blaise Pascal called *esprit de finesse*. Numerous illustrious writers, not only Karl Marx, can readily be cited in evidence. 'Not only are we aware of particular yellows, but if we have seen a sufficient number of yellows and we have sufficient intelligence, we are aware of the universal *yellows*; this universal is the subject in such judgments as "yellow differs from blue" or "yellow resembles blue less than green does"', is the dialectical way in which none other than Bertrand Russell expresses himself in his *Mysticism and Logic*. And Bertrand Russell was certainly not an advocate of any Hegelism.

Undoubtedly, arithmomorphism is an indispensable element of *modus*

[3] For details on this conception of dialectics versus arithmomorphism – an epistemological position that bears directly on the present argument – see my *Analytical Economics* (1966) and *The Entropy Law and the Economic Process* (1971).

[4] A prompt review of that volume by John T. Rader (*Quarterly Review of Economics and Business*, 1966) was proof that I was not flogging a dead horse. If I flogged any horse, that horse is still very much alive and going very strong.

operandi in science, yet not in every special discipline. Dialectics, however, is indispensable in any science, even in mathematics (*pace* the Vienna Circle). Our mind and its relation with what is outside it is such that a non-crippled knowledge needs without fail both dialectics and arithmomorphism. In the introduction of my *Analytical Economics* I opined that 'there is a limit to what we can do with numbers, as there is a limit to what we can do without them'. I did not know then that unwittingly I was echoing one of Blaise Pascal's famous tenets: the greatest absurdity is to rely only on strict reason or on no reason at all.[5]

An immediate corollary of Pascal's tenet is that the dialectical structure cannot be metamorphized into an arithmomorphic one, nor vice versa. The repulsion between these two fundamental modes of human thought is absolute, a kind not encountered in any other phenomenal domain. The failure of the centuries-old intellectual struggle to set the concept of probability on an arithmomorphic foundation is an eloquent proof of that repulsion: probability is essentially a truly dialectical concept.[6]

2. The analytical representation of production process

2.1 What is involved in setting up analytical representations?

Not only one of the pioneers of modern mathematical economics, W. Stanley Jevons, but even Joseph Schumpeter in our own time, argued that the quantitative elements are structurally present in a far greater measure than even in physics: the ordinary economic activity supplies by its very nature the numerical coefficients needed by its student. To obtain an analytical description of as many economic phenomena as possible was therefore a legitimate interest.[7]

Certainly, production, virtually a physico-chemical process, ought to have been the first choice of preference. But history, cunning as usual, has

[5] Twenty-five years ago while writing the 'Introduction' for my *Analytical Economics* (1966) I said in passing that a new Aristotle might set (if possible at all) dialectical reasoning on as solid a basis as that of the traditional logic. By a strange coincidence, one year before my volume reached the bookstores, L.A. Zadeh ('Fuzzy Sets', *Information and Control*, 1965) set a claim, now endorsed by a legion of eager followers, for having established such a logic. The claim, however, is spurious. One needs to take a look at any cognate article to see that the fuzzy set is a purely mathematical abstract, hence, a total stranger to dialectics. The very pivot of the entire enterprise – the membership function $f_A(x)$ has no objective operational value.

[6] The definition of probability developed in Georgescu-Roegen (1971, pp. 52–9), although presented analytically, is in fact Hegelian, in that it simultaneously includes both the beginning and the end of one and the same thought.

[7] As should be clear by now, an arithmomorphic representation consists most of the time of a mathematical system. So, because of this strict association, to simplify the diction, in the following I shall use 'analytical' as a synonym of 'arithmomorphic'.

arranged it so that the first analytical achievement was the economic behaviour of the individual. Whether hailing from Francis Edgeworth or from the early Vilfredo Pareto, today we have little to quarrel about the ubiquitous formula of utility:

$$U = \phi(x, y, z, \ldots, w), \tag{1}$$

where all symbols are assumed to represent numbers representing measures.

Yet in this connection we should not fail to raise some questions that, at least to my knowledge, have not been asked. Those that I have in mind are epistemological and need to be answered to ensure that our formulae are valid analytical representations of the intended phenomena.

First what kind of function is ϕ? In mathematics there are several kinds. From its general use it is clear that ϕ is tacitly assumed to be a Dirichlet function, that is, such that to every combination of valid values of the arguments there corresponds a unique value for the function.[8] This means that the individual feels a definite satisfaction (expressed on a definite scale) from the use of any basket of commodities – a fairly innocuous descriptive proposition.[9]

More precarious is the Indifference Postulate, that, over a substantial domain, the individual (not any other factor) can say how much a positive Δx would compensate his satisfaction for a negative Δy. From this it does not follow only that ϕ is continuous, but that it has a special structure – the negative inclination of the indifference lines.[10]

The basic issues associated with the analytical representation of the individual economic behaviour do not yet come to an end with what I have just said. A most important object lesson for the mathematical economist is taught by the treatment of one of Pareto's ideas. Instead of bringing the individual to a questioning session, during which he would be endlessly asked which basket from a pair he or she would prefer (the basic information of Pareto's theory of choice), we could have a sleuth follow him or her in the market and report the quantities and the prices at which they were bought. Such information can be crystallized in a total differential equation

[8] Kline (1972, p. 950). In social disciplines 'function' is used, admissibly, as a dialectical concept. Paul B. Sears, thus, began his chairmanship of a session by stating that resources and population 'are a function of the pattern of culture'. See William L. Thomas (1956).

[9] It is not wholly innocuous because it takes the human to be a perfect instrument, which does not exist even in the physical domain. For the actual imperfection of human behaviour, see section 5 of my 1936 paper, reprinted as chapter 1 in *Analytical Economics* (1966).

[10] That postulate, which once was considered superfluous for the utility theory, is actually not necessary for the theory of demand. See my 1954 paper, chapter 5 in *Analytical Economics* (1966).

$$h_1 dx_1 + h_2 dx_2 + \ldots + h_n dx_n = 0. \tag{2}$$

from which, Pareto argued, by integration one can obtain a utility function such as ϕ. Almost immediately Vito Volterra, one of the great mathematicians of the epoch, objected that integration is always feasible only in the case of two commodities. Notwithstanding Pareto's effort to mend it, the reason why only in such an economic world Pareto would be correct remained for long a famous paradox.[11] Years later, Paul A. Samuelson claimed that on the basis of his superb Axiom of Revealed Preference equation (2) is integrable for any number of commodities.[12] It is because two vital principles, one mathematical, the other epistemological, have been from the outset disregarded that Samuelson's fascinating conception has failed, nay, it was stillborn.

By his objection, Volterra implied that

$$h_1(x, y)dx + h_2(x, y)dy = 0, \tag{3}$$

is always integrable if certain very feeble conditions are fulfilled. But to be mathematically correct, we should say that under the weak Cauchy–Lipschitz theorem $h(x, y) = c$ is an integral of (3) if for most points (X, Y) of the valid domain

$$(\partial h(X, Y)/\partial X)/(\partial h(X, Y)/\partial Y) = h_1(X, Y)/h_2(X, Y). \tag{4}$$

This may not be true for some points (X, Y) that are *singular* points for the function $h(x, y)$; they may often form a whole line.[13] Outside these points $h(x, y)$ has a definite value, but ordinarily not for any singularity. A very simple example: the integral function of $xdy - ydx = 0$, which is either $y/x = c$ or $x/y = c$, has a determinate value for all finite x and y. And a simple diagrammatic representation will show that through all points of the plane (x, y) passes only one integral curve, whereas through the origin $(x = 0, y = 0)$ there pass an infinite number.

The combinations of a budget with three commodities constitute a space of two dimensions. It was with the help of this space that I proved more than fifty years ago that non-integrability was there to stay, that even for two variables (2) does not supply an ophelimity function.[14]

Let me turn now to the epistemological peccancy. The contributors to

[11] The story is splendidly outlined in John Chipman (1971).

[12] The relevant papers are of 1938 and 1946, and are reprinted in Samuelson (1966), Part I, 1 and 9. [13] Kline (1972, pp. 717–21).

[14] My paper mentioned in note 10, above. Later, Samuelson (1966, Part I, 10), stirred by a recent paper by H. Houthakker (1950), retook my result and presented it in a tale of the kind only he is capable. Houthakker presented a generalization of the Revealed Preference Axiom on the basis of which he argued that the general equation (2) becomes integrable. The claim was already refuted by Figure 1–2a, of my 1936 paper (see note 9, above).

the theory of revealed preference have followed Paul A. Samuelson in taking it for granted that if (2) happens to be integrable, the integral varieties represent indifference varieties. However, this identification by itself is unwarranted, as I had warned in advance of the theory of revealed preference.[15] More recently I constructed an even clearer example to prove the fallacy. In a community of individuals with an identical homothetic utility function, (2) considered for the whole community is integrable irrespective of income distribution. But certainly those integral varieties cannot represent the community indifference varieties. As we know, a community indifference is not an operational relation.[16] The integral varieties are indifference varieties if and only if before sending the sleuth to spy on the consumer we already know from the interrogation session that a consumer has a Dirichlet utility function. This, I believe, was Pareto's position, which Volterra seems to have ignored. The issue emerged in somewhat altered form in Samuelson's idea of revealed preference, an epoch-making idea that has nonetheless been surrounded by continuous uneasy feelings on the part of the students engaged in it. This unfortunate condition would not have ensued had Samuelson explained from the outset what it was that he thought to be revealed. If the religious connotations of the verb are ignored, as they should be, one can reveal only a *pre-existing* thing. He might have thought that the preference revealed was the classical binary preference, in which case the problem of integrability would not have presented itself. But, as it seems more probable, he thought that what is revealed is an entirely different conception from the binary one. In this case, the new preference would be associated with a set belonging to a special family, not with a pair.[17]

I believe that the fact that most of the analytical representations used in mathematical economics suffer from the peccancies mentioned in the preceding paragraphs is responsible for the illfare of that discipline, which is reflected in great part over all economics. Indeed, great disarrays result when we subject the economic formulae to valid mathematical manipulations without any restriction and then transpose the results to actuality. For faulty analytical representations there is no bridge to serve this transposition.[18]

By the preceding remarks I sought to prepare the ground for the argument that follows.

[15] See the reference in note 9, above.

[16] Georgescu-Roegen (1975).

[17] Formally the relation of revealed preference of a over b is aP_Sb, where S is some set of a given family $\mathscr{F}$. See further developments in Georgescu-Roegen (1975).

[18] Georgescu-Roegen (1979).

2.2 *The Wicksteedian production function*

I have noted earlier that an analytical representation of production activity of some effect was proposed rather late in the development of our discipline. Only in 1894 did Philip H. Wicksteed introduce the concept of production function in an acme of imprecision:

The product being a function of the factors of production we have $P = f(a, b, c, \dots)$.

Wicksteed's simple symbolism has ever since been accepted as a valid representation of the production process by the entire economic profession. Although the formula was not subjected to any customary criticism, it has been tacitly assumed that it is a Dirichlet function. Because of its mathematical nature, it has formed the point of departure for one exercise after another, and these exercises have kept accumulating in the literature on economic production. Only a few writers have thought it necessary to specify the general nature of the symbols. The field was free for all ideas, so some have taken the symbols to represent quantities, which may be written as

$$Q = F(X, Y, Z, \dots). \tag{5}$$

A smaller group thought that the symbols must represent rates per unit of time, to be written for correspondence as

$$q = f(x, y, z, \dots). \tag{6}$$

In the preceding section we saw examples of economists' lack of respect for epistemological issues. Still another example is the fact that no economic theorist has been intrigued by the wide circulation of the two opposing definitions, (5) and (6). Even such a brilliant analyst as Ragnar Frisch in his *Theory of Production* used the two definitions on one and the same page (p. 43). Yet the opposition is prominent: quantity and rate per unit of time are not equivalent concepts, although by definition they satisfy the simple relations

$$Q = tq, \; X = tx, \; Y = ty, \; Z = tz, \; \dots, \tag{7}$$

which – we should not fail to mark well – are valid for any positive value of t. And if we accept, as has been the general usage, both (5) and (6) to be valid representations of the same production process, we obtain the following *identity*:

$$tq = tf(x, y, z, \dots) \equiv Q = F(tx, ty, tz, \dots) \tag{8}$$

from which by putting $t=1$ we get

$$f(x, y, z, \dots) \equiv F(x, y, z, \dots). \tag{9}$$

Hence (5) and (6) reduce to one and the same function and, moreover, this function is homogeneous of the first degree. Therefore, if any production process can be represented analytically by either (5) or (6), absolutely any production process must be indifferent to scale.

Having been exposed by a long rote to the perfect equivalence of (5) and (6), we have naturally become so convinced of its validity that we have at first been apt to disbelieve the surprising result. To wit, Don Patinkin, the *contre-rapporteur* of my paper at the Conference of the International Economic Association (Rome 1965), after stating laconically that he could not comment on my paper because it rested on a mathematical error, simply sat down. So incredible he must have found my findings.[19]

For the problem under discussion, we may recall that Samuelson argued that the homogeneity of the Wicksteedian production does not deserve any attention. His point is that we can neither prove nor disprove its presence, which makes me wonder how many mathematical formulae in economics can be proved or disproved by a fairly acceptable procedure. Samuelson also maintains that 'double all factors must double all product' is a meaningless assertion.[20] It is indeed, but only as long as we do not specify what we mean by 'factors'. This point is forcefully illustrated by the famous – the unreservedly famous – Cobb–Douglas formula,[21]

$$P = cL^a K^{1-a}, a < 1. \tag{10}$$

If both factors, labour and capital, are measured by their services over time, certainly doubling the time of their services will double P. Also, if P represents the product of a molecular industry composed of n identical firms (a situation familiar in the theory of supply), then doubling the number of firms will double the product. But if L and K are measured in some appropriate physical units, doubling them would not necessarily double P. What kind of production process would be governed by two decision-making factors?[22]

As we have seen, several economists have explicitly described the nature

[19] To be sure, soon after the conference Patinkin realized that he had been wrong and pleaded that his statement not be published in the *Proceedings*. See 'Discussion' following Georgescu-Roegen (1969).

[20] Paul A. Samuelson (1948, p. 84).

[21] In addition to all the criticisms to which the Cobb–Douglas formula has been subjected, Saiful Islam, a thermo-dynamicist, has shown that because of the entropy law no production process can be represented by it (*Energy Economics*, July 1985, pp. 194–96).

[22] This brings to mind the unending debates about the scale of a process, an issue upon which I dwelled in some detail, Georgescu-Roegen (1964).

of the symbols of the Wicksteedian production function. Yet hardly any economist or econometrician has specified the kind of measurability that the arguments involved in their list of axioms for an essay. Samuelson is among the exceptions: 'inputs must denote *measurable quantitative* [cardinal] economic goods and services'.[23] This is the general, albeit tacit, supposition. But then, if the production process is represented by a Dirichlet function it is inadmissible to regard homogeneity as a non-problem.[24] In this connection we may note further that for a Dirichlet function the arguments need not be cardinal entities. They may be only ordinally measurable. But in this case all economic principles of decreasing or increasing this or that coefficient must go overboard. A second derivative may be either increasing or decreasing according to the scale used. We cannot say whether or not isoquants are convex towards the origin. This is the actual, although hardly apprehended, well-head of the critical importance of measurability in economic analysis.[25]

Still more critical is the issue of measure. What do we mean by 'capital', say, by K in the Cobb–Douglas function (10)? Is it, as Joan Robinson used to say, a 'putty'? Of course, we can always represent by K a vector showing the number of buildings of the type B_i, of the motors of type M_i, and similarly for L. But then we hit another hitch: what is the meaning of substituting capital for labour? There are therefore plenty of reasons to say, with Robinson, that 'the Wicksteedian production function has been a powerful instrument of miseducation'.[26]

3. The flow–fund representation

I have already pointed out that the complete view of even a material process, of a production process, is a dialectical tangle. Everywhere there is some action, some change, some vibration, far too many happenings for a manageable description. To remedy the situation we must take an absolutely necessary jump in the dark, as it were, from dialectics into analysis. In analysis a process must be defined by a substantial and temporal boundary, vacuous as I have already said. *If there is no such boundary, there is no analytic process.* Where the boundary is drawn depends on the interest of the analyst. In nature we find no seams to guide our carving, it all depends on our knowledge and purpose. But to draw in our mind (no other way) the boundary of a production process, say, of General Motors or of a quite small enterprise is not an easy exercise. But for the trend of my argument we may pass it over.

[23] Samuelson (1948). [24] *Ibid.* [25] Georgescu-Roegen (1969).
[26] Joan Robinson (1980).

Once a process has been identified by a boundary, the problem is to describe what it does. In analysis we cannot describe what happens inside a process; to do so would return us to its dialectical conception. Should we wish to know something about the internal happenings we should draw a new boundary that would divide the process into two new processes, and so forth and so on.[27]

In analysis what a process does is represented only by what happens on the boundary. For this, we take another heroic step and classify all the elements involved in a finite number of qualities. This plan is especially relevant for land and workers because they may vary very closely.

There are always elements that cross the boundary from outside the process and others that cross it from inside during a time period (O, T), which must be finite, for otherwise we would have to face the problem of the origin of the universe or wait until the end of eternity to find out what the process may have done. What we want to know from the study of a process is what it was at $t=o$ and what it has done until $T=O$. The reports of custom officials, as it were, placed along the boundary will represent a point in a functional space

$$[I_1(t), I_2(t), \ldots, I_n(t); O_1(t), \ldots, O_m(t)]_O^T, \tag{11}$$

where $I_j(t)$ is the cumulative *input* during (O, t) of factor j, and $O_k(t)$ the cumulative *output* of factor k. Let us note that the same factor may appear as input and output, as is corn in growing corn.

The representation (11) is still not easily manoeuvrable. In addition, that description of a production process would contain factors that are not commodities. This is a trouble similar to that caused by including a biological element in a discourse about nuclear reactions. The commodity plays the same fundamental role in economics as the cell plays in biology, molecule in chemistry and atomic particle in physics. All boundaries used in economics are drawn in relation to some commodity, simple or complex, for example the boundary of an *automobile* plant or that of an *automobile* industry. But in the representation (11) we would always find among outputs tired workers, worn-out tools and waste. The actual purpose of any production process is not to produce tired workers, worn-out tools or junk and garbage. None of these outputs of any process is a commodity. Excluding used automobiles and used buildings they do not have a market; they have no price and no cost of production.

The solution to the impasse lies in the analytical fiction of the static

[27] It is highly instructive to note that if we proceed with this division endlessly, we have no more analytical processes. At some point in space and in time there can be no process. The whole happening slips through our analytical mesh.

process or, as Marx more properly described it, the reproducible process.[28] Obviously, for a process to be reproducible some factors must remain strictly intact despite the change caused by the process itself. The assumption that such analytical factors remain constant is not too far-fetched. In any production process a special activity is directed towards maintenance, as it is called in bookkeeping, that is, towards maintaining in good functioning order the machines, the buildings, the furniture, etc.

To take account of this aspect of the production process, I have introduced a fundamental distinction among the factors of production. The factors that enter the process and also come out of it are *funds*; those that enter but do not come out or come out without having entered are *flows*. Clearly, there can be no other category.

In a way the funds reflect the classical factors of production: land, labour and capital. Land conceived in its perennial and indestructible qualities, that is, mere space as conceived by David Ricardo, is the archetype of fund. Obviously, it can serve in any process over and over again. Needless to add, Ricardian land does not include the top soil, nor the bodies of water. In our analytical representation, capital is also a fund, an idea that raises no difficulty if we do not forget to include among the flow inputs a maintenance flow. The problem of the labour fund is not as simple. First, we must realize that a fund must have a definite substantial existence. Hence, the labour fund will consist of workers in the most general sense, not of labour understood as effort or as labour services. There seems to be no other solution to the impasse than to take it that the workers are kept in good shape by another process, the household.

Before completing the picture sketched thus far, a few observations are opportune for circumscribing more closely the origin and the reason for the flow–fund concept. First, the analytical notion of capital fund should not be confused with the indestructible capital, which is assumed in many essays on production. Analytical capital is not indestructible; it needs a maintenance flow. Secondly, fund and stock are completely different concepts. The role of a stock is to feed a flow or to allow the accumulation of a flow. Natural resources are the typical example of stocks. The entropy law forbids them from being a fund: they cannot be maintained constant.

Irving Fisher was first to explain the difference between stock, flow and flow rate, which had been, and still is, too often ignored.[29] To wit, hard to explain though it is, relatively recently John Hicks told us explicitly that 'we do not need to distinguish between stocks and flows; for stocks and flows

[28] Recalling in this connection that in dynamics the concept of acceleration cannot be defined without that of uniform speed, we may just throw up our hands when a graduate student protests that static economics is 'valueless'. [29] See especially, Irving Fisher (1906).

enter into the determination of equilibrium in exactly the same way'.[30] But in addition to being used freely in their ordinary sense, 'stock and flow' as a pair has not been a frequent theoretical tool.[31]

One reason was there for everyone interested in the early preoccupation with linear models to see. The Wassily Leontief static input–output system and the Jan von Neumann model were not only running in parallel but were bound together conceptually. The first approach views the process as a continuous affair described only from the *outside* by flows. What was already *inside* the process at first and at the end is of no concern to the economist. The other approach consists of two snapshots, so to speak, one at time $t=0$, the other at $t=T>0$. The representation of the process is thus reduced to a two-row matrix:

$$\begin{bmatrix} A_1, A_2, \ldots, A_n \\ A'_1, A'_2, \ldots, A'_n \end{bmatrix} \tag{12}$$

where the vectors A and A' represent the *stocks* of commodities in the process at the two time instants.

A point should now be abundantly obvious: each of the two systems tells a different story. Let us consider the situation of $A=A'$. In that case it is impossible to say whether something has happened or whether the system is completely frozen. As to the Leontief system, we could not decide which of two flows is more efficient: efficiency of flows is actually the efficiency of the fund instruments that are at work. Therefore, neither model is an appropriate representation of a process. An adequate representation must therefore include both what flows and what produces the flows.[32] Flows may be divided into five basic categories: for input flows, energy and materials from nature, R, the products of other industries, I, and the maintenance supplies, M; for output flows, the products proper, Q, and the waste, W. And what transforms the input flows into output flows are the *agents*, the fund factors: land, L, capital, K, and human capital, H.[33]

According to formula (11), any given process may be represented by the functional vector

$$[Q(t), R(t), I(t), M(t), W(t), L(t), K(t), H(t)]_O^T. \tag{13}$$

A first remark is that this analytical representation includes also waste. This flow has never been considered by the old literature, so that when pollution

[30] John Hicks (1965, p. 85).

[31] Of note is the stock–flow production function set forth by V.L. Smith (1961). A too quick excursion in the 'stock–flow analysis' is the article by Robert W. Clower (1968).

[32] Georgescu-Roegen (1951, 1971).

[33] Land is indeed an agent in the proper sense. Just like a fisherman's net catches fish, land catches the most valuable item for us – solar energy. If the radius of the earth were twice as great as it is now, the amount of solar energy striking the earth would be four times as great.

struck us in the face we felt quite strange. Where did it come from; it was not in our formulae? Secondly, another factor that has been ignored (or associated in a cavalier fashion with land) is the inflow of natural resources, which has only recently become the centre of fervent attention with a slipshod treatment (as we shall see presently). Thirdly, we must bear in mind that all fund coordinates represent services expressed as the product of the size of the fund by its duration. The routine use of a 'flow of services' has also served the miseducation. In its discriminatory sense, flow pertains only to some substance. Services do not pass from one stock into another, as cloth effectively passes into a coat. But if you find an item of capital, a needle, that has flown in a pair of pants, it is certainly a regrettable accident. All these shortcomings are due to the above-mentioned lack of epistemological interest on the part of economists.

The analysis of production, like almost every other analytical endeavour, needs an elementary unit. By an elementary process I propose to understand any one of the reproducible processes by which a unit (natural or an appropriate batch) of the product in point may be obtained from some inputs.[34] The process by which a cabinetmaker makes a table from some materials with the help of some tools in his shop is the best example of an elementary process. From a minute observation we can derive the elementary process of a system as complex as that of an automobile plant.

From thinking about elementary processes we learn a fact of incalculable importance: many funds of an elementary process are inevitably idle during the process.[35] Think of the agricultural implements of a farmer or the tools of an individual cabinet shop. This idleness is technical and, hence, only a technical progress could *reduce* it. The point turns into a new problem, the economy of time in production.[36] An actual production consisting of only one elementary process can be represented by a series of curves over the interval (O, T), each curve representing the cumulative flow or the cumulative service up to t, $O \leq t \leq T$. Only one process goes on at any one time and sustained production consists of one elementary process following another. The elementary processes are arranged *in series*.

Now, in regions where farming is strictly dictated by the cycle of seasons, the elementary processes of the community are arranged *in parallel*. Idleness is then amplified in proportion to the number of farms, which

[34] Georgescu-Roegen (1969, 1970).

[35] Not to clutter the salient points of my argument with side, though possibly important, issues, I leave aside the case of joint products.

[36] The problem of the utilization of capital was broached first by Robin Marris (1964). An admirable treatment of the economy of time in consumption was one of the ignored merits of Heinrich H. Gossen. The problem surfaced recently, sadly without any reference to Gossen, in Georgescu-Roegen (1983, pp. lxxxv–lxxxvii).

constitutes the well-known plague of agriculture: the production cost must include this uneconomical and unavoidable idleness.

Turning now to the shop of an individual artisan, we find that its idleness can be reduced by a familiar method. The head artisan may bring in another, so that when one is using, say, the saw, the other may use the planer and vice versa. Then every tool will be used twice as frequently as before the coming of the second artisan. The idleness of every tool would thus be halved. Naturally, no such increase in the rate of production per unit of time would be profitable if the rate of demand per unit of time for the product did not also become greater. And if it becomes still greater more workers will be included in the production process. This, in turn, would foster a division of labour (with its increase of efficiency). This is an analytical confirmation of Adam Smith's famous proposition that the expansion of the market is the cause of the division of labour.

If the rate of demand keeps increasing it becomes profitable to include more workers in production. In the limit, the periods during which the tools are used in the elementary process may be arranged in such a way that no tool remains idle. Each worker continuously performs a task within a sequence of elementary processes that follow closely one after another.[37] These processes are arranged *in line*.

The picture is easily recognized as a *factory* process, well exemplified by an assembly line. The factory, although a very familiar sight nowadays, represents an economic, not a technological, conquest of inestimable value. A factory may be regarded as the most efficient of our exosomatic organs. Unfortunately, it cannot be used in all circumstances, for example, when the rate of demand is very small, as in the case of building ships or spacecrafts. In agriculture, as already noted, the rigidity of seasons makes the functioning of a factory impossible. However, in places such as the island of Bali agriculture operates after the factory system. We can then say that the Balinese eat at each meal the rice sown that very moment. In a factory process there is no waiting; like a music box, a factory starts to produce as soon as it opens and ceases to produce as soon as it closes. Perhaps the most eloquent proof of the unique advantage of the factory is the recent method of raising chicken by using the incubator in factory process. The chicken factories, not the chicken farms, are responsible for the 'chicken war' that ran a few years ago between the United States and Europe. Chicken factories are also responsible for the fact that in the United States the consumption of chicken has just come to equalize that of beef.

The factory also supplies us with some interesting analytical results. The

[37] See the explanatory diagram in Georgescu-Roegen (1969).

most relevant concerns the analytical representation (13). In the case of a factory that is uninterruptedly in operation from $t=0$ to $t=T$, all coordinates of that vector are obviously linear homogeneous functions of t. Hence, (13) becomes

$$[qt, rt, it, mt, wt; Lt, Kt, Ht]_{O}^{T}. \tag{14}$$

The coefficients all have a definite analytical significance. For the flows represent rates of what flows per unit of time, the same dimensional coefficients as the arguments in (6). The coefficients of funds have an entirely different dimension; they represent the quantitative size of the factors: L represents the number of works; K, the number of capital equipment pieces; and H, the number of workers. But all coordinates of (14) are quantities, as the arguments of (7) are.

At this juncture one possible slip is waiting for us. Because of its form (14) may degenerate into a simpler expression. The first is obtained by eliminating all time coordinates:

$$(q, r, i, m, w; L, K, H), \tag{15}$$

which tells exactly and simply what the process may do, not what the process does. The other degenerated form

$$(\bar{Q}, \bar{R}, \bar{I}, \bar{T}, \bar{M}, \bar{W}; \bar{L}, \bar{K}, \bar{H}; t), \tag{16}$$

where the barred capital letters represent quantities must, in contrast to (15), include time as an explicit coordinate, otherwise we would not be able to ascertain whether $\bar{Q}$ can be produced in a day or in a century. The difference between the last two forms bears upon the earlier discussion of the opposition between (5) and (6).

Either vector (5) or (6) can be looked on as a recipe of the process. We can then imagine that we set up a filing system of all such recipes for producing *the same* output with *the same* factors of production. In fact, this catalogue of possibilities constitutes the production function for the product involved, which we can write as

$$q = g(r, i, t, m, w; L, K, H), \tag{17}$$

or, alternatively, as

$$Q = G(\bar{R}, \bar{I}, \bar{T}, \bar{M}, \bar{W}; \bar{L}, \bar{K}, \bar{H}; t). \tag{18}$$

It is now seen that the quantity form (5) is unsatisfactory, because the necessary time coordinate is left out. An appropriate representation of a factory process is therefore (17), alias (6). Furthermore, since it is now clear that

$$tg = G, \tag{19}$$

the source of the paradox of homogeneity concerning (5) and (6) is brought to light. If we want to represent a production process by a function of quantities, t must be included among the arguments. Only such a function is homogeneous because – to recall – doubling the duration of a factory process doubles the quantities of inputs as well as the output. But g, alias (6), is now revealed to be the only correct form of the two traditional forms. But it is not homogeneous. The endless debate about this issue has wrongly assumed that (5) and (6) are completely equivalent. And, not to forget it, the forms (14) and (15) are valid only for a factory process. The production of Triborough Bridges, of Transatlantic Queens, can be described only by a form like (11).

Let us consider the inscription on the package of an electric bulb, say, 100 watts. It informs us what the bulb can do, not what it does. The same kind of information is supplied by many other possible processes, for motors, for speedboats, etc. The vector (15) provides the same information about a factory process. From the blueprints of the factory, which reveal the nature and the amounts of the funds, experts in that technology should deduce what rates of input and output flows are necessary for the factory process. They do not have to obtain this information from (15). This means that the arguments of (15), and hence those of (17), are not independent. Along this line of thought, we come to realize that among the variables of (17) there must exist some additional relations. The first that an expert may supply is

$$H = H(L, K). \tag{20}$$

Naturally, to staff a given equipment it is necessary to have a definite number of workers of each speciality. The structure of the equipment must also determine the rate of output of which the factory is capable:

$$q = q(L, K). \tag{21}$$

In the present perspective of the analytical representation of a production process, we must also consider the troublesome output flow of waste. This flow depends upon how much of the energy and matter of the material inputs went into the product, which can be written

$$q = F(r, i, w). \tag{22}$$

To the extent that the points (r, i, w) represent acceptable combinations, F is homogeneous of the first degree. Indeed, the equality

$$(q + w = r + i)_{\text{energy and matter}} \tag{23}$$

must exist as a corollary of the elementary laws of generalized thermodynamics. Therefore, (22) must be homogeneous of the first degree for any factory process. But if one assumes that (21), too, is homogeneous of the first degree, one grossly violates the eminent principles about the amplification of organic structures, a tradition that comes from Aristotle and was later filtered by Galileo Galilei and Herbert Spencer.[38]

The unanticipated conclusion is that even for a factory system, the most organic form of production process, the analytical representation does not consist of a surface in the commodity space, as not only the traditional forms but also our (17) form would tend to make us believe. The analytical representation of any factory process is *limitational.* This useful term introduced by Ragnar Frisch means that the production process is such that both inputs of some pairs must be increased for the product to become greater.[39] In the representation consisting of the ensemble (20), (21) and (22), two sorts of limitationalities are obvious without any ado. Clearly, a decrease of the product due to a decrease of a fund cannot be compensated *within the same factory process* by an increase of a flow input. If one sewing machine in a shirt factory is taken away, the resulting decrease of the flow rate of the product cannot be compensated by an increase of any rate of material flows, say, that of the cloth. With these remarks, the basic analytical representation assumes the following expression

$$q = q(L, K) = F(r, i, w), \; H = H(L, K). \tag{24}$$

On further thought we see that limitationality is a structural characteristic of a factory process that is much more spread than explicated by (24). To pinpoint the issue, let us think of a very simplified picture, a particular process producing q^o shoes of type S per day by using only i^o pounds of leather of the kind C per day and a daily amount e^o of energy G. Let the process also use K^o sewing machines of type M and H^o workers of type W. Since (24) teaches us to separate funds from flows, it would make no sense to represent that process in a four-dimensional space (r, i, K, H). The separation leads to the diagram of Figure 8.1, where the flows are represented by $A^o(r^o, i^o)$ in the plane (r, i) and the funds by $B^o(K^o, L^o)$ in the plane (K, L). Some other process could certainly produce exactly the same number of shoes per day by, necessarily, using some other kind of flow inputs and funds. Very likely this new process will use entirely other kinds of input – as we can learn by thinking of handmade shoes and machine-made ones. Hence, for the representation of that process we need another diagram instead of Figure 8.1. Since the new inputs are not of the same nature as the old ones, they cannot be represented by points in the spaces of Figure 8.1.

In Figure 8.1, K^o represents a definite stock of capital equipment, that is a

[38] Georgescu-Roegen (1971, pp. 105–7). [39] Georgescu-Roegen (1966, chapter 7).

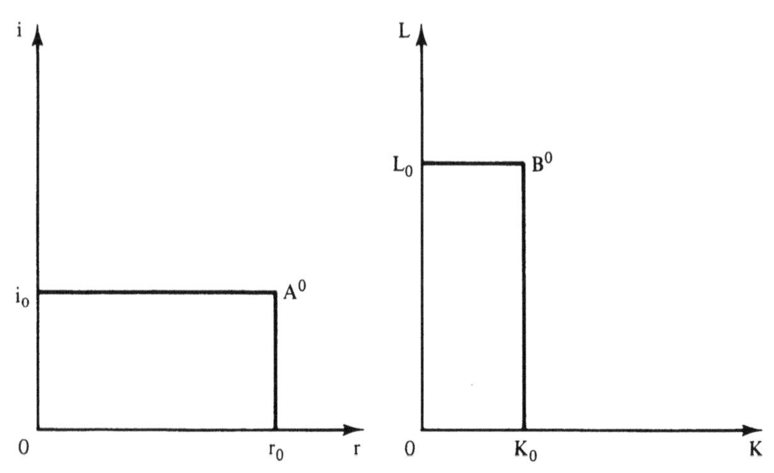

Figure 8.1 *Flow and fund utilization*

clear analytical concept. But if we speak loosely, as we all do, of the substitution of capital for labour, these words lose that quality.[40] When for the sole purpose of illustrative symbolism, we also associate the function $q=q(L,K)$ with a family of isoquants of the same form as those of the traditional, indiscriminatory theory of production, we should avow from the outset that we are adopting a substantial amount of necessary dialectics.

In some cases even this concession would be totally unjustified. The first humbug is a form that emerged after the oil embargo prompted economists to struggle to save some face about their total neglect of the economic importance of natural resources. We often met with the production function of the form

$$Q=F(H,K,R) \tag{25}$$

where H, K, are labour and capital (ordinarily, of a nature not clearly specified) and R is simply 'natural resources', assumably a flow element.[41] The simple dimensional contrast of H, K, on one hand, and R on the other should have been sufficient to stop the thought of such a formula in the cradle. But the sociology of science is full of curiosities, one being the attachment of a name to the function (25). It now circulates as the Leif

[40] On this difference – of course, with another diction – Joan Robinson (1963) has commented with her usual acumen for clarification.

[41] Proposers of this formula are many of those economists who have just become interested in the problem of natural resources, some to recognize it, some to deny its existence. For choice are Joseph E. Stiglitz and Robert M. Solow.

Johansen production function. Together with the attraction exercised by the Cobb–Douglas formula it has yielded at the hands of Joseph Stiglitz and Robert Solow

$$Q = K^a H^b R^c, \tag{26}$$

where R stands for 'natural resources'. Then,

$$R^c = Q/K^a H^b \tag{27}$$

has been used to refute the concern about the exhaustibility, by arguing (as a paper-and-pencil operation) that we can take care of the scarcity of natural resources by increasing the other factors. I hardly know any other flight of fancy as the humbug idea of producing more capital (perhaps, also feeding more people) by using less and less natural resources and thus making them actually inexhaustible.

The other humbug stemming from the traditional production theory is to write

$$Q = F(H, K, t), \tag{28}$$

for the purpose of representing by t the technological process. No one conversed in mathematics would resist taking this partial derivate of Q with respect to t and seeing in it the rate of progress.[42] This is one of the most symptomatic conjuring tricks of the economist. If t is meant to be a time index, say, one $t = 1960$, another $t = 1980$, not only the relation between Q, the product, and the factors H and K has necessarily changed during that period, but even H and K are no longer the same entities. Thus, for 1960 as well as for 1980, we should write

$$Q_{1960} = F_{1960}(H_{1960}, K_{1960}), Q_{1980} = F_{1980}(H_{1980}, K_{1980}), \tag{29}$$

when it becomes crystal clear that

$$(Q_{1980} - Q_{1960})/(1980\text{–}1960) \tag{30}$$

cannot be related to any derivative: derivative pertains to one and the same function. I have been fully justified, so it seems, to call in an early paragraph for unusual carefulness in approaching and dealing with the representations of a production process.

4. The epistemology of dynamic economics

To pass from the representation of the static process to that of the dynamic one is almost imperative. This last problem also raises delicate epistemolog-

42 Robert M. Solow (1957).

ical points, and I believe that what I have already said may be of help in pointing out the direction in which we should look.

While thinking about dynamic economics one could hardly shun the idea of the association of that discipline with the mechanics of the Newtonian sort. With the exception of Carl Menger, all the forefathers of modern economics – Jevons, Walras, Pareto – identified economics with mechanics. Not so long ago, Frank Knight spoke of economics as 'the sister science of mechanics'. These ideas have underpinned a very broad field of approaches that may be referred to as *mechanico-descriptive*. They reduce the essence of all economic phenomena to motions, hence, it is said, to mechanics. Nonetheless, the assimilation of economics to mechanics rests on thin air. Newtonian mechanics imply the presence of a force of attraction; none is found in any works on economics. Economics cannot be assimilated even to kinematics, for the study object of kinematics is the influence of forces (of any type) on the movement of the associated objects. If there is any motion in economics – besides that of any vehicle or of people themselves – it is the motion of the economist's hand from one point to another on an economic diagram. By such motion we may didactically explain the reasoning on some economic problem.

But the most important opposition between economic phenomena and mechanical locomotion is that in the economic world things not only move, most importantly, they also change in the most pertinent meaning of the term. The distinction brings to mind Joseph Schumpeter's piercing idea: there is accretion, which means that there is more (or there is less) of the same things, and there is development, which necessarily involves qualitative change.

Before bringing this essay to an end I will not fail to return to Joseph Schumpeter's magnificent philosophy, be it only within the space permitted by the architecture of this volume.

First, I must deal with the economic dynamics as initiated by Karl Marx and later perpetuated in a less vigorous style (sad to say). I propose to begin by showing that a standard dynamic model cannot be an adequate analytical representation even for pure growth. As a basis of discussion, I will choose the Leontief open input–output model because that model has the unique merit of paying some attention to the analytico-physiological aspect of the dynamic process. To prevent purely mathematical complications – irrelevant complications – to obscure the thread of my argument, I shall consider a system involving only two commodities, C_1 and C_2, and a completely undifferentiated labour, H. Table 8.1 reflects the fundamental assumption of Leontief: P_1 and P_2 are unique in each field and operate at constant returns to scale. Table 8.1 is a multi-process matrix, which I use instead of Leontief's form because the latter involves the concept of internal

TABLE 8.1 *A multi-process for an open Leontief system*

	P_1		P_2
		Flow coordinates	
C_1	$x_{11}=t_1s_1a_{11}$		$-x_{12}=-t_2s_2a_{12}$
C_2	$-x_{21}=-t_1s_1a_{21}$		$x_{22}=t_2s_2a_{22}$
		Fund coordinates	
C_1	$X_{11}=t_1s_1B_{11}$		$X_{12}=t_2s_2B_{12}$
C_2	$X_{21}=t_1s_1B_{21}$		$X_{22}=t_2s_2B_{22}$.
		Labour services	
L	$L_1=t_1s_1H_1$		$L_2=t_2s_2H_2$

flow, which is illegitimate in analysis.[43] Finally, in Table 8.1 the funds of each process are explicitly marked. They also include labour, which Leontief takes into consideration only in the static system. In Table 8.1, the funds consist of the same commodities as the flows.[44]

Accordingly, in Table 8.1 process P_1 is represented as in the earlier pattern (15), with the additional convention of representing input flows by negative coordinates. Thus, the s_i correspond to the Leontief characteristic assumption of homogeneous linearity (constant returns to scale); they measure the scale relative to the unitary processes, for which $a_{11}=1$ and $a_{22}=1$, respectively. The t_i stand for the working days of the factories (or of the molecular industries).[45] Table 8.1 brings to light a valuable teaching, namely that there are two ways for increasing the national product $(x_{11}-x_{12}, x_{22}-x_{21})$, by increasing either the working day or the scales.[46]

[43] Internal flow is indeed an illegitimate analytical concept because it does not cross any boundary. The use of this concept leads to several preposterous conclusions. On this point and on the multi-process matrix, see Georgescu-Roegen (1971, pp. 256–62).

[44] This is the assumption Leontief introduced for his dynamic system (Leontief, 1953, p. 56). He may have had in mind an idea similar to mine that lead to (21). Yet he has no valid reason to maintain (*idem*, p. 12) that static analysis, even short run analysis, may completely disregard what I have called funds. As I have pointed out earlier, whether static or dynamic, the complete picture must include both flows and funds.

[45] It is the indisputable merit of W.H. Nicholls (1948) that he long ago broke the neoclassical tradition by introducing the length of the working day into the production function. His idea could be explicated by the formula $Q=Q(L, K, H; t)$, not to be confused with Robert Solow's self-deception (28). Nicholls's t is working day.

[46] This reveals the 'secret' recipe for economic growth: a long working day. As attested by Frederick Engels this was the main lever for the spectacular economic growth of the western world during the eighteenth and nineteenth centuries. Even in the liberal Commonwealth of Massachussetts, only in 1842 did a law protect children under twelve from working longer than ten hours per day. An upshot of uppermost importance for economic planners is that, contrary to what most of them swear by, it is absurd to build another shoe factory if there are others that are not used around the clock. These remarks are what the economy of time in production teaches us.

Taking the working day as the unit of time (which implies that thereafter the working day can no longer vary), Table 8.1 yields

$$a_{11}s_1 - a_{21}s_2 = y_1, -a_{12}s_1 + a_{22}s_2 = y_2 \tag{31}$$

where (y_1, y_2) represents the national product. For $(y_1, y_2) \geq 0$, the a_{ij} must satisfy the well-known inequality[47]

$$a_{11}a_{22} - a_{12}a_{21} > 0. \tag{32}$$

In a mechanistic interpretation, for the national product to increase by $(\Delta y_1, \Delta y_2) \geq 0$, first the scales must naturally be increased as determined by the system

$$a_{11}\Delta s_1 - a_{12}\Delta s_2 = \Delta y_1, -a_{21}\Delta s_1 + a_{22}\Delta s_2 = \Delta y_2. \tag{33}$$

Secondly, the amount of the fund factors,

$$B_1 = s_1 B_{11} + s_2 B_{12},\ B_2 = s_1 B_{21} + s_2 B_{22}, \tag{34}$$

must also be increased accordingly:

$$\Delta B_1 = B_{11}\Delta s_1 + B_{12}\Delta s_2,\ \Delta B_2 = B_{21}\Delta s_1 + B_{22}\Delta s_2. \tag{35}$$

But where do the increases ΔB_1 and ΔB_2 come from? Leontief went along with the old instruction: 'Save–Invest–Grow', interpreted in the sense that the increase of the capacity of production occurs instantaneously as the additional funds have accumulated from the necessary reduction of consumption. All waiting thus occurs during accumulation. Let Δt be the time over which accumulation takes place, and (z_1, z_2) the reduced consumption flows during Δt. The increases of the funds are

$$\Delta B_1 = (y_1 - z_1)\Delta t,\ \Delta B_2 = (y_2 - z_2)\Delta t, \tag{36}$$

from which by simple elimination of Δs_1 and Δs_2, we obtain

$$\begin{aligned} z_1 &= y_1 - M_{11}(\Delta y_1/\Delta t) - M_{12}(\Delta y_2/\Delta t) \geq 0, \\ z_2 &= y_2 - M_{21}(\Delta y_1/\Delta t) - M_{22}(\Delta y_2/\Delta t) \geq 0, \end{aligned} \tag{37}$$

where the M_{ij} are positive constants of the economic system. This system shows that once we have chosen $\Delta y_1, \Delta y_2$, there is a lower limit to Δt, that is to how quickly we can reach the increased national product, $y_1^1 = y_1 + \Delta y_1$, $y_2^1 = y_1 + \Delta y_2$. Conversely, if Δt is chosen (appropriately), there are some upper limits to possible increases, Δy_1, Δy_2. From (37) it follows that no matter how small $\Delta y_1, \Delta y_2$ are and how great Δt is, the system must drop down to a lower level of consumption before pulling itself up to the higher

[47] Georgescu-Roegen (1966, chapter 9).

level of production. This is comparable to the athlete who steps back before some jumping, but it has no correspondence in the material world.

We can apply the system (37) to a series of jumps $y_k^{i+1} = y_{k'}^i + \Delta y_{k'}^i, y_k^o = y_k$, determined in connection of successive periods Δt, and obtain

$$\begin{aligned} z_1^i &= y_1^i - M_{11}(\Delta y_1^i/\Delta t) - M_{12}(\Delta y_2^i/\Delta t), \\ z_2^i &= y_2^i - M_{21}(\Delta y_1^i/\Delta t) - M_{22}(\Delta y_2^i/\Delta t). \end{aligned} \quad (38)$$

This system determines a series of increases $(\Delta y_1^i, \Delta y_2^i)$, which by cumulation determine the increasing levels of production. For the limit as $\Delta t \to 0$, (38) becomes[48]

$$\begin{aligned} z_1(t) &= y_1(t) - M_{11}\dot{y}_1 - M_{12}\dot{y}_2, \\ z_2(t) &= y_2(t) - M_{21}\dot{y}_1 - M_{22}\dot{y}_2, \end{aligned} \quad (39)$$

where, as usual, the dot shows the derivative with respect to time. All this seems simple and natural enough. Yet two snags have been concealed by our concern with the mathematical formalism. First, as we are assuming that growth can be achieved by a decrease in consumption we do not stop to ask: what item of consumption can be saved to increase capacity to produce? The application to reality of the preceding mathematical manipulation presupposed that either bulldozers are consumed by people or yogurt is a capital equipment. We seem to have forgotten the remarkable epistemology of Karl Marx, who made a strict distinction between the consumption goods produced by Department II and consumed by capitalists and workers alike, and the production goods produced by Department I and consumed in production by Department II.

Secondly, in the economic applications of (38) – or of any other dynamic system for that matter – to planning, it is always assumed that the planner first chooses the z_k's and then determines by integration how much should be produced. We know that the solution of (39) involves two arbitrary constants. These arbitrary constants, as Leontief advises us,[49] can be determined by the condition that the *newly* chosen process should begin exactly at the planning moment. The constants permit us to choose them so that $y_1(O) = y_1^o$, $y_2(O) = y_2^o$.

However, such a procedure for any dynamic system, say (39), is fully correct if, and only if, the actual process (the object of planning) was already accelerated according to (39). Therefore, we cannot use (39) to find out how we can transform a steady-state system into a growing one. The paradox stems from the fact that one weighty assumption is hidden behind (39). The assumption is that the net product starts to increase the very moment the

[48] This form is equivalent to that designed by Leontief (1953, pp. 56f). I prefer (38) to Leontief's because it directly compares the product with the consumption level.

[49] Cf. Leontief (1953, pp. 57–60).

level of consumption is lowered. This would be a quasi-explosive feature of the formal dynamic systems. For if this assumption were true in reality (in a proper approximation), then we could bring about the fantastic growth of any economy by merely decreeing one day per week, for instance, when consumer goods should not be consumed.

The major difficulty of bringing about growth is waiting. We cannot produce commodities from commodities; we can produce commodities only by accomplished production processes. A factory, for instance, is an accomplished process only after it has been primed, just as a pump must first be primed to work. And in contrast to commodities, production processes are not produced by production processes. There is no production process that would produce the process that produced the Triborough Bridge, nor one that produced the Panama Canal or even a small factory. A factory, as I hinted earlier, produces commodities without waiting; some waiting is involved mainly in processes affected by the seasonal cycle. But to set up a complete factory takes time, occasionally an enormous amount of time.

How we could make a growing process to grow faster, is a problem that is still in a very unsatisfactory state. A terrible self-deception is to believe that the system (38) teaches us how to make absolutely any economy grow faster. Yet this belief, above all others, has affected numerous specialists on economic planning.[50]

From all cases of growth (in the broad sense of the word) known from economic history one truth emerges crystal clear: growth is always due to a qualitative change or, much less frequently, to some economic import from the outside (peaceful or by conquest). Neither of these vital phenomena can be identified as dynamic. The most important of the two is qualitative change or, in other words, innovation that may be of indigenous vintage or just transmuted from outside.

An innovation must necessarily emerge in some country. How this happens is not a problem for analysis, for arithmomorphism. Mutation in the biological world constitutes a counterpart of innovation in economics. We all know by heart the most often quoted idea from Alfred Marshall's *Principles* (1961, p. xiv): 'The Mecca of the economist lies in economic biology rather than in economic dynamics.' Yet outside a few instances – the analogy of the industry with a forest is the sharpest – Marshall preached but did not apply his teaching. It is Joseph Schumpeter who, without preaching any kinship between biology and economics, proposed a theory of economic development that is on the whole a general pattern for

[50] One case that greatly surprised me was a conference at Vanderbilt University in which a renowned specialist in economic development (who must remain anonymous) claimed that even a country like Somalia can be made to grow without any aid from outside if only one knows how to begin.

economics, biology or sociology, briefly, for any phenomenological domain where there is this peculiar phenomenon called evolution. According to Schumpeter innovations are the paving-tiles of evolution. Schumpeter's definition of innovation – as a change in the methods of production, in the accessible mineralogical dowry, in any kind of institutions, or in international contacts – is familiar, at least among economists. What is almost totally ignored is Schumpeter's special elaboration on the nature of innovation. He carefully excluded from his 'innovation' all small changes, such as a new type of window-dressing, a new way of distributing newspapers to homes, etc. I believe, the most interesting point of all his talk about innovation is his admission that he cannot define in precise terms what is a small innovation, where an innovation stops to be small and becomes great, or vice versa. But in a subtle footnote (Schumpeter, 1934, p. 81) he adopted a thoroughly dialectical reasoning to point out that small and large are dialectically opposing qualities, often overlapping, yet distinct in the conditions at hand. In the same vein he protested against the idea advanced by many that 'entrepreneur' is a false concept because no one can say when that quality begins and ends. Thus Schumpeter, if judged from a very general scientific perspective, fought for the idea that only great qualitative changes, great and hence irreversible innovations, can account for evolution. In economics this is reflected by business cycles. Small innovations have no effect. In this respect, Schumpeter opposes the thesis of neo-Darwinism in biology, according to which evolution is the result of a continuous accumulation of small, imperceptible changes. According to Schumpeter evolution consists of substantially new entities, relations or activities. 'Add', he said, 'successively as many coaches as you please, you will never get a railway [engine] thereby.' (Schumpeter, 1934, 64n)

Schumpeter never preached biologism in economics, but his theory of innovation covers biology as well. Interestingly, but curiously as well, some thirty years after Schumpeter presented his theory of evolution Richard Goldschmidt, an eminent biologist, shocked his neo-Darwinist colleagues by claiming that true evolution is not the result of accumulated small phenotypic mutations, it is the result only of the emergence of 'hopeful monsters'. Goldschmidt, without having any idea about Schumpeter's theory in economics, discovered it in biology. In Schumpeter's aforementioned metaphor there is concealed Goldschmidt's idea of hopeful monster: a railway engine is indeed a monster if compared to a mail coach, but how hopeful it later proved to be.[51]

[51] Naturally, when it was set forth and even long thereafter, Goldschmidt's theory fared badly. But recently, a biologist of the highest calibre, Stephen J. Gould (1977), has modified Goldschmidt's theory into an apparently accepted theory, for which he claims that one needs dialectics.

What causes a mutation, viable or not, is still a moot question. The same is true about how an invention, the spring board of innovation, comes to a human. Nothing seems to behave like invention, for it is undeniable that Thomas Edison did not have any idea of any of his inventions before the very instant when they exploded, as it were, in his mind.

Innovations have occurred and will occur – in my opinion, not only to help us to progress, but also to help us to regress – if and when necessary. Without them there can be no change, dynamic or evolutionary. One important lesson to learn once more from Karl Marx is that after presenting his diagram of simple reproduction growth he simply presented a diagram of an economy that was already grown. It is fair to ask why he did not show how one could pass from the former to the latter. The sharp mind of Rosa Luxemburg challenged Marx by asking 'where does the increase of his demand come from?' (Luxemburg, 1951). In a different form this has been the question that I have raised about a dynamic system in relation to (39).

The lever of growth comes, as I said, from inside or outside and only after we have got hold of its nature can we use dynamic consideration to plan for its better use. While writing this, one excellent illustration came to my mind, just in time to serve as my clinching end. It was a dynamic programme (developed for the purpose) that helped the United States to solve without waging war the problems raised by the blockade of Berlin. But we should not forget that we had the necessary funds, funds in my own sense. In similar situations, concerning even more complex problems, like those pertaining to international relations, dynamics should be treated with all respect.

References

Betancourt, R.R., and Clague, C.K. (1981) *Capital Utilization. A Theoretical and Empirical Analysis*, Cambridge University Press, Cambridge.

Chipman, J.S., et al. (1971) (eds) *Preferences, Utility and Demand*, Harcourt Brace Jovanovich, New York.

Clower, R.W. (1968) 'Stock–Flow Analysis', *International Encyclopedia of the Social Sciences*, Macmillan, London and New York, vol. XV, pp. 273–7.

Fisher, I. (1906) *The Nature of Capital and Income*, Macmillan, New York.

Frisch, R. (1965) *Theory of Production*, Rand McNally, Chicago, Ill.

Georgescu-Roegen, N. (1951) 'The Aggregate Production Function and its Application to John von Neumann's Model', in *Activity Analysis of Production and Allocation*, ed. T.C. Koopmans et al., John Wiley, New York, pp. 98–115.

(1964) 'Measure, Quality, and Optimum Scale', in *Essays in Econometrics and Planning Presented to Professor P.C. Mahalanobis*, ed. C.R. Rao, Pergamon Press, Oxford.

(1966) *Analytical Economics, Issues and Problems*, Harvard University Press, Cambridge, Mass.

(1969) 'Process in Farming versus Process in Manufacturing: A Problem of Balanced Growth', in *Economic Problems of Agriculture in Industrial Societies* (Proceedings of a Conference of the International Economic Association, Rome, 1965), ed. U. Papi and C. Nunn, Macmillan, London, pp. 497–528.

(1970) 'The Economics of Production' (Richard T. Ely Lecture), *American Economic Review*, 60 (May), pp. 1–9.

(1971) *The Entropy Law and the Economic Process*, Harvard University Press, Cambridge, Mass.

(1975) 'Vilfredo Pareto and His Theory of Ophelimity', in *Convegno Internazionale Vilfredo Pareto (Roma, 25–27 ottobre 1973)*, Accademia Nazionale dei Lincei, Roma. Reprinted in N. Georgescu-Roegen, *Energy and Economic Myths. Institutional and Analytical Economic Essays*, Pergamon Press, New York and Oxford, 1976, pp. 307–49.

(1976a) 'Dynamic Models and Economic Growth' in *Equilibrium and Disequilibrium in Economic Theory*, ed. G. Schwödiauer, Reidel, Dordrecht, The Netherlands.

(1976b) *Energy and Economic Myths. Institutional and Analytical Economic Essays*, Pergamon Press, Oxford.

(1979) 'Methods in Economic Science', *Journal of Economic Issues*, 13 (June), pp. 317–27.

(1980) 'General Reflections on the Theme of Innovations', in *Economic Effects of Space and Other Advanced Technologies*, ed. T.D. Guyenne and G. Levy, ESTEC, Noordivijk, The Netherlands, pp. 47–51.

(1983) 'Hermann Heinrich Gossen: His Life and Work in Historical Perspective', in H.H. Gossen, *The Laws of Human Relations and the Rules of Human Action Derived Therefrom*, trans. R.C. Blitz, MIT Press, Cambridge, Mass., pp. xi–cxlv.

(1986) 'Man and Production' in *Foundations of Economics*, ed. Mauro Baranzini and Roberto Scazzieri, Basil Blackwell, Oxford and New York, pp. 247–80.

Goldschmidt, R. (1940) *The Natural Basis of Evolution*, Yale University Press, New Haven, Conn.

Gould, S.J. (1977) 'The Return of Hopeful Monsters', *Natural History*, 86 (June/July), pp. 22–30.

Haldane, J.B.S. (1956) 'The Argument from Animals to Man: An Examination of its Validity for Anthropology', *Journal of the Royal Anthropological Institute*, 86, Part II, pp. 1–14.

Hicks, J.R. (1965) *Capital and Growth*, Oxford University Press, New York.

Houthakker, H.S. (1950) 'Revealed Preferences and the Utility Function', *Economica*, NS 17 (May), pp. 159–74.

Kline, M. (1972) *Mathematical Thought from Ancient to Modern Times*, Oxford University Press, New York.

Leontief, W. et al. (1953) *Studies in the Structure of the American Economy*, Oxford University Press, New York.

Luxemburg, R. (1951) *The Accumulation of Capital*, Yale University Press, New Haven (1st edn 1913).
Marris, R. (1964) *The Economics of Capital Utilization. A Report on Multiple-Shift Work*, Cambridge University Press, Cambridge.
Marshall, A. (1961) *Principles of Economics*, Macmillan, London (1st edn 1907).
Nicholls, W.H. (1948) *Labor Productivity Function in Meat Packing*, University of Chicago Press, Chicago, Ill.
Robinson, J. (1963) *Essays in the Theory of Economic Growth*, Macmillan, London.
(1980) *Collected Economic Papers*, vol. II, MIT Press, Cambridge, Mass.
Samuelson, P.A. (1948) *Foundations of Economic Analysis*, Harvard University Press, Cambridge, Mass.
(1966) *The Scientific Papers of Paul A. Samuelson*, MIT Press, Cambridge, Mass.
Scazzieri, R. (1981) *Efficienza produttiva e livelli di attività*, Il Mulino, Bologna.
Schumpeter, J.A. (1934) *The Theory of Economic Development*, Harvard University Press, Cambridge, Mass. (German original 1912).
Smith, V.L. (1961) *Investment and Production*, Harvard University Press, Cambridge, Mass.
Solow, R.M. (1957) 'Technical Change and the Aggregate Production Function', *Review of Economics and Statistics*, 39 (August), pp. 312–20.
Tani, P. (1986) *Analisi microeconomica della produzione*, Nuova Italia Scientifica, Rome.
Thomas, W.L. (1956) (ed.) *Man's Role in Changing the Face of the Earth*, University of Chicago Press, Chicago, Ill.
Whitehead, A.N. (1929) *Process and Reality*, Macmillan, New York.
Wicksteed, P.H. (1984) *An Essay on the Coordination of the Laws of Distribution*, Macmillan, London (reprinted as No. 12 of the *Scarce Tracts in Economic and Political Science*, London School of Economics and Political Science, 1932).
Winston, G.C. (1981) *The Timing of Economic Activities*, Cambridge University Press, Cambridge.

9 Economic structure: analytical perspectives

MAURO BARANZINI AND ROBERTO SCAZZIERI

1. Introduction

The concept of economic structure emerges as the outcome of a complex inter-relationship between the analytical representation of the objective stock–flow network of any given economic system and the theoretical formulation of some general features of economic behaviour as may be associated with the existence of relatively persistent institutional arrangements.

In this perspective a critical linkage is provided by the distinction between horizontal and vertical patterns of integration of economic activities. The aim of this paper is to provide a critical assessment of the different intellectual traditions of structural analysis in terms of the above distinction and to evaluate the particular contribution that each tradition may provide to the analysis of economic dynamics.

Section 2 of this chapter is devoted to an appraisal of the alternative treatments of economic structure in economic theory. In particular this task is carried out by providing an appraisal of horizontal and vertical approaches to the analysis of economic structure, which consider, respectively, the circular flow of mutually dependent economic activities and the 'one-way' relationship between certain key magnitudes (such as a final consumption bundle or a vector of primary productive resources) and the associated requirements for their production or utilization. Section 3 considers the linkage between the objective stock–flow network of economic magnitudes and the institutional arrangements existing behind such a network of flows and stocks. In this section the relevance of institutional arrangements for the analysis of qualitative transformations is stressed, the relationship between the role of institutions and the 'natural' dynamics that may be associated with the objective stock–flow network is

Research support from the Institute for the Dynamics of Economic Systems (IDSE) of the Italian National Research Council is gratefully acknowledged.

examined, and finally the connection between the identification of a particular institutional set-up and the formulation of 'local models' is investigated. Furthermore, a taxonomy of institutional aspects is attempted and the analysis of transformation is put into relation with the way in which material bases and institutional set-ups react upon one another. Section 4 considers some general requirements for structural analysis and stresses the relationship between persistence and change as a fundamental requirement for the analysis of structural change. At this point the treatment of economic dynamics is introduced (section 5). This is done by first identifying the fundamental descriptive features of a dynamic economic system, then by stressing the special relationship between structural specification and dynamic analysis and pointing out that particular methods of dynamic analysis require specific ways of identifying economic structure. Section 6 provides a rational reconstruction of the different strands of structural analysis in the light of two interrelated distinctions: (i) the way in which any objective stock–flow network of economic magnitudes may be represented by alternatively focusing upon the circular (horizontal) or vertical features within it; and (ii) the way in which one may identify within any given economic system those 'objective' or 'material' features that may be analysed quite independently of particular patterns of behaviour, as well as other features that may require the explicit consideration of the institutional set-up. The interplay between these two analytical dimensions is then examined by putting them into relation with the utilization of particular methods of dynamic analysis. The final section, which brings this volume to a close, attempts a systematization of structural theories in the light of the above treatment; in particular it is suggested that the distinction between the 'anatomy' and the 'physiology' of the economic system may be related with the analytical representation of economic structure and may lend itself to the identification of different but complementary frameworks for the investigation of economic dynamics.

2. Economic structure in economic theory

2.1 'Horizontal' and 'vertical' integration of economic activities

Economic theory may be seen as a representation of the relationships among elementary economic units such as production processes and consumption activities. Such a representation might take a different form depending on the criteria by means of which such processes and activities are linked to each other. In a number of cases this integration takes the form of a circular interdependence in which the consumption activities are considered as a necessary prerequisite of the production process itself; here the notion of 'productive consumption' is relevant: corn produced in the current year has to be partly used or has to be partly re-employed for the production of corn in order to ensure that next year's output of corn will be at least as great as this year's. In this way the productive consumption of corn is in fact a requirement for future production, so that a link is established between successive time periods. What is feasible in the current period is largely determined by what has been inherited from the previous periods. This framework provides an insight into the reasons why the economic system may find itself in a stationary state (as rigorously defined in Pigou, 1935) or on an expansion path. In this picture the production of commodities is often a prerequisite for the production of other commodities, and all commodities appear to be dependent on each other's production; we could therefore say that a pattern of 'horizontal' integration has been introduced.

Yet in other cases this integration takes the form of a 'one-way' or 'vertical' relationship in which consumption of commodities appears to be the ultimate goal of the production process. Here the notion of 'productive allocation' is relevant: corn produced in the current year is the outcome of a process in which a certain number of original inputs are employed. Its level of output depends, in each time period, on the quantities of such inputs that are made available at the beginning of the period. However there is no immediate connection between subsequent time periods: for any given technique of production the output level in each period depends on the amount of available resources that are not themselves produced in the economic system. In this perspective future production is disjointed from current production, and the reasons for the dynamic behaviour of the economic system are closely connected with the availability of the productive resources at each period. (Note that resources do not depend on the productive process under consideration.) In this picture the production of commodities depends, in terms of 'one-way' causality, on the availability of resources that are independent of the productive processes. Indeed here the notion of productive consumption is void of sense: we could argue that a pattern of 'vertical integration' has been established between production and consumption.

The above argument shows that there exists a fundamental dichotomy between the two alternative, even if not mutually exclusive, notions of economic structure considered as the set of relationships among economic magnitudes (such as sectoral outputs and productive resources). The two alternatives lead to what may be called 'horizontally integrated' and 'vertically integrated' models of economic structure. At this point we may inquire into the relationship between the above dichotomy and the vision of the network of the interpersonal relationships on which the economic system is based. The use of the horizontal model has often been associated with a vision of interpersonal relationships in which the existence of functional links among social groups or classes is a prominent feature; such links are based on the mutual interdependence of production processes, a concept that is stressed in this framework. For instance, the fundamental relationships among distinct groups of income earners are grafted to production technology in models such as those of Jan von Neumann, Wassily Leontief and Piero Sraffa.

On the other hand, the use of the vertically integrated model has often been associated with the idea that the economic fabric of society is based on relationships among individuals rather than social groups. An explanation for this feature could be that the use of vertical integration draws attention away from the issues of the reproduction of the economic system and focuses upon the relationship between productive resources and their allocation. As a result individuals come to the foreground in their dual role as resources owners and consumers. Along this line we find the contributions of authors connected with the Lausanne School, such as the classical achievements of Léon Walras and Vilfredo Pareto, and the modern works of Maurice Allais and Gérard Debreu.

2.2 Treatment and specification of economic structure in horizontally integrated models

It is the aim of this section to expound the content of the specific economic structure of the most important horizontally integrated models, for which any commodity appears both on the input and on the output side of the economic system so that neither original resources nor final consumption goods play a critical logical role. In particular we shall consider the models of von Neumann (1935–7), Leontief (1941), Sraffa (1960); we shall also examine the more recent contributions by John Hicks (1965), Luigi Pasinetti (1977, 1980), Adolph Löwe (1976), Alberto Quadrio-Curzio (1986).

The model presented by von Neumann in the mid-thirties is the first complete and mathematically rigorous formulation of a fully circular view of the economic system in which neither original resources nor final consumption play a crucial role. The idea of a circular description of the economic system was at that time a rather common feature of work in economic theory, especially in Central Europe; for instance Leontief had submitted in 1926 his doctoral dissertation ('Wirtschaft als Kreislauf', 1928) written under the supervision of Ladislaus von Bortkiewicz at the University of Berlin.

The specific problem addressed by von Neumann is to establish conditions under which a circular economy may expand over time at a maximum rate. The three basic qualifications of his model are: (a) every process always requires as means of production a positive quantity of every produced commodity; at the same time every produced commodity is delivered as an output by every process; (b) natural resources needed for expansion are available in unlimited amount; (c) the distribution of income is completely exogenously defined: wages are at the subsistence level and the residual net output corresponds to von Neumann's 'interest factor'.

The path 'maximum expansion' in von Neumann's circular economy is shown to correspond to a situation in which all processes grow at the same rate, so that the structure of the economic system remains unaltered. In equilibrium the 'expansion factor' (α) is equal to the 'interest factor' (β), when $\alpha = 1 + a/100$ (a being the expansion rate) and $\beta = 1 + b/100$ (b being the rate of interest).

Von Neumann's view of the economic system is hence associated with a growth pattern that implies no structural change: the different processes of production grow at the same rate, so that their relative proportions remain constant on the maximal growth path. Such a lack of structural change provides a link between von Neumann's approach and earlier theories of the circular economy in the sense that lack of structural change on the dynamic paths corresponds to lack of structural change in a stationary state (cf. Leontief, 1928). Similarly this treatment of structure provides an important link with Sraffa's work; for also in Sraffa the conditions for the reproduction of the economic system are examined within a stationary-state framework (cf. below).

The role of institutions is to be observed, especially, in the exogenous determination of the wage rate; this introduces a kind of 'consumption barrier' that constrains the amount of social product to be used for the expansion of the economic system. It is worth noting that this institutional constraint may be left open, in the sense that its working may be analysed in both capitalist and planned economies.

At this point a clarification is in order concerning the role of structural specification in circular economic models. In the case of von Neumann structure is associated with the analysis of requirement for steady-state economic expansion; Leontief's view is associated with the use of a structure of inquiry in which 'fact finding' takes place within a conceptual framework provided by the concept of general interdependence among component parts of a given economic system (see below); Sraffa considers the reproduction conditions in the field of prices and income distribution of the economic system.

An early description of the economic system in terms of 'general interdependence' is that put forward by Leontief (1941, 1953). Here interdependence is conceived as a set of 'directly observable basic structural relationships' (Leontief, 1987, p. 860). In particular Leontief's approach focuses on detailed quantitative descriptions of the relationships among component parts of a given economic system, independently of any consideration of possible behavioural patterns from which observed phenomena can be brought about.

The stress on empirical interdependence leads to concentration of attention on the 'structural matrix' of an economic system, that is of a matrix providing

> a basis for determination of total sectoral output as well as magnitude of inter-sectoral transaction that would enable the producing sector to deliver to households and to other so-called final users a specified 'bill of goods'. (Leontief, 1987, p. 861)

This approach is associated with a view of the economic system in which provision is made for the consideration of a circular set of relationships among productive sectors. Any such sector appears in a standard input–output table both as a row and as a column, so that in principle each sector can deliver its outputs to all other sectors (including itself) while at the same time receiving inputs from all such sectors.

Circularity, in this sense, is thus an outcome of the particular description of the economic system rather than the choice of a particular theoretical framework relative to the functioning of such a system. However the circular description of the economy has been used in order to enhance the theoretical understanding of an economic system that gives emphasis to production. In particular consideration of the input–output framework has been instrumental to the discovery of the conditions under which an economic system is able to 'sustain itself', mainly to reproduce the requirements for its material existence.

This is the so-called Hawkins–Simon's condition, whose economic interpretation is that

> for a system, in which each sector functions by absorbing directly or indirectly output of some other sectors, to be able not only to sustain itself but also to make some positive deliveries to final demand, each one of the smaller and smaller sub-systems contained within it has to be capable of sustaining itself and yielding a surplus deliverable to outside users as well. (Leontief, 1987, p. 862)

The study of the conditions for reproduction of an economic system in Leontief is clearly associated with the non-dynamic description of production technology. However, Leontief explicitly tackles the issue of dynamic processes by introducing a dynamic representation of production technology, which is presented as:

A step-by-step construction of complete input–output tables of the economy for successive periods of time, each based on the knowledge of its state in the previous period, of anticipated changes in the final bill of goods and expected technological changes. In more general terms, the input–output relationship between goods produced and consumed over a sequence of successive years, can be formally described exactly in the same terms as relationship between different sectors are presented in an ordinary 'static' input–output table for a single year. (Leontief, 1987, p. 863)

This contribution of Leontief draws attention to an important feature of the reproduction model, which one often assumes to be characterized by a perfect symmetry between the input and the output side. Here on the contrary 'outputs of one year can become inputs in later years, but not vice versa' (Leontief, 1987, p. 863), which involves a precise sequence in the time profile of production of commodities and of their use as inputs for subsequent processes of production.

Economic structure in Sraffa (1960) is conceived as a set of relationships among production processes ('industries') as determined by the technology in use; the assumption being made that a fully settled position of the economy cannot be possible unless there is some kind of compatibility among techniques in use in the different industries. In other words the system of Sraffa overlooks any interdependence among different markets and emphasizes the mutual dependence among techniques in use. Take the example of a corn–iron economy considered by Sraffa in his chapter 1 of *Production of Commodities by Means of Commodities*: here production of corn requires the use of both corn and iron; symmetrically, the production of iron requires both iron and corn. The proportion of the total output of corn used either in corn or iron production is determined by technology, as are the proportions of the total output of iron used as inputs in iron and corn production. This pattern of relationships among industries implies that exchanges are carried out from one industry to the other; however the terms of exchange are determined solely by technology, independently from the market forces of supply and demand. The core model of Sraffa is to be classified among models of the horizontally integrated type since commodities are all treated on the same basis, and no original inputs nor final consumption goods are to be found.

As far as institutions are concerned we may say that Sraffa's original corn–iron model, with no net product, belongs to the level of the 'natural' economy analysis in which fundamental features of the economic system can be detected without making any assumption about the institutional framework. However institutions come into play as soon as the system generates a positive net product; their role is to ensure a distribution of the net product among industries in order to guarantee the determinacy of the price system. In particular the assumption is made that the net product is distributed among industries according to the criterion of a uniform rate of profits ('for all industries' as Sraffa, 1960, p. 6, underlines), reflecting the requirements of a capitalistic competitive economic system.

This leaves open the issue of the actual value of the rate of profit. In this connection Sraffa states that:

> The choice of the wage as the independent variable in the preliminary stages was due to its being there regarded as consisting of specified necessaries determined by physiological or social conditions which are independent of prices or the rate of profits. But as soon as the possibility of variations in the division of the product is admitted, this consideration loses much of its force. And when the wage is to be regarded as 'given' in terms of a more or less abstract standard, and does not acquire a definite meaning until the prices of commodities are determined, the position is reversed. The rate of profits, as a ratio, has a significance which is independent of any prices, and can well be 'given' before the prices are fixed. It is accordingly susceptible of being determined from outside the system of production, in particular by the level of the money rates of interest. (Sraffa, 1960, p. 33)

This view points to the possible role that financial institutions may play for the determination of the system of relative prices in the horizontally integrated scheme.

A specific feature of Sraffa's system consists in the fact that the domain of structural analysis concerns solely the determination of the system of relative prices and distribution connected with a given set of techniques in use. Long-term structural dynamics does not play a significant role, and even in the case of technical choice the stress is on comparative static analysis rather than on the analysis of the actual traverse path from one set of techniques to the other. (In this connection it may be worth recalling Hicks's distinction between the comparison of alternative (virtual) states of a given economic system and the analysis of an actual historical process.)

Common features with Sraffa's model are to be found in Hicks (1965) in which the horizontal structure of the productive system is brought to the foreground. Here Hicks describes the productive system as consisting of two interlinked sectors, one producing corn by means of corn and tractors, the other producing tractors by means of corn and tractors. Hicks emphasizes the dynamic features of the traverse from one state of technology to another, stressing in particular the possibility of bottle-necks, which derive from the fact that different technologies are associated with different proportions between productive inputs (corn and tractors respectively). As a result the transition from one steady state to another is not immediate, and the economic system is held back by the short supply of a given resource.

This particular approach to the study of economic dynamics has recently been retaken up by Hicks in his *Methods of Dynamic Economics* (chapter on structural disequilibria, 1985) and the capital-and-growth method is explicitly singled out as one of the two methods specifically suited for the analysis of the transitional path (the other method being the vertically integrated approach of *Capital and Time*, Hicks, 1973). This model is characterized by the fact that institutions do not play a significant role, as they do in Sraffa (1960); the pattern of transition from one steady-state growth to another is solely related to the technological features of the states. (In this sense Hicks's structural disequilibrium method is grafted to the system of physical quantities, which determine the dynamic feature of the system, as in Quadrio-Curzio's more recent contribution (1986).)

The logic of the pure horizontally integrated model, common to Sraffa (1960) and Hicks (1965), has been put forward by Pasinetti (1977, 1980). Here Pasinetti has integrated Sraffa's and Hicks's circular models with the representation of technology by means of input/output coefficients originally used by Leontief (1941). This approach implies two major things: first, an additional technological constraint represented by the assumption of constant technical coefficients; and secondly, a higher degree of flexibility for the examination of the complete system of inter-industry links. Such a higher flexibility allows for a more complete study of the implications of changes in the system of physical quantities over time. The institutional set-up is similar to that of Sraffa.

The analysis of interdependence in the framework of the horizontally integrated models may be connected with the distinction originally put forward by Schumpeter (1954) between 'advance economies' and 'synchronization economies', in which attention is focused either on the production of commodities by means of previous advances of capital or on the production system as a network of processes that are carried out side by side at the same time.[1] From our point of view the special cases of a circular economy provided by Sraffa are an example of a synchronization economy; while Hicks (1965) provides a first attempt to introduce an explicit link between the structure of the production system at two subsequent production periods.

Löwe's contribution is an important step towards the construction of a comprehensive treatment of the unfolding through time of a 'synchronization economy' that is subject to variations of its fundamental variables. This is achieved by formulating a particular model of the production system in which the aspects of interdependence characteristic of the horizontally integrated approach are combined with certain elements characteristic of the vertical integration approach – such as the notion of a sequence through

[1] We owe this point to our colleague Ferdinando Meacci, of the University of Padua, who has drawn our attention to this particular aspect of Schumpeter's work (see also Meacci, 1989).

historical time – thereby introducing an asymmetry between the input and the output side, which is not considered in models of the pure circular type. In particular Löwe stresses the importance of transformation processes allowing the transformation of raw materials into finished products. In this framework Löwe concentrates his attention on the study of a 'traverse' from one steady state to another. In this connection a number of characteristic features emerge:

(i) the economic system is described by means of a circular technology in which a number of produced commodities may be used as inputs in successive periods. In particular this pattern of interdependence dictates the way in which the system responds to changes in the growth rate of productive factors of production, especially of labour;
(ii) The case of an economic system that produces in the aggregate exactly as much as is needed for replacement in each period may be defined as a 'self-sustaining system'; here the system must find the exact exchange ratios among different sectors in order to avoid over- or under-production in each sector; a first case of 'traverse' may be that in which there is a change of 'technology in use', so that the economy must leave the original self-sustained state;
(iii) Löwe's attention concentrates on the traverse considered as the transition path from one growth equilibrium to another; in this case a change of technology in use makes it necessary for the economic system to change also the ratios among inputs. Such changes may entail shortages or excess capacity before a new growth equilibrium is eventually attained. In this connection a special feature considered by Löwe is the speed of traverse, which may significantly influence the timing and amounts of shortages or excess capacity;
(iv) Distribution of income among factors of production or socio-economic classes is also relevant as far as the shape of the traverse path is concerned. Löwe points out that in order to move from one growth rate to another, or analogously from one distribution to another, the transition requires a transformation of the physical capital stock. In addition an important link with distribution is provided by the fact that once the capital stock is set up there is a unique set of outputs consistent with full-employment and full-capacity utilization. (Note that, given a specific price system, the level of employment defines the relative distribution of income among factors of production and/or socio-economic classes.)

The distinction between 'advance economy' and 'synchronization economy' (see above) may also be used to introduce the contribution by

Alberto Quadrio-Curzio (1986). Here the author outlines two distinct ways of representing the production system: first the *combined techniques* method, which allows for a careful description of the linkages between techniques at any given time, and secondly the *disjointed techniques* method, in which the production system is split into a number of different sub-systems, each one associated with its 'own' particular rate of maximal growth. The combined techniques method focuses on interdependence between production processes and describes a situation in which different techniques are used side by side in order to produce the same commodity. The disjointed techniques method describes the production system by splitting it into distinct sub-systems, each of which consists of a 'complete' set of production techniques. (Complete in the sense that there is one technique for each type of produced commodity.) Schumpeter's concept of 'synchronization economy' finds an application in Quadrio-Curzio's 'combined techniques' approach since it focuses on the linkages among techniques at a given point of time. On the other hand Schumpeter's concept of 'advance economy' may be linked to Quadrio-Curzio's concept of disjointed technology, since each production sub-system is connected in time with the other sub-systems – as defined above – by means of the produced inputs that are 'carried over' from one sub-system to another, as when any sub-system generates net products that cannot be accumulated within it. Production techniques are thus described in two distinct but complementary ways: in the first case, all techniques appear to be interrelated with one another by means of 'horizontal' interdependencies, so that all techniques appear to be supplying each other's means of production on the basis of a uniform 'circular flow'; in the latter case, the interrelationship among techniques takes a different character, since a sequence of semi-independent sub-systems is now considered, in which any sub-system that has entered *its own* stationary state (so that its net product cannot be accumulated within it) may either generate residuals or feed its net product into a sub-system of 'lower rank' (that is, into a sub-system that comes after it on Quadrio-Curzio's 'efficiency ranking', which is based on the decreasing sequence of net product rates of the distinct production sub-systems; see Quadrio-Curzio, 1975 and 1986).

Quadrio-Curzio's way of looking into the structure of the economic system allows an in-depth analysis of the underpinnings of structural specification, particularly for what concerns its implications for the field of dynamic analysis. In this connection, his distinction between the horizontal' and 'vertical' specifications of the production system on a traverse path is especially worth mentioning (see also section 5 below).

2.3 Treatment and specification of economic structure in vertically integrated models

In this section we shall expound the logical characteristics and the economic implications of the most important vertically integrated models, for which a prominent feature is the analysis of the relationship between original (non-produced) resources and final consumption goods. In particular we shall consider three distinct groups of contributions. First, the modern formulation of general economic equilibrium in the tradition of the Lausanne School (in particular Allais, 1943, and Debreu, 1959); secondly, the analytical framework of temporary general equilibrium, with a special emphasis on the work of Sir John Hicks (1939); thirdly, the revival of the Smithian concept of vertical integration by Pasinetti (1965, 1973, 1981); finally, Hicks's (1973) vertical integration along the time dimension as expounded in *Capital and Time*.

The original work of Maurice Allais (1943, 1947) is rooted in the Walras–Pareto formulations of general equilibrium theory. Here economic structure is conceived as the set of data and relationships explaining how economic agents make decisions concerning the consumption and production activities. In particular, economic structure is described by (i) the set of preferences of economic agents; (ii) the set of initial resources; (iii) the set of production possibilities determining the way in which initial resources may be transformed into final consumption goods.

Here economic theory concentrates upon the existence and formation of prices within a given time period and on the basis of a given structure; and the concept of dynamics relates to the linkage between different time periods. (In the original Walras–Pareto framework the linkage between different periods of time is represented by the formation of saving and the production of new capital goods that are carried over from one time period to the next.) Here again the formation of interest plays a critical role in establishing a link between the present and the future.

This particular specification of economic structure has provided the basis for at least two distinct lines of research. One is concerned with the existence and formation of equilibrium prices; the other is concerned with the formation of surpluses and their distribution in connection with the shape of the dynamic path followed by an economic system.

The first approach stems from the work of economists such as Lindahl (1939), Hicks (1939) and Debreu (1959). Lindahl and Hicks introduced the assumption that the economic system 'extends over a finite number of elementary time intervals' (Debreu, 1959, p. 35*n*) and formulated a theoretical framework in which the formation of equilibrium prices reflects both present circumstances and expectations about the future. A most critical distinguishing feature with respect to the original Walras–Pareto framework was brought out with Debreu's description of the economic system as a set of complete markets, that is as a set of markets for all commodities at all possible dates and places of delivery (see Debreu, 1959). In the latter case:

> The economy is considered as of a given instant called the present instant. A commodity is characterized by its physical properties, the date at which it will be available, and the location at which it will be available. The price of the commodity is the amount which has to be paid *now* for the (future) availability of one unit of that commodity. (Debreu, 1959, p. 28)

A characteristic feature of Debreu's formulation is that an equilibrium state of the economy involves the specification of the set of all commodity prices. (Here it is important to stress that 'a good at a certain date and the same good at a later date are *different* economic objects, and the specification of the date at which it will be available is essential' (Debreu, 1959, p. 29).)

As pointed out above, the type of structural specification rooted in the Walras–Pareto tradition may also be used to examine the formation and distribution of economic surpluses in connection with the shape of the dynamic path followed by an economic system. In Allais's terms:

> If one looks for a common guiding principle in the research into the theory of surpluses, one is led to consider ... a more or less explicit search for an indicator to represent the global surplus realized by the economy, corresponding for the 'gains' accruing from production and exchange, whether this means 'utility gains' or gains expressed in physical quantities. This indicator would increase when 'mutually advantageous' acts of exchange and production are carried out. It should be both maximum and nil in a situation of maximal efficiency, and it ought to enable the different possible economic situations to be ranked in order of increasing efficiency. (Allais, 1986, pp. 150–1)

Within this framework, two major issues emerge:

(i) The relationship between the identification of distributable surpluses and the structural specification of the economic system: 'the necessary and sufficient condition for [a state of the economy] to be of maximum efficiency for the set of operators under consideration is that the distributable surplus ... be negative or zero ... for every feasible modification ... that is compatible with the structural relations of the economy.' (Allais, 1986, p. 144)

(ii) The relationship between distributable surpluses and economic dynamics, which is essentially conceived as the search for the realization and distribution of surpluses.

In this respect, a distinctive feature of Allais's theory of surpluses is the stress on the dynamic processes in the course of which surpluses may be generated. This entails a move away from Walras's general equilibrium theory and a reappraisal of early contributions such as those of David Ricardo and Arsène Dupuit. This contribution clarifies a logical possibility within the structural specification of the Walras–Pareto theory that had previously escaped the economists' attention, and points towards the building of a general theoretical framework in which the focus of interest is the study of economic dynamics rather than the issue of price formation; in particular this theory

> replaces the search for a certain system of prices, the same for all operators, by the search for a situation in which no surplus is realizable. The concept of prices is relegated to the background of the analysis and only plays a subsidiary role. It is the concept of surplus which plays the major role in the new formulation. (Allais, 1986, p. 159)

The different contributions considered so far in this section point to the possible uses of an essentially common structural specification of the economy of markets in which the basic characteristics of the system are described by the set of given resources, by the set of feasible techniques and the ordinal preferences of the economic units. The economic process may therefore be described as 'a one-way avenue that leads from "factors of production" to "consumption goods"'. (Sraffa, 1960, p. 93)

It is worth stressing that the approaches considered so far concentrate attention on general interdependence among economic units in which the type of commodity descriptions may be exhaustively carried out; however such a fine classification of commodities does not yet imply the consideration of an economic structure based on the 'circular flow' of production and consumption at the level of the economic system as a whole. For example, intermediate commodities (such as machines, tools and semi-finished goods) are explicitly considered, and in specific cases 'sub-systems' may be identified in which a set of markets includes the market for a final commodity as well as those in which the same commodity is used as a means of production and therefore performs the role of an intermediate commodity. However, circularity implies interdependence of a 'technological' type at the level of the economic system as a whole; in this perspective the model of general equilibrium considered cannot avoid assuming a given set of initial, non-produced resources which allows us to distinguish between the role performed by the interdependence of markets in this approach and the role performed by the interdependence of production processes in the economic theories of the 'horizontal' type (see subsection 2.2 above). The 'vertical' relationship between original inputs and final consumption goods, which is implicit in the Walrasian treatment of production processes as processes by means of which non-produced inputs are transformed into final consumption goods, is given a more general and rigorous formulation in the economic theories explicitly based upon the concept of vertical integration of production processes. Here the approaches followed by Pasinetti (1965, 1981) and Hicks (1970, 1973) ought to be distinguished.

Pasinetti introduces a vertical integration of production processes that allows a reclassification of the inter-industry commodity flows so that the intermediate input requirements for each produced commodity are reduced to the corresponding quantity of labour input and to a certain residual quantity of physical means of production. This procedure can be performed more than once so that eventually one is left with a negligible residual of physical means of production and with the quantity of labour input directly and indirectly required to produce the commodity under consideration. In the particular case in which the starting point is provided by a production technology in which commodities are produced by means of labour and other produced commodities, one is left with an economic system of the 'pure labour type'. This approach, which was initially sketched by Adam Smith, has recently been taken up by Pasinetti, who has proposed a vertically integrated model explicitly derived from the elimination of inter-industry flows of intermediate commodities (see, in particular, Pasinetti, 1973).

In a simple case the economic system is reduced to:

> a society of individuals [who] carry out an activity of production and an activity of consumption. All consumption goods are made by labour alone; labour is therefore the only 'factor of production'. (Pasinetti, 1986b, p. 421)

The one-way directionality of the production process is here presented in its purest form: human beings produce commodities by means of their activity alone, and the produced commodities are used only for their personal consumption. As a result, no intermediate products need to be taken into account. However, the same 'one-way' picture of the overall technology can be maintained if the procedure of vertical integration, which has been outlined above, is applied to a production technology in which commodities are produced by means of labour and other commodities (labour and intermediate inputs). For in this case the produced commodities that may be used as inputs in each other's production are reclassified depending on the type of *final* consumption good in whose production they are indirectly used. (For example, the corn used as an input for the production of machine tools to be used in the textile sector will now appear as a quantity of corn directly used in the textile sector.)

This procedure allows economic analysis to 'break' the structure of the 'circular flow' and to bring forth the unidirectionality underlying the process of social production. Once this result is achieved, only one other logical step is required in order to obtain an increasingly smaller residual of produced inputs by iteration of the vertical integration procedure outlined above (see Pasinetti, 1973).

Pasinetti's contribution to the study of vertical integration outlines in a rigorous way the logic of unidirectionality in the specification of economic structure. Therefore Pasinetti's merit is to provide two important insights into the concept of economic structure:

(i) a classification of the concept of unidirectionality in the analysis of the relationship between production and consumption process;

(ii) the presentation of a method of inquiry that allows for the consideration of the aspects of unidirectionality in the framework of circular economic structure. (This means also that unidirectional linkages may be focused upon both in a completely circular structure and in a vertical structure including sub-systems of a circular type.)

A second way of dealing with the role of intermediate inputs within the framework provided by vertical integration is that put forward by Sir John Hicks (1973) in his 'new-Austrian' approach to capital theory. A characteristic feature of this contribution of Hicks is that, as in Böhm-Bawerk (1889) and Hayek (1941), the 'general productive process' is conceived as 'being composed of a number (presumably a larger number) of *separable elementary processes*' (Hicks, 1973, p. 7). However, while in the original Austrian treatment each elementary process is associated with 'a unit of output, forthcoming at a particular date', and with 'a sequence of units of input at particular previous dates' (Hicks, 1973, p. 7), in Hicks's own framework an elementary process is introduced 'that converts a sequence (or stream) of inputs into a sequence of outputs' (Hicks, 1973, p. 8).

An example of Hicks's way of describing an elementary process may be provided by considering 'a process which consists in the construction of a plant, its operation over a period of years and its ultimate dismantling' (Hicks, 1973, p. 15). In this case:

> There is an initial construction period, with large inputs but no final output; it is followed by a running-in period, in which output rises from zero to a normal level, while input falls to its normal level (constructional labour being laid off while the labour force which is to work the plant is being built up). There follows a period, probably a long period, of normal utilization. Finally, as a result of a fall in the output curve or of a rise in the input curve, the process comes to an end. (Hicks, 1973, p. 15)

An important implication of Hicks's reformulation of Austrian production theory is that one avoids the explicit consideration of intermediate inputs, thus bringing to the fore an important feature of vertical integration of productive processes. As a matter of fact, according to Hicks, the explicit consideration of intermediate processes can be avoided by taking into account that:

> The sales of capital goods, such as the sale by the firm which produces a raw material (or machine) to the firm which uses it, result from the *disintegration* of the productive process; in a (vertically) integrated process they would not occur. (Hicks, 1973, p. 5)

Hicks's vertical integration, as expounded in *Capital and Time*, is rooted in the explicit consideration of the time structure of production. This allows for the elimination of intermediate inputs (Hicks's 'capital goods') in a way that is different from the approach followed by Pasinetti in his construction of a vertically integrated model that breaks the circular structure of inter-industry relationships. A remarkable implication of the fact that circularity is eliminated by means of conceiving the productive process 'as a pair of flows, of inputs and outputs ... varying over time, (Hicks, 1973, pp. 14–15) is that a particular approach to the study of economic transformation is introduced, an approach that places great emphasis upon the role of complementarities over time. As a result, Hicks's method lends itself quite naturally to the analysis of transition paths from one state of the economy to another. Transformation of the productive structure is described as a process in which 'the funds which would have been used for replacement of capital goods of the old sort, or for investment in such capital goods, may be transferred to finance the production of capital goods of the new kind' (Hicks, 1973, p. 11). In this way a precise relationship is established among the vertical concept of economic structure, the role of time in production and the study of economic transition.

3. Institutions in economic theory

3.1 The significance of institutions in structural analysis

3.1.1 Institutional arrangements and the objective stock–flow network

The description of economic systems lends itself to the identification of two distinct but interrelated patterns of economic relationships; one is represented by the *objective* network of the flows of produced commodities and services and of the stock of real assets existing at any given point of time; the other is represented by the *institutional arrangements* behind such a network of flows and stocks.

Institutions, which may be defined as 'prevalent habits of thought with respect to particular relations and particular functions of the individual and of the community' (Veblen, 1953, p. 132; as quoted in Georgescu-Roegen, 1988a, p. 308), are at the basis of the specific forms taken by economic activity in relation to the processes of production, consumption and accumulation.

The first type of structural specification, calling attention upon the objective stock–flow network of economic activities, allows for a most general treatment of the features of different economic systems, thus making them comparable on the basis of a set of limited and precisely identified empirical characteristics. The second type of specification in which institutional arrangements play a fundamental role, permits a careful identification of the distinguishing features that characterize any given form of economic activity.

In this section we shall deal specifically with contributions in which attention is focused upon the role of the institutional set up in determining the characteristics of economic structure as an objective stock–flow network of economic activities, and the path of structural change associated with any given type of structure. In this connection we start with the issue of how it is possible to treat any actual process of economic dynamics in terms of a theoretical framework in which the different types of structural description mentioned above are combined.

3.1.2 Quantitative changes and qualitative transformations

Georgescu-Roegen has recently put forward the thesis that 'economic growth involves not only quantitative changes but also qualitative transformations' (Georgescu-Roegen, 1976, p. 235; 1st edn 1974). This may be linked with the interplay between objective and institutional features of economic structure, in so far as purely quantitative changes are an insufficient basis for describing and explaining first the intrinsic characteristics of each dynamic process, and secondly the concrete transformations occurring from one specific path to another.

The relevance of institutional features for the study of economic change is provided by the lack of similarity between the productive organization in agriculture and industry:

> One may grow wheat in a pot or raise chickens in a tiny backyard, but no hobbyist can build an automobile with only the tools of his workshop. Why then should the optimum scale for agriculture be that of a giant open-air factory? In the second place, the role of the time factor is entirely different in the two activities. By mechanical devices we can shorten the time for weaving an ell of cloth, but we have as yet been unable to shorten the gestation period in animal husbandry or (to any significant degree) the period for maturity in plants. Moreover, agricultural activity is bound to an unflinching rhythm, while in manufacture we can very well do tomorrow what we have chosen not to do today. Finally, there is a difference between the two sectors which touches the roots of the much discussed law of decreasing returns (in the evolutionary sense). For industrial uses man has been able

to harness one source of energy after another, from the wind to the atom, but for the type of energy that is needed by life itself he is still wholly dependent on the most 'primitive' source, the animals and plants around him. (Georgescu-Roegen, 1976, pp. 107–8; 1st edn 1960)

This passage stresses the relevance of any particular form of productive organization considered as a 'cluster' of technological, institutional and physical features of the production process. Such a cluster of features gives identity to economic structure at any given point of time and brings about two specific characteristics of dynamic processes in the economic field: one is the crucial role of qualitative transformations, such as the shift from an agrarian-based to an industrial-based type of production (which implies that the specific cluster of features of the industrial production becomes the dominant pattern of economic activity); the other is the lack of perfect reversibility of dynamic processes taking place through real time.

In this connection Georgescu-Roegen has pointed out that reversible paths are generally derived by committing the 'fallacy of misplaced concreteness, by which Whitehead understands "neglecting the degree of abstraction involved when an actual entity is considered merely so far as it exemplifies certain [preselected] categories of thought"' (Georgescu-Roegen, 1971, p. 321). In the case of economics this type of fallacy involves that '[A] few extremely simple structures, beginning with that represented by a stationary (reproducible) process have been found to constitute a sufficient working base for a series of results' (Georgescu-Roegen, 1976, p. 237; 1st edn 1974), thus bringing about the simplification that economic changes are of a reversible type and may be studied independently of the explicit consideration of qualitative transformation. However the mutual dependence of dynamic processes and qualitative transformation may be conceived as a necessary condition for any actual self-sustained process of growth:

Mere growth – i.e., change confined to *quantity* – cannot exist in actuality continuously. The same is true even for the so-called stationary state. Briefly, continuous existence in a finite environment necessarily requires qualitative change. And it is this qualitative change that accounts for the irreversibility of the economic process. (Georgescu-Roegen, 1976, p. 237; 1st edn 1974)

3.1.3 Institutional 'middle principles' and determinacy of economic behaviour

The relevance of the institutional framework for the analysis of the way in which the objective stock–flow network of economic activities is shaped is stressed by Löwe's treatment of 'sociological middle principles'. Such principles are identified with the institutional features of the economic structure under consideration, and these determine the specific outcomes of economic behaviour and thus the particular network of stock–flow relationships characterizing any economic system at a given point of time. This type of analysis leads Löwe to identify the precise 'cluster' of institutional features governing the working of the market economy. Here Löwe points out that two fundamental sociological principles are at the basis of the 'exact laws of the market': 'the economic man on the one hand, competition or mobility of the productive factor on the other hand' (Löwe, 1935, p. 58).

Such principles are essential in establishing the determinacy of economic actions and reactions within the framework of the 'society of exchange' (Löwe). As a matter of fact it is pointed out that even in the absence of these principles 'occasional exchange actions may take place' (Löwe, 1935, p. 59); however it would be impossible to explain 'the functioning of exchange as the general order of an economic *system*' (Löwe, 1935, p. 60). In particular the determinacy of market laws is specifically related with the existence of a particular cluster of institutional features:

> The market system can persist as general and permanent economic organisation only if the impulses of every member as to quantity and quality of production, expressed by his price offers, are reacted to in a determinate manner ... [E]xchange cannot be efficient and cannot even continue as a basic form of an economic system, unless the permanent interrelationship between the partners is secured and substantially guided by ... a general working rule of bargaining behaviour. (Löwe, 1935, pp. 61–2)

A characteristic feature of Löwe's approach is that the determinacy of economic behaviour, which may be found in association with the 'exactness and calculability of the market relations' (Löwe, 1935, p. 73), is derived from the introduction of particular assumptions concerning the structure of society. In this way Löwe gives shape to his 'society of exchange', which is characterized as follows:

> Civil liberty, private property rights, free decision of the individual as to his bargaining, at the same time a structure of the material equipment that does not prevent shifting, whenever a change in the market conditions suggests a change in business and work – a concrete idea of social psychology, of the political and legal constitution is combined with a definite conception of technique: small-scale organization of many independent producers. (Löwe, 1935, pp. 58–9)

The function of a precise identification of the institutional set-up is brought to the fore by the 'instrumentalistic' approach that Löwe associated with modern economic analysis. The backbones of such an instrumentalistic approach have been described by Löwe as follows:

It picks out imaginable constellations of data and deduces therefrom movements and states of rest under varying hypotheses. Any such constellation implies a set of sociological premises. But the conditions of the origin and persistence of these constellations are intentionally disregarded, and equally their connection with the system as a whole and any influences which might arise from outside the particular set of data under consideration ... We call [this method] instrumentalistic, because it does not directly depict real structure, but tries to build up possible types of market order by pursuing individual movements under the assumption of a typical constellation of the whole. (Löwe, 1935, p. 140)

The above argument rests upon the belief that economic analysis cannot be carried out unless a precise 'constellation' of parameters has been identified, such as free decision making on the part of individuals or the free disposal of resources. However a more detailed analysis of the specific institutional requirements for each particular aspect of the working of the economic system leads Löwe to distinguish between two different levels of economic analysis. The first relates to the implications of any given technological set-up for the functioning of the economic system both at any given point of time and along a dynamic path (such implications may be examined independently of any detailed institutional specification); the second relates to aspects of economic activity that cannot be investigated unless particular institutional assumptions are introduced.

In the first case, where the technological set-up is the prevailing structuring element, it is possible to carry out an investigation of those conditions concerning the objective stock–flow network that must be satisfied 'if the transformation of the initial into the stipulated terminal state is to be achieved' (Löwe, 1976, p. 17). The second case, which requires the explicit formulation of institutional assumptions, deals with the way in which the actual dynamics of any given economic system reflects particular behavioural and motivational features.

It is the analysis of actual dynamic paths that

raises economics above the level of a mere engineering science by studying the patterns of behaviour and motivation that initiate and sustain the motion of the system along the structurally determined path. These patterns themselves are closely related to the prevailing social structure that defines the institutional frameworks within which economic activity is to operate. (Löwe, 1976, p. 17)

An example of the importance of the above distinction is provided by the analysis of the adjustment path that may be followed by an economy in its transition from one dynamic equilibrium to another. The reason is that, for any given technological set-up, there is normally a *plurality* of such adjustment paths, each of them satisfying a specific normative requirement: 'One path maximizes speed of adjustment, another minimizes waste of resources, and a third minimizes the impact on consumption during the interval of capital formation.' (Löwe, 1976, p. 106) This implies that different institutional set-ups bring about different ways of possible adjustments, so that the identification of a precise 'goal-adequate motion' (Löwe) depends on which institutional framework is taken for granted. (Different types of institutions may constrain the adjustment path in different ways, in the sense that the number of feasible paths compatible with given institutions may differ from one case to another.) On the other hand, this perspective leads to the problem of which institutional set-up is more appropriate in order to reach any specific 'terminal state'. This issue is especially prominent when it comes to devising strategies of economic planning that can lead the economic system from a given initial state to a desired terminal state. Here the following distinct and logical steps may be singled out: (i) the introduction of a specific configuration of the economic system as the desired terminal state; (ii) the identification of the set of feasible paths, on the basis of the existing structure and of the assigned goals; (iii) the introduction of 'behavioural patterns which will set the system on goal-adequate trajectories' (Chakravarty, 1987, p. 42).

An important feature of Löwe's approach to the analysis of the relationship between economic structure and economic institutions is that structural analysis may be carried out independently of the institutional framework as long as attention is focused on the structural requirements associated with the objective characteristics of technology. However, Löwe-type structural analysis is restricted to the identification of the set of feasible adjustment paths leading the economic system from one state to another. On the other hand, the study of a completely determinate trajectory presupposes the explicit introduction of institutional factors restraining the set of feasible behaviours.

3.1.4 The 'natural' dynamics and the role of institutions

The interplay between objective aspects and institutionally determined aspects of economic dynamics has been further investigated by Pasinetti (1964–5, 1981) in his formulation of a theory of economic structure and structural change. Here Pasinetti stresses that economic relationships belong to two distinct categories, each leading to a different method of inquiry. The first is the set of relationships that may be defined independently of the institutional set-up of the economic system: examples may be found in the 'structural interdependencies linking the industrial branches of the economic system; or the relationships among increases in average productivity, increases in the wage-rate, investment and general price-level. Such relationships may be stated in terms of objective efficiency or ... in "natural terms". They thus are unaffected by the institutional set-up.' (Pasinetti, 1964–5, pp. 247–8) The second set of relationships identified by Pasinetti concerns the economic arrangements that are specific to any particular institutional set-up, such as the demand-and-supply mechanism of price determination within the framework of the market economy.

Furthermore, according to Pasinetti (1964–5, p. 248) the 'natural' and the 'institutional' economic relationships may be associated with two different types of causal frameworks; whereas 'natural' relationships lend themselves to the identification of causal chains, in which a precise direction of causality may be established between fundamental explanatory variables and their relative impact upon structural interdependencies, the 'institutional' relationships may be associated with 'mutual causality' (Hicks, 1979, p. 19) among all the variables that reflect the simultaneous working of a given institutional mechanism.

The distinction between natural and institutional relationships is applied to the analysis of structural economic dynamics, namely to the study of those transformations of the objective stock–flow network that reflect the basic characteristics of technological, demographic and consumption factors and are considered to be independent of the institutional framework; in this perspective the analysis of structural change is carried out by starting

> from an evolving technology, a growing population and an evolving pattern of consumers' preferences. From these natural forces, and from nothing else, a series of structural movements have been derived which may indeed be called the *natural features* of a growing economic system. They are represented by: i) an evolving structure of commodity prices; ii) an evolving structure of production; iii) the time path of the wage rate and of the rate – or rates – of profit. (Pasinetti, 1981, pp. 127–8)

According to Pasinetti, the determinacy of the natural dynamic path is warranted by the assumption that structural change satisfies the conditions for full-employment and full-capacity utilization, thereby obtaining the two specific necessary conditions for natural-path dynamic, namely: 'a series of *sectoral* new investment conditions, defining the evolving structure of capital accumulation'; and 'a *macro-economic* effective demand condition, referring to total demand in the economic system as a whole' (Pasinetti, 1981, p. 128).

A distinctive feature of Pasinetti's 'natural dynamics' is that the determinacy of any given path of structural change is obtained by means of specific 'equilibrium' requirements (the full-employment and full-capacity utilization conditions) and quite independently of the institutional set-up and thus also independently of particular behavioural and motivational features. On the other hand, a plurality of institutional frameworks may be compatible with the achievement of the natural-path conditions mentioned above. These characteristics of Pasinetti's theory may be compared with the approach to structural analysis adopted by Löwe; both Löwe and Pasinetti agree upon the distinction between two fundamental levels of analysis – the natural (Pasinetti) or structural (Löwe), and the institutional (Löwe and Pasinetti) – but in Löwe the determinacy of adjustment paths presupposes specific behavioural and motivational assumptions; whereas in Pasinetti the natural dynamic path is uniquely determined independently of institutions.

An interesting implication of Pasinetti's theoretical framework is that not necessarily all types of institutional set-ups may allow for the attainment of natural-path conditions. This result paves the way for the integration of an explicitly normative type of analysis within the framework of the theory of structural economic dynamics:

> When it is granted that it is possible, on purely logical grounds, to (conceptually) build up the framework of a natural economic system, it becomes inevitable to think that it must be one of the aims of any society to bring the actual economic structure as near as possible to the one defined by the natural economic system; i.e., to organise itself, to devise institutional mechanisms, such as to make the actual economic quantities permanently tend towards their 'natural' levels or dynamic paths. (Pasinetti, 1981, p. 154)

3.1.5 Simplifying and characterizing assumptions: 'local models' and the institutional set-up

So far we have considered the role of economic structure in relationship with the institutional set-up. More precisely, we have examined the view of scholars who have stressed the relative autonomy of structural and institutional analysis. Here the role of economic theory seems to be restricted to the study of a set of fundamental relationships associated with the objective stock–flow network characterizing any given economic system. A complementary approach to the analysis of economic institutions has recently been provided by Morishima (1984) in his contribution to the identification of 'local models' for the analysis of industrial society. The general methodological framework of Morishima is provided by the idea that general economic theory may be too abstract to allow for a specific interpretation 'of the way in which the real economy operates' and of 'the best way to bring about a change in direction in this operation' (Morishima, 1984, p. viii).

The identification of the local model that is relevant for each particular economic system is derived from the distinction between 'simplifying and characterizing assumptions':

Simplifying assumptions are those which make discussion simple and the analytical perspective clear; characterizing assumptions are those which remove extraneous factors so that we can isolate the special characteristics of an economy. (Morishima, 1984, p. 135)

Assumptions that, in spite of their power to simplify an argument, are liable to alter the line of reasoning substantially may no longer be regarded as purely simplifying assumptions. They are rather assumptions of the characterizing type since:

While illuminating the special features of the economy about which [they are] made, [they] allow us to pursue a course of analysis that is only valid under the assumption, and to draw particular conclusions on the basis of [them]. (Morishima, 1984, p. 135)

The identification of characterizing assumptions leads one to separate between 'essential' and 'non-essential' features of an economic model. The former cannot be disregarded if the fundamental conclusions of any given theory have to be retained; they are thus those assumptions that correspond with crucial features of any particular institutional set-up. The latter type of features are not so closely associated with the type of economic society under consideration, but they may help to describe a whole cluster of different economic systems so that analysis is facilitated even if 'it is precisely when appropriate characterizing assumptions are made that theory is refined and makes substantial progress' (Morishima, 1984, p. 136).

One way of applying the distinction between simplifying and characterizing assumptions is to consider the size of industrial countries as an indicator of the cluster of essential assumptions that may be used to explain the working of an economic system associated with a given institutional set-up. The hallmark of 'large capitalist countries' is that 'countries such as the United States which are rich in natural resources ... are more or less self-sufficient, having virtually no dependence on any other country'; thus their economic system 'can develop any industrial sector that should be necessary' (Morishima, 1984, p. 3). The characterizing features of 'medium-sized industrial nations' is that 'land area is small'; thus these countries 'are perforce dependent on other countries for many of their industrial raw materials and fuel', while being 'strong enough to be able to develop domestically all sectors of industry' (Morishima, 1984, p. 3). Finally '[s]mall industrial countries are unable to produce all industrial commodities. Some of them may be unable to produce capital goods and have to purchase machines from abroad, while others may be unable to produce certain kinds of consumer goods and have no choice but to import these consumer goods from other countries to satisfy demand from the people. In as far as its population is small, a small-sized country will not possess the labour force adequate for the domestic production of all kinds of industrial products, so such small countries are likely to be forced into the position of "small industrial countries."' (Morishima, 1984, p. 4)

It is worth noting that Morishima's distinction among the above three types of economic systems may also be associated with a specific description of structural economic dynamics in a development process. In particular, development may induce change in the basic institutional features of the economic system, thus requiring change in the characterizing assumptions of any type of economic theory relevant to the analysis of the actual development process.

> There ... exist countries, which, while they may be sizeable in terms of population, cannot, for reasons such as the low level of education, develop those sectors of industry which require particular skills. Some industrial countries in the process of development become 'small industrial countries' for this reason, and many of these countries may easily before long become 'medium-sized industrial countries' if the opportunity offers. Some may even progress to become 'large countries'. (Morishima, 1984, p. 4)

The above appraisal of the relationship between the historical framework and the theoretical analysis of any given economic system calls attention to the specific role of the 'restricted abstraction approach' (Scazzieri, 1988, p. 154) in the use of economic theory. In particular the role of 'local models' is highlighted, and the relationship between economic history and economic theorizing appears to be one in which history provides the economist with a number of alternative institutional frameworks, thus emphasizing those 'characterizing assumptions' that give shape to the type of historically specific economic theories relevant for the analysis of any given economic situation (see Sylos-Labini, 1984).

3.2 A taxonomy of institutional aspects: analytical framework and economic dynamics

3.2.1 The 'analytical map' of interpersonal relationships

The role of institutions and their relevance for the analysis of economic dynamics may be assessed by introducing a number of general principles concerning the formulation of a suitable analytical framework. In this connection it is worth mentioning that 'each special science should build its analytical framework on those elements which represent atomic units within its particular domain. They are the elements that, if divided further, cease to reflect the very phenomena in which the corresponding discipline is interested' (Georgescu-Roegen, 1976, p. 205; 1st edn 1965).

The fundamental elements of a theory of economic institutions grafted into the analysis of structural economic dynamics may be derived from the conceptual framework originally formulated by Georgescu-Roegen (1976, pp. 205–6; 1st edn 1965). According to this theory, it is possible to identify in principle all institutional relations R_i that may exist between any pair of individuals A_i and A_j; however not all such relations always hold in practice. This allows for the identification of a 'dominant' set of 'true relations' that gives shape to a specific institutional set-up:

> The analytical map of the true relations $A_iR_kA_j$ will immediately separate the whole structure into several distinct nuclei ... The analytical separation results from the fact that the number of relations true for any pair A_j, A_j of the same nucleus exceeds by a significant magnitude the number of relations applicable to internuclear pairs. (Georgescu-Roegen, 1976, pp. 205–6; 1st edn 1965)

A possible application of this conceptual scheme is provided by considering the fundamental institutional relationships in a peasant society. Here individuals may be related to one another by means of a plurality of different interpersonal relations; however the number of relations connecting the members of the same village is greater than the number of relations existing among individuals belonging to different villages:

> A whole group of villages may be related so as to form a tribe; or the families of the same village may be associated in clans which in turn may cut across a number of villages. Yet the relations applicable to families belonging to the same village outnumber by far those between the families of the same clan but of different villages. (Georgescu-Roegen, 1976, p. 206; 1st edn 1965)

3.2.2 Three types of economic society

A comprehensive theory of economic institutions ought to cover the fields of consumption, production and accumulation. The relative importance of these three aspects of economic activity is to be connected with the emergence of a dominant set of interpersonal relations. Such a dominant set may be different according to whether attention is focused on primitive communities (in which the organization of production provides the dominant set of interpersonal relations); on commercial societies (in which market relationships among individuals undertaking exchanges of consumption goods give shape to the fundamental institutional set-up); or on modern industrial societies (in which the pattern of formation and accumulation of net output determines the prevailing set of institutional arrangements).

The interplay between the structural or 'natural' features of an economic system and the corresponding institutional set-up is especially manifest in the study of those institutions that are directly relevant to the organization of productive activity. Thus it provides a first logical step for the analysis of the relationships between 'material' and 'institutional' aspects of any given economic system.

An example of the way in which the dominant set of relations determines the identity and the structure of any given set of institutional arrangements is provided by the consideration of traditional peasant communities. In this case:

> The economic activity of the village forms a unit of production as close-knit as a simple workshop. A peasant household can perform practically no economic activity independently of those of others. On the contrary ... all must move in step, whether it is for cultivating the fields, mowing the meadows, cutting wood from the forest, or depasturizing the animals. (Georgescu-Roegen, 1976, p. 206; 1st edn 1965)

The above description stresses the characteristics of organization of production in a peasant community and provides a justification for the remaining institutional features of traditional societies, in which:

> In all economic respects, not only in respect to production, the village is not a granular mass of households, much less of individuals, loosely connected through anonymous markets, factories, banks, or other similar urban institutions. Above all it is not a civil society. On the contrary, it is an indivisible social and economic whole. (Georgescu-Roegen, 1976, p. 206; 1st edn 1965)

In other types of societies the organization of production is no longer in the foreground of the existing institutional arrangements. An example is provided by a 'commercial society of individuals reciprocally connected by a network of differentiated and interdependent exchange activities. In this case there exists a plurality of productive units (within which production relations still determine the dominant set of institutional arrangements), and these units are reciprocally connected by means of exchange-based institutions such as commercial markets and financial arrangements. Finally we may consider a modern industrial society in which production and accumulation come to the fore and the dominant set of interpersonal relationships reflects the existing arrangements concerning the formation and distribution of the net output (that is the excess of total production over the share of production fed into consumption and replacement). In this perspective the dominant set of interpersonal relationships once again comes to be grafted into the material bases of production. This represents a major institutional shift with respect to the institutional set-up of a 'commercial society', in which any 'particular merchant may indeed employ some fixed capital, an office, a warehouse, a shop or a ship; but these are no more than containers for the stock of goods on which his business centers. Any fixed capital that he uses is essentially peripheral.' (Hicks, 1969, p. 142)

The distinguishing features of modern industrial society may be identified by considering that a major shift occurred during the first industrial revolution, which again brought to the fore the set of institutional arrangements associated with the material bases of production. This aspect has been stressed by Sir John Hicks:

> What happened in the Industrial Revolution, the late eighteenth-century industrial revolution, is that the range of fixed capital goods that were used in production, otherwise than in trade, began noticeably to increase. It was not a single increase, that was over and done with in a single phase; the increase has continued. It is this, not simply an increase in capital accumulation, but an increase in the *range and variety* of the fixed capital goods in which investment was embodied, which I maintain to be the correct economic definition of the change we are considering. (Hicks, 1969, pp. 142–3)

The above typology is based upon a distinction between two different sets of economic relationships; one is the 'dominant' set of institutional arrangements, namely the set that constitutes the most tightly connected network of interpersonal relationships (see the analysis by Georgescu-Roegen referred to above). The other is the 'residual' set of relationships whose characteristics are determined by the dominant set.

3.2.3 Actual economic dynamics and institutional set-up

The identification of the dominant set of relationships within any given economic system is essential in order to analyse the actual dynamic path that may be followed by an economic system under a different set of circumstances. This may be seen by considering the three types of economic societies (peasant, commercial and industrial) that have been introduced above. In the case of a peasant society the dominant set is represented by a specific pattern of coordination of production among households making up the village community; that is by what may be called simple cooperation among different persons performing different types of activity. (This aspect of productive organization was originally analysed in considerable detail by Gioja, 1815–17 and Wakefield, 1835–43.) Since in this type of society 'all must move in step' (Georgescu-Roegen, 1976, p. 206; 1st edn 1965) it follows that innovation and growth are relatively difficult as it would require a perfect coordination among different individuals and households in the case of decisions concerning the organization of new production processes as well as in those concerning accumulation and growth.

In the case of a commercial society the dominant set consists of the interpersonal arrangements associated with the network of market relationships. A specific feature of trade is represented by the existence of a set of independent decision-making units so that a prior coordination of economic action is not required, thus leaving scope to the potential for change that may be associated with the actions of individual units. In particular the overall productive activity within this framework may be carried out by production units acting independently from one another and interacting by means of trade. In this way the cooperation among different producers may take the form of what may be defined as complex cooperation, whereby producers perform specialized tasks and processes and relate with one another by means of market or non-market types of exchange. Here production activity shows the operation of a more sophisticated pattern of coordination among producers (division of labour).

In the case of an industrial society the dominant set of interpersonal relationships is made up by the set of arrangements constituting the material basis of production, thus going back to a feature that had already characterized peasant society. However in the case of industrial societies such a set appears to be related with production units, such as the factory, rather than with agricultural village communities. Three relevant features emerge here: the pattern of division of labour; the role of accumulation of capital; the type of economic dynamics. In the case of an industrial society the division of labour becomes a prominent feature of productive organization; in particular it allows for a 'decomposition' of the production process into elementary components that may then be carried out by means of mechanical devices. In this way division of labour leads to what has been called 'analysis of the production process', thus establishing a critical link with the accumulation of capital and related processes of mechanisation, and with the advance of technical and scientific knowledge (see Leroy-Beaulieu, 1896 and Scazzieri, 1988). An important consequence of an increased division of labour among productive units is that such units come up with an increased ability 'to concentrate on a limited range of products possessing certain specified properties, performing specific functions, and meeting highly specialized requirements' (Rosenberg, 1976, p. 143). As a matter of fact such a pattern of productive organization appears to be conducive to the introduction of highly specific types of capital goods, such as those produced by the machine-tool industry. As Sir John Hicks has pointed out, it is especially in connection with the production of sophisticated capital goods that the constraint on division of labour, deriving from the extent of the market, is particularly significant.

It is only the simplest sorts of capital goods (building material being the obviously important case) which can expect to command a market ... sufficient to enable their production to be carried out at an efficient size. One has only to consider that there are plenty of countries that can produce textiles efficiently; but there are very few countries which can keep a textile machinery industry going without considerable reliance on an export market. This is the kind of situation which repeats itself with one sort of specialized capital good after another. (Hicks, 1959, p. 205)

The division of labour is also associated with a more significant role performed by capital accumulation in moulding productive organization. As a matter of fact the availability of sufficient capital funds is a necessary condition for the introduction of the more sophisticated types of 'complex cooperation', especially those associated with utilization of a wide range and variety of fixed capital goods. In addition, the increased division of labour is generally associated with the formation of an increasing rate of net output due to the higher productiveness of the economic system as a whole: this factor allows for an increased rate of capital accumulation. The latter result is also made possible by a higher rate of saving associated with higher levels of per capita disposable income.

The specific features of dynamic paths characterizing the industrial society result from the link among productive organization, capital accumulation and economic growth. Here Smith's doctrine of the natural order of investment is particularly significant; as a matter of fact Smith maintains that an economic society paying constant attention to the growth potential inherent in the organization of production ought to follow a definite path of economic dynamics giving priority first to agriculture, then to manufacture and finally to the 'carrying trade'. The reason for this specific sequence is that:

> The natural order of investment is concerned exactly with how the capital accumulation leads to improvement in productivity due to the division of labor, it is [thus] clear that investment must start in a most unspecialized, self-sufficing industry and gradually proceed so that industries are more and more subdivided and specialized ... When enough capital is accumulated to support a manufacture as an independent, specialized industry ... investment should be and actually is made so as to develop the occasional jobs in the neighborhood of artificers into a regular manufacture for more distant sale ... As capital accumulates more, the division of labor advances to interdistrict specialization of local manufactures ... Investment in home trade should be done ... only when the accumulation of capital has already reached the stage when interdistrict specialization is possible. The highest stage of the division of labor is that of international trade based on the international division of labor. (Negishi, 1985, pp. 30–2)

The taxonomy of three different types of 'economic societies', and the above description of each type of society, brings out an important feature of the relationship between the two levels of analysis that have been outlined in this section; that is the 'structural' or 'natural' analysis on the one hand, and the institutional analysis on the other. In particular, it emerges that the analysis of actual economic dynamics requires the integration of structural and institutional types of analyses. The actual motion of any given type of economy results from the behavioural characteristics associated with any specific pattern of integration between structure and institutions, according to the dominant set of interpersonal relationships in the type of society under consideration. In the case of 'peasant' economy the principle of 'simple cooperation' brings about a type of dynamics characterized by the proportional motion of all different elements of the economic system; in the case of a 'commercial' society the principle of 'complex cooperation' allows for the separate and non-uniform motion of different units; in the case of 'industrial society' the relevance of complex cooperation is reinforced by the importance of the capital stocks necessary for the construction and utilization of fixed capital goods, thus bringing to the fore the special role of capital accumulation in determining actual economic dynamics in this type of society.

3.3 Morphology of economic systems and the analysis of transformation

3.3.1 'Material bases' and institutional set-up: a framework for a classification

It may be argued that a fundamental issue in structural economic analysis is the interaction between the material bases and the institutional set-up. We shall use the concept of material bases referring to the matrix of objective conditions defined by (i) natural and environmental resources and (ii) technological skills and capabilities, and determining the technological set-up. Material bases, as defined above, interact with the institutional set-up considered as the system of procedures by means of which existing availabilities of produced and non-produced resources come into relationship with the allocation of these resources between consumption and investment. Here the concept of productive organization emerges as a critical component of any given institutional set-up; in particular, productive organization is the factor determining the way in which any given material basis comes into relation with the institutional set-up.

We shall expound our argument by maintaining that, from a general point of view, the degree of specificity of productive organization is connected with the degree of determinacy by which the institutional set-up is linked with a corresponding material basis. More specifically, the material basis generally leaves scope for a plurality of institutional set-ups when it is associated with a 'primitive' organization of production (by 'primitive' it is meant that the component tasks of each productive activity and their combination into specific production processes do not require a sophisticated pattern of division of labour). On the other hand, it may be argued that more determinate patterns, by which tasks are combined into processes leading to a more sophisticated type of productive organization, involve a more definite link between any given material bases and the corresponding institutional set-up. In particular this is due to the fact that in the case of a complex and relatively rigid arrangement of productive tasks, the division of labour among individuals and social groups may take a precise shape, thereby implying a specific type of institutional set-up (which may not be compatible with other types of material bases).

The relationship between types of material basis and forms of task-adequate institutional set-up may be highlighted by outlining a taxonomy of forms of productive organization. Such a taxonomy will be based upon a combination of the following three different types of classification: the first relates to a description of the time sequence of transformations of any given material from the initial to the final production stage; the second relates to the way in which productive tasks (that is elementary productive operations) are arranged through time so as to carry the 'product in transformation' from its initial to the final stage; the third brings out the difference between two alternative types of operational and hierarchical structures of the division of labour.

The first classification of forms of productive organizations has recently been expounded by Joan Woodward (1980), who distinguishes among the following three types of production systems: the 'one-at-a-time' technology, the 'large-batch' or 'mass production' technology, and the 'continuous-process' technology. The first type relates to a situation in which one single output element is produced at any given point of time, as in shipbuilding or book publishing. The second type describes the case in which a large number of output elements of a given type are produced simultaneously, such as in the car-assembly production line. Finally, the third type refers to production processes in which there is a continuous stream of output independent of any specific productive operation, as in the production of a number of technical products, electricity and petrol.

The second scheme of classification was originally proposed by Georgescu-Roegen (1969a), who distinguishes three types of time arrangements of 'elementary productive processes', that is processes made up by a sequence of tasks leading to one particular unit of finished output. Here Georgescu-Roegen describes (a) the 'in-series' production system in which elementary production processes are operated one after the other without overlaps; (b) the 'in-parallel' production system in which a number of identical processes are simultaneously carried out and repeated in exactly the same way after a certain time interval; (c) the 'in-line' production system in which the elementary processes are started at regular time intervals and are partially overlapping in time. The first type of arrangements may be found in production processes of a primitive type or in processes leading to a single output element per unit of time (such as shipbuilding). The second type of arrangements may be that of a bakery or of a chicken battery. The third type may be that of a car-assembly line of production of the Ford type.

A third scheme of classification is that of Arthur L. Stinchcombe (1959,

1983). He retains two types of hierarchical arrangements of tasks within any given unit of production: the 'bureaucratic' and the 'craft' types of productive organization. The ways in which institutions, allowing for the specific pattern of hierarchical task–arrangement required by the specific characteristics of production technology, become an essential feature of productive organization, have recently been considered by Stinchcombe. One concerns the 'craft' type of productive organization:

The one-at-a-time industries, generally speaking, have something approaching a craft system, and quite often there is a good deal of subcontracting. The central requirement on the system as a whole is that it be capable of adjusting its activities quickly and responsively, according to the plans for the particular project that they are making. In the movie industry, this plan is, of course, the script, and the skill involved is to turn it into a pattern of activity in front of the cameras. But for the most commodities, the plan comes in the form of a drawing, and either the manual worker or the foreman has to be able to read those plans and adjust activities to them. In addition, the activities of the whole organization have to change as the project advances – as, for instance, a skyscraper moves from the excavation stage, to the frame-construction stage, to the attachment-of-the-shell stage, to the internal finishing stage. This necessity for adapting the whole organization to what is essentially a different task each day tends to result in subcontracting as a typical administrative system ... The reason such firms generally have short hierarchies is that the activity of the lowest levels has to adapt very rapidly to decisions at the highest levels as the higher levels take on new jobs. (Stinchcombe, 1983, pp. 112–14)

The second type of productive organization concerns the 'bureaucratic' arrangement of productive tasks. This pattern may be found in association with two different types of technology. The first case is described as follows:

Mass production systems can be thought of as people-driving systems. That is, the management has to run the activities of people in a systematic fashion. The activities that make up the continuous production line are interdependent, so that one person has to do his or her job before others can do theirs. Workers have to do their jobs rapidly and reliably or the entire line will slow down; supervisors have to solve problems immediately or else everybody will stop working. In general, then, management has to drive supervisors to solve problems fast in order to run such a system successfully. This results in a strong line authority structure supervising semiskilled workers who, generally speaking, do the same thing today that they did yesterday. A long line hierarchy – often with up to eight or ten levels – is fairly typical. But also the continuous, large-scale character of the production process means that there are meaningful long-range problems. (Stinchcombe, 1983, pp. 114–15)

The second case of 'bureaucratic'-type organization may be found in association with continuous-process technologies:

> In the continuous process industries such as beer, oil, or chemicals, we have essentially a self-regulated production system. It is here that the extreme form of a system that runs itself is approximated; effort goes into innovation and changing the system ... The hierarchies in continuous process industries tend to be very long, and they do not have the same significance they do in mass production industries. The hierarchy is set up, essentially, to *solve problems* rather than to *run people*. Relative to mass production or one-at-a-time production, there is almost no line structure; everyone is either staff, planning what new to do in the long run, or maintenance, planning what to do about imperfections in the old plan. (Stinchcombe, 1983, p. 115)

The three schemes of classification discussed above suggest the possibility of a comprehensive analytical framework for the analysis of the relationship between material bases of economic systems and institutional set-up. This may be achieved by using Georgescu-Roegen's concept of 'institutional matrix'; this is defined as the relatively invariant patterns of relationships among distinct technological, organizational and behavioural features of a given economic system. An important qualification of this approach to the analysis of economic structure concerns the plurality of distinct institutional set-ups that may be compatible with any given institutional matrix. In this way one may consider significant changes in institutional features within the same institutional matrix. This point has an important implication for the relationship between material bases and institutional framework:

> The resiliency of the institutional matrix ... does not prove that all institutions spring up with a rigid necessity from material conditions ... The point is that an institutional matrix has the peculiar power of transforming into an institution some rather indifferent event that has by accident occurred with some regularity over a period of time. (Georgescu-Roegen, 1976, p. 218; 1st edn 1965)

An instance of the way in which institutional matrices may be derived in relation with production activity is provided by the distinction between 'job-shop' production and 'straight-line' production; the former relates to a type of production in which productive operations may be arranged in different ways, according to necessity and depending on the characteristics of the type of commodities that have to be delivered, within the same institutional matrix; the latter relates to forms of productive organization in which productive operations must be arranged in a unique manner so as to ensure the continuity of the flow of product in transformation as well as of the factor utilization compatible with the given institutional matrix (see Scazzieri, 1983).

The first type of institutional matrix (the 'job-shop' matrix) is compatible with a great variety of concrete productive organizations and product specifications. For example it may be found in the traditional peasants' communities, in the artisan workshop and in modern activities of machine-tool production of the 'standing order' type. In this type of productive organization there seem to emerge a cluster of distinguishing features, such as: a) technology is generally of the 'one-at-a-time' pattern; b) lines of hierarchies tend to be relatively short; c) continuous-factor utilization is achieved by operating a flexible structure rather than a rigid one; d) there is a relatively short planning horizon of productive activities.

The second type of institutional matrix (the 'straight-line' matrix) is compatible, in general, with a restricted range of concrete productive organizations and with a narrower range of product specifications. Examples may be found in mass production activities such as car assembly and the production of small tools, or in continuous processes such as refining, chemical activities or electricity production. Another cluster of distinguishing features emerges here: a) technology is either of the 'mass production' or 'continuous-process' type; b) lines of hierarchies tend to be relatively long; c) continuous-factor utilization is always obtained via the existence of a relatively rigid structure of production; d) there is a relatively long planning horizon of productive activities especially connected with significant amounts of fixed capital investment.

The foregoing analysis suggests two different types of relationships between any given material basis and a compatible institutional set up in relation to the two types of institutional matrices considered above. The straight-line matrix requires a relatively sophisticated and goal-specific institutional set-up; this is due to the rigid character of the corresponding arrangements of productive tasks and production processes, so that specific coordinating operations have to be preliminarily set up. On the other hand the job-shop matrix allows for a relatively simple and 'loose' institutional set-up as far as the technical execution of production is concerned; as a matter of fact productive tasks and processes constitute complex arrangements leaving scope for a plurality of distinct technological set-ups. (See Abruzzi, 1965; Scazzieri, 1983 and Landesmann and Scazzieri, 1990.)

3.3.2 Morphology of economic systems and types of economic dynamics

The above analysis of the interplay between material bases and institutional set-up has been confined to the study of institutions specifically associated with productive activities. A remarkable outcome of our analysis is the identification of a characteristic feature of the objective stock–flow network of economic activity; namely that the field of structural economic analysis cannot be restricted to the material bases of any given economic system. As a matter of fact in any economic system associated with a sufficiently sophisticated material basis the role of the institutional set-up becomes crucial, the reason being that in this case production processes cannot be carried out without the existence of an articulated network of institutional arrangements, such as property rights and associated patterns of wealth accumulation; the interpersonal distribution of resources and opportunities of exchange; the distribution of currently produced output; family size and structure; cultural traditions and inherited skills. In addition the political dimension of social institutions (such as the mechanisms of formation of collective choices) may also be considered.

It may be useful to introduce at this point the analytical device of an institutional matrix providing a systematic arrangement of the above-mentioned institutional features. Any such matrix consists in a general system of ordering of data concerning the institutional features so as to obtain a comprehensive range of theoretically possible clusters of such different features. In this way it is possible to identify a plurality of different institutional set-ups along any given dynamic path followed by an economic system. In addition, it may be possible to identify a number of distinct institutional matrices with which any given set-up may in principle be associated. More specifically, it becomes possible to follow any given economic system along a dynamic path associated with transformations in a number of its institutional features, thus determining whether such a system is moving within the boundaries of a given institutional matrix or whether it switches to a different matrix (the latter case will be dealt with in the next subsection, as an instance of morphogenesis).

We may now introduce the types of economic dynamics that are associated with particular institutional set-ups. As pointed out earlier, the analysis of structural economic dynamics requires the distinction between 'material' features of economic organization and those features that are associated with the institutional set-up under consideration. In this connection we may recall Löwe's and Pasinetti's attention to the implications of alternative institutional frameworks on the dynamic features of the economic system. In particular it may be argued that different institutional set-ups are associated with different ways in which the economic system may follow a given trend, undergo a given rupture or find itself on a traverse from one position to another. (The respective characteristics of the above three types of dynamic patterns will be considered in subsection 4.1 below.)

A comparison of distinct institutional set-ups within the framework of structural analysis leads us to identify a number of different types of economic dynamics. For instance one may distinguish among institutional set-ups depending on whether (a) priority is given to the maximization of current consumption versus future consumption and economic growth; (b) priority is given to the maximization of present employment versus the rate of mechanization and productivity increase; and (c) the existing economic structure gives scope to a plurality of transformation possibilities or is bound to a more narrowly determined path of economic change.

The relationship between current consumption and economic growth may be illustrated by considering a number of distinct clusters of institutional features that lead to different institutional set-ups. For instance we may consider first a cluster in which production is oriented towards final consumption goods; the process of wealth accumulation is not encouraged; distribution of disposable income is relatively equalitarian and the family structure is such that the young cohorts of ages are well represented: here one may argue that current consumption is given prominence relative to growth maximization.

Another example of the relationships between institutional set-up and dynamic pattern is provided by the stress laid upon mechanization and increase in productivity by means of an institutional set-up characterized by a productive organization oriented towards the use of fixed rather than circulating capital; an intensive process of wealth accumulation; a relatively less equalitarian distribution of property rights and disposable income. A third framework is provided by a relatively wide distribution of property rights generally implying a lower rate of wealth accumulation and a pattern of inherited skills that gives scope for a more flexible structure of human capital, which may encourage a more flexible organization of the production process. (This feature may imply a switch back to the emphasis upon circulating capital, an emphasis that characterized some of the pre-industrial forms of productive organization.)

It is worth pointing out that the above considerations have focused upon the comparison of distinct institutional set-ups in their connection with dynamic analysis, without examining the way in which such institutional set-ups have been brought about, and without dealing with the way in which processes or morphogenesis may take place starting from a given initial state.

3.3.3 Structural change as morphogenesis

The issue of structural change is deeply rooted in the relationship between two distinct concepts of economic structure: the objective stock–flow network characterizing any given state of the economic system, and the interpersonal set of arrangements setting up the 'social fabric' of any given community. The above relationship may be analysed by considering two important aspects. First, there exists a precise relationship between the institutional set-up and the corresponding material basis: once a certain degree of sophistication in productive organization is attained, the material basis, which is expressed by means of an objective stock–flow network, takes shape according to the possibilities implied by the existing institutional set-up. An important consequence is that changes in the material bases of the economic system may require corresponding changes of the institutional set-up; on the other hand modifications of the institutional set-up may sometimes be impossible unless a corresponding change of the material basis takes place. Indeed, there are circumstances under which changes in the material basis lead to an institutional set-up that does not belong to the previous institutional matrix (this concept has been introduced in subsection 3.2 above).

The above argument leads us to introduce the issue of structural change as morphogenesis: in many cases structural change may not be adequately examined by restricting oneself to consideration of changes in what has been called the objective stock–flow network of the economic system, since important features of change are associated with transformations of the existing institutional set-up, in spite of the fact that in certain cases such transformations may appear as changes in the material bases. The interplay between institutional framework and material bases suggests a first possible approach to the study of morphogenesis, that is to the analysis of the actual processes by which new institutions may emerge from a previous institutional framework, either as an outcome of endogenous determination or as an outcome of deliberate actions taking into account existing structures and their implicit potential for change.

A first important distinction has to be made between two different types of institutional transformation (or morphogenesis): on the one hand, such a process may be restricted to the formation of new clusters of institutional features within the existing – and unaltered – institutional matrix; on the other hand, the transformation of the institutional set-up is assoicated with the formation of new clusters so that the resulting institutional matrix is different from the original one. The former type of transformation is simply the outcome of a new combination of already existing institutional features, such as productive organization, the structure of property rights, the pattern of wealth accumulation and so on. For example we could refer to a simple institutional matrix consisting of two dimensions: the distribution of property rights (equalitarian or unequal) and the size of agricultural units of production (small or large). Initially the institutional set-up may consist of a cluster of two different types of combinations of features: small-sized farms are associated with a relatively equalitarian distribution of property rights; while large-sized farms are generally associated with a less equalitarian distribution of property rights. This institutional matrix may also be associated with a different cluster of features, such as one in which the two above combinations coexist with an additional one, one in which large farms are compatible with an equalitarian distribution of property rights (the case of agricultural cooperatives may be an example).

The second type of institutional transformation is the one associated with a modification of the original institutional matrix, that is with the emergence or disappearance of a number of institutional features. For instance with the transition from a pattern of common landownership, such as the one observed in many instances of medieval production and in a number of contemporary agrarian economies, to a system in which property rights are privately assigned to families, there emerges a new type of institutional matrix with the possible rise of new combinations of institutional features. In particular, one may find that property rights come to be distributed unequally among families and individuals, and that each specific pattern of landholding is generally associated with a distinct type of production organization:

In poor agrarian economies, the pattern of landholding is a major correlate of political power structure, social hierarchy and economic relations. Possession of land confers on the possessor the mutually reinforcing attributes of political privilege and social prestige. The aggregate pattern of landownership, furthermore, determines the manner in which land and labour are combined for production purposes, with consequences for the quantum and distribution of the product. These, in turn, have implications for the relative and absolute material well-being of the population, particularly as food is the major product of land. (Ghose, 1983, p. 3)

The change of the institutional matrix may also be associated with the disappearance of institutional features existing in the traditional matrix. Always referring to the 'development process' of a rural economy one may mention the fact that rural non-agricultural activities, such as the production of textiles, have often shown a tendency to disappear as a result of the development of an urban industrial sector.

We may now move to the appraisal of the actual dynamics of institutional set-ups. Here we may distinguish between two different types of morphogenesis. One is associated with the formation of new clusters of features within the existing institutional matrix. These are generally the outcome of the continuous operation of dynamic factors, such as population increase, the change in the composition of demand as income levels rise and certain instances of productivity change. Given the operation of this type of factor the institutional matrix may be subject to increasing pressure, but it generally shows a certain degree of resiliency.

There may, however, be a building up of internal pressure that turns out to be incompatible with the existing institutional matrix. At this point the second type of morphogenesis comes into play. The switch to a new type of institutional matrix shows the interaction of the gradual formation of a certain potential for change within the previous matrix with a set of deliberate actions aimed at taking advantage of such potential for change in order to bring about the transformation of the institutional matrix. Such deliberate actions, which mould economic dynamics at certain critical phases where this type of morphogenesis is required, are often not of a purely economic nature but necessitate the action of political institutions.

4. Persistence and change in the analysis of structure

4.1 Static analysis and 'open' structural specification

The aim of this section is to provide a comprehensive framework for the analysis of structural change in economic theory. The concept of structure may in fact be associated with consideration of a fixed pattern of relationships among component parts of the economic system ('static' analysis) and of an 'open' structural specification, in which provision is made for the description of changes of the fundamental patterns of relationships among the different parts of a given economic system. This latter concept of structure draws attention to two distinct ways of dealing with structural change in economic analysis.

One is the consideration of structural change as a *historical* process in the course of which the relationships among component parts of the economic system are subject to change for reasons external to the structural specification that has been adopted. A case in point is Leontief's 'dynamic' description of production technology, in which '*all kinds* of structural change, including elimination of old and introduction of entirely new goods' can be introduced (see Leontief, 1987, p. 863; our italics).

The other is the consideration of structural change as a process characterized by the internal dynamics of structure, that is by changes in the pattern of relationships among component parts of the economic system, changes that are induced by a causal mechanism embedded in the conceptual framework adopted for the analysis. A case in point is Pasinetti's theory of structural economic dynamics, which starts from a particular description of production structure in terms of vertically integrated 'sub-systems', and then integrates this description into a general theory of how structure is modified on the assumption that the economic system operates under a specific set of conditions (a given pattern of population and productivity growth along a full employment equilibrium dynamic path).

In both cases (Leontief's and Pasinetti's) the issue of structural specification comes to the fore, since the way in which a given economic system is described determines which particular relationships among component parts are considered, thus significantly influencing the specific features of the dynamic paths considered in economic analysis.

There is a close relationship between the types of structural specification and the types of structural change that can be considered. The analysis of this relationship is a specific task, that we shall undertake in this chapter, especially from the point of view of how the 'objective' stock–flow network characterizing any given economic system may lead to alternative structural descriptions, as well as of the way in which these descriptions may be related with given institutional set-ups and thus with the 'settled practices' determining the behaviour of the economic system over time. (The relationship between structural specification and structural change has also been considered by Landesmann and Scazzieri in chapter 4, above. They draw special attention to the relationship between structural invariance and structural change, as well as to the particular requirements to be satisfied in the identification of dynamic structures.)

However this issue does not exhaust the topic of this section. In particular the actual dynamic path of structural changes is often left undetermined unless one explicitly introduces the consideration of settled patterns of behaviour as expressed by the institutional set-up.

4.2 Persistence of structural set-up

The above arguments lead us to the analysis of 'persistence' of any given structural set-up. This may arise within two different frameworks, depending on whether a 'closed' or an 'open' specification of economic structure is adopted. In the former case, the identification of a given economic structure depends on the persistence of fixed relationships among the elements of that structure. An example may be that of a standard input–output matrix where the patterns of technical relationships are described in terms of specific physical input requirements for the production of each particular unit of different commodities. A similar structural permanence is to be found in Quesnay's *Tableau économique*, where the inter-sectoral output flows are linked to the existence of a particular technological and institutional set-up within a circular and stationary framework. Here the existence of specific distribution arrangements guarantees a constant reproduction (year after year) of the same level of output as well as the persistence of the same productive structure through time. If part of the surplus is invested in the expansion of productive activities, the system may reach a higher level of output, without any change in its technological or institutional set-up. In this last case the persistence of economic structure is guaranteed.

We may now turn to the consideration of persistence in an 'open' structural specification, one in which the fundamental patterns of relationships among the elements of a given economic system are allowed to change. This is made possible by the fact that the elements of economic structure are identified in a way that leaves scope for transformations of the individual elements of the given structure while leaving the structure itself unchanged. For instance, the model of vertical integration of production processes (outlined above) allows for consideration of a pattern of technical change in which the coefficients of a standard input–output matrix would be changing while the fundamental relationships among factors of production on the one side and 'final commodities' on the other side remain constant through time. Such a constancy of fundamental relationships is consistent with a dynamics of technical coefficients, production prices and income distribution.

In this way one avoids the extreme situation of either the completely static analysis of the workings of a given economic system on the basis of a 'closed' structural specification or the description of a structural dynamics that is entirely determined in an exogenous way (and hence solely attributable to the operation of exogenous shocks). Here structural dynamics may be studied in a context where the continuity of some fundamental relationships allows for the appraisal of the internal dynamics of another set of relationships.

4.3 Structural change

The above argument leads to the following distinction concerning the factors determining structural change within any given economic system. First, the case of an exogenous determination of structural change, as in the case of technological shocks or sudden emergence of natural scarcities. Second, the case of an internally determined modification of structure.

The analysis of an internally determined modification of structure requires a complex theoretical framework, such as in Smith's *Wealth of Nations* where the dynamics of productive structure is associated with an increasing division of labour. This in turn is made possible by an expansion of the 'extent of the market'. This framework has recently been taken up by Kaldor (1966 and 1967) and Negishi (1985). Kaldor underlines the link between the scope for an increasing division of labour in the different productive sectors and a precise pattern of structural change with a contraction of low-productivity activities (such as agriculture) and the expansion of higher-productivity activities (such as manufacturing); in this way the change in labour productivity is the outcome of internally determined movements of productive resources across different sectors. Negishi has recently reconsidered the Smithian theory by proposing an analytical framework in which the dynamics of development of an economic system is associated with a precise sequence in the expansion of its different sectors: first agriculture, then manufacturing and hence commerce and services. His approach is clearly a development of Smith's view that there is a different scope for division of labour in different sectors, and this feature suggests a precise sequence in the 'natural progress of opulence' (Smith) of the various countries.

Another instance of internal determination of structural change may be found in Ricardo's theory of accumulation and growth. Here the external factor is represented by the non-reproducibility of land, which sets an upper limit on the quantity of land available for the expansion of the economic system; and the dynamics of economic structure is brought about by the interplay of this exogenous constraint with endogenously determined prices and income distribution. In this connection, an important element for making structural change 'endogenous' has been pointed out by Sraffa (1960, chapter 11) and Quadrio-Curzio (1967 and 1980), who have both shown that there is in general no natural ranking of lands in terms of fertility; therefore techniques of production have to be ranked by taking pricing and distribution into account. In this way, 'fertility' becomes an economic characteristic and cannot be uniquely associated with given physical characteristics of production technology.

A third instance in this framework is connected with the theories of structural dynamics based on the empirical generalization according to which the composition of consumer demand changes in the long run and in a systematic way as a result of a persistent increase in real per capita income (Engel's law). Such modifications in the composition of demand are then reflected in the composition of production in the presence of a long-run, 'fully settled' adjustment between productions of commodities and use of commodities. In this perspective we should mention the works of Pasinetti (1965, 1981) and Leon (1967).

4.4 Concluding remarks

It has been maintained throughout this section that external and internal determination of structural dynamics provide two distinct frameworks for the analysis of the dynamics of economic structure. It is the purpose of this short paragraph to stress that a complete theory of structural economic dynamics must be constructed on the basis of the integration of both elements. More precisely, it is impossible to confine such a theory to the analysis of linkages among different structural set-ups brought about by means of purely external determination. For instance, a theory of technical change based exclusively on external shocks is bound to focus on the effects of parameter changes on equilibrium states of the economy; and the determination of these shocks remains external to the field of economic theory. In a similar way, the purely internal determination of structural dynamics might lead to a different problem, since here structural change could be associated with the pattern of parameter changes that an economic system may undergo during an adjustment process through time. In this case, however, there would be no reason to allow for structural change if Alfred Marshall's 'theoretically perfect long period' (Marshall, 1961, p. 379*n*) is considered. If exogenous parameter changes are not taking place and sufficient time for adjustment is allowed, there would be no theoretical reason for admitting a state of the economic system different from the stationary state, 'in which the requirements of a future age can be anticipated an indefinite time beforehand' (Marshall, 1961, p. 379*n*; see also Pigou, 1952, pp. 123–34). Therefore it seems that a comprehensive study of structural dynamics should require a blend of internal and external determination (see Quadrio-Curzio and Scazzieri, 1990). In particular, the consideration of internal mechanisms ensures that the study of structural dynamics is conceived within the framework of economic theory; conversely the consideration of external factors inducing parameter changes does not confine the model to a stationary state but allows for an examination of the truly dynamic process of structural change.

5. The features of economic dynamics: representation and method

5.1 Economic dynamics: features and patterns

The primitive components of economic dynamics may be identified with the three following dimensions of a changing economic system:

(i) a pattern of approximately continuous variation of certain economic magnitudes such as national income, employment and productivity; such a pattern generates a specific *trend* if it is possible to identify a constant direction of change.

(ii) a *transition* from one well-identified trend to another; such a transition is generally characterized by a non-constant relationship among economic magnitudes, in a sequential dynamics where causal relationships are based upon the directionality of time. A special case of such a transition is where a given economic system, which is initially in equilibrium, is disturbed by an external impulse that displaces the system from its original state, thereby pushing it towards a different equilibrium state. This transition from one equilibrium path to another is the Hicksian 'traverse', which may be considered as a 'smooth passage' to the new equilibrium (Hicks, 1985, p. 132).

(iii) the *rupture* of established patterns of change. As such the rupture does not allow for precise identification of a new trend nor for the possibility of converging to a new pattern of continuous variations.

These three different dimensions of change may be considered as features of a given economic system that is undergoing a transformation. As a matter of fact, an economic system may appear to be simultaneously on a trend or transition path or undergoing a rupture in its previously followed dynamic path.

As maintained by Sir John Hicks (1965, 1985), there are various ways in which processes of economic change may be analysed; this provides scope for a plurality of 'methods of dynamic economics'. Each method involves a concentration of attention on a certain dimension of change to the exclusion of all others; indeed, a comprehensive account of such processes involves the use of a plurality of methods and cannot be obtained with one method alone.

A particular instance in which the analysis of a complex dynamic process requires the coordination of different perspectives is to be found in connection with those processes characterized by alternating movements of expansion and contraction (*economic cycles*). In this case, the description of the process of change takes advantage of a precise distinction among dimensions of economic dynamics. In particular, any given economic system may be described as a 'moving system' that is undergoing 'cycles' whenever its fundamental variables are subject to a process of change that shows the following characteristics: (i) there are trend paths that are relatively short with respect to the time horizon under consideration; (ii) such short trend paths are separated by 'ruptures' that start a different trend path on which the economic variables under consideration undergo a continuous variation in the opposite direction; (iii) each short trend may be considered as a sort of transition between two distinct types of ruptures (such as the 'up-swing' and the 'down-swing').

It may also be said that the study of the cycle represents a particular way of describing a more general framework within which the analysis of dynamic processes may be carried out. In fact a comprehensive analysis requires first the identification and selection of the relevant features of economic dynamics, and secondly the identification of patterns of change emerging on the basis of the particular features.

In this connection the identification and selection of dynamic features set the basis for the identification of patterns of change. For example more emphasis may be placed on the process of change of the network of technological interdependence than on the processes by which factor endowments do change through time. In fact, in the former case, there could emerge a pattern showing a high degree of discontinuity associated with possible bottle-necks in the supply of certain types of produced inputs, or with difficulties in the 'blending' of distinct technological set-ups; in the latter case the patterns of change are mainly associated with changes in the rate of change rather than sharp 'ruptures' in the pre-existing dynamic processes: this leads us to consider the implications of alternative structural specification. Any given economic system may hence be described in terms of alternative structural specifications, which may in turn appear to be either 'open' or 'closed' with respect to the processes of change under consideration. More precisely, the structural specification is 'closed' with respect to the dynamics of technical change if the structure of the productive system is described by a set of 'input–output' relationships: once inputs and outputs are precisely identified by a particular technology, the latter is precisely described by the existing proportion among inputs and outputs in each process or industry. As a result one is bound to identify a structural break whenever there is (a) a change of identity of inputs or outputs; or (b) a change of the proportion of existing elements of production. Conversely, the structural specification is 'open' with respect to the dynamics of technical change if the structure of production is primarily described by a set of factor endowments so that inputs and outputs are identified independently of their relative proportions. In this way a process of technical change appears to have a much more continuous character than in the former case: the dynamics of technology influences the rates at which inputs such as labour or capital are progressively fed into the economic system. However structural breaks are bound to appear less prominent since the change of technology simply affects the rate of change of input supply and input utilization.

It turns out that the choice of structural specification is not independent of the identification and selection of specific dynamic features and patterns. The relevance of the method of economic dynamics may hence not be assessed independently of an appraisal of the particular structural specification in terms of which the analysis of dynamic processes is carried out.

5.2 *The representation of economic structure*

It has been argued in the previous section that a complex process of economic dynamics can be reduced to a number of fundamental components such as trends, transition paths and ruptures. The way in which these components may be combined so as to generate definite patterns of change critically depends on the description of economic structure. In particular, it is here important to recall our previous distinction between 'horizontal' and 'vertical' schemes of structural specification. As a matter of fact, it is possible to show that the patterns of economic dynamics that can be considered are different depending on the particular scheme of structural specification adopted.

An immediate implication of the above distinction is linked with the analysis of the structural rigidities to which economic systems are bound. When economic structure is identified with a set of vertically integrated sectors the production system appears as a sequence of successive processes by means of which a number of original inputs (such as labour and land) are transformed into final consumption goods. On the other hand, when economic structure is identified with a set of interdependent and horizontally integrated sectors, the production system may be represented as a network of sectoral interdependencies in which circularity of production comes to the fore. Different types of bottle-necks are associated with this distinction: first, the focus on transformation of original inputs into consumption goods draws attention to the bottle-neck relating to the endowment of original factors or the level of final demand. Secondly, the focus on circularity and accumulation draws attention to relative scarcities internal to the production system (this may be due to the inadequate supply of a given sector with respect to other complementary factors).

As Sir John Hicks (1985) has pointed out, any given economic system is normally subject to both 'horizontal' and 'vertical' structural rigidities. According to him, they are normally both present even if little is known in this case. 'Still, it is helpful to have both in mind.' (Hicks, 1985, p. vi) In this connection, as Quadrio-Curzio and Scazzieri have pointed out, it may be possible to identify different dynamic patterns depending on whether the economic system is subject to an impulse acting upon bottle-necks of a horizontal or vertical type:

> A slowdown of the process of growth may be principally due to a bottle-neck in the supply of original factors; in this case the need for the change of structural apparatus emerges. On the other hand, when the slowdown is principally due to a phase of 'climacteric' of the structural apparatus, the direct relationship between original factors and final consumption goods comes to the fore; while the structural apparatus itself shifts into the background. (Quadrio-Curzio and Scazzieri, 1982a, b, p. 27)

The above distinction between 'horizontal' and 'vertical' schemes of structural specification may be used to analyse the three fundamental components of economic dynamics (trend, transition paths and ruptures) and the way in which their combination brings about definite patterns of economic dynamics.

Let us first consider the generation of trends. We may recall that trend is meant to be a pattern of approximately continuous variation of certain economic magnitudes in which it is possible to identify a constant direction of change. In this way any given trend may be connected with a cumulative and self-propelling movement.

In the vertically integrated scheme attention is focused on synthetic indicators such as total capital, labour supply and employment, national income and population as well as ratios like capital per capita, output per capita and saving propensities. A particularly important implication concerns the treatment of technical progress, which is often linked with the so-called 'factor augmenting' bias. This is due to the fact that the analysis of a process of cumulative change tends to exclude the consideration of structural breaks, so that technical change is often associated with increased effectiveness of factor utilization. The use of a restricted number of synthetic indicators makes the identification of the trend component of economic dynamics easier and provides a direct link with macro-economic conditions.

The horizontally integrated scheme, which is based on the concept of circularity and reproducibility, draws attention away from the fairly simple trend-generating mechanism of the vertical scheme, by bringing to the fore the endogenous nature of the process by means of which commodities are produced and accumulated within an economic system.

In this way a process of cumulative change may no longer be described as the outcome of externally generated movements of a cumulative type, such as capital accumulation, population increase and technical progress, since the basic determinants of economic movements are not to be found outside the system. The analysis of dynamic processes thus becomes much more complex: on the one hand emphasis is placed upon elementary economic movements of a more disaggregated nature than in the vertical model; on the other hand a complete analysis of dynamic paths becomes difficult in the absence of a comprehensive theory of causation mechanisms.

5.3 Structural specification and structural change

In this section we concentrate on the methodology according to which economic dynamics may be *studied*, having already discussed the features and patterns of economic dynamics and the different conceptual frameworks by means of which economic dynamics may be *described*. A general indication deriving from the previous analysis is that the precise identification of the principal components of an economic system and of their interrelationships (economic structure) is a fundamental prerequisite for an adequate assessment of the identity of the economic system under consideration.

We may also say that in the field of economic inquiry, structural analysis reduces the arbitrariness of description (see also Thom, 1974, p. 132). In this way the role of the structural specification comes to the fore, since we may say that different descriptions of a given economic system correspond to the identification of what may be conceived as alternative ways of identifying the economic system under consideration. In particular, a precise identification of economic structure calls attention to a limited set of critical features and allows the reconstruction of economic dynamics in terms of definite causal mechanisms. A fundamental distinction is that between the 'circular' and 'vertical' descriptions of economic structure (introduced above). In this connection, we aim at showing that this distinction allows for a distinct reconstruction of the primitive components of economic dynamics that have previously been identified with trends, transitions and ruptures (cf. subsection 5.1 above).

Let us consider the trends first. Since the first Industrial Revolution the processes of economic dynamics have been associated with certain long-run trends such as the progressive contraction of the primary sector and the increase in average per capita output. However such long-run trends are characterized by changes in the rates of change, which are themselves essential features of the dynamic processes under consideration. For instance, the decline of the employment share of the agricultural sector in the British economy has shown remarkable changes of speed since the beginning of the nineteenth century. In a first phase (1811–31) changes of the structure of employment are associated with a sharp decline of the share of the primary sector; a second phase (1831–1914) is characterized by a constant reduction of agricultural employment without significant variations in the rate of change; a third phase (1914–50) is also characterized by a slow decline of agricultural employment (see Deane and Cole, 1967). Behind such different 'regimes' definite patterns of inter-sectoral shifts of resources may be identified: in the first phase the contraction of agricultural employment is associated with a transfer of workers from agricultural to manufacturing activities which are themselves growing at sustained rates; the second phase is associated with a transfer of workers towards manufacturing activities characterized by modest rates of expansion. The last phase shows a rise of manufacturing employment at a rate higher than the rate of increase of the overall labour force and is associated with the transfer of workers from the sector of personal services (see Deane and Cole, 1967, p. 142).

Such trends may be analysed in different ways depending on the kind of structural specifications adopted. In particular the 'circular' and 'vertical' descriptions of economic structure allow for the identification of different features, and thus for alternative interpretations of the underlying causal mechanism. Both approaches highlight features that may be critical in interpreting the observed trend. The relevance of either the 'circular' or 'vertical' approach in identifying critical features cannot be judged on *a priori* considerations, since it depends on how specific clusters of features determine economic dynamics in any given historical circumstance. (Note that the types of causal relationships highlighted by the two approaches are not necessarily incompatible with each other; they may often be of a complementary nature.) In general we may say that interpretations based upon inter-sectoral shifts of resources imply a circular structure of the economy whereby scarcity of resources falls into the background and the modified pattern of resource allocation is based upon a modification affecting the 'circular flow' in, respectively, the agricultural and manufacturing sectors. (A higher labour productivity allows for the reproduction of circular and fixed capital needed within the agricultural 'sub-system' while requiring a decreasing share of overall employment.)

On the other hand, interpretations based upon the consideration of scarcities and bottle-necks affecting the overall availability of certain productive resources (such as labour) imply a vertical structure of the economic system in which the pattern of resource allocation falls into the background. (For instance increased employment in manufacturing may be compatible with constant overall employment and labour productivity, provided that there is a sector of the economy – such as personal services – that gives up part of its reproductive capacity and enters a phase of long-run decline.)

Transition phenomena generally presuppose the possibility of the rupturing of established patterns of change. Significant instances of the rupture of established paths of economic dynamics are associated with the emergence of bottle-necks in the supply of certain essential inputs. For instance, it is well known that the development of the British iron industry in the second half of the eighteenth century originated from the bottle-neck in the supply of wood, which was an essential raw material in the traditional iron-producing technique. Already at the beginning of that century the British iron industry was stagnating, if not declining, owing to the high cost of production brought about by the increasing scarcity of wood. Such a rupture of an established trend of production was the prerequisite for the subsequent adoption of a new iron-producing technique and for a new trend of growth for the iron industry.

The historical sequence of innovations leading to the transformation of the technological set-up is described by Phyllis Deane:

Abraham Darby had successfully smelted iron with coke as early as 1709. In a sense this was the beginning of the end of the charcoal iron industry. But it was only the beginning. Even when the iron-masters had learned first to select the types of iron ore and coal so as to produce an acceptable quality of pig-iron, and then to get rid of impurities in the final cast-iron by resmelting the pig in foundry furnaces, the innovation was still not profitable enough to persuade existing producers to move from their woodlands to the coalfields. Coke was a slow-burning fuel compared with charcoal and needed power to secure an adequate blast. Water-power was used, of course, but was subject to seasonal variations. It was not until Boulton and Watt had developed an efficient steam-engine, around 1775, that the furnaces were able to generate a blast strong enough and continuous enough to make coke-smelting a manifestly more efficient way of producing pig-iron in any circumstances. Till then the use of coke was confined to only a few furnaces while the majority still used charcoal. (Deane, 1969, p. 101)

Finally, in the years 1783–4.

Henry Cort patented a puddling and rolling process, which permitted the large-scale production of bar-iron with coal fuel, [and] it was possible to produce wrought-iron, at a price and quality which effectively killed the charcoal industry (and also the industry based on imported ores) for all purposes except high-grade steel. (Deane, 1969, p. 107)

In this case too it is useful to see how a given feature of economic dynamics may lead to alternative interpretations, depending on whether the circular or the vertical concepts of economic structure are used. In particular, the circular specification of economic structure calls attention to the existence of different patterns of reproducibility of essential inputs in distinct technological set-ups, whereas the vertical specification gives emphasis to the total availability of such inputs and to their scarcity in relation to production requirements.

Alternatively, the bottle-neck in wood supply may be interpreted as the outcome of different periods of reproducibility in the cases of wood and iron (circular concept of structure) or as the outcome of a shortage or scarcity of a non-produced raw material (wood) with respect to the corresponding production requirements (vertical concept of structure).

Similarly the transition to the coal-using technique of iron production may be interpreted through either the vertical or the circular approach. In the first case, the bottle-neck due to the scarcity of wood is overcome by means of technical innovations that allow the substitution of coal (a raw material in abundant supply) for an increasingly scarce raw material such as wood. (Emphasis is thus placed upon the relative degree of scarcity of two essential and virtually non-reproducible inputs.) In the second case, the above transition appears as the substitution of a technology based upon the utilization of a non-reproducible input (coal) for a technology based upon the utilization of a reproducible type of fuel such as wood. In this case the transition from a slow-growth trend to a high-growth trend requires the adoption of a technology that is in a sense 'less viable', since it relies more heavily on the existing availability of non-producible and relatively limited resources. As a result we may say that the high-growth trend is attained at the cost of a decrease in the overall reproducibility of the economic system.

5.4 Economic dynamics: methods of inquiry

The above arguments have shown that the process by which economic structure is identified significantly reduces the 'arbitrariness of description' of actual economic dynamics and directs attention to certain causal mechanisms rather than to others. The aim of this subsection is to provide a general assessment of the robustness of the above argument by considering whether the identification of structure is related to the adoption of a clearly defined method of dynamic economics. In particular, we shall attempt to answer the question whether the adoption of a specific concept of economic structure is independent of the dynamic question we want to consider.

As Sir John Hicks has pointed out:

> A method ... is a family, or class, of models. A model is a piece of theory, a theoretical construction, which is intended to be applied to a certain range of facts ... Models may thus be classified according to the facts to which they are intended to refer ... the particular grouping which I have in mind relates to the dynamic character of the model. I think we shall find that for that kind of grouping the term *method* is appropriate. (Hicks, 1985, p. 1)

Following Hicks we may say that the identification of a particular method of dynamic analysis presupposes a clearly identified question and a precisely devised strategy of inquiry. As a result a method of dynamic economics in Hicks's sense is clearly distinguished from the adoption of a particular description of economic structure, since the latter relates only to the 'form' that economic inquiry introduces into the economic system, not to the identification of specific mechanisms by which dynamic features and patterns may be interpreted.

At this point we may attempt to associate a specific method of dynamic economics to both types of structural specifications considered so far, namely the circular and the vertical. In the case of a vertical economic structure, the arbitrariness of description is drastically reduced by establishing an immediate connection between the original inputs (considered one by one as independent bundles of productive capabilities) and the final consumption goods, thus avoiding the description of the complex pattern of interlinked tasks and transformations making up the production process at both the individual and the social level. An important outcome of using such a concept of economic structure is that the dynamic phenomena appear to be determined externally (in the sense that dynamic features and patterns cannot be interpreted by focusing purely upon a system of mutual constraints operating among the different components of the economy). Here the shape of dynamic phenomena depends almost exclusively upon the operation of forces that economic theory *per se* is unable to explain (such as technological progress or increase in population). At the same time this approach appears to be suitable for the appraisal of specific and punctual impulses as they affect the dynamic performance of the economic system. This implies that under any circumstance the internal structure of the economic system ceases to exert an explicit role; such a role is performed implicitly by the reaction mechanisms that are built upon the original impulses. An important field of application of the concept of vertical economic structure may be found in the idea that upswing and downswings in the level of economic activity may be separated into a number of distinct fluctuating patterns for separate branches of production activities (or 'development blocks', as originally defined by Dahmén, 1950):

An examination of the history of economic cycles shows that during each period of expectation, each boom, there have always been a few branches of industry which especially aroused interest and therefore were developed to an enormously greater extent than the rest. Many of the booms during the nineteenth century thus took colour from the intensive railway construction which absorbed the bulk of the savings. The rationalization of steel manufacture by new methods of production lies behind other cyclic upward movements, while the vigorous development of the electrical industry during the eighteen-nineties sets it stamp on the international crisis at the turn of the century. The crises which occurred between the beginning of the twentieth century and the outbreak of the Great War are particularly characterized by a rapid increase of building activity, while the most recent boom was noticeably influenced by the growth of the motor-car industry. (Åkerman, 1932, pp. 57–8)

In this connection it has also been observed that:

certain industries, for example, the motor-car industry, in the present Century do on the average increase their proportion of production all the time. Even after a depression and its retrenchments, growing industries will ... play a larger part than during the previous depression. (Åkerman, 1932, p. 59)

As shown in the dynamic patterns that have been described above it may be useful to analyse the system of inter-industry linkages in order to highlight the separate dynamic of individual branches or development blocks. The vertical concept of economic structure is particularly suitable to this purpose since it allows for an investigation of the separate dynamic of individual branches of the production system. The reason is that, by means of vertical integration, one can investigate the final product and immediately relate it to its direct and indirect requirements, quite independently of whatever is going on inside these requirements ... From this standpoint, the circular process, however complicated it may be, appears to be of secondary importance, as it simply reproduces those means of production that existed already at the beginning of each period. It can therefore be taken for granted and kept in the background. (Pasinetti, 1986a, p. 11)

In the case of a circular economic structure a more ambitious undertaking is attempted since arbitrariness of description is reduced without at the same time playing down the existence of a complex network of relationships among the components of the economic system. An important feature of the circular description is that the economic system is directly conceived as a set of coherent activities that are interlinked with one another in order to deliver a given social product. As a result the internal structure of the economic system comes to the foreground and the dynamic behaviour of each part of the system appears to be mutually dependent on the behaviour of all other parts of the same system. In this framework the analysis of dynamic patterns tends to be associated with the working of an existing structure that partly determines economic dynamics by itself (for instance by means of changes of the accumulation process) and partly moulds externally generated impulses according to its internal rules. (For instance the introduction of a new technological set-up may generate a higher rate of net output, thus allowing for a higher rate of accumulation and economic expansion. At the same time the substitution of one technological set-up for another may reflect the operation of externally given constraints, such as the existence of bottle-necks in the supply of certain primary inputs.)

An important application of the concept of circular economic structure to the study of economic dynamics may be found in the idea that technological change is associated with substitution of one technological set-up for another, and that the resulting overall dynamics reflects the way in which the circular structure of each technological set-up is compatible with that of the other. In this connection Ricardian dynamics, which is 'based on the relative scarcity of natural resources on which, nevertheless, technical progress was able to operate' (Quadrio-Curzio, 1986, p. 312), introduces an important instance of a dynamic pattern in which the principle of relative compatibility of different technological set-ups is brought to the fore.

In particular the attention for the circular structure of the economic system allows for the analysis of the reproducibility requirements of each separate technology, thus highlighting the circumstances under which technical change (which is induced in this case by the relative scarcity of certain primary inputs) may give rise to 'residuals' or produced means of production that cannot be used as inputs with the new technology. The emergence of such residuals has specific consequences on the overall dynamics of the economic system:

The residual, which will ... emerge in each period ... can have various destinations; that is, consumed, placed in stocks, exported. In turn, these destinations, which can be adopted only in part, have various consequences for growth. (Quadrio-Curzio, 1986, p. 329)

In this case

The economic system may switch from situations in which the whole net output can be accumulated to situations in which residuals are generated, and again to situations in which the whole net output can be invested ... The growth rates of total and net output may increase or decrease and change their dynamic pattern more than once over time. The employment of a non-produced means of production, which is less efficient but is part of a process requiring a combination of means of production that more widely uses the available residuals, may be the source of an increase in rates of growth. (Quadrio-Curzio, 1975, pp. 2–3)

At this point we may attempt a final appraisal of the two fundamental methods of dynamic economics that have been examined in this subsection. It has been argued that the concept of economic structure can be articulated in two essentially different ways (the 'circular' and the 'vertical') and that each way is associated with a 'task-specific' method of dynamic inquiry. Task-specific in the sense that there are particular features and patterns of economic dynamics that can be more easily interpreted within one or the other framework. However, none of the methods that we have been considering 'will do for all purposes' (Hicks, 1985, p. 157). The respective independence of the 'circular' and the 'vertical' approach is in fact an important prerequisite for an adequate understanding of the complex interplay of different causal mechanisms that are generally operating behind the actual dynamic patterns of any given economic system.

6. Vertical integration and the circular flow: perspectives on the evolution of dynamic theory

6.1 Dynamic theory: conceptual frameworks and objects of analysis

The dynamics of the wealth of nations has been the object of analysis from two distinct and often complementary standpoints: first, the view that national wealth consists of commodities and facilities for personal consumption independently of whether such items are producible or not; secondly, the view that the wealth of nations consists uniquely of those commodities and facilities that can be obtained by means of production activity.

The first approach to the analysis of wealth is associated with the view that the amount of wealth may be increased or reduced depending on whether available commodities become more or less abundant with respect to the corresponding demand. An important implication of this approach is that attention is focused upon the availability of 'resources' independently of whether they are used directly as means of consumption or indirectly as means of production for final consumption goods. Secondly, the analysis of wealth may be associated with the idea that wealth depends on the effectiveness with which available resources are used in order to produce the required consumption goods. An implication of this view is that organization of production is brought to the fore and labour is often considered as 'the fund which originally supplies [every nation] with all the necessities and conveniences of life which it annually consumes, and which consist always, either in the immediate produce of that labour, or in what is purchased with that produce from other nations' (Smith, 1976, p. 10).

The above distinction emphasizes the possibility of two distinct approaches to dynamic theory: one associated with the concepts of 'scarcity' and 'allocation' of given resources among competing uses; the other associated with the concepts of 'producibility' and 'accumulation', by means of which commodities for consumption can be reproduced within any given economic system and the stock of necessary means of production can be augmented through an appropriate use of the produced commodities available in each period.

It is thus evident that economic dynamics may be approached either by focusing upon intertemporal allocation of resources (present consumption *versus* future consumption) and considering the process by means of which an adequate supply of productive factors may be ensured in each period, or by focusing upon the precise ways in which commodities may be produced by using existing inputs and considering how the existing supply of productive factors may be increased by producing these factors within the economic system. In this way dynamic theory based upon the concept of producibility deals not only with the dynamics of the producibility of consumption goods but also with the process by which productive inputs are made available through production. In this sense dynamics emerges as a multi-dimensional concept: in the case of the 'scarcity' oriented theory it depends in a critical way upon the relationship between available resources and structure of preferences; in the case of the 'producibility'-oriented theory it is determined by the internal structure of the production system (as represented by, for example, the relative proportions among productive sectors or among different types of production processes).

It is our intention to consider in the next two subsections the historical evolution of dynamic economic theory by distinguishing between the set of theories that emphasizes the direct relationship between original resources and final consumption goods by means of a concept of economic structure based upon vertical integration, and the set of theories that emphasizes the role of producibility as far as commodities and their means of production are concerned. This is done by introducing a concept of economic structure that is based upon a circular description of commodity flows from one process of production to another.

6.2 Vertical integration and dynamic theory

6.2.1 Wealth, employment and division of labour

The aim of this subsection is to present an analytical framework underlying important contributions to dynamic theory based upon the vertically integrated concept of economic structure.

An early explicit attempt to base the study of economic dynamics upon the vertical concept of structure is to be found in Smith's *Wealth of Nations*. Here we find a clearly formulated interpretation of the level of national wealth in terms of endowment of labour, of its distribution between productive and unproductive uses and of the degree of effectiveness of productive activity. In particular, the growth of national wealth critically depends on the share of productive employment in total employment. This is because in the framework of the vertically integrated model, which Smith is implicitly using, the quantity of product that is made available in order to employ 'productive workers' determines the level of investment and thus of economic growth. The share of social product going to productive workers is linked with the so-called *necessary consumption*, which consists of personal and productive use of commodities. Additionally Smith's distinction between 'necessary consumption' and 'unproductive consumption' seems to anticipate the modern distinction between consumption and investment and provides an important link between the analytical structure of Smith's dynamic theory and that of important contributions of modern theories of growth.

An important feature of Smith's dynamic theory is represented by the analysis of division of labour and of its implications for the overall dynamics of the economic system. Here a distinction is important between two different but complementary types of division of labour: the first relates to the way in which specialized workers are allocated to the performance of a particular task (or set of tasks); the second refers to the allocation of the existing labour fund among the different branches of production – such as agriculture, manufacturing and trade – which in Smith's case may be interpreted as instances of vertically integrated sectors. Complementarity between the two types of division of labour is based upon the relationship among the degree of division of labour in the case of specific production processes, the productivity (Smith's 'productive power') of labour in the production process and the extent to which the division of labour can be applied in different fields of production. In this connection Smith makes the point that an increasing division of labour leads to an increase in productivity through a better utilization of the existing labour fund and through the possibility of devising new and more efficient methods of production (technological inventions):

This great increase of the quantity of work, which, in consequence of the division of labour, the same number of people are capable of performing, is owing to three different circumstances; first, to the increase of dexterity in every particular workman; secondly to the saving of the time which is commonly lost in passing from one species of work to another; and lastly, to the invention of a great number of machines which facilitate and abridge labour, and enable one man to do the work of many. (Smith, 1976, p. 17; 1st edn 1776)

As is well known, Smith associates the degree of division of labour with the 'extent of the market' (as determined by the extent of market relationships and by the level of demand). However, there is another element that comes into play in assessing Smith's theory of division of labour: that division of labour has a different scope depending on the field of production that is being considered, for the maximum degree of division of labour in the production process varies according to the type of productive activity. In particular, according to Smith, division of labour in agriculture may be pursued to a lesser extent than in manufacturing, due to the different bearing of natural conditions on the time sequence of productive tasks. This feature provides a ground for a theory of structural dynamics since any given economic system may grow at the maximum rate that is technologically feasible, on condition that the different branches of production each grow at their own maximum feasible rate and that the set of relative growth rates of the different sectors changes over time. Starting with the expansion of the agricultural sector, once the maximum feasible division of labour is attained, the maximum overall growth rate is achieved by switching resources to the manufacturing sector where the scope for higher division of labour is greater. Eventually the same pattern will take place when the upper limit on division of labour is attained in manufacturing and resources have to be transferred to the service sector in order that the economic system maintains itself on the maximum growth path.

It is important to point out that the above scheme of economic dynamics provides the basis for a comprehensive theory of structural dynamics, in which different sectors grow at different relative rates thus determining a change in the weight of each sector over time. Such a complex theoretical formulation is based on a conception of the economic system in terms of a set of vertically integrated branches drawing upon the existing labour fund, without explicitly considering the concept of net product but focusing upon the relationship between consumption and investment both in each sector and in the overall economic system. Finally, Smith draws attention to the significance of purely technological factors in determining the dynamics of each growing sub-system as well as that of the economic system as a whole, independently of those changes in the composition of demand that may be expected in the process of economic growth. (On the concept of 'growing sub-systems' see, in particular, Pasinetti, 1988; a complex theoretical scheme considering the pattern of structural economic dynamics associated with long-run changes in the composition of demand has been provided in Pasinetti, 1981.)

The vertical concept of economic structure is also at the root of Thomas Robert Malthus's approach to economic dynamics; in particular Smith's theoretical framework is reformulated by developing Smith's distinction between necessary consumption and unproductive consumption by dropping the idea that there is an equality between ex-ante savings and investment (this aspect of Smith's theory is considered in Hicks, 1965, pp. 40–2). Smith's approach to economic dynamics is in fact based upon the idea that an increase of necessary consumption (as brought about by an increase in demand for productive labour) feeds sufficient additional demand for produced commodities, thus ensuring the maintenance of the process of economic growth. Malthus's contribution draws attention to the fact that an increase of necessary consumption is not sufficient to ensure that the corresponding total output will find its way through consumption. At the root of Malthus's approach is the idea that the quantity of labour commanded by any given amount of produced commodities (this, as is well known, is Smith's way of measuring the value of commodities) does not correspond with the quantity of labour necessary to produce such commodities; in other terms, the labour commanded by commodities entering necessary consumption is generally less than the labour commanded by the total output produced by the former quantity of labour. As a result, a process of investment is likely to generate a level of productive employment that cannot sustain itself unless there is a source of additional effective demand external to the production system.

In this way Malthus provides an important insight into the understanding of the vertical concept of economic structure by introducing an important qualification to Smith's dynamic theory:

> The powers of production, to whatever extent they may exist, are not alone sufficient to secure the creation of a proportionate degree of wealth. Something else

seems to be necessary in order to call these powers fully into action; and this is such a distribution of produce, and such an adaptation of this produce to the wants of those who are to consume it, as constantly to increase the exchangeable value of the whole mass. (Malthus, 1951, p. 367; 1st edn 1820)

The principle of saving, pushed to excess, would destroy the motive of production. If every person were satisfied with the simplest food, the poorest clothing, and the meanest houses, it is certain that no other sort of food, clothing, and lodging would be in existence. (Malthus, 1951, pp. 7–8; 1st edn 1820)

6.2.2 Resource utilization, product in transformation and effective demand

The application of the concept of vertical economic structure to the study of economic dynamics brings about a view of the production process in which the transformation of non-produced inputs and raw materials into finished consumption goods comes to the fore. Arthur Cecil Pigou gave a characteristic description of this standpoint when, at the beginning of his *Industrial Fluctuations*, he wrote:

At every moment of the working day workers by hand and brain, in association with the capital equipment available for them, are engaged in rendering economic service. Some of them are constructing and some maintaining capital goods, such as railways and ships, machinery, tools and buildings: others are extracting raw material from the earth or looking after crops and animals on its surface: others advancing material on its way from the raw state nearer to the final form designed for it, as the makers of pig-iron or of cotton yarn: others finishing consumable goods of various sorts, as the makers of clothes, bicycles and boots: others transporting goods: others dealing with them in warehouses and shops: others operating such services as the provision of gas, water and electricity: yet others rendering personal services to individuals and groups of individuals, for example, doctors, lawyers, teachers and domestic servants. At the same time that all this is happening, a stream of goods, the final fruit of a substantial portion of this process, is always flowing into warehouses and shops – institutions which we may regard, if we will, as a lake into which these things pass and in which they stay for a while. At the opposite, or purchasers', end of this lake there is also always proceeding an outflow of goods to the various persons who have claims on them. This outflow goes, in great part, to the controllers of business, who retain some of it for their own consumption or their own use as machines, hand over some to the persons to whom they are under contract to pay interest on past loans, and hand over another part to workpeople in the form of wages to induce them to carry on further work. (Pigou, 1929a, p. 1)

This remarkable passage shows a way in which the vertical concept of economic structure may influence the description of economic activity by drawing attention to the flows of 'product in transformation' that are emerging from original resources and produced raw materials. This perspective is clearly associated with a 'one-way' conception of the economic process in which the sequential character of production activity is stressed. At the same time attention is also called to the lack of continuity of the 'transformation process' as each product is 'advancing ... on its way from the raw state nearer to the final form designed for it' (Pigou, *ibid.*).

A central feature of the theory that we are expounding is the interest in the factors that determine a specific level of resource utilization and thus a particular amount of national wealth. Here a distinction must be recalled between two different approaches to this general issue: i) the level of activity is made to depend on the way in which the productive resources of no matter what kind belonging to the country are distributed among different uses or occupations' (Pigou, 1929b, p. 129); in this way supply factors come to play a crucial role; ii) the overall level of activity is associated with the level of employment, and this latter is made to depend on the level of 'effective demand', that is upon the influence exerted by expenditure mechanisms on the way in which productive resources (taken as given) are utilized. Demand factors in this framework do play a critical role among 'the forces which determine changes in the scale of output and employment as a whole' (Keynes, 1973a, p. xxii; 1st edn 1936).

At this stage we introduce the dynamic elements that are associated with the above approach to structural specification. An important reference point of Pigou's approach to economic dynamics as expounded in his theory of industrial fluctuations is the work of Tugan-Baranovsky, and in particular his stress on the role of construction activities in determining the pattern and intensity of changes in activity levels and their repercussions through all different branches of the production system.

To construct a factory or a railway it is necessary to procure materials of construction (wood, tiles, iron, etc.), machines and tools, and to engage work-people. The materials of construction, like the machines, do not fall from the sky; they are furnished by other branches of production. Thus, the more numerous new enterprises are, the greater is the demand for means of production. (Tugan-Baranovsky, as quoted in Pigou, 1929a, p66)

In this connection Pigou formulates a conceptual framework that puts into the background Tugan-Baranovsky's concept of circular economic structure and introduces a view of the linkage between construction industries and consumption industries that is characteristic of the vertical representation of economic activities. This view is clearly expressed by Pigou in analysing the repercussions of changes in the level of activity of a certain branch of production upon the remaining branches of the same production system:

To clarify the issue, it is convenient to conceive industrial groups in the following abstract form. Industry A manufactures finished goods, and has, subordinated to it and producing the materials and the machinery that it needs, sub-industries α_1, and α_2; the sub-industries in turn having other sub-sub-industries α'_1 and α'_2, which provide their materials and machinery. Alongside of A there is another finishing industry B, with a similar series of sub-industries, and yet others, C, D, and so on. Of course this rigid division and specialisation of sub-industries does not exist in real life, but the conception is none the less of service for analysis. (Pigou, 1929a, pp. 65–6)

The above conceptual framework leads Pigou to the following analysis of the dynamic process:

When the demand for B's products in terms of A's stuff (for which we assume B has an elastic demand) expands, B, in order to increase his output so as to take advantage of the increased demand for his products, will need more materials and machines. It is plain, therefore, that a stimulus to expansion will be given to sub-industries b_1 and b_2 and to the sub-sub-industries below them ... So far, therefore, as the sub-industries b_1, b_2, and so on are concerned, it is true that A's prosperity propagates itself through B among further industries. But this propagation is, so to speak, analytic and not synthetic. That is to say, in its dealings with A, B is partly a principal and partly an intermediary for b_1, b_2, and so on, distributing what A pays between itself and its subordinates according to their respective contributions towards the final B product. (Pigou, 1929a, p. 66)

From the passage above it emerges that the course of 'repercussions', that is the sequence of events following a given stimulus to demand for a particular 'finishing industry', follows a vertical path going from the finishing industry itself to the various layers of the sub-industries subordinate to it, thereby excluding the possibility of direct horizontal interrelationships among industries that are linked with one another according to the circular pattern.

As previously mentioned, another approach to structural specification within the vertical framework is provided in Keynes's *General Theory* in which Pigou's distinction among different productive sub-systems is dropped and a unique correlation is established between the level of national income and the volume of employment. In other words, in Keynes a given demand variation is assumed to have a 'neutral' effect on the relative weight of the different productive branches so that, for example, it is impossible to associate a given stimulus on demand with a specific transformation of the industrial composition of production.

This approach, which is based upon a particular simplification of the vertical concept of economic structure, calls attention to a direct link between 'primitive' factors of production and final consumption goods, as is clearly expounded in the following passage:

We take as given the existing skill and quantity of labour, the existing technique, the degree of competition, the tastes and habits of the consumer, the disutility of different intensities of labour and of the activities of supervision and organisation, as well as the social structure including the forces, other than our variables set forth below, which determine the distribution of the national income ... The given factors allow us to infer what level of national income measured in terms of the wage-unit will correspond to any given level of employment; so that within the economic framework which we take as given the national income depends on the volume of employment ... in the sense that there is a unique correlation between the two. (Keynes, 1973a, pp. 245–6)

The implications of this approach for the design of dynamic analysis are far-reaching. In fact for Pigou such a dynamics is to be connected with a series of production linkages that presuppose a given pattern of input–output relationships, even if circularity is not explicitly stressed. On the other hand, Keynes's *General Theory* may be connected with a series of consumption linkages that establish a causal connection among level of demand, volume of employment and level of income. In this way the production relationships that played such a critical role in Pigou recede into the background; whereas the expenditure mechanisms, providing a link between income levels and levels of consumption, come to play a fundamental role in Keynes.

The above elements of Keynes's structural specification are crucial for explaining the characteristic features of his approach to dynamic analysis and are associated with Keynes's own description of his object of inquiry:

I have called my theory a *general theory*. I mean by this that I am chiefly concerned with the behaviour of the economic system as a whole – with aggregate incomes, aggregate profits, aggregate output, aggregate employment, aggregate investment, aggregate saving rather than with the incomes, profits, output, employment, investment and saving of particular industries, firms or individuals. And I argue that important mistakes have been made through extending to the system as a whole conclusions which have been correctly arrived at in respect of a part of it taken in isolation. (Keynes, 1973a, Preface to the French Edition, p. xxxii; 1st edn 1939)

This type of structural specification is adopted in order to tackle an essential feature of economic dynamics, that is the fact that production and employment levels are subject to fluctuations. At the root of economic fluctuations, in Keynes's view, is the role of effective demand considered as 'the aggregate income (or proceeds) which the entrepreneurs expect to receive ... from the amount of current employment which they decide to give' (Keynes, 1973a, p. 55). In this connection, a 'unique correlation' is established between the level of production and employment in each individual branch of production and the overall level of production and employment of the economy. Such a conceptual framework allows Keynes to formulate his contribution to the theory of the 'forces which determine changes in the scale of output and employment as a whole' (Keynes, 1973a, p. xxii). In particular it provides the basis for the idea that 'the increased employment for investment must necessarily stimulate the industries producing for consumption and thus lead to a total increase of employment which is a multiple of the primary employment required by the investment itself' (Keynes, 1973a, p. 118).

Such an analytical representation of the dynamic process behind economic fluctuations is considered to hold '[u]nless the psychological propensities of the public are different from what we are supposing' (Keynes, 1973a, p. 118) and reflects Keynes's view concerning the critical role of expenditure mechanisms and consumption linkages within a given structural framework. In this way, the scale of output and employment as a whole is uniquely related to given external impulses, such as an increase in primary employment associated with an expansion of investment activities, and the analysis of a dynamic process may be carried out by considering the relationship between a given increase in one component of global expenditure and the final and overall level of effective demand.

An important implication of the above argument is that the dynamic theory of Keynes is fundamentally different from that of Pigou, not only for what concerns the general outcome of the analysis, but also in terms of the basic causal relationships that are at the root of his theory. In Pigou's approach, the repercussions that any given 'initiating cause' may produce must be studied by focusing upon the sequence of repercussions providing a link between such impulses and general industrial fluctuations as distinct from relative ones; while in the case of Keynes the analysis is carried out in terms of 'contemporaneous causality' (as defined by Hicks, 1979), so that the sequence of repercussions may be overlooked and attention may be focused upon the linkage between the different elements of overall effective demand during a given time period.

In other words, Pigou and Keynes provided two distinct examples of the way in which the criterion adopted for structural specification may significantly influence the scope and method of economic theory. In Pigou, the detailed description of production linkages calls attention to the sequential character of the adjustment process that may follow any given 'initiating cause of industrial disturbance' (Pigou, 1929a, p. 57). On the other hand, in Keynes the attention to the 'structural consistency' of the expenditure mechanism leads to a type of analysis in which the causal relationships do not significantly depend on any particular sequence of events. (We may also say that Pigou draws attention to the time-lags implicit in any adjustment process, whereas Keynes is interested in the necessary conditions that ensure the full attainment of the scale of output and employment compatible with any given variation in autonomous expenditure.)

In other terms, as Hicks points out, in the case of Keynes's theory:

> So long as the period is looked at *by itself*, all that matters about the investment, during the period, is the employment that it gives, and the income that it generates. It does not matter, accordingly, whether the form that it takes is wisely or unwisely chosen. It is only when one looks further forwards that it does matter. (Hicks, 1985, p. 60)

6.2.3 Vertical integration and the theory of continuation

The theories so far considered in this section are characterized by an explicit attention to the vertical concept of economic structure considered as a means for the classification of economic activities, as well as by application to the analysis of the relationships among different vertically integrated magnitudes. In this connection economic theory takes into account the way in which autonomous impulses may spread through the different branches of the economic system following a one-way path of diffusion.

A characteristic feature of this type of approach is that it overlooks the time profile of this diffusion process in the sense that given, for instance, a certain 'stimulus to expansion' (Pigou, 1929a, p. 66), its repercussion may be observed through the sub-system of productive processes branching out from the specific set of activities that is directly affected by the original impulse. This diffusion process is, however, considered in connection with the directionality of the whole family of repercussions and independently of the durations of the different stages of the diffusion mechanism.

The vertical concept of economic structure may lead itself to the analysis of the time structure of a diffusion process in which an explicit distinction is introduced among the different stages of the various production processes, so that the stages and their duration are explicitly considered. In this way it is possible to follow through the sequence of repercussions starting from a given original impulse by taking into account the speed of reaction of the different parts of the given economic system. This framework allows for the identification of possible 'bottle-necks' in the transition from one stage to the next, thus leading to a non-proportional dynamics of the different branches. This feature of the dynamic process brings to the fore an important aspect of the way in which exogenous impulses may influence the path followed by any given economic system through the emergence of a complicated pattern of 'propagation'. Again, consideration of the time structure of productive activities leads to the analysis of features that remain in the background whenever structural specification is confined to the static classification and typology of economic activities, as is the case with the theories of Pigou and Keynes (see above). In this way economic theory comes to grips with those specific features of dynamic paths that are associated with 'those repercussions which *must* take time to work themselves out – which are delayed, not by slowness of communication or imperfect knowledge, but by the technical duration of productive processes' (Hicks, 1946, p. 283).

It is the purpose of this section to inquire into the features that the concept of vertical economic structure must take if the sequential character of dynamic processes is to be taken into account. Here in particular we shall emphasize the importance of describing the production process as a 'one-way' stream of transformations leading from the original and non-produced productive factors to the finished commodities, passing through a sequence of intermediate stages that are *causally* related with one another. This way of looking at production activities implies that what is being done at any given time is related both to the past and to the future by means of 'material causality'; for the fact that at a given time the 'material in process' is characterized by certain precise physical characteristics implies that certain specific stages must take place beforehand (while others must be excluded) and that subsequent stages crucially depend on the current stage in the sense that the current characteristics of the 'material in process' leave scope for a set of future sequences of transformation while excluding others.

In particular, the sequential character of the production process is related with its material character, since it is of the nature of that process that a number of physical transformations cannot be undone once they have been carried out. Sequential causality has thus an important connection with the study of production, for it may be argued that it is in the field of production that the nature and scope of this type of causality reveal themselves in the clearest way. The reason for this is that the concept of a process taking place in real time, which is so essential in the theory of sequential causality, is primarily associated with the necessary character of 'material transformations' rather than with the behavioural features of expectation-formation and planning procedures. Indeed it has been argued that an excessive focus upon expectations and planning may draw attention away from consideration of the sequential aspect of dynamic processes:

[I]n dynamic analysis, telescoping is dangerous. It is essential to keep the time-sequence right. Though changes in actual prices do affect expectations, and changes in expectations do affect actual prices, cause precedes effect. The *lag* may be short, but (in principle) it is always there. In truly dynamic analysis ... there must be lags ... It is inevitable, when time is divided into single periods, that the lags should extend from one single period to another. Not necessarily from one to the next; rapidity of reaction can be varied by making the lags extend across a number of periods. (Hicks, 1985, p. 70)

The vertical concept of economic structure suggests two distinct and complementary ways in which a 'theory of continuation' may be formulated by concentrating attention upon the 'stage-structure' character of productive activities.

One is the description of the productive process as a sequence of causally related transformations of a given 'material in process' that is taken from one stage to the next, bringing it a step nearer to final completion. An important instance of such approach may be found in Adam Smith. In particular we may mention Smith's application of a 'stage-structure' view of the productive process to the analysis of the sequence of repercussions of a given change in the composition of final demand:

A publick mourning raises the price of black cloth (with which the market is almost always under-stocked upon such occasions) and augments the profits of the merchants who possess any considerable quantity of it. It has no effect upon the wages of the weavers. The market is under-stocked with commodities, not with labour; with work done, not with work to be done. It raises the wages of journeymen taylors. The market is here under-stocked with labour. There is an effectual demand for more labour, for more work to be done than can be had. It sinks the price of coloured silks and cloths, and thereby reduces the profits of the merchants who have any considerable quantity of them upon hand. It sinks too the wages of the workmen employed in preparing such commodities, for which all demand is stopped for six months, perhaps for a twelvemonth. The market is here over-stocked both with commodities and with labour. (Smith, 1976, pp. 76–7; 1st edn 1776)

A second way of describing the productive process in terms of sequential causality is by focusing upon the time profile in the utilization of original inputs. Such an approach, which may be traced back to certain classical contributions such as that of David Ricardo (here Ricardo's attention to the proportions between fixed and circulating capital is especially relevant), is generally associated with the Austrian theory of production and capital.

The essential features of this theory may be identified with:

The definition of capitalistic production as time-using production; of the amount of capital employed as an indicator of the amount of time employed; of the effect of a fall in interest on the structure of production as consisting in an increase in the amount of time employed. (Hicks, 1946, p. 192)

A distinguishing feature of the latter approach (with respect to the former) is a more abstract view of the productive process, which is not directly described as a precise flow of 'material transformations', but is associated with a 'time-integration' of productive activities. In this way attention is not concentrated on the actual tasks performed at any given time and on their outcome, but upon the time distribution of dated original inputs among the different stages of the productive process. Here the stress is upon the time duration of the whole time-integrated process that permits the production of finished goods through the utilization of direct labour inputs as well as of productive instruments (such as machinery) that must be produced within the same process. By taking labour as the relevant original input we may say that a time-integrated process of production consists of two distinct and consecutive phases: one is the 'construction period', in which labour inputs are used in the building up of productive equipment but no finished commodity is being delivered; the second is the 'utilization period', in which no productive equipment is being constructed and the existing equipment is utilized by means of direct labour in order to produce a certain amount of finished commodities. (See Hicks, 1973, pp. 14–15; as quoted in subsection 2.3 above.)

Hicks's contribution allows us to identify a remarkable difference between the two types of sequential analysis that are associated with the concept of vertically integrated structure. On the one hand, in the case of Smith, vertical integration leads to a 'forward-looking' description of the actual transformation process; whereas in the case considered by Hicks vertical integration leads to a 'backward-looking' description.

Each way of tackling the sequential aspects of economic dynamics relates to important but not exhaustive aspects of the 'theory of continuation'. The relationship between the two above-mentioned methods of analysis may be illustrated by considering that, in general, the input sequence described in the 'backward-looking' approach is made up of quantities of inputs that are in turn partly the outcome of previous stages of transformation:

> Initial equipment will consist, to a large extent, of goods at the intermediate stage of production; work has already been done on them with the object of converting them in the end into a certain kind of product; if this process is at all far advanced, the degree to which its ultimate object can be changed will be limited ... This characteristic puts a limitation upon the nature, and perhaps also the timing, of the nearer parts of the output stream which can be got from the given equipment; since further inputs will generally be needed in order to complete these particular outputs, it puts a limitation on the nearer parts of the prospective input stream as well. Even if input prices rise unexpectedly, it will pay to finish processes which have been started but not finished, so long as the rise in input prices is not very large; even

though it may sometimes be possible to find a middle way between pure continuance of the preceding plan and complete cessation of processes, it will take some time before the entrepreneur has a really free hand to deal with the new situation. (Hicks, 1946, p. 211)

Important insights into the interplay of the 'backward-looking' and 'forward-looking' uses of vertical integration may be found in Friedrich August von Hayek's contribution concerning the concept of productive structure and its dynamic applications. Hayek, in particular, introduces the concept of 'producers' goods', which relates to the stock of all goods existing at any given time in the economic system and used as inputs in production processes, independently of whether they are original inputs or unfinished goods used as intermediate inputs. In this way Hayek comes to grips with the two-sided nature of sequential causality in the dynamics of productive structure. In particular, the concept of 'producers' goods' allows Hayek to deal with the consequences of a shortening or lengthening of the production process by considering that the changes in the duration of productive processes also affect the stock–flow structure of production activity:

The term production I shall always use in its widest possible sense, that is to say, all processes necessary to bring goods into the hands of the consumer. When I mean land and labour, I shall speak of *original means of production* ... When I use the expression *producers' goods*, I shall be designating all goods existing at any moment which are not consumers' goods, that is to say, *all* goods which are directly or indirectly used in the production of consumers' goods, *including* therefore the original means of production, as well as instrumental goods and all kinds of unfinished goods. Producers' goods which are not original means of production, but which come between the original means of production and consumers' goods, I shall call *intermediate products*. (Hayek, 1967, pp. 36–7)

It may be worthwhile at this point to reconsider the whole argument of the theory of continuation in relation to the method of vertical integration. We have seen that the theory of continuation requires the utilization of a sequential concept of causality so that we may be able to establish systematic links between subsequent time periods, and that such a requirement is generally met by introducing a type of vertical integration in which different stages of the productive process are integrated along the time dimension. However, the latter approach leads to two kinds of development, which we have associated with Smith and Hicks. An important feature of temporal integration is that it tends to overlook the interrelatedness among the *different* productive processes of the economic system, so that the complex network of technical complementarities among distinct activities recedes into the background, and economic theory is primarily applied to the analysis of linkages among different time periods or stages of production (such as in Hicks's inquiry into the relationship between 'substitution over time' and 'complementarity over time').

The analysis of technical interrelatedness may also require explicit consideration of the linkages among different productive activities at any given point of time. However, such linkages are generally associated with the existence of 'stationary complementarity' among productive activities on the basis of a given 'circular flow'. (In a stationary economic system, successive stages of the same vertically integrated productive process may be represented as different processes carried out side by side.) We may conclude that the vertical concept of economic structure is open to a variety of different applications, and that important issues of dynamic theory seem to require some coordination between the concept of 'vertical integration' and that of 'circular flow'.

6.2.4 Vertical integration and the theory of production in dynamic theory

In economic theory the concept of vertical integration has sometimes been applied to the description of the whole economic system rather than that of specific productive processes. In particular, we may recall the theories of Smith, Malthus, Pigou and Keynes as relevant instances of an application of the concept of vertical integration in order to classify productive activities into distinct vertically integrated branches. The above authors also provide a theoretical framework for studying economic dynamics in terms of changes in the relative proportions among vertically integrated branches as well as for analysing the repercussions following an autonomous impulse both at the level of the whole economic system (Keynes) and at that of the various vertically integrated branches (Pigou).

A modern formulation of the concept of vertical integration as a method for classifying productive activities into distinct branches and for analysing economic dynamics as a process of transformation simultaneously affecting the various branches has been put forward by Pasinetti (1965, 1973). A specific feature of Pasinetti's contribution is the attempt to provide a rigorous and comprehensive method for analysing the different ways in which vertical integration had been implicitly applied in economic literature.

A common feature of economic theories making implicit use of vertical integration is the exclusion of produced means of production and of replacement processes that are taking place within the 'circular flow'. Léon Walras and Keynes provide significant examples of such a procedure:

> The notion of vertical integration is implicit in all discussions on the theory of value of the Classical economists. The same thing can be said of the marginalist economists. When, for example, Léon Walras adopted the device of eliminating intermediate commodities from his analysis of production, he was making use of the logical process of vertical integration. (See 'Elements of Pure Economics', W. Jaffé, ed., pp. 241 and ff.) Keynesian macro-economic analysis is also generally carried out in terms of vertically integrated magnitudes (net national income, net savings, new investments, consumption, etc.). Very rarely, however, is the logical process of vertical integration explicitly discussed. Generally it is simply taken for granted. (Pasinetti, 1973, p. 1)

Pasinetti's formulation is based upon the view that the physical quantities produced and consumed in any given economic system may be classified in two different ways, depending on whether one follows the criterion of the 'industry' or that of the 'vertically integrated sector'. The first criterion provides a type of classification leading to immediately observable aggregates, while the second provides a schematic representation of the economic system in terms of a set of aggregates that are not to be observed directly but provide a more synthetic description of the overall economic system. When classified according to distinct vertically integrated sectors, the magnitudes making up each economic system are disaggregated into separate components depending on the specific type of final use (consumption or net investment) to which they may be associated. For example, the overall quantity of labour employed in the economic system at any given time is split into a number of separated labour quantities, each of which may be associated with specific components of the net output vector (made up of final consumption and net investment). The same procedure is followed when dealing with the stocks of intermediate commodities that are used in the economic system. In this case the stock of each particular intermediate commodity (performing the role of capital goods in this model) is also split into distinct components depending on the final use with which they may be associated. For example, the total quantity of steel used as an intermediate commodity in the whole economic system has to be split into as many parts as there are possible final uses. As a result the overall economic system ends up being split into as many sub-systems as there are final uses. Each such sub-system or 'vertically integrated sector' consists of the corresponding vertically integrated labour coefficient (which 'expresses in a consolidated way the quantity of labour directly and indirectly required in the whole economic system to obtain one physical unit of [a particular commodity] as a final good' (Pasinetti, 1973, p. 6) and of a particular composite commodity called 'unit of vertically integrated productive capacity' relative to the same sub-system. (Such a composite commodity 'expresses in a consolidated way the series of heterogeneous physical quantities of [all] commodities ... which are directly and indirectly required as stocks, in the whole economic system, in order to obtain one physical unit of [a specific commodity] as a final good' (Pasinetti, 1973, p. 6).

Pasinetti's theory of vertical integration provides a precise analytical formulation to a way of representing the economic system that has been of critical importance for the development of dynamic analysis since the early applications of this method in Smith's *Wealth of Nations* (see above). An especially important feature of Pasinetti's formulation is that a number of critical assumptions and essential logical steps, which were only implicit in the earlier economists, may now acquire a definite meaning.

At this stage it may be recalled that the concept of vertical economic structure, in its dynamic applications, has been mainly associated with the analysis of technological requirements for economic expansion (Smith), or with the technological interrelatedness in its implications for the diffusion of particular impulses (Pigou). On the other hand, vertical integration has been linked with the autonomous role of effective demand on the dynamic path (Malthus and Keynes). The analytical formulation introduced by Pasinetti provides a logical framework in which both technological and demand conditions may be integrated in order to give a comprehensive interpretation of the dynamics of the 'wealth of nations', concerning both its absolute level and possible changes in its composition (structural economic dynamics).

In a more specific way the exclusion of intermediate commodities (characterizing Pasinetti's theory) provides an analytical 'short cut' that permits the establishment of a direct link between the technological conditions determining the 'productive power' of any given economic system (as influenced by technical progress) and the level and composition of effective demand.

In particular the method of vertical integration allows for the consideration of technical progress without upsetting the relationship between changes in the productive capacity of the whole economic system and variations in the level of disposable income, and thus in the level and composition of effective demand.

The logical implications of the vertical integration of productive activities – as far as the structural dynamics of the productive system is formulated – may be set out as follows:

In the general case of production of all commodities by means of fixed capital goods and of technical progress of the most general type, the relation between ordinary physical capital goods and capital goods in units of productive capacity breaks down at the end of each period and the problem arises of what meaning one can give to the physical operation of replacement of the capital goods. Clearly 'replacement' ceases to have any meaningful sense in terms of ordinary physical units. On the other hand, 'replacement' does continue to make sense in terms of physical units of productive capacity. Even in the midst of a maze of physical and qualitative changes, we may indeed continue to say that replacement of used-up capital goods has taken place if, at the end of each period, the economic system has recovered the same productive capacities as it had at the beginning.

The analytical consequences of these remarks are far-reaching. With technical progress, any relation in which capital goods are expressed in ordinary physical units becomes useless for dynamic analysis. But relations expressed in physical units of productive capacity continue to hold through time, and actually acquire an autonomy of their own, quite independently of their changing composition. At the same time the elaborations of the previous pages provide the way for a return to the ordinary physical units any time that this is necessary, within each period ... Of course a different result will be obtained for each single period. (Pasinetti, 1973, p. 28)

6.3 The circular flow and dynamic theory

6.3.1 The stationary state and the circular flow

This subsection will consider the analytical structure of dynamic theories based upon the explicit consideration of the circular network of input–output relationships within the economic system.

It may be possible to associate the consideration of the circular flow with a specific feature that emerges from 'time-related sequences' of productive transformations when the economic system fulfils the requirements for the stationary state. In this way the circular flow may be introduced as a special case of a dynamic economic system, as a special case of an economic system in which productive processes are described as sequences of time-related transformations of original factors into finished output. This point has been stressed, among others, by Sir John Hicks:

It is true that factors are actually employed in processes which will only result in future output, and that it is the expectation of future vendibility which provides the stimulus to their employment. But, nevertheless, in a stationary state the factors currently employed do seem to produce the current output; for they make it possible to produce that output, subject to the condition that the stock of intermediate products (fixed and working capital generally) shall not be diminished in consequence. As in Professor Pigou's famous illustration, the stock of intermediate products is a 'lake' fed by the input of current services, drained by the output of current products. Although the water generally remains in the lake a certain length of time, nevertheless, if we impose the condition that the total amount of water in the lake should be kept constant, there is a direct relation between current input and current output. So long as we make the 'stationary' assumption that capital is maintained intact, the technical production function becomes a relation between current input and current output – we are back in the 'static' world.

One thing, however, is evident when we look at this stationary economy, which was not evident in the static theory when time was left out of account altogether. This is the dependence of the input–output relations (the production functions) on the quantity of intermediate products carried by the system. (Hicks, 1946, p. 118)

Hicks's remarks call attention to an important feature of dynamic paths, namely the close association between the specific conditions of the stationary state (absence of structural change) and the possibility of precisely describing the role of intermediate products in the reproductive mechanism of the economic system. In particular, the assumption of stationary state allows the economist to avoid the oversimplification of reducing the whole set of productive activities carried out in the economic system to a set of semi-independent sequences of productive transformations. This is due to the nature of circular interdependence that is brought forward under the stationary-state assumptions, where the actual sequence of stages characterizing any actual transformation process is mapped into a circular structure in which each stage of production is carried out simultaneously with all other stages. At the same time this approach brings to the fore the proportions among different types of current output (say the output of corn and that of steel) that are compatible with the existence of given transformations of productive resources into finished consumption goods.

The circular structure of the productive system, which has been described above in connection with the assumption of stationary state, is also compatible with the consideration of steady-state dynamics. The specific features of steady-state dynamics have been analysed in von Neumann's 'model of general equilibrium' as well as in the subsequent literature that has developed von Neumann's approach. The essential difference of this case with respect to the stationary state is that the economy produces more than the minimum necessary for replacement' (Sraffa, 1960, p. 6) and the associated net output is reinvested, thereby increasing the overall productive capacity of the economic system. The dynamics of capital accumulation is examined by von Neumann under the assumption that productive capacity is proportionately augmented in all sectors, thus maintaining unchanged the relations among such different sectors. As a result, von Neumann is able to focus his attention:

on a state of long-run equilibrium where all sectors of the economy are in harmony with each other, and hence the economy changes only in scale but not in composition. [The model of von Neumann] is useless as a theory of short-run fluctuations, but may effectively describe the long-run growth. (Morishima, 1969, p. 105)

Von Neumann's results concerning the optimal properties of the balanced growth path (which is shown to coincide with the maximum growth-rate path) are associated with a number of restrictive assumptions relative to the technological set-up and to consumer behaviour. In the first case it is assumed that production processes are carried out by using a fixed-coefficient technology and, furthermore, that 'the natural factors of production, including labour, can be expanded in unlimited quantities' (von Neumann, 1945–6, p. 2). In the latter case von Neumann assumes that 'consumption of goods takes place only through the processes of production which include necessities of life consumed by workers and employees' (von Neumann, 1945–6, p. 2).

Von Neumann's simplifying assumptions, together with a particular representation of fixed-capital goods as joint products, makes it possible to analyse the complete 'dynamic structure' of the circular model without considering the complications associated with the existence of 'funds' (such as old machinery) that are not themselves produced in the *current* period. (In von Neumann, '[a] process that uses capital equipment is regarded as a process that converts a bundle of "inputs" into a bundle of "outputs"; inputs are defined to include capital goods left over from the preceding period and outputs are defined to include qualitatively different capital goods left over at the end of the current period' (Morishima, 1969, p. 89). At the same time, the 'dynamical potential' of any given circular structure of the productive system may be analysed without having to deal with factors of change that are external to the network of input–output flows such as a changing structure of preference on the part of consumers in the presence of a rising level of income. In connection with the latter point, it is worth stressing that von Neumann's assumption of a fixed consumption basket, needed to support one worker's activity, establishes a direct linkage between the scale of the overall productive activity and the level of 'final demand'. The importance of such an assumption has also been confirmed by subsequent research in which the consumer's choice is explicitly considered. In particular, Morishima has shown that, in this case, the balanced growth of the economic system on the assumption of positive workers' (and capitalists') savings requires 'the proportionality between [worker's] consumption and his income' (Morishima, 1969, p. 98). Indeed, it is found that such a proportionality involves that 'a proportional change in the quantities of goods does not give rise to any change in the preference ordering' (Morishima, 1969, p. 98). As a result, von Neumann's apparently unrealistic assumption concerning consumers' behaviour turns ultimately to be a suitable simplification if the economist's attention is focused upon the 'dynamic potential' of any given circular network of productive processes.

In spite of the interesting results outlined above, von Neumann's model leaves scope for possible refinements, especially in the direction of the analysis of non-steady-state economic dynamics. As a matter of fact, the concept of circular economic structure has so far been considered in connection with the assumption of an economic system that is either stationary or moving along a proportional-dynamics path. It is now time to turn to the issue of whether the circular theory allows for a comprehensive treatment of historically relevant features of actual economic dynamics (such as trends, ruptures and traverses from one long-run position to another). In this connection we may note that steady-state analysis does not directly allow for an exhaustive consideration of the uneven dynamic processes that characterize transition paths, nor does it allow for the explanation of switches from one regime of the economic system to another. As far as trends are concerned, the above theory makes it possible to consider only simplified dynamic paths along which the economic system maintains a fixed composition among elementary components; thus excluding those processes that affect only specific branches of the economic system.

6.3.2 Structural dynamics and circular-type analysis

As we have seen above, in its original formulation, the approach of von Neumann cannot accommodate the endogenous analysis of structural change. This feature has already been outlined in the previous discussion concerning the proportionality between consumption and income, and the underlying assumption that the elasticities of demand with respect to income are unity for all goods (see above). This excludes possible changes in the composition of demand due to variations in the level of real income – such as those associated with Engel's law, according to which the share of income allocated to the purchase of any type of goods and services changes with increases in real per capita income (Engel, 1857).

Recently, this aspect of real economic dynamics has been taken up by Pasinetti's (1981) work on structural change. However an important feature of Pasinetti's contribution is the idea that the pattern of structural dynamics associated with Engel's law may be adequately examined within a vertically integrated framework. In Pasinetti's view the structural implications of Engel's law lead to a type of economic analysis in which attention may be focused not on the conventional industries of circular theories, but on vertically integrated sectors in which

[a]ll inter-relations which can be observed in the real world are looked at as parts of a process which has not yet come to an end. Any process reaches its completion only when the product which comes out is a final commodity (consumption or investment good). A vertically integrated sector is, therefore, from an inter-industry point of view, a very complex 'sector', as it repeatedly goes through the whole intricate pattern of inter-industry connections. However, from the point of view of the homogeneity of the inputs, it becomes a very simple one, as it eliminates all

intermediate goods and resolves each final commodity into its ultimate constituent elements: a (flow) quantity of labour and a (stock) quantity of capital goods. It may be interesting to recall that this procedure was used by Léon Walras himself in his *Eléments*, although in a more rudimentary way. (Pasinetti, 1981, p. 110)

Pasinetti's contribution shows that important features of structural dynamics may be examined without explicitly considering the complex inter-relations among different productive processes as they are described in the circular representation of the economic system. This is achieved by setting into the background the role of intermediate products, which are at the centre of the circular approach.

An alternative view of structural change, in which the starting point is provided by von Neumann's framework and where the role of intermediate products is maintained in the foreground, has been provided by Quadrio-Curzio (1975, 1986). In this contribution it is stressed that:

The *interdependence* between raw materials, primary commodities and produced goods means that the raw materials themselves act as an aspect and, indeed, a constraint on production processes. The latter constraint thus results from an interdependence in which means of production of all kinds assume a combined role with relative substitutability. (Quadrio-Curzio, 1986, p. 312)

Clearly at the centre of this approach is the idea that means of production (including intermediate products) play a critical function in explaining the working of any given economic system and the processes of structural change taking place within it. In this connection it may be noted that Quadrio-Curzio's use of the circular approach leads him to the formulation of two distinct types of analytical framework: the 'global technologies' framework and the 'composite technologies' framework. In the former case 'technology is represented so as to make it possible to describe the physical system in a synthetic way. The essence of this method . . . is that of enclosing in a single technological matrix the processes with NPMPs [non-produced means of production] . . . together with the processes producing commodities without the use of NPMPs' (Quadrio-Curzio, 1986, pp. 322–3). In this perspective, it is assumed that changes in the scale of the economic system bring about the simultaneous use of different processes using different types of the same non-produced means of production but delivering the same type of output. This kind of situation is described by a special type of technological matrix that contains both the standard technical coefficients of the Leontief type as well as the 'splitting coefficients', namely the coefficients used to split the standard technical coefficients according to proportions that depend on what share of any given produced raw material (such as corn) is delivered by the different types of non-produced means of production (such as lands of different degrees of fertility).

The second framework of analysis is based on the consideration of 'composite technologies', in which the overall economic system is described as a set of distinct sub-systems of productive activities where each sub-system is a 'miniature productive system' containing all commodities produced in the complete system and a number of production processes equal to that of produced commodities. Here there is a one-to-one correspondence between the number of produced commodities and the number of production processes; whereas in the complete economic system, which provides the starting point of analysis, processes outnumber commodities in the case of a growing economy with a number of non-produced means of production. (The latter statement holds true when the early stage of expansion has been overcome, and at least two different processes *need* to be operated in order to provide a sufficient amount of at least one commodity.)

In this case the linkage among different sub-systems is provided by the process of capital accumulation. The different sub-systems are considered to be

> connected in time, in that they rely upon the means of production of techniques already activated. These disjointed, but temporally connected techniques, will give rise to composite technologies which ... represent a fair approximation to reality when account is taken of the non-produced means of production. (Quadrio-Curzio, 1986, p. 327)

This framework allows for an exhaustive inquiry into some of the most relevant features of economic dynamics when the latter is described as a process in which variations in the level of activity are associated with structural changes of the production system. As a matter of fact such a process may be split into a number of different dimensions, which the above analytical framework may highlight. On the one hand, a number of distinct production techniques may be simultaneously operated, particularly when changes in the productive structure are progressively taking place; on the other, intermediate products delivered within a given technological set-up may be used as means of production in a different technological set-up.

The analysis of the former aspect is made possible by the use of the 'splitting coefficients' of the global-technology approach; while the identification and analysis of the latter is facilitated by the use of the 'composite-technology' approach. For example it may be possible to inquire into a process of technological diffusion by stressing the relevance of the different input proportions to be ascribed to distinct sources of supply (say the quantity of steel produced with a new method and that delivered by an already obsolete method still in operation); in this case 'splitting coefficients' may be a relevant analytical tool. However there is another aspect of the diffusion of new technology that may be explained within the framework of 'composite technologies'; here an example may be provided by the dynamic implications of the connections among distinct productive techniques, which may be highlighted by explicitly considering the circular nature of any alternative technological set-up and thus the specific role of intermediate products in providing a linkage between the old and the new technology. In this way the diffusion of a new technology may be analysed by combining two different but complementary perspectives: one is associated with a description of the economic system in transition at any given point of time; the other refers to the dynamic linkages between old and new technologies, from which relevant consequences may obtain for the process of capital accumulation and thus for the overall pattern of expansion.

So far we have considered analytical schemes that were not formulated with the aim of a direct empirical implementation. However, the circular concept of economic structure lends itself to a utilization for 'direct structural analysis' (Leontief, 1966, p. 39; see also 1954), that is for empirical assessment. The role of circularity in this type of analysis is made clear by the logical steps followed by Leontief in his attempt to derive an empirically oriented analytical framework starting from a purely theoretical formulation. Leontief's starting point is the analysis of productive interdependencies within the economic system. In this connection it is pointed out that

Economic theory tells us that in order to trace through such a chain of relationships, one must determine the actual shape of the transformation (production) functions of all the individual sectors of the economy in question, insert them into an appropriate system of general equilibrium equations and finally compute the effect which the assumed increase or decrease in final demand would have on the output in question. (Leontief, 1966, p. 41; see also 1954)

In this connection Leontief expounds a methodological standpoint according to which 'the reduction in qualitative variety is attained at the cost of ever increasing quantitative indeterminacy' (Leontief, 1966, p. 55; see also 1959).

The reduction in quantitative indeterminacy is thus obtained by increasing the level of detail of qualitative descriptions. This procedure is illustrated by carefully analysing the relationship between 'an intricate quantitative system with many variables' and 'several simpler relationships – each involving fewer variables' (Leontief, 1966, p. 151; see also 1947). The analytical procedure followed by Leontief may be described by taking as a starting point his own account of the process of steel production. In this case:

The final output depends ... on a very great number of different inputs. If one goes back far enough, these will comprise the quantities of various kinds of labor, machinery, explosives, and other auxiliary materials used in extraction of coal; they will also include a not less heterogeneous collection of cost factors of the iron-mining industry. To be complete this list should contain as well a long array of tools, labor skills, and materials used directly in the operation and maintenance of blast furnaces and open-hearth units. (Leontief, 1966, p. 151; see also 1947)

The relationship between increasing qualitative variety and greater quantitative determinacy is analysed by Leontief starting from the consideration of a general, overall steel production function in which the quantity of finished steel is made to be dependent on the exact amount of all the distinct individual inputs entering the different stages of steel production. It is at this point that the relevance of intermediate commodities is clearly brought to the fore:

The various material processes covered by this formula are so many and so different from each other that even a verbal description of such a vast technological complex would hardly be possible without reference to intermediate commodities such as coal and ore. The over-all relationships between the set of the independent variables $x_1, x_2, \dots, x_8$ and the dependent variable, y, can be conveniently thought of as a combination of many separate, intermediate relationships involving not only these original but also some additional, intermediate variables. Let, for example, x_1, x_2, x_3 represent those of the eight factors which are actually used in the production of coal and x_4, x_5, x_6, x_7 those which constitute the cost elements of the iron-mining industry. Let, furthermore, z_1 stand for the amount of coal and z_2 the quantity of ore going into the production of steel and x_8 be the amount of labor used in servicing the blast furnaces. (Leontief, 1966, p. 152; see also 1947)

The above quotation shows the important association between the increase in the degree of detail of the description of the production process and the explicit treatment of the 'internal structure' of functional relationships describing material transformation processes. In this connection, it is worth stressing that the greater determinacy acquired by the new type of structural description leads Leontief to introduce 'intermediate production functions'. Of these,

[t]he first describes the output of coal in terms of the original factors – 'original' means in this context a factor represented by one of the independent variables in the production function ... – actually used in the coal industry; the second gives an analogous description of iron mining. The last is a production function of the steel industry but in contrast to the over-all function ... it does not have among its independent variables any of the original factors used either in the coal or in the iron industry. It describes the output of steel in terms of the two new intermediate variables, coal, z_1, and ore, z_2, combined with one 'original' factor, x_8, which does not appear in either one of the two other production functions; as stated before, x_8 represents labor employed on the blast-furnace crews. (Leontief, 1966, p. 152; see also 1947)

This type of detailed structural description gives relevance to the role of intermediate and produced commodities that are themselves used as productive inputs in other production processes; and in this way a systematic connection may be established among the different quantities of produced inputs entering the different productive activities and providing a basic underlying unity to the whole and complex network of input–output relationships existing in any given economic system. As a result, a 'circular' specification of the economic system is explicitly substituted for the simplified 'vertical' descripiton that provided Leontief's original analytical starting point.

The circular nature of Leontief's input–output approach is also essential in the formulation of dynamic theory. In particular, the relevance of a circular productive structure is shown by the consideration of 'stock–flow relationships' that are themselves considered to be reducible to 'fixed structural lags'. These lags are associated with the existence, in the whole economic system, of reproductive cycles for the different commodities, the length of which may vary depending on the different patterns of utilization of the various commodities as productive inputs. The specifically dynamic feature of structural stock–flow relationships (to be distinguished from the type of stock–flow relationships usually considered in economic analysis in association with the accumulation and decumulation of stocks of unsold or overdemanded commodities) is shown by the fact that 'the dependence of the future on the past states of the system' (Leontief, 1953, p. 54) is sometimes associated with 'the operation of primary structural lags' (Leontief, *ibid.*):

> The fluctuation in the amount of 'work in progress' (which is a stock of intermediate products) observed in the shipbuilding industry, for example, can be successfully explained on the basis of the structural lag measured by the time which elapses between the laying of the keel of a vessel and its final completion. Conversely an observed lag between the variation in the stream of inputs absorbed by an industry and the corresponding changes in the level of its output can often be traced back to its changing capital requirements based on the technologically determined stock–flow ratio between the amounts, i.e. the stock of equipment, building, and inventory of materials, on the one hand, and the corresponding capacity to turn out the actually observed stream of finished products, on the other. (Leontief, 1953, p. 54)

Leontief's vision of dynamic analysis shows a clear interest in the relationship between the explanation of dynamic paths and the identification of a specifically relevant type of economic structure, which may be taken as given when dealing with dynamic issues. This perspective allows for the determination of 'the empirical law of change of a particular economy from information obtained through the observation of its structural characteristics at one single point of time' (Leontief, 1953, p. 53). (In this connection it is relevant to mention that, according to Leontief, the equilibrium proportions along a dynamic path 'between the outputs of the individual industries are dependent upon the structural properties of the economy only; because of that, they can be determined without the knowledge of any initial conditions' (Leontief, 1953, p. 62).)

Summing up, Leontief's approach to dynamic analysis is based on two distinct but closely related hypotheses.

The first concerns the idea that the distinguishing feature between static and dynamic theory is that the former deals with changes in endogenous variables on the basis of 'observed changes in the underlying structural relationships' (Leontief, 1953, p. 53); whereas dynamic analysis deals with changes in endogenous variables 'on the basis of fixed, i.e. invariant, structural characteristics of the system' (Leontief, 1953, p. 53). Such a perspective stresses the specific role of structural invariance in a theoretical scheme dealing with economic change in a proper dynamic method.

The second hypothesis refers to the belief that a comprehensive analysis of structural dynamics ought to build the law of change into the structure of the explanatory scheme, so that economic change appears as a dynamic process to be explained in terms of a fixed 'higher order structure'. As a result, the analysis of economic change is closely associated with the issue of structural specification; and structural change, which appears as an instance of parametric change in static analysis, may now be considered as the outcome of the working through time of specific dynamic mechanisms that are built into the general description of the economic system under consideration. This leads Leontief to stress that differences in methods may ultimately be reduced to differences in theories, and that alternative theoretical frameworks may lead to the identification of distinct but closely related empirical bases:

> It is important to remember that [the distinctions among alternative treatments of economic change] refer to differences in theories, that is, to different methods of describing and explaining the observed facts rather than to some intrinsic properties of the observed reality itself. Alternative theories, instead of being mutually exclusive, might furthermore be hierarchically related to each other. A dynamic theory could, for example, treat the data of the less general, static theory as its variables and thus, taking up where the latter leaves off, reduce what in the first instance appeared to be a structural change to a dynamic law. Such generalization of a theoretical approach would necessarily have to be accompanied by a corresponding widening, or rather deepening, of its empirical basis. (Leontief, 1953, p. 17)

6.3.3 Accounting frameworks for structural analysis

The specific role of the theoretical framework in establishing appropriate empirical bases for the application of the circular process of economic structure has also been stressed by Richard Stone in his contribution on the foundations of national and social accounting. More precisely, the role of economic theory in empirical analysis has been pointed out by Richard Stone and Giovanna Stone as follows:

> The economic aspects of social accounting is concerned with a comprehensive, orderly, consistent presentation of the facts of economic life, in which the concepts, definitions and classifications adopted lend themselves to actual measurement and, within this limitation, correspond to those which appear in economic theory and so can be used for economic analysis. Thus even if we start from an empirical point of view we shall find ourselves listening to the suggestions of theory at every turn: it is not the facts themselves that lead us to distinguish between current and capital expenditure, we do so at the suggestion of theory despite the difficulties involved in carrying out the distinction; nor is it the facts themselves that lead us to emphasize the national income as the basic total both of a country's income and of its contribution to world production. And so it is all the way through. The facts we present and the way we arrange them depend a great deal on considerations of theory. (Stone and Stone, 1977, p. 163)

The contribution of Stone and Stone to the introduction of schemes aimed at 'a comprehensive, orderly, consistent presentation of the facts of economic life' is rooted in the circular concept of economic structure, which may be traced back 'to the Political Arithmeticians in England in the second half of the seventeenth century and in particular to the work of William Petty and Gregory King' (Stone and Stone, 1977, pp. 152–3).

The logical procedure in terms of which it is possible to gain information relative to economic structure starting from data concerning overall magnitudes such as national income and 'other income totals' (Stone and Stone) is laid out by stressing the role of disaggregation as a prerequisite for structural analysis; since it is by defining 'the constituents of these totals', and by showing 'how they are related to each other to form a closed network of flows', that it is possible to gain 'some insight into the basic structure of an economic system' (Stone and Stone, 1977, p. 31). In particular, the classification of productive activities ought to meet given conceptual prerequisites (which are themselves rooted in economic theory) if 'an interconnected set of production accounts' (Stone, 1961, p. 33) is to be useful in carrying out structural analyses. As a matter of fact, a coherent set of production accounts (that is, an input–output table)

> is not required just to provide more detailed information about production but information of a particular kind. It should provide, as far as possible, an

unambiguous and stable picture of industrial structure in such a way that it is possible to trace the implications in different lines of production of a change in the demand for any particular product. (Stone, 1961, p. 33)

The procedure of disaggregation may lead to a description of the circular network of productive structure by introducing a suitable way of splitting the consolidated production accounts of the whole economy so as to emphasize intermediate product flows. In this perspective, input–output accounting may be introduced as a specific basis for the study of the set of circular interrelationships within any given economic system:

If we want to study the productive system in detail we must retrieve [information concerning all the flows of intermediate products], since in most industries a considerable part of the costs of production consists of purchases from other industries and in many industries a considerable part of the revenue from production comes from sales of other industries. We can do this by subdividing the production account so that we have one account for each branch of production. If we arrange these accounts in matrix form in such a way that the elements in a given row relate to the revenues (outputs) of a particular industry and the elements in the corresponding column relate to the costs (inputs) of the same industry, we obtain the familiar type of input–output table. In addition to the industry rows and columns, this table will contain an extra row and column whose elements will be respectively the primary inputs into the different branches of production and the final outputs emerging from them. (Stone and Stone, 1977, p. 155)

This view of intermediate-product relationships lends itself to a description of those specific features of the economic system that emerge in the dynamic working of circular economic structures, in which a central role is performed by the process of accumulation:

Production, consumption and accumulation are the three basic forms of economic activity. Its ultimate aim is consumption, but since production requires the services of durable equipment it is necessary that this equipment should be maintained and increased if consumption is to be maintained and increased. If a large part of production is accumulated it is to be expected that the capacity to produce will rise so that in the future more products will be available for consumption. On the other hand, if no part of production is accumulated it is to be expected that the capacity to produce will remain constant, and if the stock of durable equipment is not even maintained, the capacity to produce will fall. In practice, of course, other forces, social, political, scientific or natural, may affect productive capacity but, other things being equal, the larger the part of final product devoted to accumulation the larger the future consumption as compared with present consumption. (Stone and Stone, 1977, p. 32)

Richard Stone's contribution has called attention to the relevance of a suitable classification scheme in order to carry out the description of dynamic processes in which the crucial role of accumulation within the circular flow is brought to the fore. In particular he has stressed the need for a logical step 'implying the transition from a *single magnitude*, the basic total of income, to a *structure* in which this magnitude is related to others of similar kind' (Stone and Stone, 1977, p. 161).

6.3.4 Structural analysis of dynamic processes: stocks and flows

The importance of specific accounting frameworks for structural analysis may be further investigated by introducing the distinction between flow-based and stock-based types of accounting. In the former case the description of the economic system relates to the amounts of goods and services that are 'produced, consumed, due to be paid, due to be received, transferred, lent, borrowed, etc., *per unit of time*' (Stone and Stone, 1977, p. 158). In the latter case account is taken of stocks 'not in the limited sense of products awaiting sale or use but in the more general sense of *assets* and *liabilities* existing *at a point in time*; that is to say, we must set up a national *balance sheet*' (Stone and Stone, 1977, pp. 158–9).

The need for integrating a flow-based description and a 'balance-sheet description' of the economic system has been stressed by Löwe (1976) in his outline of 'A schema of industrial production'. In this connection, Löwe points out that at any given point of time a particular productive system exhibits a complex pattern of relationships between the physical stocks of wealth and the physical flows of production. In the former case a complete description of the productive system leads to the identification of a number of different stocks of physical assets:

> If at any point in time we were to undertake a census of an industrial community's wealth in physical terms, we would find four different stocks of real assets: a stock of labor; a stock of natural resources; a stock of durable-equipment goods, such as plant, machinery, residential buildings; and a stock of other goods of rather diverse physical forms and economic uses, which needs further specification. (Löwe, 1976, p. 24)

At the same time, if we consider the ongoing processes of production, the economic system exhibits a complex network of input–output relationships characterized by the existence of interdependent input and output flows and the critical role of produced and intermediate commodities. According to Löwe a complete description of the productive system needs to incorporate both such elements; such a requirement is outlined in the following account of the production process:

> A continuous process of production requires that the industrial sectors, the various stages of completion into which each sector is subdivided, and the portions of each of the four basic stocks of goods and services assigned to the individual productive

units in every stage of every sector be arranged in a definite order. We shall call a *schema of production* the model that depicts the reproduction of the principal stocks and flows in the technically required sequence. (Löwe, 1976, p. 27)

The above integration of stock-based and flow-based descriptions of an economic system lends itself naturally to dynamic analysis.

As a matter of fact a systematic linkage is thereby provided between the successive time periods of a dynamic sequence by means of the 'heritage' of physical assets that is transferred from one time period to the next. As already mentioned in the first part of this section, it is by means of the introduction of stock–flow relationships that it becomes possible to drop the 'stationary state' fiction underlying the circular-flow analysis and to explicitly introduce the treatment of historical sequences as a transition to dynamic analysis. (As pointed out in subsection 6.3.1 above, when dealing with Pigou's contribution quoted by Hicks in *Value and Capital*, a specific type of stock–flow relationship is associated with the accumulation of intermediate products into a stock progressively 'fed and drained' by current inputs and outputs.)

The pattern of integration between circular input–output relationships and the processes by which the 'industrial wealth' of the economic system is progressively accumulated (or depleted) is described by Löwe when expounding the conditions to be fulfilled in order to achieve the continuity of production processes:

First, the 'active' factors, labor and equipment, have to operate in a technically predetermined manner upon the 'passive' factor: natural resources, both in their original form and in their successive transformations as working capital. Second, the stocks of labor, equipment, and natural resources must be continuously replenished in proportion to what they release currently as input flows into actual production. (Löwe, 1976, p. 29)

The particular type of structural specification in Löwe is linked with the identification of a precise method of dynamic analysis in which the principle of relative structural invariance performs a major role. An important instance of the functioning of this principle may be found in the influence of technically specific inputs (such as workers with given skills or machinery with given capabilities) in determining the reaction pattern of the economic system to dynamic impulses (such as a 'once-over' increase in the growth rate); the reason why the corresponding dynamic path or traverse is influenced by the existing productive structure is that 'the initially prevailing technical coefficients of production can be altered only by a productive process that itself is conditioned by these very coefficients' (Löwe, 1976, p. 10).

The pattern of such a dynamic path is based upon a succession of states that brings about a well-identified process of transformation:

> [T]he path itself, the dynamics of configuration, appears then as a sequence of structured states, each stage describing the physical and price relations between the state variables: inputs and outputs in the aggregate and for relevant sectoral subdivisions, employment and incomes, savings and investments, etc. From stage to stage these variables undergo expansion or contraction in the aggregate, or relative shifts, until they assume the configuration of the terminal state. (Löwe, 1965, pp. 258–9)

At this stage we may consider the methodological implications of the type of approach put forward by Löwe whereby the pattern of dynamics is significantly determined by the principle of relative structural invariance and by a relative rigidity of the economic structures undergoing transformation processes. In this connection there are important implications concerning both the description of empirical dynamic paths and the corresponding theoretical frameworks introduced for their explanation. Such implications have been outlined as follows:

> To the extent to which the technical structure is unalterable in the short period, the prevailing degree of factor specificity determines each stage of the growth path. Therefore, what in retrospect appears as a secular process is, in fact, an abstraction derived from a sequence of short-term movements, the latter being the only 'real' processes. We have long been accustomed to this kind of reasoning in statistical trend analysis. It is time to realize that it applies with equal force to the theoretical treatment of growth. (Löwe, 1976, p. 10)

The type of economic structure envisaged by Löwe, characterized by the coexistence of elements (such as specific industries or sub-systems) with different levels of rigidity with respect to external shocks, implies the adoption of a level of aggregation that is intermediate between that implied by aggregate analysis of the macro-economic type and that implied by the precise description of the complete network of input–output relationships. Löwe's analysis of economic dynamics concentrates upon particular problems of growth such as:

> the building up and wearing down of fixed capital, the accumulation and decumulation of working capital, the relationship between these capital stocks and the flows of output, the effect of technical change on capital formation and employment capacity, and related topics. (Löwe, 1976, p. 22)

The related issue concerning the adoption of a suitable level of aggregation in the description and analysis of the problems of growth is expounded as follows:

It cannot be denied that each of these problems has also a micro-economic aspect. But our investigation will, on the whole, concentrate on those macro-economic issues that are independent of the peculiarities of individual units or even industries. For this reason the level of aggregation chosen here is very much higher than the one applied, for example, in input–output analysis. At the same time the Keynesian model is too highly aggregated for our purpose. Dealing with production problems we require a model that depicts not only the 'value dimension' of income–expenditure flows and asset stocks but also the 'physical dimension' of technically differentiated inputs and outputs. (Löwe, 1976, p. 22)

The approach to dynamic analysis presented in Löwe's work shows a significant utilization of a circular type of theoretical framework for the investigation of sequences of productive transformations in which there emerges a clear directionality of causation mechanisms, associated with the 'linear' aspect of productive processes. Such processes are in fact considered as a sequence of connected stages by means of which a given material is progressively shaped into a finished commodity. Such a view introduces the consideration of vertical features of productive activity within a theoretical framework maintaining a basically circular structure. This is introduced by the particular accounting that combines the description of interdependent flows of intermediate products with the consideration of 'the system's basic stocks' (Löwe). Here it is possible to find the coexistence of vertical and horizontal flows, since non-produced resources are followed through the process of progressive transformation stages leading to the stage of finished commodities; however, the continuity of such a vertical flow presupposes the coexistence of a simultaneous horizontal flow of fixed-capital goods needed to replace the worn out capacity that is used up at every stage of the vertical material-transformation process already described.

6.4 Vertical and circular approaches: tools for dynamic analysis

It is now time to assess the relative merits and the mutual relationship between the two analytical frameworks respectively represented by the circular and vertically integrated approaches to the theory of production. We shall take into consideration the way in which economic theories built upon either representation of the structure of production allow for the analysis of dynamic processes.

Any appraisal of actual economic dynamics must be based upon the utilization of a specific analytical framework, which suggests the identification of a limited number of critical features and the discovery of a chain of causal relationships behind the process under consideration. As Hicks has pointed out, economic theories in general and dynamic models in particular always presuppose a selective concentration of attention upon certain crucial aspects and relationships (see Hicks, 1975 and 1985). This is also true in the case of the application of circular and vertical models to the study of economic dynamics. Here we may underline the fact that actual processes of economic change (such as trends, ruptures and traverses) always show a cluster of 'circular' and 'vertical' features. In this connection it is relevant to recall that the 'analytical picture' of an actual economic situation is often distinct from the 'realistic picture' of the same situation, since it may be difficult to disentangle a plurality of interlinked causal mechanisms of a complex system when a comprehensive description of the latter is attempted. An instance of this problem is provided by Jeremy Bentham:

> In the order of history labour precedes capital: from land and labour everything proceeds. But in the actual order of things, there is always some capital already produced, which is united with land and labour in the production of new values. (Bentham as quoted in Hayek, 1934, p. 227)

The relationship between the circular and vertical perspective, which is already implicit in Bentham's passage, has been carefully examined by Nurkse, who has called attention to the complementarity of the two perspectives. As far as the vertical description is concerned it may be argued that such a description:

> Fits circulating capital excellently: here we can indeed in most cases point to a highest stage (in the sphere of what in everyday language is well named 'primary' production), where no raw materials or semifinished goods are taken over for further treatment from an earlier stage. (Nurkse, 1962, pp. 25–6; see also 1935)

However a possible descriptive failure of the vertical approach may be identified when fixed capital goods are explicitly considered. In this case fixed capital goods would be conceived as 'intermediate products moving essentially in the same way to "become" consumable goods and services' (Nurkse, 1962, p. 26; see also 1935). This implies that the associated *Tableau économique* would exhibit two types of deficiency:

> First, the origin of fixed capital goods is left obscure in the triangular picture. Second, the linear representation does not adequately show the place of the productive services of durable instruments in the structure of production. (Nurkse, 1962, p. 26; see also 1935)

The above considerations lead Nurkse to suggest that in a number of cases a realistic picture of the structure of production ought to consider the circular aspect of the productive process. In this connection Nurkse stresses that a comprehensive appraisal of the productive process requires:

A recognition of the fact that fixed capital not only adds value to the circulating capital (i.e., the 'goods in process') to which, in common with the 'original' factors, it is applied, but that it *reproduces itself* (in the sense to be developed presently). For 'production is in reality no such linear process from the original factors to the consumable commodity. The iron and machine industry, for example, produces for the lower stages (for the consumption industries) as well as for the preceding stages, e.g., for the mining industry ... The process of production takes no straight path; its course is, rather, a circular line which turns back into itself any number of times before reaching the final stage of consumption.' (Nurkse, 1962, p. 26; see also 1935. Quotation from Haberler, 1933, pp. 98–9.)

In spite of the important role of 'self-reproduction' in the case of fixed capital, a purely circular description of the productive system misses one essential aspect of the production process, that is the fact that any type of productive activity is based upon the cooperation between active and passive factors of production, such as instruments and materials respectively. Instruments bring about a sequence of coordinated transformations in the 'raw material basis' of the process. As a result a realistic picture of such a process requires consideration of the time structure of production, especially as far as the succession of transformations is concerned.

For this reason it may be argued that the vertical approach highlights a critical aspects of production that cannot be eliminated from a comprehensive analytical framework. As a matter of fact a purely circular framework may draw attention away from a number of conditions that production activity must satisfy if given objectives are to be reached. Löwe has stressed this point as follows:

One needs only to consider an increase in the aggregate demand for coal, that is, growth, in a system in which all real capital is fully utilized. Then we see at once that the critical bottleneck 'in the hierarchy of production' arises in the machine tool stage and that only after capacity has been increased there, can the output of ore-steel-extractive machinery and, finally, coal be increased. (Löwe, 1976, p. 34n)

The reason is to be found in the time-constrained sequence of transformations associated with coal-production technology:

It is true that coal, as a 'finished equipment good' in the sense previously defined, is required for the production of iron, but the converse is not true. What we require for the production of coal is extractive machinery, in the production of which iron is an intermediate good, itself derived from the natural resource 'ore' and transformed into extractive machinery with the help of the truly circular factor 'machine tool'. (Löwe, 1976, p. 34n)

The description of the relationship between 'vertical' and 'horizontal' features of productive activity has been further examined by Vasily Nemchinov, who stresses that both perspectives are essential for the representation of productive structure and that from a historical point of view the distinction yields to the discovery of an important feature of actual economic dynamics. The 'complex and varied' nature of the production process is described as follows:

Each commodity in order to be produced requires the consumption of other commodities, such as raw materials, fuel, electricity, whose production is in turn connected with the consumption of yet other commodities. In this way a complex productive network is formed, in which one may identify a vertically integrated and highly articulated productive sector associated with each commodity ... The fabrication of each consumption good, that is of all goods making up the material fund of national income, is associated with complex production linkages ... In all productive processes, besides the vertically integrated sector, there exists a horizontally integrated set of activities, which is made up of enterprises simultaneously functioning and exchanging the results of their work with one another. (Nemchinov, 1969, section 3.1)

The dual character of the productive process may be connected with the division of labour among productive units performing specialized tasks, since we may describe any given set of interdependent productive activities alternatively as a set of distinct but simultaneous processes performed within productive units reciprocally connected by exchange, or as a set of successive stages of production all leading to a given final commodity. Such a duality allows for the emergence of alternative types of productive organization depending on whether the set of vertically connected sectors coincides with the set of horizontally integrated activities. Here Nemchinov argues that the consideration of historical development allows for the identification of distinct stages of the division of labour:

In the early stages of development of human society, the vertically integrated sector was not clearly identifiable. In a sense such sector was to be found within each individual enterprise only, in which the independent producer divided himself his own labour time into a series of operations: extraction and transformation of the basic raw commodity, fabrication of the working tool, and so on ... Social division of labour became more complex as society reached a higher stage of development, and each vertically integrated sector became increasingly more complex, until it did no longer coincide with the set of horizontally integrated activities. (Nemchinov, 1969, section 3.1)

The above argument suggests that the relationship between circular and vertical theories may be based upon the relationships already examined between circular and vertical features. As a matter of fact the flexibility in the application of economic theories to the study of specific features of economic dynamics is highlighted by the fact that it is possible to use alternatively the circular or the vertical types of model for the analysis of both vertical and circular features. For instance it may be possible to apply a circular (horizontally integrated) model to the analysis of a basically vertical description of the economic system. On the other hand one may also apply the vertically integrated theory to inquiry into the mechanisms of an economic system as described by a circular framework. Significant instances of such a flexible utilization of distinct theoretical schemes may be found in Löwe (1952, 1976) and Pasinetti (1973, 1981). Löwe's 'schema of industrial production' starts from a basically circular model of the productive system and applies it to a vertical description of the stage-structure of the productive process. On the other hand Pasinetti's multi-sectoral theoretical scheme is constructed upon a vertically integrated conceptual framework that provides an analytical device to inquire into the structure of a self-reproducing system described as a circular economy.

7. 'Anatomy' and 'Physiology' of the economic system: a framework for economic dynamics

It is now time to attempt a critical assessment of the various conceptual strands that have emerged in the foregoing analysis of the relationships between structural change and economic dynamics. One fundamental perspective is provided by the distinction between two complementary concepts of structure in economics: the 'set of objective economic magnitudes', which is associated with the 'stock–flow network', and the 'social fabric' giving shape to the patterns of interaction among individuals in any given economic system. Such a distinction provides a common thread underlying the various themes dealt with in the previous sections.

More specifically the above distinction provides a unifying framework for assessing the mutual compatibility between structural features, institutional arrangements and patterns of economic dynamics. It is at this stage that the full implication of the distinction between two fundamental ways of representing the objective stock–flow network may be highlighted. As a matter of fact it is possible to argue that there is a relationship between the way in which the objective stock–flow network is described and the manner in which the actual working of the social fabric may be reconstructed within economic theory.

A clue to this relationship is provided by setting into a framework the horizontal and vertical representations of economic structure. In fact it may be argued that in the case of the vertical representation of structure attention is called to the basic linkage between human needs and the provision of goods: in this way certain features of social organization come to the fore. For instance most of the elements of the institutional set-up emerge in an immediate way, particularly because individuals are described as the core of economic structure and emphasis is placed upon the way in which emerging needs may be satisfied by establishing certain patterns of interaction among individuals. On the other hand, in the case of the horizontal or circular representation of the objective network of economic magnitudes, the 'technological order' (Nurkse) of society comes into the foreground to determine the way in which the self-replacement and possible expansion of the system takes place. More specifically, this type of description focuses on the role of technological and social linkages among groups of individuals especially linked to the organization of production and less directly associated with the satisfaction of human needs (the latter being the case of the vertical representation).

At closer scrutiny it appears that certain aspects of institutional elements (see section 3 above) are better highlighted in the case of the vertical representation, while others come to the fore in the case of the circular representation. For instance the form of property rights may differ according to the type of representation adopted: in the instance of the vertical approach the distribution of existing assets is emphasized; while in the case of the circular approach the property rights over productive capacity play a more important role. A similar distinction may be applied to distributional patterns: functional or personal distribution of income and wealth are stressed by, respectively, circular and vertical approaches.

Moving on to dynamics we may stress that the distinction between types of representation of the productive system can be linked with the identification of different types of motion of the whole economy. Such linkage is connected with the distinction between 'natural' and 'institutional' set-ups; that is between those features that are associated with uniform and constant causal mechanisms independent of historical circumstances (as in the case of Pasinetti and Löwe) and those behavioural characteristics that depend on the historical and institutional aspects of economic society. Consequently we are now in a position to argue that the linkage between the two levels of analysis will determine the way in which, in a dynamic context, the institutional features – and thus the behavioural principle governing the motion of any given economic system – may be associated with a given representation of the objective stock–flow network (vertical or circular). As a matter of fact, vertical and circular representations suggest the consideration of distinct clusters of institutional features, thus calling attention to a specific configuration of dynamic principles.

The way in which alternative descriptions of 'material bases' may be helpful in identifying distinct dynamic features of economic systems may be illustrated by considering the processes of propagation of given impulses and the way in which these crucially depend on the specification of economic structure. Sir John Hicks has called attention to the relevance of a stage-structure theory of the production process taking place through time to show the conditions under which the Keynesian multiplier applies. The basis of Hicks's analysis is the contention that 'the multiplier is not instantaneous; it takes time to operate' (Hicks, 1974, p. 10). The sequential character of the multiplier mechanism is closely related with the fact that productive activities take time to go through the distinct transformation stages leading to finished goods. The role of produced commodities behind the working of a multiplicative process is highlighted by the fact that the employment effects of an increase in investment expenditure presupposes either the availability of adequate stocks of intermediate products or a readily expanding production of such intermediate products. This may be observed in the case of additional investment taking place in the building industry; here it is clear that employment may not be increased unless sufficient amounts of building materials are available for construction. For example it will be impossible to increase employment 'at a time when all bricks that are currently being produced by the brickmakers are already being used' (Hicks, 1974, p. 11); in this case the multiplicative process may take place provided that 'the bricks are in fact acquired by drawing on stocks' (Hicks, 1974, p. 11) and that in due course 'as the brickmakers find their stocks of bricks diminishing, they . . . take steps to expand their output of bricks' (Hicks, 1974, pp. 11–12). The time-related structure of productive processes is at the root of the role of bottle-necks in slowing down the course of economic expansion rising from a given increase in investment expenditure: '[i]f there are no surplus stocks of bricks, there can be no extra house-building, and no extra employment on house-building, until extra bricks have been produced. If there are ample materials for producing bricks, the extra bricks can be produced, but only after a delay. If there are not ample materials for producing bricks, these also have to be produced, and the delay is longer. The bottle-necks slow up the expansion in output, and also in employment.' (Hicks, 1974, p. 18)

The role of bottle-necks in a Keynesian process of employment expansion stresses the advantages of a vertical description of economic structure in considering crucial features of actual economic dynamics; however a comprehensive account of the conditions under which dynamic processes (such as employment expansion) may take place requires the consideration of features that are characteristic of the circular theory of economic structure. For instance the Keynesian multiplier may be analysed independently of an explicit consideration of stocks whenever, as presupposed by Keynes himself, a depressed economy is described. For '[o]ne of the symptoms of depression is an abundance of stocks, at many stages of the productive process – stocks which cannot be used, because the will (or the incentive) to use them is lacking' (Hicks, 1969, p. 152n). However if abundant stocks are not available a more immediate link is established between simultaneously operated productive processes. Additionally, the existence of simultaneous input requirements along a fully adjusted dynamic path comes to the fore. This may be shown by the consideration of a stationary state of a circular economy; here the mutual requirements of their respective outputs as essential inputs in a number of distinct but interrelated industries may be explicitly analysed.

At this point it may be worth stressing that alternative states of the economy (for instance depression or full employment) lend themselves to distinct dynamic features and thus suggest the utilization of distinct analytical tools. For instance a situation in which there exist underutilized productive resources, such as idle machinery and unsold stocks of intermediate products, may be easily dealt with within the framework of a vertical description of economic structure, since the input requirements of an industry undergoing output expansion may be satisfied by using already existing means of production without taking into consideration the whole network of inter-industry relationships. On the contrary when idle resources are not available any expansion sets into motion the whole set of inter-industry relationships, thus bringing to the fore the circular character of economic structure.

Moving on to the specific dynamic issues that may be highlighted by taking into consideration a circular theory of the economic system, it is worth noting that certain aspects of industrial fluctuation lend themselves to analysis by dropping the vertical representation of the productive system, in which the latter is described as a set of vertically integrated sectors, and the production process appears as a sequence of fabrication stages. A distinguishing characteristic of circular theory is the adoption of a view of the productive system in which the stage structure of production loses the prominent role it has in the vertical approach and is substituted by the explicit consideration of the network of interdependent productive activities. A simple instance of a circular economy is provided by an economic system in which the overall process of production is split into two distinct productive sectors: one delivering means of production, the other finished consumption goods. Here the circular character of the economic system is grafted onto a network of inter-sectoral flows, in such a way that the first sector (investment sector) delivers means of production both to itself and to the other sector (consumption sector). Here we may underline the coexistence of certain features of the vertical approach (a 'triangular' structure of input–output flows, which implies the existence of a one-way causal relationship from the investment sector to the consumption goods sector) with characteristic features of circular theory such as the explicit consideration of the self-reproduction mechanism for the investment-good sector.

This view of the productive system allows for a careful examination of a number of crucial aspects of the dynamics of industrial fluctuations. For instance it provides an explanation for the cumulative or self-reinforcing character of both expansionary and contracting phases of such fluctuations; here the crucial role is performed by the self-reproduction of the investment-good sector. A characteristic feature of this sector is that a share of its output is fed back into the same sector, whose productive capacity is thereby increased; this brings to the fore a most prominent feature of the productive system: '[T]he circular character of the structure of production makes it possible that new machine factories, power plants, iron works, etc., are constructed to produce more machine factories, power plants, and iron works. And this piling up of capital equipment in the investment industries ... is in fact a characteristic feature of the boom.' (Nurkse, 1962, p. 37n; see also 1935) A symmetrical cumulative process takes place during the slow-down, in which 'the original contraction of demand for the output of [the investment-good sector] may, owing to the circular nature of the self-reproduction of capital, lead to a cumulative shrinkage of replacement demand within [the investment-good sector] itself' (Nurkse, 1962, p. 39; see also 1935).

This specific feature of circular-type models draws attention to an important difference between the circular and vertical-type models as far as the analysis of economic dynamics is concerned. The cumulative character of expansion and contraction provides an example of a dynamic feature, which may be considered in circular theories but may not be adequately dealt with in theories of the vertical type. As a matter of fact the latter type of theory lends itself to the analysis of the process by which a given impulse fades itself out through a sequence of repercussions, without giving rise to self-reinforcing feed-backs.

At this point we may suggest a possible extension of the above argument to include the relationship between institutional features and types of economic dynamics. Here we may refer to Hicks's view concerning the link between the role of stocks of finished and unfinished storable commodities and the mechanism by which a given impulse propagates itself through the different parts of the economic system (see above). Here the distinction between 'flexprice' and 'fixprice' markets plays a relevant role since in the case of flexprice markets 'traders ... are intermediary traders, neither producers nor final consumers; the price is established by trading between them, rising when the stocks that have come into their possession are less than they desire to hold, falling when they have more' (Hicks, 1988, p. 3). On the other hand, in the case of fixprice markets the role of traders is significantly diminished, prices are ultimately dependent on the producers' cost and commodity stocks do play a less strategic role in determining the dynamic pattern of the economic system.

The above argument lends itself to a conjecture concerning the relationship between the flexprice–fixprice distinction and the representation of the productive system. Flexprice markets are to be conceived as 'traders' markets', in which stocks tend to separate demand and supply of goods from their production; so that the production process is better represented in terms of the vertical model (in which there is a clearly identifiable final stage and the relationships between different and interdependent productive processes are mapped into a precise 'stage structure' of any given process). On the other hand, fixprice markets, which may be taken to be 'producers' markets', establish a more direct link between demand and supply on the one side and production organization on the other side; here the production process may be better represented in terms of a circular model (in which, provided production and consumption activities are fully interlinked, it is no longer possible to clearly identify a final stage of production and the pattern of interdependence among productive processes replaces the 'stage structure' characterizing the performance of such a process through time).

In this way the institutional set-up appears to be related with the type of structural specification most suitable for the analysis of each particular economic system, in the sense that it draws attention to those structural features that are most important for the explanation of the dynamic patterns characterizing the system under consideration.

References and bibliography

Abruzzi, A. (1965) 'The Production Process: Operating Characteristics', *Management Science*, 11, pp. B 98-B 118.

Åkerman, J. (1932) *Economic Progress and Economic Crises*, Macmillan, London.

Allais, M. (1943) *A la recherche d'une discipline économique. Première partie: L'économie pure*, Ateliers Industria, Paris, 2 vols; 2nd edn: *Traité d'économie pure*, Imprimerie Nationale, Paris, 1952 (2nd edn identical to 1st edn, except for new introduction).

(1947) *Economie et intérêt*, Imprimerie Nationale and Librairie des Publications Officielles, Paris.

(1986) 'The Concepts of Surplus and Loss and the Reformulation of the Theories of Stable General Economic Equilibrium and Maximum Efficiency', in *Foundations of Economics. Structures of Inquiry and Economic Theory*, ed. M. Baranzini and R. Scazzieri, Basil Blackwell, Oxford and New York, pp. 135–74.

Amendola, M., and Gaffard, J. L. (1987) *The Innovative Choice*, Basil Blackwell, Oxford and New York.

Bacharach, M. O. L. (1986) 'The Problem of Agents' Beliefs in Economic Theories', in *Foundations of Economics. Structures of Inquiry and Economic Theory*, ed.

M. Baranzini and R. Scazzieri, Basil Blackwell, Oxford and New York, pp. 175–203.

Baldone, S. (1990) 'Vertical Integration, the Temporal Structure of Production Processes, and Transition between Techniques', in M. Landesmann, R. Scazzieri et al., *Dynamics in Production Systems*, 1990 (forthcoming).

Baranzini, M. (1982) (ed.) *Advances in Economic Theory*, Basil Blackwell, Oxford.

(1990) *A Theory of Wealth Accumulation and Distribution*, Clarendon Press, Oxford.

Baranzini, M., and Scazzieri, R. (1986) (eds) *Foundations of Economics. Structures of Inquiry and Economic Theory*, Basil Blackwell, Oxford and New York.

(1986) 'Knowledge in Economics: A Framework', in *Foundations of Economics. Structures of Inquiry and Economic Theory*, ed. M. Baranzini and R. Scazzieri, Basil Blackwell, Oxford and New York, pp. 1–87.

Bliss, C.J. (1975) *Capital Theory and the Distribution of Income*, North-Holland Publishing Company, Amsterdam and Oxford.

(1986) 'Progress and Anti-Progress in Economic Science', in *Foundations of Economics. Structures of Inquiry and Economic Theory*, ed. M. Baranzini and R. Scazzieri, Basil Blackwell, Oxford and New York, pp. 363–76.

Böhm-Bawerk, E. von (1889) *Positive Theorie des Kapitales* (*Kapital und Kapitalzins*, Part 2), Wagner, Innsbruck. (Translated as *The Positive Theory of Capital* (1891), Macmillan, London.)

Chakravarty, S. (1982) *Alternative Approaches to a Theory of Economic Growth. Marx, Marshall and Schumpeter*, Orient Longman, Delhi.

(1987) *Development Planning. The Indian Experience*, Clarendon Press, Oxford.

Dahmén, E. (1950) *Svensk industriell Företagverksamhet. Kausalanalys av den industriella utvecklingen 1919–1939*, Swedish Industrial Institute for Economic and Social Research (IUI), Lund.

Deane, P. (1969) *The First Industrial Revolution*, Cambridge University Press, Cambridge.

Deane, P., and Cole, W.A. (1967) *British Economic Growth, 1688–1959. Trends and Structure*, Cambridge University Press, Cambridge.

Debreu, G. (1959) *The Theory of Value*, John Wiley, New York.

Engel, E. (1857) 'Die Productions- und Consumptions-verhältnisse des Königreichs Sachsen', in *Zeitschrift der Statistischen Bureaus des Königlich Sächsischen Ministerium des Inneren*, Nos. 8 and 9, No. 22, republished in *Bulletin de l'Institut International de Statistique*, IX (1895).

Georgescu-Roegen, N. (1960) 'Economic Theory and Agrarian Economics', *Oxford Economic Papers*, NS, 12, pp. 1–40.

(1966) *Analytical Economics*, Harvard University Press, Cambridge, Mass.

(1969a) 'Process in Farming versus Process in Manufacturing', in *Economic Problems of Agriculture in Industrial Countries*, ed. U. Papi and C. Nunn, St. Martin's Press, New York, pp. 497–528.

(1969b) 'Institutional Aspects of Peasant Economies: An Analytical View', in *Subsistence Agriculture and Economic Development*, ed. G.R. Wharton, Jr., Aldine Publishing Co., Chicago, pp. 61–93. (A Seminar on Subsistence and Peasant Agriculture, Honolulu, March 1965.)

(1971) *The Entropy Law and the Economic Process*, Harvard University Press, Cambridge, Mass.
(1976) *Energy and Economic Myths – Institutional and Analytical Economic Essays*, Pergamon Press, New York and Oxford.
(1986) 'Man and Production', in *Foundations of Economics. Structures of Inquiry and Economic Theory*, ed. M. Baranzini and R. Scazzieri, Basil Blackwell, Oxford and New York, pp. 247–80.
(1988a) 'The Interplay between Institutional and Material Factors: The Problem and Its Status', in *Barriers to Full-Employment*, eds. J.A. Kregel, E. Matzner and A. Roncaglia, Macmillan, London, pp. 297–326.
(1988b) 'Closing Remarks: About Economic Growth – A Variation on a Theme by David Hilbert', *Economic Development and Cultural Change*, 36 (3), Supplement, pp. S291–S307.
Ghose, A.K. (1983) 'Agrarian Reform in Developing Countries: Issues of Theory and Problems of Practice', in *Agrarian Reform in Contemporary Developing Countries*, ed. A.K. Ghose, Croom Helm, London, pp. 3–28.
Gioja, M. (1815–17) *Nuovo prospetto delle scienze economiche*, Pirotta, Milan.
Goodwin, R.M. (1989) *Essays in Nonlinear Economic Dynamics*, Peter Lang, Frankfurt/Bern/Las Vegas.
Haberler, G. (1933) Paper (untitled) contributed to *Der Stand und die nächste Zukunft der Konjunkturforschung. Festschrift für Arthur Spiethoff*, with foreword by Joseph Schumpeter, Duncker and Humblot, Munich, pp. 92–103.
Harrod, R.F. (1939) 'An Essay in Dynamic Theory', *Economic Journal*, 49, pp. 14–33.
Hayek, F.A. von (1934) 'On the Relationship between Investment and Output', *Economic Journal*, 44, pp. 207–31.
(1941) *The Pure Theory of Capital*, Routledge, London.
(1967) *Prices and Production*, Routledge and Kegan Paul, London (1st edn 1931).
Hicks, J. (1932) *The Theory of Wages*, Macmillan, London.
(1939) *Value and Capital. An Inquiry into Some Fundamental Principles of Economic Theory*, Clarendon Press, Oxford.
(1946) *Value and Capital. An Inquiry into Some Fundamental Principles of Economic Theory*, Clarendon Press, Oxford (2nd edn).
(1959) *Essays in World Economics*, Clarendon Press, Oxford.
(1965) *Capital and Growth*, Clarendon Press, Oxford.
(1969) *A Theory of Economic History*, Clarendon Press, Oxford.
(1970) 'A Neo-Austrian Growth Theory', *Economic Journal*, 80, pp. 257–81.
(1973) *Capital and Time. A Neo-Austrian Theory*, Clarendon Press, Oxford.
(1974) *The Crisis in Keynesian Economics*, Basil Blackwell, Oxford.
(1975) 'The Scope and Status of Welfare Economics', *Oxford Economic Papers*, 27, pp. 307–26.
(1976) '"Revolutions" in Economics', in *Method and Appraisal in Economics*, ed. S.J. Latsis, Cambridge University Press, Cambridge, pp. 207–18.
(1977) *Economic Perspectives*, Clarendon Press, Oxford.

(1979) *Causality in Economics*, Basil Blackwell, Oxford.
(1983a) 'Preface', in *Classics and Moderns*, vol. III of *Collected Essays on Economic Theory*, Basil Blackwell, Oxford, pp. xiii–xvi.
(1983b) 'A Discipline not a Science', in *Classics and Moderns*, vol. III of *Collected Essays on Economic Theory*, Basil Blackwell, Oxford, pp. 365–75.
(1985) *Methods of Dynamic Economics*, Oxford University Press, Oxford.
(1986) 'Is Economics a Science?', in *Foundations of Economics. Structures of Inquiry and Economic Theory*, ed. M. Baranzini and R. Scazzieri, Basil Blackwell, Oxford and New York, pp. 91–101.
(1988) 'Introductory Remarks', given at the International Economic Association Conference '*Value and Capital* Fifty Years Later', mimeographed, Bologna.
Hildenbrand, W. (1983) 'Introduction', in G. Debreu, *Mathematical Economics. Twenty Papers of G. Debreu*, Cambridge University Press, Cambridge.
Hont, I., and Ignatieff, M. (1983) (eds) *Wealth and Virtue. The Shaping of Political Economy in the Scottish Enlightenment*, Cambridge University Press, Cambridge.
Johansen, L. (1960) *A Multi-Sectoral Study of Economic Growth*, North-Holland Publishing Company, Amsterdam.
Kaldor, N. (1966) *Causes of the Slow Rate of Economic Growth of the United Kingdom. An Inaugural Lecture*, Cambridge University Press, Cambridge.
(1967) *Strategic Factors in Economic Development*, New York State School of Industrial and Labor Relations, Cornell University, Ithaca, N.Y.
Kantorovich, L.V. (1965) *The Best Use of Economic Resources*, Pergamon Press, Oxford (Russian original published in 1959).
Keynes, J.M. (1973a) *The General Theory of Employment, Interest and Money*, Macmillan, London (1st edn 1936).
(1973b) *The Collected Writings of John Maynard Keynes*, ed. A. Robinson and D. Moggridge, Macmillan, London; Cambridge University Press, Cambridge.
Keynes, J.N. (1890) *The Scope and Method of Political Economy*, Macmillan, London.
Kirman, A. (1989) 'The Intrinsic Limits of Modern Economic Theory: The Emperor has no Clothes', *Economic Journal*, 99, pp. 126–39.
Koopmans, T.C. (1951) 'Analysis of Production as an Efficient Combination of Activities', in *Activity Analysis of Production and Allocation*, ed. T.C. Koopmans, Yale University Press, New Haven and London, pp. 33–97.
(1957) *Three Essays on the State of Economic Science*, McGraw-Hill, New York, Toronto and London.
Landesmann, M.A. (1986) 'Conceptions of Technology and the Production Process', in *Foundations of Economics. Structures of Inquiry and Economic Theory*, ed. M. Baranzini and R. Scazzieri, Basil Blackwell, Oxford and New York, pp. 281–310.
Landesmann, M.A., Scazzieri, R., et al. (1990) *Dynamics in Production Systems* (forthcoming).
Leon, P. (1967) *Structural Change and Growth in Capitalism*, Johns Hopkins University Press, Baltimore, Md.

Leontief, W.W. (1928) 'Die Wirtschaft als Kreislauf', *Archiv für Sozialwissenschaft und Sozialpolitik*, 60, pp. 577–623.

(1941) *The Structure of American Economy, 1919–1939. An Empirical Application of Equilibrium Analysis*, Harvard University Press, Cambridge, Mass.

(1947) 'Introduction to a Theory of the Internal Structure of Functional Relationships', *Econometrica*, 15 (October), pp. 361–73.

(1953) (ed.) *Studies in the Structure of the American Economy*, Oxford University Press, Oxford and New York.

(1953) 'Static and Dynamic Theory', Part 1 of *Studies in the Structure of the American Economy*, ed. W.W. Leontief, Oxford University Press, Oxford and New York, pp. 1–90.

(1954) 'Mathematics in Economics', *Bulletin of the American Mathematical Society*, 60 (May), pp. 215–33.

(1959) 'The Problem of Quality and Quantity in Economics', *Daedalus*, 88, pp. 622–32.

(1966) *Essays in Economics. Theories and Theorizing*, Oxford University Press, New York.

(1987) 'Input–Output Analysis', in *The New Palgrave. A Dictionary of Economics*, ed. J. Eatwell, M. Milgate and P. Newman, Macmillan, London and Basingstoke, vol. II, pp. 860–4.

Leroy-Beaulieu, P. (1896) *Traité théorique et pratique d'économie politique*, Guillaumin, Paris.

Lindahl, E. (1939) *Studies in the Theory of Money and Capital*, Allen and Unwin, London.

Lombardini, S., and Nicola, P.C. (1974) 'Income Distribution and Economic Development in Ricardian and Walrasian Models', in *Proceedings of the 11th Polish-Italian Conference on Applications of System Theory to Economy Management and Technology*, Pugnochiuso, Italy, pp. 294–320.

Löwe, A. (1935) *Economics and Sociology. A Plea for Cooperation in the Social Sciences*, Allen & Unwin, London.

(1952) 'A Structural Model of Production', *Social Research*, 19, pp. 135–76.

(1955) 'Structural Analysis of Real Capital Formation', in *Capital Formation and Economic Growth*, ed. M. Abramovitz, Princeton University Press, Princeton, pp. 581–634.

(1965) *On Economic Knowledge. Toward a Science of Political Economics*, Harper and Row, New York (2nd enlarged edition, M.E. Sharpe, White Plains, New York, 1977).

(1976) *The Path of Economic Growth*, Cambridge University Press, Cambridge.

Malthus, T.R. (1951) *Principles of Political Economy* (1st edn 1820), in *The Works and Correspondence of David Ricardo*, ed. P. Sraffa with the collaboration of M.H. Dobb, vol. II, Cambridge University Press, Cambridge.

Marshall, A. (1961) *Principles of Economics*, ed. C.W. Guillebaud, Macmillan, London (1st edn 1890).

Marx, K. (1969) *Theories of Surplus Value*, Lawrence and Wishart, London (German original 1905–10).

(1983) *Capital. A Critique of Political Economy*, vol. I, book 1, Lawrence and Wishart, London (German original 1867).
Meacci, F. (1989) 'Irving Fisher and the Classics on the Notion of Capital: Upheaval and Continuity in Economic Thought', *History of Political Economy*, 21, pp. 409–24.
Meade, J.E. (1966) 'The Outcome of the Pasinetti Process: A Note', *Economic Journal*, 76, pp. 161–5.
Morishima, M. (1964) *Equilibrium, Stability and Growth*, Clarendon Press, Oxford.
(1969) *Theory of Economic Growth*, Clarendon Press, Oxford.
(1973) *Marx's Economics. A Dual Theory of Value and Growth*, Cambridge University Press, Cambridge.
(1984) *The Economics of Industrial Society*, Cambridge University Press, Cambridge.
(1989) *Ricardo's Economics*, Cambridge University Press, Cambridge.
Mukherji, B. (1982) *Theory of Growth and the Tradition of Ricardian Dynamics*, Oxford University Press, Delhi.
Negishi, T. (1985) *Economic Theories in a Non-Walrasian Tradition*, Cambridge University Press, Cambridge.
(1989) *History of Economic Theory*, North-Holland Publishing Company, Amsterdam and New York.
Nell, E.J. (1976) 'An Alternative Presentation of Löwe's Basic Model', appendix to A. Löwe, *The Path of Economic Growth*, Cambridge University Press, Cambridge, pp. 290–325.
Nemchinov, V.S. (1969) *Obščestvennaja stoimost i planovaja tsena* (Social Value and Planning Price), Nauka, Moscow.
Neumann, J. von (1935–7) 'Über ein Ökonomisches Gleichungs-System und eine Verallgemeinerung des Brouwerschen Fixpunktsatzes', in *Ergebnisse eines Mathematischen Kolloquiums*, Vienna, vol. VIII, pp. 73–83.
(1945–6) 'A Model of General Equilibrium', *Review of Economic Studies*, 9, pp. 1–9 (German original 1935–7).
Nurkse, R. (1935) 'The Schematic Representation of the Structure of Production', *Review of Economic Studies*, 2, pp. 232–44.
(1962) *Equilibrium and Growth in the World Economy*, ed. G. Haberler and R.M. Stern, Harvard University Press, Cambridge, Mass.
Pareto, V. (1906) *Manuale di economia politica, con una introduzione alla scienza sociale*, Società Editrice Libraria, Milan.
(1911) *Economie mathématique*, in *Encyclopédie des sciences mathématiques*, book I, vol. IV, Gauthier-Villars, Paris.
Pasinetti, L.L. (1962) 'The Rate of Profit and Income Distribution in Relation to the Rate of Economic Growth', *Review of Economic Studies*, 29, pp. 267–79.
(1964–5) 'Causalità e interdipendenza nell'analisi econometrica e nella teoria economica', *Annuario dell'Università Cattolica del S. Cuore*, Milan, pp. 233–50.
(1965) 'A New Theoretical Approach to the Problems of Economic Growth', in *Econometric Approach to Development Planning*, North-Holland Publishing Company, Amsterdam, pp. 571–696.

(1973) 'The Notion of Vertical Integration in Economic Analysis', *Metroeconomica*, XXV, pp. 1–29; reprinted in *Essays on the Theory of Joint Production*, ed. L.L. Pasinetti, Macmillan, London; Columbia University Press, New York, 1980.
(1974) *Growth and Income Distribution. Essays in Economic Theory*, Cambridge University Press, Cambridge.
(1977) *Lectures on the Theory of Production*, Macmillan, London (Italian original 1975, Il Mulino, Bologna).
(1980) (ed.) *Essays on the Theory of Joint Production*, Macmillan, London (Italian original 1977, Il Mulino, Bologna).
(1981) *Structural Change and Economic Growth. A Theoretical Essay on the Dynamics of the Wealth of Nations*, Cambridge University Press, Cambridge.
(1983) 'The Accumulation of Capital', *Cambridge Journal of Economics*, 7, pp. 405–11.
(1986a) 'Sraffa's Circular Process and the Concept of Vertical Integration', *Political Economy. Studies in the Surplus Approach*, 21, pp. 3–16.
(1986b) 'Theory of Value – A Source of Alternative Paradigms in Economic Analysis', in *Foundations of Economics. Structures of Inquiry and Economic Theory*, ed. M. Baranzini and R. Scazzieri, Basil Blackwell, Oxford and New York, pp. 409–31.
(1988) 'Growing Subsystems, Vertically Hyper-Integrated Sectors and the Labour Theory of Value', *Cambridge Journal of Economics*, 12, pp. 125–34.
Pigou, A.C. (1929a) *Industrial Fluctuations*, Macmillan, London (1st edn 1927).
(1929b) *The Economics of Welfare*, Macmillan, London (1st edn 1920).
(1935) *The Economics of Stationary States*, Macmillan, London.
(1952) *Employment and Equilibrium. A Theoretical Discussion*, Macmillan, London (1st edn 1941).
Quadrio-Curzio, A. (1967) *Rendita e distribuzione in un modello economico plurisettoriale*, Giuffrè, Milan.
(1975) *Accumulazione del capitale e rendita*, Il Mulino, Bologna.
(1980) 'Rent, Income Distribution, Orders of Efficiency and Rentability', in *Essays on the Theory of Joint Production*, ed. L.L. Pasinetti, Macmillan, London, pp. 218–40 (Italian original 1977, Il Mulino, Bologna).
(1986) 'Technological Scarcity: An Essay on Production and Structural Change', in *Foundations of Economics. Structures of Inquiry and Economic Theory*, ed. M. Baranzini and R. Scazzieri, Basil Blackwell, Oxford and New York, pp. 311–38.
Quadrio-Curzio, A., Manara, C.F., and Faliva, M. (1990) 'Production and Efficiency with Global Technologies', in M. Landesmann, R. Scazzieri et al., *Dynamics in Production Systems* (forthcoming).
Quadrio-Curzio, A., and Scazzieri, R. (eds) (1977–82) *Protagonisti del pensiero economico*, vols. 1–4, Il Mulino, Bologna.
Quadrio-Curzio, A., and Scazzieri, R. (1982a) 'La formazione delle "idee cardine": rivoluzione industriale e economia politica', in *Protagonisti del pensiero economico. Rivoluzione industriale e economia politica (1817–1848)*, ed. A. Quadrio-Curzio and R. Scazzieri, Il Mulino, Bologna, pp. 11–42.

(1982b) 'La formazione delle "idee cardine": struttura produttiva, scambio e mercati', in *Protagonisti del pensiero economico. Struttura produttiva, scambio e mercati (1848–1872)*, ed. A. Quadrio-Curzio and R. Scazzieri, Il Mulino, Bologna, pp. 11–48.

(1984) 'Sui momenti costitutivi dell'economia politica', *Giornale degli Economisti e Annali di Economia*, NS, 43, pp. 37–76.

(1986) 'The Exchange–Production Duality and the Dynamics of Economic Knowledge', in *Foundations of Economics. Structures of Inquiry and Economic Theory*, ed. M. Baranzini and R. Scazzieri, Basil Blackwell, Oxford and New York, pp. 377–407.

(1990) 'Profili di dinamica economica strutturale', in *Dinamica economica strutturale*, ed. A. Quadrio-Curzio and R. Scazzieri, Il Mulino, Bologna (forthcoming).

Quesnay, F. (1758) *Tableau économique*, Versailles.

Resta, M. (1954) *Struttura, sviluppo e ciclo*, Cappelli, Trieste-Bologna.

Ricardo, D. (1951) *On the Principles of Political Economy and Taxation* (1st edn 1817; 2nd edn 1819; 3rd edn 1821), vol. I of *The Works and Correspondence of David Ricardo*, ed. P. Sraffa, with the collaboration of M.H. Dobb, Cambridge University Press, Cambridge.

(1951–73) *The Works and Correspondence of David Ricardo*, 11 vols, ed. P. Sraffa with the collaboration of M.H. Dobb, Cambridge University Press, Cambridge.

Robertson, D.H. (1915) *A Study of Industrial Fluctuation*, P.S. King and Son, London. (Reprinted with a new introduction in 'Reprints of Scarce Works on Political Economy', London School of Economics and Political Science, London, 1948.)

(1961) *Growth, Wages, Money*, Cambridge University Press, Cambridge.

Robinson, J. (1956) *The Accumulation of Capital*, Macmillan, London.

(1962) *Essays in the Theory of Economic Growth*, Macmillan, London.

Rosenberg, N. (1963) 'Capital Goods, Technology and Economic Growth', *Oxford Economic Papers*, 15, pp. 217–27.

(1976) *Perspectives on Technology*, Cambridge University Press, Cambridge.

Samuelson, P.A. (1947) *Foundations of Economic Analysis*, Harvard University Press, Cambridge, Mass.

Samuelson, P.A., and Modigliani, F. (1966) 'The Pasinetti Paradox in Neoclassical and More General Models', *Review of Economic Studies*, 33, pp. 269–301; and 'Reply to Pasinetti and Robinson', ibid., pp. 321–30.

Say, J.B. (1817) *Traité d'économie politique*, 3rd edn, Déterville, Paris (1st edn 1803).

Scazzieri, R. (1982) 'Scale and Efficiency in Models of Production', in *Advances in Economic Theory*, ed. M. Baranzini, Basil Blackwell, Oxford, pp. 19–42.

(1983) 'Economic Dynamics and Structural Change: A Comment on Pasinetti', *Rivista Internazionale di Scienze Economiche e Commerciali*, 30, pp. 73–90.

(1987) *Tasks, Processes and Technical Practices: A Contribution to the Theory of the Scale of Production*, Oxford, D.Phil. Thesis.

(1988) 'Economic Theorizing', in *Contributi di Analisi Economica*, ed. M.

Baranzini and A. Cencini, Casagrande, Bellinzona, pp. 149–57.
(1989) 'Classical Traverse Analysis', in *Dynamis*, Istituto di Ricerca sulla Dinamica dei Sistemi Economici, CNR, n. 6. (Forthcoming in *Structural Dynamics of Capitalist Economies*, ed. M. Landesmann and R. Rowthorn, Oxford University Press, Oxford.)
(1990a) 'Funds, Processes and the Structure of the Productive System', in *Beyond the Austrian School*, ed. P. O'Sullivan, Macmillan, London (forthcoming).
(1990b) 'Vertical Integration in Economic Theory', *Journal of Post Keynesian Economics* (forthcoming).
Schumpeter, J.A. (1954) *History of Economic Analysis*, ed. from manuscript by E. Boody Schumpeter, Allen and Unwin, London.
(1974) *The Theory of Economic Development*, Oxford University Press, Oxford and New York (German original 1912).
(1976) *Capitalism, Socialism and Democracy*, Allen & Unwin, London (1st edn 1942).
Smith, A. (1976) *An Inquiry into the Nature and Causes of the Wealth of Nations*, ed. R.H. Campbell, A.S. Skinner and W.B. Todd, Clarendon Press, Oxford (1st edn 1776).
Sraffa, P. (1960) *Production of Commodities by Means of Commodities*, Cambridge University Press, Cambridge.
Stinchcombe, A.L. (1959) 'Bureaucratic and Craft Administration of Production', *Administrative Science Quarterly*, 4, pp. 168–87.
(1983) *Economic Sociology*, Academic Press, New York and London.
Stone, R. (1961) *Input–Output and National Accounts*, Organization for Economic Cooperation and Development, Paris.
(1970) *Mathematical Models of the Economy and other Essays*, Chapman and Hall Ltd., London.
Stone, R., and Stone, G. (1977) *National Income and Expenditure*, Bowes & Bowes, London (1st edn 1971).
Sylos-Labini, P. (1984) *The Forces of Economic Growth and Decline*, MIT Press, Cambridge, Mass.
Thom, R. (1974) *Modèles mathématiques de la morphogénèse*, Union Générale d'Editions, Paris.
Tugan-Baranovsky, M.I. (1894) *Promyshlennye krizisi v sovremennoi Anglii* (Industrial Crises in England), I.N. Skorochodova, St Petersburg.
Usher, A. (1954) *A History of Mechanical Inventions*, Harvard University Press, Cambridge, Mass.
Veblen, T. (1953) *The Theory of the Leisure Class*, Viking, New York (1st edn 1899).
Vinci, F. (1945) *Gli ordinamenti economici*, Giuffrè, Milan.
Wakefield, E.G. (1835–43) *'Commentary' to An Inquiry into the Nature and Causes of the Wealth of Nations, by Adam Smith, LL.D., with a commentary by the author of 'England and America'*, Charles Knight, London.
Walras, L. (1874–77) *Eléments d'économie politique pure*, Corbaz, Lausanne.
Williamson, O. (1985) *The Economic Institutions of Capitalism. Firms, Markets, Relations, Contracting*, The Free Press, New York and London.

Woodward, J. (1980) *Industrial Organization. Theory and Practice*, Oxford University Press, New York.

Zamagni, S. (1984) 'On Ricardo and Hayek Effects in a Fixwage Model of Traverse', *Oxford Economic Papers*, 36 (November supplement), pp. 135–51.

(1987) 'Georgescu-Roegen, Nicholas', in *The New Palgrave. A Dictionary of Economics*, ed. J. Eatwell, M. Milgate and P. Newman, Macmillan, London, vol. II, pp. 515–16.

Ziber, N.I. (1871) 'Teoriia Tsennosti i Kapitala D. Ricardo' (David Ricardo's Theory of Value and Capital), *Universitetskiia Izviestiia* (Kiev), nos. 1–2 and 4–11.

Name index

Abraham-Frois, G., 140
Abramovitz, M., 170, 328
Abruzzi, A., 262, 324
Åckerman, G., 133
Åkerman, J., 280, 324
Allais, M., 6, 19, 105n, 119, 133, 140, 230, 238–40, 324
Amendola, M., 164–6, 168, 324
Anderson, P.W., 102, 119
Arensberg, C.M., 43
Aristotle, 2, 201n
Arrow, K.J., 119, 140
Ayres, C., 39n

Bacchi, M.C., xiii
Bacharach, M.O.L., 324
Baldone, S., 115, 119, 166, 168, 325
Baranzini, M., v, vii, ix, xi–xii, 1, 6, 17, 19–20, 39n, 41, 43, 73, 91, 119, 121–2, 225, 227, 324–7, 330–2
Barbeyrac, J., 26n, 42
Bartolus, 2
Beber, M., 23n
Beccaria, C., 32
Becher, J.J., 30, 41
Belloc, B., 115, 119, 140
Bentham, J., 316
Bergson, H., 199
Berrebi, E., 140
Betancourt, R.R., 224
Bhaduri, A., 140
Bidard, C., 142
Blaug, M., 140
Bliss, C.J., 325
Blitz, R.C., 225
Böhm-Bawerk, E. von, 40n, 41, 69–70, 72, 91, 119, 122, 126, 132–6, 140–1, 149–50, 168, 242, 325
Boody Schumpeter, E., 92, 332
Bortis, H., vi, ix, 9–10, 64, 77, 80, 91
Bortkiewicz, L. von, 230
Boulton, M., 278
Bousquet, G.H., 140
Brennan, G., 27n, 41
Brentano, L., 170
Brody, A., 120
Brunner, O., 30, 41
Buchanan, J.M., 27n, 41
Bücher, C., 32
Burchardt, F.A., 69–70, 72, 91, 112, 119, 148, 148n, 149, 149n, 150, 150n, 151, 151n, 167n, 168
Burmeister, E., 140

Campbell, R.H., 332
Carter, A.P., 120
Cassel, G., 23n, 119
Cauchy, A.-L., 203
Cecil, A., 287
Cencini, A., 20, 332
Chakravarty, S., 109, 119, 168, 248, 325
Chipman, J.S., 203n, 224
Chng, M.K., 167n, 168
Clague, C.K., 224
Clark, D., 148n, 168
Clark, J.B., 106, 119, 135, 140, 150n, 169
Clower, R.W., 210n, 224
Coase, R.H., 37, 41
Cobb, C.W., 134, 206, 206n, 207, 217
Cole, W.A., 193n, 196, 276, 325

Collard, D.A., 171
Colm, G., 148n
Commons, J.R., 39n
Cort, H., 278
Cournot, A., 62
Craver, E., 148n, 169

Dahmén, E., 280, 325
Darby, A., 277
Dasgupta, A.K., 176–7, 196
Davenant, C., 1, 3
Deane, P., 193n, 194n, 196, 276–8, 325
Debreu, G., 19, 119, 230, 238–9, 325
De Luca, G.B., 31, 41
Diehl, K., 170
Dirichlet, P.G.L., 202, 205, 207
Dobb, M., 142, 167, 167n, 168–9, 171, 328, 331
Domar, E.D., 151–2, 158, 167n, 169
Dore, M., 109, 119
Dorfman, R., 71, 91, 133, 140, 146n, 169
Dotsey, M., 35, 41
Douglas, P.H., 135, 206, 206n, 207, 217
Duchin, F., 112–13, 119
Dupuit, A.J.E.J., 240
Dutailly, J.C., 127, 142

Eatwell, J., 41, 44, 167n, 171, 328, 333
Edgeworth, F.Y., vi, viii, 9, 47–8, 57–60, 62, 202
Edison, T., 224
Effertz, O., 134
Eltis, W., 109, 119
Ely, R.T., 225
Engel, E., 4, 60, 76, 86, 167, 270, 303, 325
Engels, F., 25n, 42, 219n
Etzioni, A., 108, 118–19

Faliva, M., 330
Farrell, M.J., 60, 62
Feinstein, C.H., 142
Fel'dman, G.A., 167, 167n, 168–9
Ferrara, F., 32, 41
Filangieri, G., 32
Fisher, F., 100, 119
Fisher, I., 147n, 209, 209n, 224, 329
Foxley, A., 43
Freeman, C., 35, 41
Freyer, H., 24n, 41
Friedman, M., 37n, 41
Frisch, R., 112, 119, 148n, 205, 215, 224

Gaffard, J.L., 165, 168, 325
Galilei, G., 215
Garegnani, P., 53n, 62, 140
Garvy, G., 148n, 169
Gehrke, C., 144
Genovesi, A., 32
Georgescu-Roegen, N., vii, ix, 15–16, 107, 119, 198, 198n, 201n, 204n, 206n, 207n, 210n, 211n, 212n, 215n, 219n, 220n, 224–5, 243–5, 252–5, 259, 261, 325, 333
Ghose, A.K., 266, 326
Gifford, C., 140
Gioja, M., 255, 326
Goldschmidt, R., 223, 223n, 225
Goodwin, R., 109, 113, 119, 326
Gossen, H.H., 77, 211n, 225
Gould, S.J., 223n, 225
Gram, H., 72, 92
Grandmont, J.M., 103, 119
Graunt, J., 3
Groenewegen, P., 30, 41
Guillebaud, C.W., 37n, 41, 63, 120, 328
Guyenne, T.D., 225

Haberler, G., 317, 326, 329
Hagemann, H., vi, ix , 12–13, 144, 154n, 155n, 157n, 160n, 169–70
Hague, D., 142
Hahn, F.H., 100, 119, 176, 196
Haldane, J.B.S., 199n, 225
Harcourt, G.C., 140
Harris, D.J., 153, 169
Harrod, R.F., 105–6, 106n, 107, 119, 151–2, 152n, 158, 160, 178, 178n, 191, 196, 326
Hawkins, D., 125, 232
Hawtrey, R.G., 147n
Hayek, F.A., 26n, 41, 133, 135–7, 140–1, 143, 147, 148n, 171, 242, 296, 316, 326, 333
Heilbroner, R.L., 163n, 169
Heiner, R.H., 27n, 41
Helmstädter, E., 151n, 169
Henderson, A.M., 44
Hicks, J., ix, 8, 11–12, 19, 23n, 41, 47, 49, 51, 53–4, 62, 96, 103, 103n, 104, 106, 106n, 107, 113–15, 120, 122, 126, 128,

Hicks, J., (*cont.*)
130, 133, 136–9, 141, 144, 144n, 152–3, 160, 160n, 165, 166n, 169, 209, 210n, 225, 230, 234–5, 238, 241–3, 249, 254–6, 272, 274, 279, 282, 286, 291–7, 300–1, 313, 315–16, 320–1, 323, 326
Hilbert, D., 326
Hildenbrand, W., 6, 19, 327
Hintze, O., 32, 41
Hirschman, A.O., 37n, 42–3
Hirschleifer, J., 141
Hohberg, W.H. von, 29n, 42
Honegger, H., 40n, 42
Hont, I., 327
Houthakker, H, 203n, 225
Huncke, G., 140

Ignatieff, M., 327
Intriligator, M., 119
Islam, S., 206n

Jaffé, W., 63, 197, 298
Jeck, A., 155n, 157n, 169
Jevons, W.S., 9, 47, 58, 77, 122, 126, 132–3, 141, 201, 218
Johansen, L., 112, 120, 217, 327

Kähler, A., 148n, 151, 170
Kahn, R.F., 88, 103
Kaldor, N., 74, 135, 141, 269, 327
Kalecki, M., 5, 44, 158, 170
Kalmbach, P., 169–70
Kantorovich, L.V., 3, 20, 327
Keynes, J.M., vii, 1–2, 4–5, 14, 20, 23n, 76, 83, 86–8, 91, 146, 147n, 148n, 163, 169, 178, 178n, 188, 190–1, 196, 288–93, 297, 299, 327
Keynes, J.N., 327
King, G., 3, 310
King, J.E., 30, 42
King, R.G., 35, 41
Kirman, A., 6, 20, 327
Klimek, C., 122
Kline, M., 202n, 203n, 225
Klundert, T. van de, 141
Knight, F.H., 28n, 42, 134–5, 141, 218
Koopmans, T.C., 224, 327
Kregel, J.A., 326
Kuczynski, M., 121, 171
Kurz, H.D., 144, 154n, 160, 169–70
Kuznets, S., 146, 146n, 170

Laing, N.F., 140
Lalor, J.J., 43
Lamare, N. de, 31n, 42
Landesmann, M.A., vi, ix, 11, 95, 119, 262, 268, 325, 327, 330, 332
Landry, A., 134
Latsis, S.J., 326
Leon, P., 270, 327
Leontief, W.W., 1, 3, 16, 20, 65–7, 76, 88, 112, 120, 148n, 151n, 152, 170, 210, 218–19, 219n, 220–1, 221n, 225, 230–3, 235, 267–8, 304, 306–9, 328
Lerner, A.P., 37
Leroy-Beaulieu, P., 256, 328
Levhari, D., 140
Levy, G., 225
Lindahl, E., 103–4, 106, 113, 120, 238, 328
Lipschitz, R., 203
Lombardini, S., 328
Lorenz, H.-W., 102, 120
Los, J., 109, 120
Los, M.W., 109, 120
Löwe, A., vi, 13, 24n, 38, 42, 112, 120, 141, 144–6, 146n, 147, 147n, 148, 148n, 149–50, 150n, 151–2, 152n, 153, 153n, 155–7, 157n, 158, 158n, 159–60, 160n, 161–3, 163n, 164, 165–7, 167n, 168–71, 230, 235–6, 245–8, 250, 263, 312–15, 317, 319–20, 328–9
Lundberg, E., 141
Lutz, F., 141–2
Lutz, V., 141
Luxemburg, R., 109, 120, 224, 226

Machiavelli, N, 29n
Mackenroth, G., 142
McPherson, M.S., 43
Magnan de Bornier, J., vi, ix, 12, 114, 120, 122, 126, 137–8, 142
Mahalanobis, P.C., 224
Maier, C.S., 43
Maine, H.J.S., 27n, 44
Malinvaud, E., 163n, 166n, 170
Malthus, T.R., 106, 120, 286–7, 297, 299, 328
Manara, C.F., 330
Marris, R., 211n, 226
Marschak, J., 133, 142, 148n
Marshall, A., 1–2, 9, 11, 47–8, 53–6, 56n, 57–8, 62, 101, 103–5, 105n, 106–7, 120, 222, 226, 271, 325, 328

Marx, K., 2, 5, 13, 25n, 42, 56n, 63–5, 67–9, 74, 76, 78, 81, 88, 91, 109, 110n, 119–120, 132, 146, 148–9, 150n, 151n, 152, 157n, 168–70, 200, 209, 218, 221, 224, 325, 328–9
Mathur, G., 167, 170
Matteucci, N., 35n, 36, 42
Matzner, E., 326
Meacci, F., 235n, 329
Meade, J.E., 5, 20, 37, 53, 329
Meek, R.L., 121, 171
Meinecke, F., 29n, 42
Menger, C., 77–8, 132, 141–2, 218
Merhav, M., 168, 170
Mettelsiefen, B., 151, 170
Metzler, L.A., 113, 120
Miglio, G., 27, 29n, 42
Milgate, M., 41, 44, 328, 333
Mill, J.S., 2
Mirrlees, J., 143
Mises, L. von, 34n, 42, 147
Mitchell, B.R., 193n, 194n, 196
Mitchell, W., 44
Mixter, C.W., 34n, 43
Modigliani, F., 5, 20, 331
Moggridge, D., 327
Montfort, J., 127, 142
Morgenstern, O, 35, 40n, 42, 148n
Morishima, M., vii, ix, 14–15, 50n, 51, 52n, 63, 109, 120, 175, 192n, 193, 195–6, 250–2, 301 2, 329
Mukherji, B., 329
Myrdal, G., 103, 103n, 120

Negishi, T., v, ix, 8–9, 47, 49n, 56n, 57n, 63, 257, 269–70, 329
Neisser, H., 148n
Nell, E.J., 329
Nemchinov, V.S., 317–18, 329
Neumann, J. von, 109–10, 110n, 119 20, 124, 154n, 166, 180, 210, 224, 230–1, 301–4, 329
Newman, P., 41, 44, 328, 333
Nicholls, W.H., 219n, 226
Nicola, P.C., 328
Niphus, A., 2
Nunn, C., 225, 325
Nurkse, R., 150, 150n, 167n, 171, 316–17, 320, 323, 329
Nuti, D.M., 142

Oakeshott, M., 26n, 34n, 42
Oakley, A., 144, 170–1
O'Donnell, G, 43
Oestreich, G., 26n, 42
Ohlin, B.G., 148n
Olson, M., 35, 42
Oncken, A., 66, 91
Oppenheimer, F., 40n, 42
Orestano, R., 26n, 42
Ornaghi, L., v, ix, 7, 23, 29n, 40n, 42
Ortes, G., 32
O'Sullivan, P., 332

Page, A.N., 43
Palmström, A., 147
Pantaleoni, M., 23n, 40n, 43
Papi, U., 225, 325
Pareto, V., 23n, 43, 202–4, 218, 225, 230, 238–40, 329
Parsons, T., 44
Pascal, B., 200–1
Pasinetti, L.L., 4, 20, 39, 43, 65–6, 73–6, 83–4, 88–9, 91, 115–17, 120, 129, 142, 157, 166–7, 171, 230, 235, 238, 241 3, 248–50, 263, 267–8, 270, 281, 286, 297–300, 303–4, 319–20, 329, 331
Patinkin, D., 206, 206n
Pearson, H.W., 43
Perrot, J.-C., 30, 43
Perroux, F., 26, 35n, 43
Petty, W., 1, 3, 29, 310
Phelps Brown, E.H., 44
Pigou, A.C., 117, 121, 229, 271, 287–93, 297, 299–300, 313, 330
Pines, D., 119
Pizzorno, A., 36, 43
Plato, 198
Polanyi, K., 31n, 33, 43
Porta, P.L., 29, 43
Pufendorf, S. von, 26n

Quadrio-Curzio, A., 28, 34, 34n, 43, 111, 117, 121, 230, 235, 237, 270–1, 274, 281–2, 304–5, 330–1
Quesnay, F., 1, 4, 13, 65–7, 76, 109, 121, 146, 148, 171, 268, 331

Rader, J.T., 200n
Radner, R., 103, 121
Rae, J., 34n, 43, 133
Rainelli, M., 127, 142

Rao, C.R., 224
Reichardt, R., 43
Resta, M., 331
Ricardo, D., vii, 2, 14, 74, 78, 107, 111, 122, 132, 142, 157n, 160, 160n, 170–1, 178, 178n, 179–80, 183–4, 192–4, 196, 209, 240, 270, 294, 328–9, 331, 333
Robertson, D.H., 103, 331
Robinson, A., 327
Robinson, J.V., 20, 74, 142, 145, 167n, 171, 207, 207n, 216n, 226, 331
Roll, E., 79, 92
Roncaglia, A., 326
Roosevelt, F.D., 148n
Roscher, W., 38, 39n, 43
Rosenberg, N., 107n, 121, 256, 331
Rowthorn, R., 332
Russell, B., 200

Salvati, M., 35, 44
Samuels, W.J., 39, 44
Samuelson, P.A., 5, 20, 71, 91, 142, 146n, 157n, 169, 203, 203n, 204, 206, 206n, 207, 207n, 226, 331
Sartori, G., 35, 44
Say, J.B., 14–15, 147, 175, 182–4, 186–8, 193–6, 331
Scazzieri, R., v–vii, ix, xi–xii, 1–2, 6, 11, 17, 19–20, 28, 34, 34n, 39n, 41, 43, 73, 91, 95, 119, 121–2, 171, 225–7, 252, 256, 261–2, 268, 271, 274, 324–7, 330–1
Schaik, A., van, 141–2
Schiera, P., 30n, 44
Schmitt, E., 43
Schmoller, G., von, 32
Schulze, R., 31, 44
Schumpeter, J.A., 23n, 77–8, 82, 92, 142, 199, 201, 218, 222–3, 226, 235, 237, 325–6, 332
Schwier, A.S., 43
Schwödiauer, G., 225
Scitovsky, T., 61n
Sears, P.B., 202n
Sella, E., 24, 44
Sen, A, 142
Sennholz, H., 140
Simon, H., 125, 232
Skinner, A.S., 332
Small, A.W., 30n, 44
Smith, A., 1–2, 30, 65–7, 76, 78, 88, 91, 107, 117, 212, 241, 257, 269–70, 283–6, 294–7, 299, 332
Smith, V.L., 210n, 226
Solow, R.M., 53, 71, 91, 142, 146n, 169, 178, 178n, 192, 196, 216n, 217, 217n, 219n, 226
Sombart, W., 32, 44
Sordi, B., 33n, 44
Spaventa, L., 143, 153, 171
Spencer, H., 215
Spiethoff, A., 148n
Spulber, N., 169
Sraffa, P., 4, 20, 65–7, 71–2, 76, 88, 92, 115, 121, 124–5, 129, 143, 146n, 150–2, 154n, 157, 160, 166, 171, 196, 230–1, 233–5, 240, 270, 301, 328, 330–2
Stern, N.H., 143
Stern, R.M., 329
Steuart, J., 30, 30n, 4
Stigler, G., 135–6, 143
Stiglitz, J.E., 216n, 217
Stinchcombe, A.L., 259–61, 332
Stone, G., 310–12, 332
Stone, R., 1, 3, 310–12, 392
Stucken, R., 147
Swan, T.W., 53
Sylos-Labini, P., 252, 332
Szyld, D.B., 112–13, 119

Tani, P., 226
Thom, R., 278, 332
Thomas Aquinas, St, 2
Thomas, W.L., 202n, 226
Tinbergen, J., 37, 148n
Todd, W.B., 332
Tönnies, F., 24n, 44
Torrens, R., 124
Treitschke, H. von, 36n, 44
Truman, H.S., 148n
Tugan-Baranovsky, M.I., 109, 121, 288, 332

Usher, A., 332
Uzawa, H., 53, 178, 178n, 197

Veblen, T., 39n, 79, 243, 332
Verri, P., 32
Vinci, F., 332
Volterra, V., 203–4

Wagemann, E., 148n
Wakefield, E.G., 255, 332
Walras, L., vii, 9, 47–9, 51–4, 57–8, 62–3, 73, 77–8, 92, 178, 178n, 183–4, 197, 218, 230, 238–40, 297–8, 304, 332
Walsh, V., 72, 92
Watt, J., 278
Weber, M., 25, 25n, 44
Weber, W., 32, 44, 141
Weiss, F.X., 41
Weizsäcker, C. von, 130–1, 143
Wharton, G.R., jr. 325
Whitehead, A.N., 200, 226, 245
Wicksell, K., 11, 52, 63, 103, 103n, 133, 141, 143, 147n
Wicksteed, P.H., 205, 226
Wieser, F., 33, 40n, 44
Williamson, O., 332
Winston, G.C., 226
Wolin, S., 32, 44
Woodward, J., 259, 333
Wyler, J., 153n, 171

Xenophon, 2

Yasui, T., 52–3, 53n, 63

Zadeh, L.A., 201n
Zamagni, S., 166n, 171, 333
Ziber, N.I., 333
Zincke, G.H., 30n, 44
Zwiedineck-Südenhorst, O., 40n, 44

Subject index

accounting frameworks, and structural analysis, 310–12
actions
  individual and social, 78–83
  and institutions, 78–83
adjustment paths, and normative (institutional) requirements, 247–8
aggregation, and structural change analysis, 314–15
agriculture, 178–84, 193–6
anatomy
  of the economic system, 319–24
  see also physiology, of the economic system
arbitrariness of description, 95–8
arithmomorphism, *see* dialectics
auctioneer, 60
Austrian (neo-) model
  structure of production, 144, 149–50, 165–6
  see also vertical model
Austrian theory of capital, 122, 126, 132–6, 137
average period of production, 132–3

basic(s), industry or sector, 153, 155, 159, 164, 167–8
biological analogy, 54, 57
bottle-necks, 107n, 292, 321
business-cycle theory, 147, 148n

Cameralistic science, 30n
capital, 124
  accumulation, 19, 263
  accumulation society, 18–19
  goods, 256
  time structure of, 126–8, 132–6
  theory, 242
capitalism, 176–7
capitalists, 181
causality
  contemporaneous, 104
  sequential, 102–4, 242
  vertical and horizontal, 10, 83–9
change, 64–5, 83–9
  and structure, 5–7
characterizing assumptions, as distinguished from simplifying assumptions, 15–16, 18, 250–2
chicken factory, vs. chicken farm, 212
choice, possibilities of, 64, 89–90
circular flow, 240
  and economic structure, 228–30, 230–7
  and the stationary state, 109–11
classical
  economic theory, 2–3, 178–84, 184–90, 193–6
  economics, 176, 178–84
closed, or open, model, 125, 127
combined techniques, as an analytical representation of production technology, 237, 304–6
commercial society
  defined, 254
  dynamic features of, 254–5, 255–6
commodities
  produced by processes, 222
  production vs. consumption, 221
communication structure, 47, 57–60, 60–2
  in duopoly, 60–2
  of Edgeworth's theory, 57–60

concepts, 200
  Hegelian, 201n
  structural, alternative uses of, 1
congruence, between economy and economics, 175–8
constitutional political economy, 27n
consumption
  good industry, 180
  good curve, 155, 158
  'necessary' and 'unproductive', 284–6
consumption linkages
  and contemporaneous causality, 291
  and dynamic analysis, 289–91
continuation, theory of, 292–7
  in relation with the 'backward-looking' and 'forward-looking' views of vertical integration, 295–6
  and time profile of input utilization, 294–5
  and time profile of production processes, 292–7
  and transformation stages of the material in process, 293–4
contract, vs. status, 27n
cooperation, 65
cumulative processes, 11, 112
cycle
  political-economic, 35–6
  see also business cycle

Dasgupta's interpretation of economic history, 176–8
'decomposition', of Marshall's economic dynamics, 106
deductive-behavioural approach, in economic investigation, 100
demand–supply condition, 181, 186–9, 190 2
descriptive–analytical approach, to structural change analysis, 11, 98–101, 118
determinism, 64, 89–91
development block, 280
development vs. accretion, 218
dialectics
  vs. arithmomorphism 200–1
  and evolution, 222, 223n
  and production process, 207
  and production theory, 216
disjointed techniques, as an analytical representation of production technology, 237, 305–7
distribution
  classical view of, 74–6
  neoclassical view of, 77–8, 78–80
division of labour, 65
  and extent of the market in modern industrial society, 256–7
duality, 158
duopoly, 59–62
dynamics, in Ricardo and Keynes, 195–6
dynamic economics, 217–21, 300–9, 315–19
  and Kinematics, 218
  and Leontief system, 218–9
  and Newtonian mechanics, 218
dynamic processes, of and within the economic structure, 33–4
dynamic structure
  defined, 97
  and the analysis of productive interrelationships, 108–18
  and hierarchically related sub-systems, 104–5
  and the interrelationship of dynamic forces, 105–8
  and methods of dynamic analysis, 101–2
  and sequential causation, 102–4
  and time differentiation, 101–2
dynamic theory, 309

economic action
  as creative action, 24, 36–8, 40
  in Max Weber's definition, 25, 25n
  temporal horizon of, 36–8
economic cycles, 272
economic dynamics, epistemology of, 16, 217–21
economic fabric, of society, 1–2, 230
economic history, 175 8, 193–6
economic order, 31
economic policy, theory of, 36–8
economic society, types of, 1–3
economic structure, 17–19, 25, 25n, 33
  and institutional framework, 3–5
  in Marxist terminology, 24–5, 25n
  see also structural specification
economic system, 25
  a realistic theory of, 24n
economic theory
  Dasgupta interpretation, 176–8
  and structure and change, 5–7

economics
  from 'economics' to political economy, 29
  as a part of politics, 38–9
  philosophy of, 24n
  and psychology, 23n
economy of time
  in consumption, 211n
  in production, 211–12, 219n
  see also factory process
Edgeworth's
  box diagram, 59
  equivalence theorem, 57–60
elementary production process
  in Austrian theory, 242
  in Georgescu-Roegen's flow–fund approach, 16
  in neo-Austrian theory, 242–3
  separable, 242–3
empiricism, theoretical, 18
endogenous structural change, 270
Engel's law, and structural change analysis, 270
epistemology, 16, 205
  of dynamic economics, 217–24
epochs, in economic theory, 193–6
equilibrium
  dynamic, 144–5, 147, 152–8
  flow, 145, 152n, 155n
  partial, 48, 53–4
  stock, 145, 152n, 155n
evolution, 222–3
exchange, 82
exosomatic organs, 198–9
  and the economic process, 198–9
  evolution of, 198
expectations, 145, 163–4

'fabric' of economic society, 1–2
'factor augmenting' bias, 275
factory process, 212–15
fertility, of land, 270
filière, 127
final commodities, 269
fixed capital goods, 144–5, 149–51, 152–3, 159–60, 165–6
fixwage path, 138, 139
flow, 209
  internal, 219
  maintenance, 209, 210
  of services, 211
flow–fund model, 16, 207–17, 219n
force analysis, 163–4, 167–8
  its relation with structural analysis, 14
forms of production organization, taxonomies of, 259–61
framework, institutional, 3–5
free goods, rule of, 184
full-capacity utilization condition, for natural economic dynamics, 249–50
full-employment
  condition, for natural economic dynamics, 249–50
  equilibrium, 187–8
  path, 138–9
function
  in dialectic sense, 202n
  Dirichlet, 202, 204, 205
functional
  degenerate, 213
  relationships, internal structure of, 307
  space, 208
fund, 209
  agents, 210
  vs. stock, 209–10
fuzzy sets, 201n

general economic equilibrium, 49, 52, 58
  and the analytical representation of the economic system, 300–3
  and the circular flow, 301–3
  and communication structure, 9
  of credit and capital formation, 50–3
  of exchange, 49
  of production, 48–9
  and time structure, 8–9
growth, 220–1, 222
  and differential systems, 221–2
  and division of labour, 212
  and increased demand, 224
  and Leontief system, 218–20
  and waiting, 222

Harrodian dynamics, and the interrelationship of motive forces, 105–8
historical conditions, of capital accumulation, 149

'hopeful monsters', 223
horizontal integration of economic activities, 9–10, 17
  and dynamic theory, 9–10, 300–3, 321–4
  and time structure of production, 111–13
  see also vertical integration of economic activities
horizontal model of production, 123–5

idleness of funds, 211–12
impulses, 274–5
  and the circular concept of economic structure, 281
  and economic dynamics, 271–3, 279–80
  and relative structural invariance, 313–14
  and the vertical concept of economic structure, 279–81, 289
increasing returns, 55–6, 57
indifference postulate, 202, 202n
industrial evolution and economic theory, 175–96
innovation(s), 160–7, 222–4
  capital-displacing, 161, 162, 166
  irreversible, 223
  labour-displacing, 161–2, 164–5
  process, 161, 166
  product, 161–2
input–output analysis/method/model, 151–2, 167–8, 306–9
institution
  vs. action, 38, 39
  definition of, 26, 26n
  as goal-oriented procedure, 27, 33
  and structure, 35
  see also political institutions
institutional arrangements
  and economic change, 244–5
  and the horizontal concept of structure, 319–20
  and the objective
    set of economic relationships, 3–7, 17, 19
    stock–flow network, 243–4
  and relative structural invariance, 118
institutional
  economics, 38–9
  features, taxonomy of, 262–4
  framework, 3–5
  'middle principles', 245–8
  rules, and equilibrium, 27n
  set-up, 3–5
institutions, 3–5, 78–83
  and repetitive actions, 10
instrumental analysis, 163
  in economic investigation, 246–7
  see also structural analysis
integrability, 203, 203n
integration, of economic activities, 228–43
inter-industry approach/model, 144, 146n, 148–9, 153, 164–7, 315–19
interdependence, 306–9
  empirical (Leontief), 309
  theoretical, 309
  see also economic structure
interest, political, 29n
intermediate
  commodities, 242–3
  production functions (according to Leontief), 242–3, 306–9
  products, 242–3, 307
  see also working capital
interpersonal relationships
  their analytical map, 252–3
  and economic structure, 1–2
intertemporal, complementarities or rigidities, 122, 131–2
invention, 223–4
investment function, in Keynes, 164

Keynesian economics, 5, 176–7, 190–3, 195, 288–92, 321
  equilibrium conditions, 190–1
  and the role of entrepreneurial class, 5
Keynesian model, with undercapacity and underemployment, 191–2
Kiel School, 146–51

labour
  division of, 284–5
  and national wealth, 284–7
  productive and unproductive, 284–7
  services, 209
  supply and demand, 188–90
laissez-faire, 31n
landlords, 178
large economy, 60

Leontief system
dynamic, 219n
static, 210
life-cycle theory of firms, 57
limitational process, 215
linear production model, 144, 145, 149–51
local models, 228, 250–2

machine–labour ratio(s), 144, 155–7, 164–5, 164n
machine tool(s), 144, 150–1, 153, 160n, 165–6, 167–8
machinery problem, 151, 161
maintenance, *see* flow
market
-day model, 48, 53
extent of, 285
markets
economy of, distinguished from the market economy in Allais, 105n
and the formation of surpluses, 238–40
Marshallian stationary state, 57
material basis (of an economic system)
alternative descriptions of, 320–4
see also institutional set-up
matrix, of institutional features, 262–4
maximum expansion path, and proportional economic dynamics (von Neumann)
and inter-sectoral division of labour (Smith, Negishi), 257, 285
and structural change (Quadrio-Curzio), 304–5
measurability, 207
methods of economic dynamics, 279–82
model, as a theoretical construction, 279
modern industrial society
defined, 255
dynamic features of, 255–6
see also capital accumulation society
money, 208
morphogenesis, and structural change, 17, 264–7
morphology of economic systems, 258–62
and economic dynamics, 262–4
multi-process matrix, 219n

natural economic dynamics, 248–50
natural order of investment, and capital accumulation in Smith, 257
natural resources, 209, 211, 216–17, 217n
necessary consumption, 284–7
neo-Austrian model, *see* Austrian model
neoclassical economics, 176
net product, 281–2
see also surplus
Neumann (von)
equilibrium condition, 180
model, 210
non-price competition, 47, 62
non-produced resources
and horizontally integrated models, 230–7
and structural change, 269–70
and vertically integrated models, 238–43
numéraire, 181

objective set of relationships, and economic structure, 3
oligopoly, 62
order
civil, 29
economic, 2, 31, 35, 40
good, of a community, 30–1
natural, 29
political, 25, 29, 35, 40
of the state, 31–2, 40
organization theory, and the principle of relative structural invariance, 118
output, and employment determination, 77

partial equilibrium, 48, 53–4
peasant community
defined, 254
dynamic features of, 255
period of production, 152n
persistence, 11
as a characteristic feature, 267–8
in relation to change, 269–70
of structural relationships, 269–70
see also relative structural invariance
physiology, of the economic system, 18–19, 319–24
see also anatomy of the economic system
planned traverse, 139
plans, in economics,
their execution, 104
their formation, 104
and the temporary equilibrium approach to economic dynamics, 102–4

political economy
its 'interfering concepts', 24
its 'terminal problems', 24, 40
political élite, 35n
political institutions, 26–9
as a 'limit' imposed upon the economic structure, 36–8
the surplus value of, 24
see also institution
political power, 29–31, 38–40
politics
and economics, 28
and '*Policey*', 30
power, organization of, 29–31
price
equations, 156–7
system, in Ricardo, 178–84
prices
in horizontally integrated models, 300 9
in vertically integrated models, 283–4
probability, concept of, 201, 201n
process, 200
and analytical boundary, 207
concept of, 16
and dialectics, 207, 209
processes, elementary and separable, 242–3
producibility
creative, 34
vs. scarcity, 34
production, 73–7, 77–8
Austrian view of, 69–70
as a circular and social process, 65–9, 69–73
coefficients, 179
life activity, 198–200
linear and individualistic view, 65–6, 69–73
period of (Böhm-Bawerk), 69–70, 152n
process, 125–8, 129–30, 131
Walrasian view of, 73
production and exchange, 18–19
different treatment of, in 'circular' and 'vertical' theories, 9–10
and economic structure, 17–18
production function
Cobb-Douglas, 206–7
and entropy law, 206n
of factory, 213–15
Johansen, 216 17
of stock flow, 210n
and technological progress, 217
Wicksteedian, 205–7
production linkages
and dynamic analysis, 288–90
and sequential causality, 291
production process(es), 201–4, 208–9
and dialectics, 207, 216
elementary, 211
and flow and fund, 209
horizontal integration of, 111–13
interrelationship among, 108–9
in line, 212
in parallel, 211
reproducible, 209
in series, 211
vertical integration of, 69–73, 228–30, 238–43, 284–330
productive
allocation, 229–30
consumption, 229–30
profit-maximizing behaviour, 124
profitability rule, 180
property rights, 37
proportions among sectors, 75–7

qualitative transformation
and economic dynamics, 169
and quantitative changes, 244–5
qualitative variety, and quantitative determinacy, 306–7
quantitative determinacy, and qualitative variety, 306–7
quantity equations, 154–5

rational expectations, 28n
relative structural invariance, and structural change analysis, 95–7, 118, 314–15
repercussions, *see* impulses
representative firm, 55, 57
reproduction model, 232–3, 236
residuals, in economic dynamics, 281–2
revealed preference, 202, 203n, 204, 204n
Ricardian
economics, 178–84, 184–90, 193–6
land effective agent, 210n
risk, 28, 28n
roundabout methods of production, 134–5
ruptures, as features of economic dynamics, 272–3

saving function, 158, 257
Say's law of markets, 175, 186, 193–6
schema of production, as the analytical representation of the principal stocks and flows (Löwe), 312–13
schemes of reproduction
  in Böhm-Bawerk, 149–50
  in Marx, 146–8, 152, 157n
  in Quesnay, 148
sector-based model, *see* horizontal model
separable elementary processes, 242–3
simplifying assumptions, 18
  as distinguished from characterizing assumptions, 250–2
simultaneity of production and consumption, 135–6
singular points, 203
social sciences, autonomy and isolation, 23–4
society of exchange, 17–18, 246
splitting coefficients and structural change analysis, 304–5
stages of production
  and repercussion through time of economic impulses, 292–7
  and traverse analysis, 113–15
state
  historical origins of, 29
  modern, and capitalism, 32–3
  welfare, 35n
static theory, its relation with dynamic analysis, 309
stationary state, 28, 37, 231
  and the circular flow, 300–3
  Marshallian, 57
  and population dynamics, 107–8
  Walrasian, 52–3
steady-state dynamics, 230–1
stock
  and the entropy law, 209–10
  vs. fund, 209–10
stock–flow
  network, of economic magnitudes, 18–19, 319–24
  relationships, and economic dynamics, 308–9
stocks and flows, in structural change analysis, 310–15, 319–24
structural analysis, 146, 158–62, 168
  in economic investigation, 247–8
  see also instrumental analysis
structural apparatus, 34
  and economic dynamics, 274–5
structural change analysis
  and accounting frameworks, 310–12
  and analytical representation of an economic system, 1–7, 275–82
  and circular-type analysis, 303–15
  and empirical investigations, 306–9
  and identification of 'higher order structure', 308–9
  and vertical integration of economic activities, 284–300, 315–19
structural equivalence, of economic systems (in a dynamic sense), 97
structural specification
  of the 'closed' type, 268
  of the 'open' type, 268–9
  and patterns of economic dynamics, 95–118, 273–5
  see also structural change analysis
structure, 3–7, 64, 78–83, 83–89
  in Marxist terminology, 24–5
  as the set of relationships among economic magnitudes, 3
  transformation duality, 28
sub-industries, and Pigou's theory of industrial groups, 287–9
sub-systems, 101, 286, 297–300
  growing, 286
surplus, 66, 179, 281–2
  see also net product
surplus, distributable (in Allais), 239–40
surplus value, 24
synchronization economy, as distinguished from advance economics, 235–6

tâtonnement, 54
technological
  externalities, 37
  unemployment, 161–4
temporary equilibrium, 51, 53, 102–4, 191–2
theoretical empiricism, and structural analysis, 18
thermodynamics and factory process, 214–15
time
  and creative action, 38
  historical, 145, 164
  logical, 145
  in political processes, 36–7

time-based model, *see* vertical model
time structure, 62
  of Marshallian theory, 53–4
  of Walrasian theory, 50–3
tools, 199
transformation apparatus, 34
  of original factors into final consumption goods, 274–5
transformation processes, 108–18
  and the objective stock–flow network of an economic system, 313–15
  of raw materials into finished products, 236, 287–92
  and the theory of industrial fluctuations, 288–90
  time structure of, 8–9
transitions, as features of economic dynamics, 271–3
traverse, 139, 154
  analysis, 144–5, 146, 152n, 158–62, 166, 243, 272
  defined, 114
  and economic theories of the circular type, 303, 305
  speed of, 236
  and the stage structure of production, 113–15
  types of, 139
trends, as features of economic dynamics, 271–3
tripartite (three-sectoral) model, 146–7, 152–7
two-sector growth model, 178

uncertainty, 28, 28n
undercapacity, in Keynesian model, 190–1
underemployment, in Keynesian model, 190–1
utility function, 202–4
Uzawa's growth model, 178

value
  classical view of, 74–7
  neoclassical view of, 77–8, 78–80
vertical integration of economic activities, 17, 125–8, 144, 148–51, 152–3, 164–7, 168
  and dynamic theory, 9–10, 284–300, 319–20
  model of production, 125–8
  see also horizontal integration of economic activities
vertical model of production, 125–8
vertically integrated sector
  and economic dynamics, 298–300
  and structural change analysis, 115–18, 298–9

wage–profit curve, 153, 156
waiting, 133–5, 211–12, 222
Walrasian
  investment function, 52
  model, 48–53, 184–90
waste outflow, 210–11
wealth of nations
  and the productivity view, 282–3, 300–15
  and the scarcity view, 282–4, 284–300
working capital, 144, 145–6, 153, 157n, 159, 163–4
working day, and growth, 219, 219n, 220

Lightning Source UK Ltd.
Milton Keynes UK
UKHW011020191222
414111UK00029B/652